MISSISSIPPIANS IN THE MIGHTY EIGHTH

A COLLECTION OF STORIES BY AND ABOUT YOUNG MEN FROM
MISSISSIPPI WHO SERVED IN THE EIGHTH AIR FORCE
DURING WORLD WAR II

Illustrated with photographs from World War II and others.

N. KENNETH NAIL, EDITOR

PUBLISHED BY THE MISSISSIPPI CHAPTER-
EIGHTH AIR FORCE HISTORICAL SOCIETY
214 North Madison
Tupelo, Mississippi
1999

This collection of stories is respectfully dedicated to our brothers who fell in combat in the skies over Europe and, thus, were unable to finish their missions and come home as we did.

> *"They shall not grow old, as we that are left grow old;*
> *Age shall not weary them, nor the years condemn.*
> *At the going down of the sun and in the morning*
> *We will remember them." (Binyon)*

ACKNOWLEDGMENTS

There are so many people to whom we are grateful for the part they played in the preparation and publication of this volume: First of all we must thank the almost sixty contributors of stories, poems, and letters. All the members of the Board of Directors and the Officers of the Mississippi Chapter gave us their unqualified support as we proceeded. The MIME Committee worked in all the areas of this effort; to list them is very faint praise and small thanks, but we must do at least that. They were:

> Ernest J. Adcock
> Bettye Duke Jackson
> William H. Johnson, Jr.
> Homer C. King
> William F. McGuire
> Ethelda Nail
> Howard Richardson
> George Roberts
> Eugene Spearman
> John L. Walker
> Dr. W. W. Walley
> Joan Wilson

Every one of the members of this committee deserves the thanks of all of us for the work they did. Many of the stories submitted to us were circulated and reviewed by the committee members, who made valuable comments and suggestions for their improvement.

A few of the committee members, however, are to be given special acknowledgment. Bettye Duke Jackson submitted stories she had written. But she also worked with several other veterans of the Eighth to help them produce their stories. Bettye also has worked tirelessly in editing the manuscript as it neared completion. For all of these things, for her constant encouragement, for her help with all sorts of small problems, we give her our heartfelt thanks.

George Roberts, though suffering from a hearing problem shortly after we began this project, has provided invaluable help in editing the stories, offering suggestions for format improvement and tremendously valuable encouragement.

Ethelda Nail has been right in the center of the activity from the outset of the Committee's work. She wrote stories, she helped interview and write stories for some of our members, she acted as our secretary at committee meetings, she stayed loyal to the project through all the hard work and problems that occurred, she never gave up on us when the prospects looked formidable. As the manuscript nears completion, Ethelda is giving it a final "read," marking it up with a red pen where commas are needed, helping us to be consistent with our usage throughout. Besides all that, she still cooks and keeps house for me and helps run the bookshop!

Our daughter, Susan Bozeman, not a member of our chapter nor the Committee, has offered a great deal of encouragement as we proceeded. As this effort comes to its conclusion, she has been helping tremendously with the final edit.

Mary Catherine Whitley, who is a high school junior, is an absolute whiz with the computer. Without her, we would never have been able to get the manuscript ready for the printer, we would certainly never have been able to get the pictures scanned in, we just could not have completed this task without her. We salute Mary Catherine and offer her our sincerest thanks and appreciation for all she has done.

Thanks to all who have submitted stories, poems, letters, pictures. Especially do we thank Craig Harris who, though he now lives in North Carolina, is a Mississippian with the best of us. Craig submitted several wonderful stories.

Our thanks go also to Phil McGuire who served admirably on our Committee and, also, submitted some very valuable essays for our collection.

We salute all of these, all the Committee members, all the Chapter members who have sent in stories and completed questionnaires, to all who pre-subscribed to our book and thus helped us finance its publication.

To all who had a part in our mime project, your Editor offers his most sincere gratitude.

N. Kenneth Nail,
Editor

CONTENTS

CONTENTS (CONTINUED)

CONTENTS (CONTINUED)

CONTENTS (CONTINUED)

FOREWORD

By Lieutenant General E. G. Shuler, Jr., USAF Retired
Former Commander of Eighth Air Force

My fascination with military aviation began during the terrible days of World War II, when the airmen serving with the Eighth Air Force were so courageously writing air power history in the terror filled skies over Europe. Although my father served in the Pacific during the war as a naval officer in the Seabees, I was always interested in airplanes and followed the later stages of the air war with keen interest. Thus, this was the genesis of my desire to become an Air Force pilot and later a career that spanned 32 years from 1959 to 1991. Little did I realize in those formative years of my youth, that some 44 years later, I would be privileged to command the very unit that prosecuted the air war against Nazi Germany, The Mighty Eighth. It was also a special honor to command the Eighth Air Force, while its units were actively engaged in combat, in the Panama Operation Just Cause and the Persian Gulf War Operations Desert Shield and Desert Storm.

Since my retirement on the first of June 1991, I have been closely associated with the creation and operation of The Eighth Air Force Heritage Museum near Savannah, Georgia. This rare opportunity for me, which began in April of 1992 and continues to this day, has brought me into very close contact with many truly remarkable Eighth Air Force veterans of WW II. My associations with these men and women, including ground crew, aircraft maintenance, support as well as flying personnel, has served to deepen my respect and appreciation for what they accomplished under difficult odds and severe hardships during those perilous days from 1941 to 1945. My admiration and affection for these heroes is unbounded.

It is my distinct honor to pen this Foreword and commend to you the stories emanating from the WW II era of many brave Mississippi veterans of the Eighth Air Force and those of their family members. These are touching and poignant stories of rock solid, down to earth people of the great State of Mississippi, who with their colleagues from other states, arose to meet a challenge unprecedented in the Twentieth Century. As you read these stories, reflect deeply on the personal sacrifice, shortened lives, intestinal fortitude, love of nation above self, unshakable determination, family devotion, and so many other positive attributes of this remarkable generation. All Americans owe them an everlasting debt for the freedom we enjoy today. These stories represent an absolutely unique and magnificent legacy, which no one can erase from the history of the United States. I commend the members of the Mississippi Chapter of the Eighth Air Force Historical Society and all others who put forth the effort, to record and preserve the personal accounts in this wonderful anthology. My life has been enriched from reading these stories and personally knowing several of the participants.

PREFACE

By Colonel Billy J. Jones, Chaplain

Our Chaplain, Col. Billy J. Jones, was born in Luxora, Arkansas. He served in the Army in the latter part of World War II, being part of the army of occupation of Japan when it was over. After the war, he earned a BA degree from Mississippi College and a ThM degree from Southern Baptist Seminary. He served as a pastor in Duck Hill from 1956-1961, then entered the Air Force as a Chaplain. He served in the Air Force in places literally all over the world, retiring in 1979. He now lives in Jackson with his wife, the former Winnifred Gunn.

Chaplain Jones acquired a Hammond organ from an Eighth Air Force chapel which was being replaced when he was serving in Guam. He has now made a donation of the organ to the Mighty Eighth Air Force Heritage Museum, to be used in the soon to be built "Chapel of the Fallen Eagles."

They came, they carried out their mission well, some of them died, they must not be forgotten.

I was introduced to the Mississippi Chapter - Eighth Air Force Historical Society, by Colonel Howard Richardson, friend and associate as a real estate broker, membership in the Retired Officers' Association and participation in Broadmoor Baptist Church. He invited me to attend a dinner meeting of the relatively new Chapter. I observed, listened to stories of yesterday and learned of future plans to preserve their page in history. I soon realized that the same enthusiasm and dedication displayed by this group was that which had brought an end to World War II. These individuals and their families portrayed a patriotism unlike others with whom I had been associated. Some of the men recounted their experiences with exuberance and excitement as if it was yesterday; others spoke through abject silence of incidents too horrible to remember, yet too justifiable to forget. As an infantryman in the Pacific Theater, I sorted through my own memories and what had led me to become an Air Force Chaplain in 1961, making me a part of today's Eighth Air Force. I was not prepared for the invitation to become the group's Chaplain. Could I find the time in my busy schedule?

A new door for service had opened and I accepted with humility and gratitude. My only regret is that we did not find each other earlier. Some had died whom I would have been pleased to know. They are remembered at our Memorial Services and are regularly in our hearts, as are the crew members who gave their lives in service to our great country. As God was with them in death, may he continue to be with us who live, so that there will always be a tomorrow.

To all of the members of the Mississippi Chapter, I sincerely thank you for the privilege of being your Chaplain. The association through meetings, the pleasure of your company on historic trips, the sharing of mutual aches and death of loved ones, the response to worship services - all have added a colorful enhancement to my military career.

MISSISSIPPIANS IN THE MIGHTY EIGHTH

An Introduction

In introducing this collection of stories by, and about, the young men from Mississippi who served in the Eighth Air Force during World War II, it is appropriate, I think, to tell something about who and what the Eighth Air Force was, and still is, and how it came to be referred to as *The Mighty Eighth.*

When the Eighth Air Force was first constituted in January, 1942, it was anything but "mighty." In fact, it had no aircraft, no bases from which to fly and practically no personnel: no pilots, navigators, bombardiers, no flight engineers, no radio operators, no gunners. All it had was was its Commanding Officer, General Ira C. Eaker, and a small staff. This contingent was sent right away to England to organize a fighting force to destroy the German Air Force, the Luftwaffe, and to destroy German airfields, industry, oil refineries, and munitions works, thus to curtail the ability of Nazi Germany to defend itself, if and when the Allies could invade the continent of Europe.

This new fighting force was to join with Great Britain's Royal Air Force in this monumental endeavor. The British were bombing German cities by night; the Americans proposed to bomb by day, precision bombing against specific German military targets. The British felt, however, that daylight bombing could not succeed; it would be too vulnerable to enemy anti-aircraft fire, or "flak," and to German fighter attacks. They believed that daylight raids could be nothing more than a waste of scarce planes and men. *They came very near to being right!*

It was July, 1942, before the Americans were able to launch the first bombing attack against an enemy target. This raid consisted of a squadron of twelve B-17s, and the target was just across the Channel to Rouen, in France. This first effort was successful, in that the target was hit effectively, and no planes or men were lost. But the Eighth Air Force had a long way to go.

Throughout 1942 and well up into 1943, without long-range fighters, the Eighth raids were limited to strikes just across the Channel, to targets in the occupied countries of Holland, Belgium and France. However, during this period the British were building bases for the arriving groups of American airmen. Back home, the great industrial capacity of our country was awakening after the long, deep depression of the 1930s and was turning out literally thousands and thousands of bombers and fighter planes. Young men from all over America, who had always been fascinated by flying, who were highly motivated to do so, were beginning to graduate from schools that trained them as pilots and air crews. They formed into bomb groups and fighter groups and many of them flew their planes across the Atlantic. They came in ever increasing numbers and moved into the air bases prepared for them all over "East Anglia," mostly in Suffolk and Norfolk, but extending back toward the Midlands. Some of these young men on this mass migration were from Mississippi; a *lot* of them were!

As the number of bomber crews in East Anglia and the Midlands grew and as the fighter groups arrived, as well, raids into Germany were staged. And they became larger and larger raids and more frequent. But the fighter planes arriving in 1943, while being very effective in combat with the Luftwaffe, did not have the range to accompany the bombers on these long trips into Germany.

The first Schweinfurt raid, deep into Germany, in August, 1943, consisted of 300 heavy bombers. Since the escorting fighters did not have sufficient range to accompany them into Germany, they were vulnerable to German fighter attacks, from the Channel all the way in and out. Losses were tremendous, with intense flak as well as fighter attacks. Sixty of our bombers were lost. Another sixty were lost three months later when the mission was again to Schweinfurt. These losses were almost persuasive that the British were right that daylight bombing was not feasible.

Then, the tide began to turn with the coming of 1944. Long-range P-51s began to arrive on the scene; they could escort the bombers all the way to the target and on the return, even on the deepest penetrations. More and more bombers arrived; more and more pilots and navigators and gunners arrived. The Eighth Air Force grew to over forty heavy bomber groups and over twenty fighter groups. Over 350,000 young men and women, including air crews and ground personnel, were serving in the Eighth. Missions were flown into the deepest sections of Germany, into Poland; shuttle missions were flown to Russia. The size of the bomber stream grew; one-thousand plane raids became common. By the end of 1944, the Eighth was able to mount a mission of over 2,000 heavy bombers and over 1,000 fighters. The bomber stream reached from England all the way to the target. No one had ever seen such a sight as the bomber stream passing overhead, with contrails streaming behind each engine. No one had ever heard such a sound as the throaty roar the airplane engines were producing. No one had ever seen the likes of that air armada; no one ever will again. British friends began to refer to it as *The Mighty Eighth.* They still do!

These huge fleets of bombers and fighters left nothing but complete destruction of the rail yards, airfields, munitions plants, oil refineries and the like in their wake. The Luftwaffe was not completely eliminated but was greatly diminished and rendered very ineffective. When General Eisenhower gave his message to the troops landing on the Normandy beaches, he was able to assure them that, at least, they wouldn't have to worry about German air attacks; if they saw any planes, they would be ours.

And there were Mississippians in those great streams of bombers. There were a lot of them! And there were young men from Mississippi flying fighter sweeps and escorting the bombers in the P-51s, the P-47s and the P-38s. There were a lot of them! This collection recounts just some of their stories.

The stories tell about the great air armada. They tell about flying in a B-17 or a B-24 at heights up to 30,000 feet, with temperatures as low as 60 degrees below zero; they tell about flying through flak, black clouds of flak; they tell about fighter attacks. You can feel the fear with which all these young men were faced on every single mission. You can read an account of a crew fighting to make their plane hold together to get back to England, or even to get back to the Channel where they had to ditch in very cold, rough water. Some tell about bailing out and being captured and suffering privation and humiliation in a prisoner of war camp for the rest of the War. Others tell of bailing out over occupied territory and being rescued and sheltered by a friendly and very courageous underground. Some tell of relations with the wonderful English people they got to know in the villages where the airbases were located.

And these are all stories of Mississippians, many of whom had never been very far from the town or countryside in Mississippi where they were born. They all volunteered to fly.

I feel sure they all would have elected to go to England and fly in *The Mighty Eighth* had they been given a choice. All are exceedingly proud of their service in *The Mighty Eighth.*

The Eighth Air Force still exists today, headquartered at Barksdale Field, Louisiana. It served our country throughout the Cold War, in Korea, Vietnam and Desert Storm.

****

In December of 1990, three Mississippi veterans of *The Mighty Eighth* were visiting in the home of one of these veterans. As is very often the case when old "war-birds" get together, their talk was largely of some of their experiences during the War. They learned that all three were members of The Eighth Air Force Historical Society, as well as their respective bomb group associations: the 305th, the 95th and the 457th.

All three felt that these organizations were splendid, but they discussed the difficulty of getting to the reunions these groups held each year, which might be in any city in the USA or, indeed, sometimes in England. As a result of this discussion, the men decided to look into the possibility of forming a Mississippi Chapter of the Eighth Air Force Historical Society. This would enable Mississippians to have the fellowship and other benefits of the Eighth Air Force Historical Society and group reunions without having to travel so far.

By mid-January of 1991, the three had set up a meeting for anyone interested in forming a chapter; 19 veterans and their wives attended. This small group elected to call an organization meeting in April, give it good publicity and try to have a representative attendance to actually form the Chapter. The Mississippi Chapter has grown from that meeting. It has met twice each year; two of the meetings have been chartered bus trips. A newsletter is published quarterly, under the name of *Contrails & Propwash.* The

meetings and the newsletter and other contacts have produced an outstanding fellowship and a wonderful bonding.

The Chapter organization came into being at about the same time as the initial fund-raising effort for the Mighty Eighth Air Force Heritage Museum, which has since been built near Savannah, Georgia. The Chapter began at once to espouse the cause of building the Museum as a primary chapter project, and has made every effort to participate fully in that cause. All members have been urged to become members of the Museum and to make contributions of as much money as they could, as well as memorabilia. At every reunion of its members, the Chapter holds a raffle, sometimes raising over $1,000; all proceeds have always been given intact to the Museum. In 1997, the Chapter raised over $6,000 to erect a Mississippi monument in the Memorial Gardens at the Museum.

The Chapter's current project, the collecting of stories for this anthology, has been the largest effort it has undertaken to date. It is done with the purpose of preserving these stories for posterity, and we believe that there is no better way to preserve the legacy of those young people from Mississippi who served in *The Mighty Eighth,* over fifty years ago.

****

When the decision was made three years ago to put together this anthology of stories by young Mississippians who served in the Eighth Air Force during World War II and, subsequently, our first question had to do with who would be included, whose story or stories would be eligible for inclusion in this volume. This involved the definition, geographically and otherwise, of the term, *Mississippian.*

Easily recognized as Mississippians are those individuals who were born and grew up in

Clarksdale or Grenada or Hattiesburg or Biloxi or Holcomb or Clara; went to serve their country, returned to a job within our state or to complete their education at Ole Miss or Mississippi State or Millsaps or Delta State, and have lived in Mississippi ever since. However, we felt we must allow stories from some of our finest young men who moved on after World War II, for one reason or another, to go to school or work somewhere else. There are several such in this volume, and we are very honored to have them included; some are among the finest stories we have. Also considered as Mississippians are some who have chosen to *become* Mississippians. Stories from these Mississippians by choice were welcomed.

What limits were we to place as to the time period in which stories or incidents took place? Clearly, most of the stories would cover the time of World War II. However, since the Eighth Air Force continued to exist after the war and served our country in every subsequent military engagement (Korea, Vietnam, Panama, Grenada, Desert Storm,) we decided that we would not exclude stories from those occasions. One story is about an incident of the Cold War. We would have welcomed more, as we felt that *The Mighty Eighth* served an important role in that part of our history.

We accepted stories as written by many of our participants with very little editing. Some stories were given to us on tape; we transcribed those and edited them for inclusion. Some stories first appeared in newspaper accounts which, with additional comments by the veteran, we have retold for this volume. Some stories were written by our committee members from interviews; in some the interview has been presented just as it was recorded by the interviewer. We have included a few poems written by our participants and a few letters written to the folks back home. We have also included vintage photographs when they were

available to us, especially if they were illustrative of the story presented.

We have not limited our story-tellers to just one story; if our participants wanted to write multiple stories, we have been happy to include them whenever we could do so. Some stories as submitted were rather long; in such cases we often asked the writer to shorten his story. In other cases, the editors excerpted some events from such lengthy stories for inclusion. Other long stories were, we felt, unique in subject matter or so very good that we included the entire story.

This anthology includes approximately ninety different stories, from about sixty different veterans of *The Mighty Eighth*. We did not get all the stories we had hoped for from those still living. We do have stories that concern Mississippians who fell in battle, written by family members or others. We were very conscious of the fact that some of the stories, about our greatest heroes, have not been told and will never be told. We can't say enough about these Fallen Eagles. We can only hope that the reader of the stories herein will realize that much is missing, that much has been lost because a B-17 or a B-24 exploded before the young boy from Mississippi, flying one of his combat missions, could escape. We will never know the true story of some fine young man from the Delta or the Coast or the hills of Northeast Mississippi who was murdered by his captors or who died while in captivity. We will never know the thoughts of a young farm boy from our State when he was able to bail out of his bomber, only to find that there was no land below but only the cold waters of the Baltic Sea, in which one can survive for no more than fifteen or twenty minutes. We can only imagine the agony of a splendid young college student from Mississippi, who could not bail out from his out-of-control aircraft because the centrifugal force as it spun was too great to overcome, as he clawed and struggled to reach the escape hatch. The committee who put this anthology together have dedicated their efforts in memory of all those fallen Mississippi heroes.

We also know we are missing some outstanding accounts from those of our number who have passed on within the last few years after living productive lives as citizens of our great State and the wonderful country we all fought for and served in both war and peace. We regret not having their stories for this anthology.

****

The editorial committee for this anthology made an effort to get from our participants a good variety of stories; however, we knew at the beginning that we might have a preponderance of some types of experiences. We just hope the reader will find a special and unique flavor in the telling, even though the subject matter may be similar. Several of the stories cover experiences in prisoner of war camp; some of these tell of other occurrences. We have one major account of an airman who evaded capture and with the help of a friendly underground sat out the war with friendly people in one of the occupied countries.

We have accounts which tell of the everyday activities of airmen serving in their separate crew assignments. Other stories tell of making friends with the English people. Two stories were written by a British war bride telling of her romance with a Mississippi boy and then of her journey from England to Mississippi. Another wife who grew up in Mississippi tells about "her war." One writer tells much about day-to-day events in the life of an aircraft maintenance crew.

One of the Mississippi young men started home from a mission in a crippled aircraft but was unable to make it across the North Sea, having to ditch in those cold waters. One young man arrived in England early in the life of the Eighth Air Force and served in the control tower at his airbase. Some tell of their trip over the Atlantic taking new B-17s or B-24s for service over Germany.

We tried to select a variety of stories; we just hope that you will have a memorable experience as you read these accounts by some of Mississippi's finest young men as they battled the cold and deprivation at high altitude, as they fought off German fighter planes, as they flew through flak "so thick you could walk on it."

"Little Friend"

East Anglia

13

ALL KINDS OF HELL

By Ernest J. Adcock

Ernie Adcock, who grew up in Ridgeland, entered the Armed Forces at Camp Shelby and took his basic training at Keesler Field. After completing gunnery school he was assigned to a crew which proceeded to fly a new B-24 Liberator to England via Central America, South America, Africa, and into Tibenham, England and the 445th Bomb Group, arriving in November,1943. He had been married, to Jean Maxwell, two months before this flight. He and Jean have two sons, both living in Ridgeland, as do Ernie and Jean. After the war, Ernie successfully owned and operated an asphalt paving company. He retired from that career on March 6,1989, the 45th anniversary of the day he was shot down over Berlin.

March 6, 1944, is a date that will long be remembered by the survivors of Neal Serkland's B-24 crew attached to the 8th Air Force, 445th Bomb Group, 700th Squadron stationed at Tibenham, England.

It was the usual foggy, rainy, cold morning as everybody hustled to breakfast and then filed into the briefing room to get all the details. There were groans from the assembled crews when the

Major uncovered the map to reveal, in large, black letters, "BERLIN."

"Gentlemen," he began, "this will be your toughest assignment yet—to continue our pressure on Hitler and his forces by carrying the war to his front doorstep. You will encounter flak like you've never seen before—solid, black walls of it—and the enemy fighters will go all out to penetrate our formations and give you all kinds of hell."

14

"This is by far the largest number of aircraft the 8th Air Force has ever mustered for any mission," the Major continued. "We are determined to render a knockout blow to the enemy, and you will deliver that blow." After giving us all the usual formation, he ended by saying, "Good luck and God bless."

We left the briefing room, boarded our respective airplanes, and taxied to take-off. Soon we were airborne, seeking our place in the formation. Everyone moved into position like clockwork, and we were on our way to Hitler's capital city of Berlin. After three hours of smooth sailing, the pilot suddenly radioed to the crew that we had just lost our left outboard engine, and he was unable to feather the prop. At that moment, our ship was rocked by a huge blast of flak that destroyed the outboard engine on the right side. The prop disappeared completely.

The pilot automatically dropped out of formation and informed the crew that we would abort the mission and head back to England. Our visit to Berlin would have to wait. We didn't realize just how long that wait would be.

We dropped down to about 8,000 feet, struggling to maintain enough speed to stay in the air. God only knew what was ahead for us. We jettisoned our bombs into an open field and lightened our load as much as possible, but our ship was vibrating, moaning, and groaning. How long could old "Balls o' Fire" remain airborne? We soon found out.

Six German ME109s moved in for the kill. We were blasted with fire power from our right side giving us no chance of escape. Our ship was headed down in flames, and the pilot gave the order to bail out. Fortunately, my bottom turret was turned in the right direction to allow me to unlatch the door and climb into the waist section of the plane.

I was wearing only the electric flight suit and helmet. There wasn't room in the turret for shoes or a heavy flight suit. Scrambling out into the smoke-filled waist area, I felt for my parachute and shoes. I found the chute quickly but couldn't locate the shoes. The heat from the fire was growing more intense, and the smoke was suffocating. I knew I had to get out of that inferno.

Snapping on my chute, I crawled on my belly toward the rear of the plane. The two waist gunners were nowhere to be found, but the floor was covered with blood. As I eased my way through the blood, I saw that the bottom hatch was open and headed for it. Above me there was a gaping hole in the tail section where the tail turret had been completely blasted from the plane. I dove through the open hatch and into the cold, empty German air.

As I fell through space, I began to feel a burning sensation on my forehead. My helmet was on fire. I jerked it off, and the wind ripped it from my grasp. Now I had no helmet, no shoes, and no clothing other than the electric flight suit. I knew I was in for a decidedly uncomfortable visit to the snow-covered ground that was swiftly looming up toward me. After several seconds, I pulled the ripcord and floated toward the earth.

When I hit the ground just outside a small wooded area, I thought the impact had broken every bone and dislocated every joint in my body. I forced myself to gather up my chute and head for the woods, where I fell into a ravine. As I pulled my chute in on top of me, I heard the sounds of voices and barking dogs nearby. Gingerly raising my head above the rim of the ravine, I saw a search party with dogs, looking for me.

I quickly lay back out of sight and stayed quiet as they approached. Although they came close enough for me to reach out and touch the dogs, they passed by without spotting me and moved on into the woods. Trying to decide what I should do next, I wrapped myself in the chute for warmth and, after an hour or so, drifted off to sleep.

When I awoke, night had fallen; but the moon was shining brightly through the trees. I decided to hide my chute as well as I could and, following the direction of the rising moon, slip into Holland or Belgium before daylight. I had no real idea of my location, but I felt that we had flown long enough to be near the border of one of those countries. The air was bitterly cold, and my feet were freezing, but I gritted my teeth and headed out.

After walking for what seemed to be miles upon miles, I came upon a farm with an open barn where I might be able to warm up for a while and possibly save my feet from frostbite. Easing into the gloom of the barn's interior, I made out the shapes of a pair of cows and sat down next to them. I leaned back against a post, stretched out my legs, and pressed my feet against the side of one of the cows. Thankfully, she didn't move. Gradually, my feet began to warm up and I dropped off to sleep.

I don't know how long I slept, but I woke up to see the moon almost directly above me, and I wasn't sure in which direction I should travel. I waited awhile to establish my bearings, then headed out into the frigid darkness. As I trudged through the snow, I stayed off the roads and away from the villages. I stopped to rest occasionally, but I knew that I had to keep on the move so that I wouldn't freeze.

The moon was going down, and daybreak was approaching when I came upon a small village with several farm houses in the area. I crawled under a hedgerow by a fence along a country road and fell into an exhausted sleep. I awoke to the sound of barking dogs and knew for certain I was a dead duck.

Then I saw a man watching me from his porch. He called off the dogs and beckoned me toward him. As I crawled wearily from my hiding place, I realized that I must be in the hands of the underground forces that helped American airmen to safety. He called out, "Americano?" When I answered, "Yes," he came to meet me and led me inside his small cottage. When he offered me a slice of black bread with some type of spread on it and a glass of milk, I suddenly realized that I

was ravenously hungry and thirsty and accepted with gratitude.

We attempted to communicate for some time, but with little success. Finally, he motioned for me to follow him, and we left the house and headed up the street. At first, I had no clue where we were going, but I found out soon enough as we entered a building decorated with a large swastika. The Nazi headquarters. The man who had brought me there spoke briefly with the German officers, gave me a smile, and disappeared out the door. Then one of the German officers turned to me and said, in heavily accented English, "For you, the war is over."

Thus began 14 months of imprisonment in the hands of the German government. I underwent interrogation at Frankfurt, then rode a railroad boxcar to Stalag VI Heydekrug in Lithuania. I was on the horrible Baltic Sea cattle boat transfer from Stalag VI to Stalag IV in Grosschow, Poland. I was also part of the death march from Stalag IV, which lasted from February, 1945, until we were liberated by British forces on May 5, 1945, three days before the war ended.

The words of the Major back in the briefing room will always haunt my memory: "Good luck and God bless." Our encounter with the German fighters cost the lives of our bombardier, tail gunner, and one waist gunner. The other waist gunner was critically wounded. I was one of the lucky ones, and I know I was truly blessed.

"BLACK THURSDAY"

By George G. Roberts

There is a bond which unites a crew. Some say it is called crew integrity; others call it loyalty. I think it is not just a bond, but a fear. Fear of failure or not measuring up causes a pain much greater than the battle itself.

We were advised just after the Munster raid that a front was moving across the continent, and there would probably be a respite for a few days. This was welcome news, and the miserable, foggy weather became our ally. There had been rumors among the airmen that it was time to hit one of the most important targets of the war, and everything depended on the weather. We were alerted on the evening of October 12th, Tuesday; but the morning saw only fog and drizzle and a relief from the alert. On Wednesday the 13th, we again got the warning; but seeing no changes in the weather at Thurleigh, we figured it too would be canceled. The bright and shining CQ, alerting us to a 0700 briefing the next morning, put a quick damper on this thought. As I walked to the chow hall, I encountered Captain Reecher, Group Operations Officer, who asked me how long I had been a Staff Sergeant. Telling him it was about four months, he said, "When you get back from today's mission, you will be a Technical Sergeant; and I will have the orders cut while you are gone." I attached no important significance to this generous offer, but later reflected that, "He sure is a fine officer." Our pilot, Kirk, had already been notified that he was promoted to Captain, and we congratulated him on his promotion.

At the briefing, our group commander, Colonel George Robinson, led off by saying this was to be the most important mission for the Eighth and carrying it off successfully could dramatically shorten the war. Our target was to be the ball and roller bearing factories at Schweinfurt, Germany. The name meant little to me, but again the long red string across the war map told me that we were in for a long flight over enemy territory. Weather over England was to remain cloudy all day; but as we approached the French Coast clouds would break up and we would have CAVU (Ceiling and Visibility Unlimited). Group Intelligence Officer, Major Bairnsfather, cautioned us to expect strong fighter opposition, moderate to intense flak and a minus 50 degree temperature at our bombing altitude of 24,000 feet. With this dire information, we donned our flying gear; checked out parachutes, codes and escape kits and went by truck to the hard stand where our B-17, "Cavalier" was again ready for duty. One bit of good news was S Sgt Weber who had been wounded on our first mission had been returned to duty and would again be our right waist gunner. Tom Hill, ball turret gunner was also on board after flying the previous mission with another crew. The ground crew, headed by M Sgt Ed Gregory, sensed that this was to be a big mission and said that our bomb load was high explosive types; and we would have a full fuel load with an extra supply in wing Tokyo tanks. His last reminder was, "Bring her back, guys." We quickly assembled our guns, loaded our gear and checked out our positions. The radio equipment seemed to be working OK, and all systems said go. Captain Kirk then met with us under the wing to give us last minute instructions and said we could expect a rough mission and to stay cool. With that, we were ready to board for crew check-in and await engine start-up. At 0900 hours we were advised of a weather delay; so we left the plane, congregated around the tents and smoked one of those all important cigarettes. We all expected and hoped that this one would be scrubbed until another day. Promptly at 1000 a green burst from the control tower shattered our hopes, and the roar of Wright Cyclone engines filled the air. Eighteen B-17s of the 306th Bomb Group taxied toward the end of the main runway, ran up the engines and

Crew of B17-F "Cavalier," October 1,1943

waited their turn for takeoff. The base was still socked in, it was misting, and the ceiling was limited to one hundred feet. Near the end of the runway, "Cavalier" with its crew of ten, full Tokyo tanks and six one thousand pound high explosive bombs left the ground. After feeling the familiar bump of the retracting landing gear, our fighting lady ascended into the solid overcast. With a climb rate of 500 feet per minute, and on instruments, our three squadrons broke through the cloud cover at 8000 feet and made a delayed but routine assembly over the base.

This was mission #115 for the Eighth Air Force and was being led by the 40th Combat Wing composed of the 92nd, 305th and 306th Bomb Groups. A group was usually composed of three squadrons, each having six planes. Hence a three group wing had 54 bombers. While our 306th group assembled without too many problems, Captain Kirk could locate only 30 aircraft and saw none from the 305th group. Despite the firing of many assembly flares, there were numerous stragglers. Before departing the English coast, Col. Budd Peaslee, Air Commander flying with the 92nd Group, noting the large number of missing planes, called the 41st Combat wing just behind us to take over the

lead while he made a 360 degree turn to try to find the missing 305th group. While making this turn to allow the 41st Wing to move ahead of us, Col. Peaslee spotted the missing 305th group who had attached themselves to another combat wing through error. With the bad weather and SNAFU assembly, I listened intently on the radio for an expected recall from Station 7MT, First Bomb Division. It never came. We departed the coast just North of Felixstowe at 1230 hours and after a few minutes were cleared to test fire our guns. The clouds began to break up; and crossing the enemy coast near Helgoland, I noted the ugly puffs of flak coming from the coastal batteries. I spotted P-47 Thunderbolt fighters doing their familiar zigzag patterns above and to the rear of our formation. These "Little Friends" did not stay long, and the next fighters noted were German FW-190s and ME-109s. These were soon followed by ME-110s, JU-88s and ME-210s. The lead aircraft in our squadron developed a runaway supercharger and was the first to abort; so Capt. Kirk took over the squadron lead. A few minutes later, the last plane in our squadron, piloted by Lt Davis and flying tailend Charlie, was hit on this first attack, broke formation and turned back to England.

That left us with only four bombers from our squadron to continue on to the target.

The German fighters then began flying directly through the group formations, ignoring the intense fire of our 50 caliber machine guns. It was the most daring attack I had witnessed to date, and it was apparent the Hun knew where we were going. They were prepared to stop our formations at any cost. In the ensuing hours, we noted 200 to 300 fighters attacking us from all directions and planes from our other two squadrons of B-17s began to go down. Twin engine fighters flew above and in front of us and fired their rockets into the bombers while the single engine fighters lined up on the tail section from six o'clock high to fire in their 20mm cannons. It was apparent from the tracer bullets and rapidly appearing holes that "Cavalier" was taking a lot of hits. Quite suddenly the plane shuddered from an explosion in the waist section. In looking back, I noted Sgt. Weber, our right waist gunner, had been badly hit in the left leg; and a 20mm shell had made a hole in the right side of the fuselage big enough for a man to fall through. The left gunner, Kelly, and I applied a tourniquet to the leg, administered a shot of morphine and covered him with a blanket. As I returned to my gun in the radio room, a 20mm shell exploded in the transmitter and literally blew up the communications equipment and oxygen system. I plugged the small feeder hose into a 15 minute emergency bottle, and by inhaling oxygen only when necessary; this bottle would take me through the next two hours. The tail, waist, upper and ball turrets announced they had no more ammunition, and we had not yet reached the target. Since most of the attacks were now coming at the tail and we were out of ammunition, Captain Kirk told us that he would take violent evasive action every time a fighter lined up his guns on our plane. Sgt Poff in the tail and I in the radio room called out on the intercom each time we saw tracer bullets being fired in our direction. I saw two of our planes in the second element peel off and leave our formation. One had an engine on fire. Sgt Poff then called Pilot Kirk to say, "Sir, there are no more planes behind us," and I heard him answer,

"We are the only plane left from the squadron and only five total from the original group of eighteen." Our five planes then tacked on to 13 other planes from the lead 92nd Group for added protection and increased fire power.

As we approached the bomb run, the German fighters appeared to fly right through the ugly black puffs of flak; I could hear and feel the concussions, and the familiar "woof" followed by the peppering effect on the fuselage. In looking out of the left window, I saw seven parachutes at 9 o'clock low and one of our planes in a spin. The plane disappeared from sight under the wing, while the parachutes appeared to be hanging still. Following the welcome call of "bombs away," I checked the bomb bay and discovered that the doors would not close electrically. Additionally, wearing no oxygen mask, the direct air blast was causing frost bite on my chin and in my nostrils. After a bit of cranking by the bombardier and the engineer, the doors closed; and the rush of minus 50 degree air tapered off. As we made the turn for home, I glanced around for B-17s with our familiar tail and fuselage markings. I saw none with our squadron markings, and only three planes assigned to the other squadrons in our group. It was evident that the German fighters could finish us off with our small numbers and extremely limited firepower. The only guns we had left with any ammo were in the navigator's compartment and the radio room. Strangely, many of the fighters left us to rearm and attack other formations. Those that did stay with us did not seem to press their attacks as viciously as they did prior to the bomb run. As I looked out the left window to see how many planes were flying with us, I noted several feathered props, smoking engines and holes in the fuselages and counted only five 306th planes in the sky. It was apparent that "Cavalier" had received major damage, but she kept on flying. With one engine out and another with limited power, she began carrying us back toward England.

Nearing the English Channel, the clouds began to thicken, and we were once again in foul weather. Captain Kirk decided to break for our home base at Thurleigh on his own and began a gradual let down through the cloud cover. We had difficulty seeing the edge of the wings, and a light rain was coming in the radio room from the open gun cover. Suddenly a break in the clouds appeared, and the green countryside became a welcome sight. Using landmarks and a magnetic radio heading, it was not long before we spotted the spire of Keysoe Church which marked the end of our main runway at AAF Station 111, Thurleigh. I noted no other B-17s in the landing pattern; and after a short peel off, we fired a red flare to signal that we had wounded aboard. In bad weather, descending darkness and flying a badly damaged airplane, Captain Kirk managed a bumpy but safe landing. As soon as our plane rolled to a stop, the ambulance met us, the medics boarded and placed Weber on a stretcher and carted him off to the hospital. He was conscious but groggy from the morphine. At the hardstand, as Kirk shut down the engines, we were greeted by the group commander and operations officer. They told us that only five of our group's 18 airplanes reached the target, ten were shot down enroute, and "Cavalier" was the only plane assigned to the Clay Pigeon Squadron to bomb Schweinfurt and make it back to base. In spite of severe damage by seven 20mm hits and over 300 holes by enemy aircraft fire and flak, this gallant lady had brought her crew back, but she would fly no further missions for our crew. Sgt. Weber was transferred from Thurleigh Hospital to a regional center to recover from his wound. It was his second Purple Heart in two missions flown.

In only four missions, our Clay Pigeon Squadron had five crews shot down; 50 airmen missing in action; major battle damage to every plane; and, worse still, a rather demoralized number of airmen who honestly felt that there was no chance of completing a tour of 25 missions. At our present loss rate, we would be extremely lucky to finish 10 missions. Back in our Nissan hut we had only eight of twenty people left. The snapshots of the missing were taken down from the door, personal effects turned in, and spoils divided among the survivors. Being the highest ranking airman after four missions, I got the coveted cot next to the entrance. Our engineer

was a nervous wreck and said he had to quit. "I will never fly another mission, regardless of the cost," he told me that night while lying in his bunk. This was not because of his personal fear but a fear that he would crack, not be able to perform his job and let down his crew in the middle of a battle. Considering his reduction in rank back to private and his removal from flying quarters, this demanded as much courage as going into battle itself. As I started on missions, I always said a small prayer, "Lord, get me back from this one, and I will never fly another." Still, when it came time for me to fly with my crew on the next mission, there was never any hesitation. Loyalty always overcame fear.

One hundred of my friends did not return to Thurleigh that afternoon. While we learned later on the BBC News that the Schweinfurt ball bearing factories had suffered major damage, I suddenly realized that we could lose the war. True to tradition, the 8th USAAF was not turned back by enemy action; nevertheless, our loss rate in this savage air battle over Europe was the highest ever recorded; and we knew this could not continue. While Bomber Command attributed 60 aircraft downed as a result of enemy action, the 40th Combat Wing which consisted of our 306th and two other groups lost 30 of it 53 bombers dispatched. Many of the returning 23 planes carried wounded, suffered major damage and landed at emergency bases. Understandably, Air Force Historians refer to October 14, 1943, as "Black Thursday." Others call it "The Glory and Tragedy of the Air Force."

SUMMARY
Mission 115, Black Thursday, October 14, 1943

B-17s DISPATCHED   317 (1ST BD 163)

(3RD BD 154)

B-17s ENTERING GERMANY   257

B-17s BOMBING TARGET   229

B17s LOST ENROUTE   28 to target, 31 on return

One B-17 ditched in channel, five were unable to land due to battle damage or fields closed by fog. Three of the five crews bailed out over England, two crews crashed with their plane. Total B-17s lost 65. This was 25% of those that entered combat. 1st Bomb Division had 45 planes shot down over enemy territory and five more crashed in England. Seventeen additional B-17s suffered Category E battle damage and never flew again.

594 airmen listed as missing over enemy territory, 5 dead and 43 wounded on returning aircraft, ten of these so critical that their survival was questionable.

Summary of 40th Combat Wing (92nd, 305th & 306th Bomb Groups.)

92nd BG, Podington: Dispatched 19; One abort, six shot down, one crashed in UK. Ten returning planes had four wounded aboard.

305th BG Chelveston: Dispatched 16; One abort, thirteen shot down, two planes bombed target & returned to base. The other plane made an emergency landing at another UK base.

306th BG Thurleigh: Dispatched 18; Three aborts (one of these following enemy attack), ten shot down, five bombed target, all five returning to base had wounded aboard. Of the 100 missing airmen, 35 were killed and 65 became prisoners of war.

306th BG Planes returning (5) used 29,290 rounds of 50 cal. ammunition. The group was taken off operational status the next day because there was not enough equipment or crews to fly.

The Schweinfurt raid destroyed "455,000 sq. ft. of floor space in the UKF and Kugel-Fischer ball-bearing plants." (Fortune Magazine, Vol. 31, no. 1, p. 246.)

Marcus L. Shook, from Belmont, flew as a gunner on a B-17 Flying Fortress with the 390th Bomb Group at Framlingham. On a mission to drop food and supplies to the Polish patriots during their uprising in Warsaw; his plane was badly damaged by flak. Marcus and a fellow crew member were in the bomb bay when they saw that the plane was on fire; flames were ready to engulf them. The two bailed out, managing to clear the plane before it exploded. None of the remainder of the crew got out. On the way to the ground the two crewmen were constantly shot at by the Germans as they descended. Marcus was severely wounded. The other airman was killed before he reached the ground. Marcus spent the rest of the war in a P.O.W. camp, most of the time in the hospital.

When later to be President, George Bush, was serving as Vice President, he was invited to Warsaw by the Polish government, for the dedication of a monument the Polish people were erecting in honor of the brave airmen who dropped food and supplies to them in their time of need. Marcus was invited to accompany the Vice President in Air Force II, and was given special honors and recognition by the Polish government.

Marcus passed away a few years ago. This Fallen Eagle is remembered by all who knew him as a kind and gentle man who served his country honorably and well in the skies over Europe.

STALNAKER'S SURVIVAL

By Harold Stalnaker

Harold Stalnaker moved to Tupelo after the War, where he had a distinguished career with the Pitney-Bowes Company. Harold and his wife Peggy have two daughters and one granddaughter. He is active in the P.O.W. organization and is past president of the State chapter. Harold is now retired, and he and Peggy still live in Tupelo.

I was born on a farm in Pontotoc County, on December 19, 1922. Just over 20 years later, on December 31, 1942, I was drafted into the military at Fort Oglethorpe, Georgia. After a few days there we went to Miami Beach, Florida, for basic training in the Army Air Corps. After finishing my basic training, we went to Buckley Field, Colorado. There they taught us how to synchronize a machine gun to fire through the propeller on a fighter plane with it running. When I graduated from there we went to Lowrey #2 where we studied turrets and bombs for heavy bombers.

After graduation we went to Panama City, Florida, Tyndale Field, where we learned to fire air to air, gunnery school. Before we graduated, they didn't have enough room for us; so they carried a group of us to Apalachicola to an old CCC Camp. They had built a runway down there, and that's where we took our air to air gunnery.

After finishing that school, we went to Salt Lake City, which took us five nights and four days. After being there for a few weeks, we were transferred to Gowan Field at Boise, Idaho. We were assigned to our crew there. We trained for a while and came back to Salt Lake City, Wendover Field and on to Tonopaw, Nevada, where we met up with some other crews, only one squadron. The other three squadrons trained at other places. We met there, and that completed the formation of the 458th Bomb Group.

We did our training, bomb runs, high altitude. On December 24, 1943, we received our new bomber. After training for a while, we had to go to Sacramento, California, Hamilton Field, to have our plane modified. After a week or two, we started our route overseas.

S/Sgt. Harold Stalnaker

The Crew of "Wabbit Twacks."

We went on then to Homestead Field, Florida, where we stayed for a few days. We had our plane decorated with Bugs Bunny lying on the side of it eating a carrot. We named the plane, "Wabbit Twacks."

After Homestead we went to St. Lucia Island, Trinidad, Belem (Brazil), Fortelazia, and Natal. We crossed the Atlantic to Dakar in French West Africa and then on to Marrakech. From there we went to England, just outside of Norwich to our base at Horsham-St. Faith.

We started then making missions across the Channel. We made bomb runs on railroad yards, fuel dumps, factories, and you name it. One day we made a run deep into Southern France. They were waiting for us: "Ack-Ack! !" We got back, and we had about a hundred holes in our plane. Some of them were a foot long. We dropped our bombs about 2:00 and at 3:30 I could still see smoke from where we hit.

Hitler said we'd never bomb Germany. We did. He said we'd never bomb Berlin. On March 6, 1944, we hit Berlin. The B-17s hit it one way and the B-24s hit it going another way. We took some deep runs. The longest run I made was 14 hours at high altitude. The temperature was more than 60 degrees below zero. On April 8, 1944, there were 1,000 heavy bombers, 750 fighters that crossed the English Channel. When we went over Belguim, the tail-end of the formation was just leaving England. We split up. Our target was an airfield in Brunswick, Germany. On our bomb run two fighters attacked our plane. One set number 3 engine on fire, and the other one destroyed my tail turret. Under those conditions, the life expectancy of a tail gunner is 30 seconds. It blew my oxygen mask off; I had no oxygen at all. So we had to bail out.

I fell several thousand feet. When I first bailed out, I said, "Oh, Mama!" After falling several thousand feet, it dawned on me to pull my rip-cord. I was falling about 120 - 150 miles an hour. It was such a jolt when my parachute opened that I blacked out. When I came to, I said, "O God, help me!"

I went on and hit the ground. The German Air Force was waiting for me. They took us in to a little air field, put us in solitary confinement; there was a wooden bed, and that was it. We stayed there about four or five days. We fell out one morning to catch a train. There were only nine men

there when we should have had ten. About an hour later we got to Brunswick, and there stood our tenth man. He had broken his leg. His foot and leg were in a cast. We told the Germans that he was one of ours and they let him come in our little compartment. The navigator prayed the sweetest prayer I think I ever heard.

We went from there to Hanover. We had to wait outside the town for the Eighth Air Force to get through bombing it. All the railroad stations were underground. We got out of that train, got to ground level and here came a German just screaming and hollering. The guard that we had with us had a gun with a clip about a foot long. He threw that on him and said, "Go!" Afterward we asked him what he would have done if they had attacked us. He said, " I would have shot them." He said, "My orders are to get you fellows to Frankfurt-on-Main. I intend to."

At Frankfurt, I don't even remember getting a meal. We were just piled in there, just hundreds of us. Finally, they got us out and put us on a "Forty and Eight." That's what they called the train car. They had twenty P.O.W.s in one end and eight guards in the other. We slept on the straw in shifts. I don't know how many days it took us to get to the camp at Krems, Austria; we got there and signed in late at night. They had "lights out" at 9:00, but they left them on for us.

I got up the next morning and they were going to move us to another camp. I saw a boy throw an old softball across the field. I said, "Who is that fellow?" They said, "I don't know, but they call him Pat." I said, "Call him over here." I had my head clipped, hadn't had a shave, and I was dirty. He came over there, and I said, "How're you doing, Pat?" He said, "O.K. How're you?" He turned and started off and I said, "L.T." and he whirled around and said, "Harold, what are you doing here?" I said, "I might ask the same thing of you." When I wrote home I would say, "When have you seen Mr. Fred?" That was his Dad. He would write and ask, "When have you seen Mr. Horace?" That was my Dad. Our folks were able to figure out that we were together.

We stayed there for one year. The buildings were built in World War I. Wind whistled around the windows and under the doors. We slept on wooden beds with two thin German blankets. Every morning - roll call! We would go out to roll call; when we went back in, they would bring some German coffee. It tasted like it had acorns in it. In a little while they would bring a loaf of bread and that loaf of bread was to serve twenty men. At lunch we would get three potatoes. That night we might get a ten gallon wooden bucket full of hot water with a rutabaga turnip in it or dehydrated cabbage with worms in it. That was our diet from the Germans. If we hadn't received Red Cross parcels once in a while, I wouldn't be here today.

We would walk around in the compound out behind our barracks, just walk, if the weather would permit. We had to keep going. Walk and talk. If it was raining, we would just sit there in that barracks. Our end of the building had 150 men piled into it. We would get a bath once a month. They would take us down, de-louse us, cut our hair and give us a bath. We kept our hair cut. Somebody would come in and say, "They're cutting hair." It cost two cigarettes to get your hair cut.

We lived through air raids. The Fifteenth Air Force came over every day going to Czechoslovakia toward Vienna or toward Romania. One night the RAF came over. They dropped those "chandeliers," and it lit that place up like you wouldn't believe. Then it dawned on the bombardier who dropped the "chandelier" that he had lit up the wrong target; so he made a quick circle and dropped red, red, red flares. Then we could hear the bombers coming. In a few minutes, just up the valley, we heard the bombs go off from the air field up there.

One day the 15th Air Force turned and were going a different direction; they bombed the little old town of Krems. The railroad yard was flattened. The old German Major who was in charge of our camp had a hotel down there in Krems and all the windows were blown out. He wanted us to save all the cardboard from our Red Cross parcels. We

saved it to sweep the floor with. They wouldn't give us a broom. When it rained, it was muddy. Mud would get about two or three inches deep around the front door, and they would let us have a shovel to clean that mess up. But, anyway, we gave him all the cardboard we could find and thought we could spare. You know what, some dogface slipped up there and stuck a match to it. Man! He got mad! Well, anyway, this was our routine. Just absolutely miserable. They were always searching the barracks; just anything to harass you.

We had one boy who tried to escape. They shot him in the leg. He was lying there begging that guard not to shoot him again; but the guard did, and killed him. Well, they had his funeral, and he came by with an American flag draped over his casket. (We did not know where they got that American flag.) We had a fellow in the camp called Father King. He had a chaplain's uniform, so I guess he was the real McCoy. When they started the march down through there with that flag, a German walked up and put a wreath on top of the flag. Father King walked over and took it off and said, "Nothing goes above the American flag!" The German didn't put it back on. We asked him what would you have done if he had put it back on. He said, "He would have had to do it over my dead body." That's how strong a man he was.

On April 8, 1945, we heard the Russians shelling Vienna 30 miles away. The Germans started marching us West, 500 to the group. We would walk 45 minutes, rest 15. Down the Danube Valley. They would feed us, maybe, every third day. We walked in rain and what have you. And wherever night caught us, that's where we would lie down, in a field, in a pasture. Once in a while we would get lucky and stay in a barn. The Germans told the people we were "Luftgangsters" and that we bombed women and children.

We had some Swan soap that we had got out of Red Cross parcels. There were 5 bars to one parcel. We didn't need that many. We gave a lady a bar of soap, and we gave a man a pack of Roy or King or some other off-brand cigarettes. The next morning when we started to leave, the woman cried and said, "I wish you would stay." But we had to move on.

One night we slept out in the yard behind a house, right by a little creek. And we heard this girl singing. She was a Polish girl, a forced laborer. The next day we looked by the door on the back side of the house and saw a jug of white stuff. When we moseyed over there, we found out it was buttermilk. We had our little tin cans hanging on our belts; this was our cup as well as our plate. Anyway, we took care of that jug of buttermilk. When we looked back a little bit later, there was another jug there; we let some other boys have it.

We would start walking early in the morning. One morning we were going along and saw a five gallon can sitting on the side of the road. We looked to see that no guards were watching us. They were looking the other way; so we picked the can up. It was milk. We finally got the top off of it and passed the can around and several boys got a cup of good milk. We tried the same thing another morning. This was a smaller bucket. When we lugged it up the hillside, we found out that it was pure cream. We couldn't drink that!

This went on for days and days. In fact, we went through Lenz, Austria, and other towns to Braunau and went about four or five miles down a gravel road. There they put us right out in the woods, with nothing. It rained, sleeted and snowed. We made lean-tos. We slipped out and borrowed axes or stole axes or anything we could get our hands on to make a lean-to or something to keep dry, but the weather just came on through, anyway. Of course, it wasn't as cold there as it was back in camp. On Christmas Eve, 1944, snow was 18 inches deep; the temperature was 30° below zero, and we had no heat. We just had to suffer through that.

Right after we got in those woods, about 4,000 of us in all, here came 6 Army trucks painted white, loaded with Red Cross parcels. Boy, that fixed us up. At least we had something to eat. We had more than we needed, so we gave some of them to some other people on the march, other nationalities, down in the valley there.

We stayed there about two weeks. You had to go about a half a mile down to this river to get good water. If you had an old bucket or something it was hard to get back up the slippery, muddy bank. If we fell down and spilled the water, we just had to go back and try it again.

Finally, one day we looked up, and there came a little green Piper Cub with a big white star. I said, "Boys, look a there!" The next day we looked across the river, and there were big tanks with white stars on them. That night we heard a bomb go off. Every bridge had a bomb on it. We crossed a lot of bridges in that 22 days and 288 miles that we walked. When we heard that bomb go off, I said, "Now we've had it." But we knew the Americans were on the other side of the river. We looked up one morning, and here came a German car down a little gravel road with two German soldiers sitting out on the fender. They stopped and an American officer got out. He said, "Boys, I can't help you but I'll radio back. I'm trying to hook up with a tank outfit out of Italy, and that will complete the loop around their necks." A couple of days later six jeeps pulled in; it was GIs! The Germans laid their guns down, and the Americans took them to town and put them in jail. There was one boy there, a little fellow, but he had a long old gun and a big pistol on his hip. He looked about 20 feet from him, and there sat his brother. Now, you talk about whooping and hollering and carrying on; they did it!

We stayed there for a few days, had to dig trenches for our toilets and all that stuff. I mean we had nothing! They finally started marching us into town. I got food poisoning and ended up in a Red Cross station. The rest of them went into an old bombed-out factory, an aluminum plant. They fixed up steam boilers, and we had steam baths. One boy got an old steam engine, and he was crossing the river to Braunau every hour and coming back on the half hour. A fellow came in one day and said, "If you don't get those Americans out of there, they're going to fly an airplane out of there."

Several days rocked by, and a doctor came in and gave me a shot. I got on the truck, and we went up to this big pasture. We sat there and waited for C-47s and C-46s to come in and get us. From then until I got to Camp Lucky Strike in France, I remember nothing. That must have been some kind of shot he gave me! I thought we flew all the way, but some of them told me we just flew over the mountains, and then we were on a train for two days and two nights.

When we got to Camp Lucky Strike, an officer met each truck as it came in. He said, "Welcome home, boys. How about two weeks furlough?" I said, "That would be nice!" He said, "How about a month? How about two months?" Man, I couldn't stand it; I had never had a furlough of any kind.

They de-loused us, burned our clothes and cleaned us up as best they could. They had a place for us to eat special food. One boy asked, "Aren't y'all going to give us a physical?" The answer was, "No. You aren't going to live very long anyway." I knew we looked terrible, but I didn't think we looked that bad. Anyway, we stayed there several days and then caught a boat in Le Havre, went to Southampton, then to New York. Nine days.

When we got to New York, they put us on a ferry to Camp Shanks, New Jersey. The folks in the mess hall there had been cutting steaks all day long, getting ready for us. It takes a lot of steaks to feed 4,000 men. What they didn't know was that we couldn't eat. Two or three bites of that steak, and that's all you could eat – *just could not eat!*

We stayed at Camp Shanks for a few days and then went by train to Atlanta. We missed our connection there. However, a semi-retired engineer there said, "Give me the Green Hornet." This was a steam engine painted green. He was going to take the two cars of P.O.W.s and four cars of veterans on furlough and he was going to Birmingham. He did take us to Birmingham, *in a hurry!*

We then caught a train to Hattiesburg and went out to Camp Shelby. After being checked there, we were given leave to go home. We only had a little bit of money to get home on. A boy from south of

Oxford and I went in the Continental Trailways bus station, bought our ticket, and sat down at a table. We ordered some cornbread and buttermilk. The waitress said, "I don't think I've got any." I said, "Lady, we haven't had any in two and one-half years." She got out cornbread and buttermilk.

A fellow came in the bus station and asked, "Anybody want to go to Jackson?" If I rode the bus I would not get to Pontotoc until the next afternoon; so I turned my ticket in and got my money back, and that fellow carried me to Jackson. I went in the bus station there and called the train station. I asked them if the Rebel had run yet. The agent said, "No, it's late." I got a taxi and went down to the train station, bought my ticket and when I walked out on the platform, I heard it blow.

I got to Pontotoc Sunday morning about daylight. I wondered how I was going to get home, but when I got off the train, there stood my mother's brother. His brother-in-law was on the train sitting in the same car as I was. I walked up and touched him. Fellow, he grabbed me and you could have heard him holler a mile away. He said, "Get in this car and let's go home!" The car was a little old black '38 Ford. I thought he was going to wreck it going down that gravel road.

We got home, but Papa and Mama'n 'em wasn't up. I jumped out and ran in the house. Papa was trying to get his overalls on and couldn't get one leg in, and Mama had just got up and was standing there crying. I said, "Mama, don't cry. I'm not going back."

Everything finally kind of calmed down. What had disturbed them was that my uncle had started blowing the horn about half a mile before he got there. He told everybody from there to where he lived that I was home.

Mama went in and fired that old wood stove up and cooked a breakfast like she always did. Forty biscuits! I ate one egg and half a biscuit. She started crying and I said, "Mama, it's not your cooking. I can't eat." My brother was sitting over there, about 17 years old, already ate 6 or 8 biscuits. He'd eat biscuits and molasses until they came out even.

I stayed around home, and people started coming in. This went on for three days and nights.

I appreciated this, but one of them asked my Dad, "What are you going to make Harold do?" He said, "Not a you-know-what thing!" I stayed at home my 60 days, then I got a 30 day extension.

I finally went back to serve out the rest of the war in various places. Nothing too unusual, though.

Amzie Jones, who lives in Shaw, grew up in Ruleville. He flew as a tail gunner on a B-17 Flying Fortress, with the 95th Bomb Group at Horham. He didn't quite make it to the end of his tour of 25 missions; he says he flew 24½. He was shot down while returning from a mission to Augsburg on March 14, 1944. Amzie could have jumped from the tail; but since the hatch was small, he decided to go up to the waist gunners to jump. There he found one of the waist gunners who told him he just couldn't jump. Amzie said, "I know you can't, but here you go," and pushed him out. The next 14 months were spent in P.O.W. camps. He was liberated by General Patton's army when it reached the camp.

William Bryant Ridgeway grew up in Jackson and still lives there with his wife Nita. Bryant had CPT training before entering the Air Corps and was already in pilot training as a cadet when the war began. In combat he flew a B-24 Liberator in the 467th Bomb Group at Rackheath. He tells about a rough mission:

On one of my first missions, we carried 4-2,000 lb. bombs to get a bridge in Germany. We made our run on the primary target and dropped bombs. One bomb hung up in the bombbay. We could not get it to drop. After we left the target area, I asked permission to pull out of formation and try again to get the bomb to drop. Still no luck. Over the English Channel, we again asked permission to leave the formation and try to dislodge the bomb with no success.

I called 467th control, told them what my problem was and requested instructions. They told me to fly around in the area after the rest of the group landed, use up most of my gas and then come in for a landing. On my final approach to land, I saw fire trucks and ambulances moving to the end of the landing runway. We made a good landing, but the slight jar was sufficient to loosen the bomb, and it fell out on the runway. I knew that using brakes I was going to stop the plane before the bomb would be ready to drop so we applied full throttles, took off, made a tight pattern and came back in for landing. The bomb slid to the end of the runway and did no damage. There was some talk that they might give me an award as the only man in the 8th Air Force to bomb his own airfield.

AN ENGLISH FAMILY

By Homer C. King

Homer King was born in Roxie, but grew up in Natchez where he graduated from high school in 1939. During high school, Homer served as second captain of the high school band. He has served in offices in the Natchez High School PTA, the Adams County T.B. Association, the Mississippi T.B. Association, the Natchez Rotary Club, the Andrew Jackson Lodge #2, F.&A.M. He is a retired executive and a 46 year employee of a local wholesale automotive parts warehouse. He is a past president of Mississippi Automotive Parts Wholesalers Association, past board member and vice-president Adams county Water Association, former chairman and deacon, Parkway Baptist Church, board member and past president of Mississippi Chapter of The Eighth Air Force Historical Society, member of board of directors of 490th Bomb Group Association, and a member of the Natchez - Adams School Board of Trustees from 1992 - 1997.

February, 1944, began a series of events that remain with me to this day. Some I am still trying to forget, and others I love to remember. This began for me when the *Queen Elizabeth* docked in Greenock, Scotland, where I disembarked, dressed in full uniform, armed with gas mask, weapon and helmet and loaded down on legs that were still wobbly from the voyage over. I didn't recognize this as being the type of *invasion* that we were trained for. These people were like those on Main Street back home, and the men weren't wearing kilts and bonnets as I thought all Scots did.

Homer King outside "Tech Supply"

We boarded a train for a night run to Stone in England, a suburb of Birmingham, which was a repo-depot for those of us sent over under the Bradley Plan. We were processed in a few days and we were off to Eccles Road where construction was underway. We were assigned to a Nissan hut that had no ends or doorways, just a slab of concrete with a half barrel roof - in other words, a "wind tunnel." It was landscaped with a sea of mud, had no heater, but did have wind that never stopped blowing. We stood in line for hours in a mess line for something they call "S.O.S." served by GIs who had eye problems. They just couldn't seem to see a mess kit. However, they succeeded in doing what months of training had failed to do. They succeeded in making me a *"fighting man."* They reassigned me after a short while to a Sub-

Depot Squadron attached to the 445th Bomb Group at Tibbenham near Tivetshall, which was the residence of Major James Stewart, CO of the 703rd Bomb Squadron, better known for his association with the movie business. I was introduced to *"bomb shelters"* and *"Tannoy systems"* that almost nightly announced alerts that Jerry was about the business of disturbing our sleep with his bombing raids. You were expected to run for the shelter when the "alert" first sounded; but after my first experience in which I put on my helmet, my overcoat over my long-johns, and my unlaced boots and ran for the shelter, down the steps and into a foot of ice-cold water, I decided I would much rather meet my Maker in a better frame of mind and in the prone position. After some "on the job" training with the 445th, I was selected as *one of 36*

28

men in an advance party to prepare the "tech" site of Broome Airfield that had just been completed by 2000 black U.S. Army Engineers. This was near the village of Eye. We were awaiting the arrival of the 490th Bomb Group from Mountain Home, Idaho, with their B-24s. They would later make a transition to B-17s.

We quickly learned that we were now going to live under a new life-style where war left devastation, inconvenience, anxiety, shortages, death and despair. We became a part of this awesome fighting machine where men and machines covered the skies as far as you could see. Civilians and military alike were mobilized in some effort to defeat a way of life that would ruin dreams and enslave the world. Each of us had an assignment, and we had to perform that duty. This was certainly not your typical 8 to 5 job. We were in a new dimension where nothing seemed normal and, much worse, it wasn't going to be normal. We fought the enemy, weather, boredom, no mail, off-brand cigarettes, no heat, cold showers, lousy grub, irregular sleep, and every day was bringing more of the same or worse. Nothing really made sense. We had two bathtubs on the base, one in the Group Commander's quarters and the other in consolidated mess where we peeled and measured potatoes. In 1944, East Anglia officially had four days of sunshine. The weather was always in a state of change.

Homer, front row left, and the Whant family of Eye

Then into this setting God placed me into the midst of an English family. These were the people who viewed us as uncouth and ill-mannered, and described us as over-paid, over-fed, over-sexed and over here." I met Ned and Lucy Whant and their family through Master Sergeant Lawrence Tanner,

Chief of the Supply Division of our unit. Larry was an organist from Mesa, Arizona, who got permission from the Rector to practice and play the church organ. Permission to do this was a great step forward for Anglo-American relationships, because Mr. Adams, the church organist, didn't relinquish that right to just anyone. I accepted an invitation and accompanied Tanner to the church to listen while he played. Lucy Whant had observed and met Tanner at the church previously and invited him to visit with the Whant family when in Eye. We stopped for a visit on the way back to the base and started a friendship that has lasted to this day. Lucy was a retired school teacher, and Ned was the chief registrar for the County of Suffolk. Their daughter, Dene was completing her schooling as a teacher and dated Harley Hughes, a New Yorker, who was also a member of our Squadron. We three Yanks spent many hours in the Whant home learning from them about England, and they were learning from us about our country. We shared mutual interests; we met the locals; we went to church in Eye; we shared their anxiety about their son, Louis, in the RAF in Australia, from whom they rarely received information. We would go with the Whants two at a time in their little Anglica Ford to Norwich to the Theater Royal or the Hippodrome for an evening's entertainment. These escapes to reality were precious to us and the Whants were simply great people! !

The expression that "wherever you go, you will find someone from home" proved true one evening when two passing GIs recognized each other as being from Natchez. Adrian Trimble and I relived Natchez on every occasion we could get and kept our minds occupied with all the pleasant memories we could steal. We "sweated out" his missions together !

The events during and after D-Day kept us really busy but gave us hope that this show would soon be over. Things began to get tough as winter came, and weather began to deal us a lot of misery. Christmas time was approaching and gloom set in. The Nazis were making a last ditch effort, and it affected everybody. Missions were called and canceled because of the weather. The combat troops were in need of everything, and we were called on to surrender blankets, socks and blood to an effort that later became know as the Battle of the Bulge. Two days before Christmas, Adrian came in with a bottle of spirits to celebrate the finishing of his tour of missions and return to the States. With him went my last bit of hope of getting home in the foreseeable future. I didn't have time to think on this as we were scavenging from aircraft graveyards and 3rd Air Division Depot for AOG parts to get aircraft back on the line. I had just returned from one of these trips Christmas Day, 1944, and found my hut empty. I had received an invitation to join the Whant family for Christmas dinner that evening along with their adopted Yanks, but I was in a "Sad Sack" frame of mind and just sat down on the side of the bunk to write my wife a cheery letter.

I heard the door open and heard a voice say, "Kingie, get into your clothes; we are waiting dinner for you." It was Ned Whant and that wide ear-to-ear smile let me know that he would never accept "no" for an answer. I crawled into that English Ford and we sped to Eye where the festivities had begun. The house was filled with people and all of them were enjoying food and beverage they had saved from their meager rations. I contributed the remains of a "care" package Helen had sent and enjoyed a cigar that was pressed on me by Ned's brother. The Yule tree was decorated with hand-made ornaments that had been made by hands many years before. Light from the fireplace glowed from the first *coal* I could remember seeing in the house since *coke* was commonly used. Tanner played appropriate music that we knew on a portable piano borrowed from the Lion Hotel, and we

sang together tunes that were common to all of us. We ate pork from the pig that rested on the table, Yorkshire pudding, and a number of dishes brought by different members of the family. There were sweets that I hadn't seen over there before, and everyone was insisting that I partake. I felt somewhat guilty knowing that much austere behavior was practiced just to enjoy this day. If there was any doubt about "the British" that day, it was all put away just to be plain "home folks" with our cousins from across the waters.

From left, Ned and Lucy Whant, Homer King

Ned died in the late fifties, and Lucy died a few years ago at the healthy age of 93. We had corresponded to the last and now correspond with her daughter, Dene, who is a retired School Mistress and who has three sons: a doctor, an engineer and a commercial artist. Her husband works with the Rank Studios, and they live at Southwold on the Channel. Helen and I have visited them several times since the war, but none has meant more than that Christmas in 1944 with the Whants! !

4-3-2-1

By Bettye Duke Jackson

I have always loved flying. I guess it was because my brothers loved airplanes. They were always building models, and I was their "go-for." I remember when I was very young, I happily agreed to "pilot" the "sure-to-soar-the-skies" wooden apple crate my brothers had ready to launch from the roof of our two-story house. Only the command from our second mother, Mammy Iona, to "get that baby out of that contraption, and come down offen that roof fo' I tears you up" saved me from an unknown fate.

The four - back when.

When I was about ten, my brother Ken was in the "Flying Rebels" at Ole Miss. He would take me out to the airport, and his instructor, Mr. Champion, would let us fly over Oxford. I had to promise not to tell Mom.

A lazy Sunday afternoon found me curled up in front of the big old Philco radio listening to a ballgame. My dad and brothers had gone to Memphis to see the game. It was the 7th day of December, 1941. You know the rest of the story. I had two brothers, Homer and Kendel, students at Ole Miss and one brother, Billy, a senior in high school. Homer and Ken joined the Air Force, Homer soon to become a radio operator with "the Bloody Hundredth," and Ken went to the Pacific as a P-38 pilot where he would give his life for his country. When Billy completed a year at Ole Miss and turned 18, he joined his brothers and eventually piloted the "Iron Duke," an ill-fated B-24 shot down on the 7th mission.

It's impossible to explain what having my brothers leave home did to me. I was always the "tag along," and they never seemed to go anywhere without hollering, "come on, Bug." Our house was always the gathering place for kids as the four of us grew up. Most of the time boys were there to play some kind of sports; so I grew up in a male environment.

When my brothers left for service, the big old fourteen room house echoed with loneliness. The first letter I got "just to me" and not "Dear Folks" was the continuing of a special relation among three brothers and their kid sister. One of the first things my brothers did was set up a special bank account for me. This was not to be spent until I graduated from high school. I learned years later what a special and unselfish act of love this was because of the little pay soldiers actually received.

Most Saturdays found my Mom and me baking and packing boxes not only for my brothers but for their friends. I often helped on Saturdays at the ration office signing up people for their ration books. Sometimes I got to go with my Dad on his check of the neighborhood when the practice air raid whistle blew. All windows had to be darkened. William Faulkner would fly over in his little plane to see if Oxford was secured.

31

Oxford was a small town, and the memories I have of the town's support of its service men and women are heart-warming. The newspaper was only a weekly, and we couldn't wait to read the news of the service men and women - where they were stationed, what schools or assignments they had, if they were being shipped out and what clues as to where.

My brothers kept writing letters to me and I have a few of those. Sometimes they would ask me to shop for their girl friends or the family. Most of the time they would write about how much they loved flying. I remember Ken saying, "when you get above these clouds, sometimes you never want to come down." One day he didn't.

You know, it's hard to remember the emotions I felt when the telegram came that Lt. Andrew Kendel Duke had lost his life when returning with one engine; he spun in and crashed. I just remember feeling so guilty because I had dreamed so often that he wouldn't get home. Homer and Bill were still stateside and came home for Ken's memorial service. This was August, 1943.

I couldn't guess how many letters I wrote to my brothers after Ken's death. I wrote my brothers, I wrote their friends, and when a convoy from Camp McCain came through town, guess who was out in the Square picking up addresses thrown from the Army trucks and jeeps. (My dad did a lot of "supervising" the answers I received!)

As I got into high school, I really felt the void in my life now that I was the only one at home. I was alone when the telegram came that Billy was missing in action. My world was shattered again. I couldn't imagine that any of my friends, not even my parents realized how devastated I was. My aunts and uncles, my brother Homer in England were constantly saying, "You have to be brave for your Mother and Dad." I didn't believe they could say that when I had one brother dead, one brother missing, and one brother still fighting a war. Who was there for me? I didn't realize until I joined the Mississippi Chapter of the 8th AFHS what those wonderful airmen went through. All I knew was that my brothers loved flying, loved their country and God was with them, not just in life, but in death, also, and their laughter and their love would always fill our home and always be in my heart.

After the war, my brother Homer flew many missions picking up P.O.W.s, always hoping to find Bill. Unknown to us, Bill had been shot by civilians the day he bailed out, February 22, 1944. When Homer came home, he wore all the sadness, the hurt, and the bitterness of one who had lost his younger brothers. I clung to his every move. We jitterbugged in the living room, and he teased every date I had, but he had changed. He left home a lot; he was easy to argue; he would often just stare into space. I couldn't understand what had happened to him; now fifty years later, I do understand. I wish I could have been more there for him than expecting him to be there for me. He was killed shortly thereafter in an automobile accident, leaving a wife and three children. I know now that he was a victim of the war in many ways.

Well, this is my story, rambling as it is: how it felt to be a younger sister who was petted and pampered by three older brothers and in just a blink of the eye, became the only sibling left. I watched my Mom as she caressed the flag with the two gold stars that hung in our window; I wrote letters, baked cookies, prayed a lot, and dreamed of getting old enough to join the WASPs. But each day I felt a void in my life that would never be filled except in my heart. The reason I titled this "4-3-2-1" is because after the death of my brothers, a haunting jingle played over and over in my brain: "Once there were 4, then there were 3, then there were 2 and then just me."

I am very thankful to all the members of the Mississippi Chapter of the 8th AFHS for taking me as a member. All the members have helped me in ways they will never realize. I consider myself fortunate to be a part of this anthology and in gaining the friendship of some special people. I pledge that I shall make a continuing effort to keep the story of *The Mighty Eighth* alive and help in any way the Chapter chooses to use me as a member.

MISSISSIPPIAN BY CHOICE
(First Lieutenant James William Schaen, 8th Air Force, 702nd Sq., 445th Bomb Group)

By Sarah Schaen Naugher

He was a Mississippian by choice and marriage and planned to live in Columbus following the war although he was from Des Moines, Iowa. In January, 1942, when the first airmen came into the Columbus Air Base, James W. Schaen came as a meteorologist. He and a fellow airman, Stanley Walker, who also married a "W" girl, Rose Houston, had heard that there was a "Woman's" College in Columbus and came out their first day to check it out. On this afternoon, my friend and I were leaving the campus for an afternoon walk. As we were leaving the campus, they were coming in the gate. They asked if they could walk around the campus. As this was a new experience for us, we didn't know, as the rules had not been made at that time. Dr. Parkinson was out in his yard and I just called across the street and asked him if it were permissible. I believe that he was in such shock at my audacity that he replied affirmatively and added, "if they don't stop."

Mary Elizabeth and I continued on our walk, emoting over how wonderful to see real, live men who weren't "too old or too young." As we re-entered the campus, they were leaving. Naturally, a few words were passed, and a short time later we met them at a near-by drug store for a coke. As my friend and I were lowly sophomores, we weren't allowed to date air base men. Nearly two years later, after Jim received his wings and was soon to become a bomber pilot, we were married on December 25, 1943, in Liberal, Kansas. I still had my exams to take at M.S.C.W. and another semester of school. However, Jim in his persuasive way, convinced my father, superintendent of the Pontotoc Schools, that I should drop out of school for that second semester of my senior year so that I could be with him out west while he trained with his crew prior to going overseas. Unbelievably, they allowed it, after I came back and took my exams.

We were together in Salt Lake City; Casper, Wyoming; McCook, Nebraska; and lastly, Topeka, Kansas. He left Topeka, with his crew, flying their B-24, on June 6, 1944, fulfilling a lifelong dream of flying across an ocean.

He joined the 8th Air Force in England and was stationed near Norwich and was in the 702nd Squadron and 445th Bomb Group. I returned to Pontotoc, discovered my pregnancy, and hurried to Mississippi State University to finish the requirement for my degree, as he had promised my parents I would do.

Jim was on his fifteenth mission on September 27, 1944, with the 2nd Bomb Division of the 8th USAAF, with 283 four-engine, long-range B-24 bombers flying to the Henschel factory in Kassel, Germany. One hundred ninety-eight fighter planes were flying escort for the bombers. In dense cloud cover, the 445th, leading the 2nd Wing, veered north and lost their fighter escort. The group of 35 Liberators was attacked in three waves with lightning speed by nearly 100 or more German fighters.

At 11:03 A.M., German summer time, the "storm" fighters, in closed formation and firing their cannons, broke through the Liberator formation and blasted it asunder. According to concurring accounts of surviving American and German airmen, "All hell broke loose within a few minutes. The sky was filled with multicolored flashes of exploding shells. Aircraft, burning or breaking apart, were plunging to the ground with deafening noise. Debris from the airplanes and items of equipment were whirling through the air towards the ground. Explosions, blazing cannons, roaring and howling aircraft engines reverberated throughout the area." The center of this air battle was located along what is now known as the East-

West German border, over the villages of Lauchroeden, Gerstungen, and Richelsdorf.

The 8th USAAF lost 30 bombers in this disaster, 25 over German territory, as well as one fighter plane which came to the rescue. One hundred eighteen airmen died, 121 survived as prisoners of war. These were the highest losses any bomber group ever suffered on any mission. The 445th Bomb Group, which was based at Tibenham, was presented the *Croix de Guerre* by the country of France at their 2nd Air Division Convention at Norwich, England, in July, 1990. Jim and four of his crewmen died in the battle. Several of his crewmen became prisoners of war, and their families were notified in about two weeks. Four months later, I was informed by the American Red Cross that the German Red Cross now reported him as killed in action. A month later, our daughter, Jima Carter Schaen was born. I continued to live in Pontotoc with my parents. Jim's remains were not brought back until January 31, 1951, when he was buried in Arlington National Cemetery.

When Jima was three years old, I was married to David Naugher of Pontotoc and he became the father she had never had. As David had been in the infantry during World War II and was a part of the invasion forces through North Africa, Sicily, Italy, France and into Germany, he had lost many friends in the fighting and a brother in the Normandy Invasion, he had all the compassion and patience Jima and I needed. He felt that he had been spared many close calls for this reason.

In 1990, following the fall of the Berlin wall, the area of East Germany was opened to visits by Americans, Ex P.O.W.s, and West Germans. Many Americans went back to the area of the air battle near Bad Hersfeld to see where they went down and where they were captured. Invariably they were put in contact with Walter Hassenpflug, the director of law and order department in nearby Bad Hersfeld. As a young boy, a Hitler youth, he had watched the battle and helped capture an American airman whose plane had been shot down. In 1986, while researching the battle, Hassenpflug again met that fallen flier, Frank Bertram, whom he

first spotted hiding in the brush near a creek. As a result of this meeting the plans for the Kassel Memorial Monument came into being, as a cooperative effort between Germans and Americans. Deep in the Hesse State Forest, where 445th Bomb Group Captain John W. Chilton's Lead Liberator crashed, a beautiful monument, composed of three huge imported Norwegian granite stones, was prepared by the Germans. American donations paid for half the cost, and provided the three bronze plaques which list the 136 fallen airmen. The 8 foot high center monument bears the plaque describing the air battle of September 27, 1944. Jima, David and I were in attendance on August 1, 1990 for the dedication of the Memorial to American and German airmen who perished in a spectacular air battle over that town.

Jim's first grave at Gerstungen.

While at Bad Hersfeld, we also visited the crash sites. We went to the city cemetery in Gerstungen where Jim was first buried with six other American airmen in a single grave by the German people. When I received a picture of the grave in 1946, pansies were growing on the grave and a marker had been carved out of wood with the names of the seven airmen. While we were there, an East German woman told us that there was a grave in another part of the cemetery where two of the German fighter pilots were buried. While we were at Bad Hersfeld, we met Martin Brunotte, whose father was one of the pilots buried at Gerstungen. Jima and Martin had many things in common and discovered that she had been born five months after the air battle in which her father died and that Martin had been born one month after his father was killed in the battle. Since that meeting in Gerstungen, Martin and his wife Sylvia have visited Jima and her husband Steve Sparks in Gaffney, SC. Jima returned to Germany for the 50th anniversary Memorial Service of the Kassel Mission on September 27, 1994. At that time she and Martin met Gerhardt Mett whose father was the other German fighter pilot buried with Martin's father at Gerstungen. This meeting between the three was pictured and written up in the Europe edition of *Stars and Stripes.*

Jim's grandchildren, from left: Adam, Leah, and David Brumfield

Jim's daughter, Jima Schaen Sparks, resides in Gaffney, SC and is a Speech Therapist with the Spartanburg, SC schools. She is now 53 years old and has three wonderful adult children. Her twins, Leah and Adam are now 29 years old and David is 28. David, the youngest, is the image of his grandfather; looks, size, disposition, artistic ability. and even appetite. They are Jim's grandchildren and he will continue to live through them.

Jima Schaen Sparks, right, with Jim's bombardier, George Collar

Jim Schaen, front row, left.

A LIFETIME AIRMAN

By William George Elder
(28 missions over Europe/ 108 Over Vietnam)

Biloxi native, William George Elder, never thought about flying as he grew up; however, on his 16th birthday, he took a $1.00 sight-seeing trip over his hometown. Perhaps this led ultimately to a twenty-six year career in the Air Force. Twenty-five of those years were spent aboard bombers.

In January, 1943, Bill Elder entered Engineering and Operations School at Ft. Logan, Colorado and later was assigned to gunnery school. Elder served with the 95th Bomb Group and was stationed in Framlingham and later in Horham. He flew as a B-17 aerial gunner and toggleer and attained the rank of T Sgt.

After combat, T Sgt Elder returned to the U.S. and entered cadet training. He trained in B-29s and later B-36s and B-52s. He flew with the strategic air command and logged 108 missions over Vietnam.

This much decorated flyer received 20 medals for his patriotism. These included recognition from Russia and Poland. Bill Elder flew shuttle missions to Russia and dropped arms and ammunition into Warsaw. Polish president Lech Walesa awarded Bill Elder The Warsaw Uprising Cross.

In February, 1969, Bill Elder retired to Biloxi. There on his game farm, he raised wild geese, swans, ducks, and pea fowls, but now lives in Gulfport in retirement, absolute.

CONTRAILS

By N. Kenneth Nail

White plumes of cloud form behind
Each engine of a thousand planes.
Silken tassels of vapor blossom and flow,
Arrows pointing to our destination.

Those vapor strings are straight
Except for "Bandits" attacking in a curve.
"Little Friends" mix it up and stir those clouds,
Roaring over and under, leaving patterns of
white.

And patterns these are of battle scene,
Relics of brave men and frightened, too.
Here's their record blooming pure,
Signs in the heavens of blameless feats.

I would see that sight again
If I could call old time to show me
Denmark ahead, Helgoland below
And endless contrails in the sky.

But now, they're gone, those strings of pearls
That bedecked the skies long ago.
No earthworks these; they didn't last.
Generations may hear; sight is gone.

There will never be another time
When *Mighty Eighth* makes all those lines
Across blue skies. No more earth tremble
As they pass, into slumbering peace.

But we do remember, we who made those trails.
We remember contrails and propwash, too.
In the innocence of early life,
We were there; we rode those skies.

DUTY WITH THE EIGHTH AF
DURING WORLD WAR II

By Howard Richardson

Howard Richardson remained on active duty for a total of 31 years. Some of his assignments included service at the Pentagon as a Personnel Officer, service overseas to USAFE in Germany and later in the 12th Air Force at Ramstein, Germany as Comptroller. He served in SAC from 1954 until 1963, where his duty included flying B-47s and B-52s as well as staff jobs. His last assignment before retirement in February, 1973, was a three year tour with Tactical Air Command.

Howard received the Legion of Merit, Distinguished Flying Cross with one Oak Leaf Cluster, Air Medal with four Oak Leaf Clusters, Air Force Commendation Medal with one Oak Leaf Cluster, Presidential Unit Citation and the European Campaign Medal with four Battle Stars.

During his Air Force career, Howard flew the AT-19, BT-13, AT-17, T-6, C-47, C-54, B-25, B-26, T-29, B-17, B-47 and B-52 aircraft. He amassed over 7000 total flying hours.

I was born on September 6, 1921, in Louisville, son of Dr. and Mrs. E. L. Richardson. Fifteen minutes later my "womb mate," David D. Richardson joined me in the new world. We were not identical twins, but we both responded to either Howard or David. I was going to Mississippi State University when Pearl Harbor was attacked by the Japanese on December 7, 1941. I had obtained a private pilot's license at Starkville in the Civilian Pilots Training (CPTP) program early in 1941. I immediately volunteered in the aviation cadet program in the Army Air Corps. Due to the number of cadets going into training, I did not enter the program until October, 1942. I was sent to the Classification Center in Nashville, Tennessee.

One night I came in late with another cadet from Bayonne, New Jersey. The Tactical Officer made us march the next night in full combat dress with rifle, gas mask and full back pack. The weather was freezing rain with plenty of mud. I ended up with viral pneumonia after arriving in San Antonio, Texas. I mention this because later I worked in the Overseas Assignment Branch in the Pentagon. An officer was coming off a tour of duty after teaching at Annapolis with the Naval Academy. He had not

been overseas so that his most likely assignment was to an overseas base. I was having lunch with the officer who was to assign him and happened to mention that this was the same officer that had me out in freezing weather with full gear and a gas mask. I told my friend that I didn't hold grudges, but he told me he would take care of this officer. I later found out that the assignment was to a remote base in Alaska. Thus, I learned that you need to be good to people as you climb the ladder, for you may meet them later on!

From San Antonio I went to Primary Training at Stamford, Texas, where we flew Fairchild PT-19 aircraft. After this, we went to Enid, Oklahoma, to Basic Training, flying BT-13 Vultee Vibrators. We then went to advanced flying school at Frederick, Oklahoma. We flew AT-17s, twin engine Cessna aircraft. One of our instructors was George Gobel, who later became a famous comic. He was once asked what part he contributed to the war effort. He replied that he was an instructor pilot at Frederick, Oklahoma; as a result, no Japanese or German aircraft came close to Oklahoma during World War II. We then proceeded to B-17 training at Sebring, Florida and

"Mississippi Miss"

then to Dalhart, Texas. It was here our entire crew of ten trained together. After this the crew went to Kearney, Nebraska, picked up a brand new B-17G and flew it to Grenier Field at Manchester, New Hampshire.

Our next stop on our trip was to Gander, Newfoundland where, after a wait for the weather to improve, we took off for Nutts Corner, Ireland. On our flight over the Atlantic, we noticed that the entire area was lighted up above us, below us and all around. We thought that it must be a German Convoy and that we might be in trouble. Our Engineer was in the top turret looking all around and accidentally pulled the trigger on the Very pistol, shooting a colored flare up in the air. We thought for sure the German Convoy would shoot us down then. After talking it over, we finally realized that this was the Northern Lights.

As we were getting close to empty fuel tanks, we saw daybreak and clouds over land. As we descended, we saw the airbase and landed immediately. We left the B-17G and caught a train and later a boat to England. We reported to the 385th Bombardment Group at Great Ashfield. This was near Cambridge; our train station was called Elmswell.

At the time of year we arrived, the weather was to improve. We were given briefings and a couple of training missions in a short period of time as the Group was short of crews.

On our first combat mission, the co-pilot and I went with experienced crews, each flying as co-pilot. The mission was to Zwichau, Germany. This was May 12, 1944, and was deep into Germany. After we turned on the IP, the flak was extremely heavy, as this was an important city with lots of heavy production for the war. After bombs away, I never saw so many enemy fighters, and they were flying through our formation and all around. Several bombers were smoking and some were going down in flames. This target was of import to our cause and our bombs were on the target with excellent results. As a result, the Group was later awarded a Presidential Unit Citation.

39

After landing, I was busy trying to find our co-pilot, Charles Manuel; we were told that the crew he flew with was missing in action. We later learned that their B-17 had shot down a German fighter, but the fighter had crashed into the B-17 causing both to go down.

From then on, our crew gave new pilots and co-pilots this same new experience, or we flew with any co-pilot who was available. We flew quite a number of missions with a co-pilot named Gorsuch. We flew some real rough missions, and we flew often. We completed a combat tour of 35 missions in almost record time.

Our crew members were from many different states, but since I was the pilot and from Mississippi, they named the aircraft the "Mississippi Miss." When we first arrived, a combat tour was 25 missions. After General Doolittle took over command of the Eighth, he increased a tour to 30 missions. After the D-Day invasion, crews were badly needed, so General Eisenhower increased this to 35 missions.

On June 5, 1944, we were awakened around 23:00 hours for a combat mission; and we proceeded to the mess hall. We were told a few days before to wear our 45 caliber pistols at all times. We were told that this was a precaution in case of German paratroopers. We were served fresh eggs because we were going on a combat mission. On the way to the briefing building, we noticed an unusual amount of vehicle traffic and many people going about their business. We arrived around 0045 hours and Colonel Elliott Vandevender, the Group Commander, was to brief us. He started out saying "Well, fellows, this is it." We all knew immediately that he was referring to "D-Day" or the invasion of Europe. This was our 12th mission, to Caen, France. We had a bomb load of 12 - 500 pound bombs. When we arrived at the aircraft the crew chief had everything ready. He and his helpers had worked all day and into the night. We started taxiing out as soon as daybreak, the B-17s started their takeoff roll. Immediately the aircraft started turning, climbing and joining in formation. We continued to climb and leveled off at around 15,000 or 17,000 feet. This was lower than we

usually leveled off; that was usually around 28,000 feet. Flight over the channel was uneventful and there was an undercast. However, there were a few breaks; and we could see solid ships below. After bombs away, we made a turn and headed back toward England. I remember seeing a lot of C-47 aircraft pulling gliders or full of paratroopers. We felt really good that we had not seen any German fighters, and we did not see any flak. This mission was one that we referred to as a "milk run" because it was fairly short with no flak or fighters, but it did count toward our 30 missions for completing a combat tour. However, we would learn real soon that a combat tour had been increased to 35 missions. We were glad that we were not the ones on the ground invading the beaches or the paratroopers that were about to bail out behind enemy lines. These soldiers and sailors were going through the worst times of any war. They deserve all the praise that we can give, for they were making the supreme sacrifice of their lives.

We landed back at our airbase, and our crew moved to another airplane. The officer crew members went in for a short briefing and headed back to the awaiting B-17. We were loaded with 16 - 300 pound bombs for this mission. We were airborne again at around 1745 hours, and we climbed out forming our flight of bombers. Our 18 B-17s crossed the English Channel; and we headed for our target of Argetan, France: in support of the soldiers that had landed on the French coast. After we released our bombs, we turned back toward the English coast. There were many aircraft in the area, and we found out later that there were 1361 heavy bombers flown that day. That did not count the fighter aircraft. Besides the B-17s and B-24s, we also had B-26s, C-47s and British aircraft. The clouds below had big holes; so we could see the many surface vessels below. It was getting darker; and as we descended, we flew through patches of clouds. Just as we were approaching the coast, we flew into a formation of B-26 aircraft and how we missed each other, we will never know. This was a miracle, and we all had minor heart attacks. Landing was around 2345 hours; and we proceeded to debriefing, the mess hall and then fell into bed.

The next day we slept late and just rested, for we had no mission that day.

I started out flying #4 position in the formation which was below the lead aircraft. Our Group insisted that we fly close formation so that maximum guns would be facing any enemy fighter. Flying this position was extremely difficult because you had to bend your neck for the entire mission. During sunrise you had a problem seeing the lead aircraft because of the sun. This resulted in a stiff and sore neck. When our crew was moved to high squadron lead, only the pilot could see below to keep in position with the other aircraft. We flew low squadron lead three days in a row to bomb Munich. I had to fly in the right seat and had to look up to fly formation. Here again the co-pilot could not help relieve me.

Contrails were prevalent at high altitude and were pretty; but if the weather was clear, this was of immense help to the German anti-aircraft gunners in aiming their guns. Sometimes the contrails were so thick we had trouble seeing the other aircraft to fly formation. If there was an undercast when we made a bomb run, we would release chaff, a silver ribbon, and the anti-aircraft guns would fire at these strips rather than our aircraft. This chaff saved many aircraft.

At the end of our mission, we would assemble at a table and an Intelligence officer would debrief our entire crew. They wanted to know where we encountered flak, fighters or any unusual event. They wanted to know if we had seen any bombers hit and crews bail out and the location of each of these. We were offered a shot of bourbon if we wanted it. It was not too tasty and we called it Old Methuselah.

All days were not the same. One such day we awakened, proceeded to the mess hall then to briefing. As we were riding out to our aircraft, we heard three explosions. When we arrived, we could see an aircraft departing the field overhead. This was a German bomber, and he had dropped a bomb that had hit the top of a hangar, exploded and destroyed a B-17 that was undergoing maintenance work. One bomb just missed a cloverleaf where

four fully loaded B-17s were awaiting their crews for take-off. The other bomb exploded in an empty field. Our engineer, Ed Brown, told me that he was tracking this plane with his two top turret guns and could have shot him down, but he thought it was a friendly British plane flying over our base. After all of this we continued on our mission and made our takeoffs on time.

We had a great ground crew chief named M Sgt Miller, a tobacco-chewing Yankee from New Jersey. He was outstanding and our aircraft, the "Mississippi Miss," received the best of treatment. I would ask him how did he feel as a Yankee taking care of a Southern Belle. He considered this aircraft as his only child. He and his crew would work all afternoon after we had landed and well into the night until takeoff time. He always had to patch a lot of flak holes after every mission. He even got some heavy metal that he put under my seat, and I actually have a big piece of flak that he dug out of the bottom of my seat in the cockpit. These hard-working crew chiefs never got the recognition they so richly deserved.

Late one afternoon we were in our barracks and heard a buzz-bomb fly past. We saw some B-24s returning from a mission; all of a sudden, we saw one of the aircraft stream down and crash. The field nearby was close enough for us to see the aircraft in the landing pattern. We saw another B-24 with a German fighter on his tail, firing and shooting him down. It turned out that some German fighters followed these aircraft, and when they were in the traffic pattern, they started shooting them down. I think we saw about three B-24s shot down that evening. I guess flying was not too safe at all times. Another morning we saw a fully-loaded B-17 takeoff on a mission; soon after he cleared the ground, something happened causing him to fly back into the ground, explode and cause a big fireball.

On my time off between missions, I would hop on a train at the Elmswell Station; and before boarding I would get a hot cup of tea that was always available. I would head for London where my cousin, Major Henry McGraw, worked for the American Embassy. He had an apartment in

London and would give me a key and I would stay with him. He worked for a General Officer that was head of procurement and supply; Henry would always take me in to see him, and he would always be interested hearing about my missions. In wandering around London, I would hear the buzz-bombs and their peculiar sounding engines. When the engine stopped, everyone had to head for cover because their controls were then locked in a down position. Soon afterwards you would hear an explosion. I think these were referred to as V-ls. The V-2s were sent to London often, and they were rockets and had no warning that they were on the way to London. They did a lot of damage and kept the people on edge at all times. The British were great people and were brave also. One thing they told me that was hard to believe was that they no longer fired antiaircraft shells at these buzz-bombs, for the shrapnel falling from the antiaircraft shells did more damage than the bombs did.

Colonel Elliott Vandevender was our Bomb Group Commander. His father was a West Point graduate as well as his son. Colonel "Van" had flown B-17s in the Pacific Command, and they had picked him to form this new group in the States. After their training was completed and they had their aircraft, they proceeded to England. He was promoted to full Colonel on his 26th birthday, which made him one of the youngest Colonels in the military. He was a great leader, and he picked some of the toughest missions to fly as mission commander. There was also a Major Septine Richard who was from Jackson, and I got to know him well.

All of our 10 crew members finished a 35 mission combat tour; and only the ball turret gunner, Felton Watkins, from Alabama, was wounded. He got hit by flak on one of his last missions. It was not too serious, but he did receive a Purple Heart. After I completed my combat tour, I was asked if I wanted to go to the 4th Bomb Wing and work in operations. This was at Bury St. Edmunds and not too far from our base. I had received the Distinguished Flying Cross and the Air Medal with four Oak Leaf Clusters as well as the Presidential Unit Citation and a campaign ribbon. We had flown our first mission on May 12, 1944 and the 35th mission on August 11, 1944; so I felt that this was too soon to go back to the States. Brig. General Castle was the Wing Commander, and he was later shot down on a mission in December, 1944. He was attacked by many German fighters, and he made the crew bail out while he stayed with the aircraft. He was later awarded the Congressional Medal of Honor, and the air base in California was renamed Castle Air Force Base in his memory. General Robert Burns replaced him. I later served again with General Burns in the Pentagon in 1947. We had five B-17 Groups in our division and were the largest division in the theater. In April, 1945, the war was winding down; so I decided to return to the United States, where I was assigned to Memphis, Tennessee.

My family consists of my wife, Vivian Ann Richardson, my son William K. Richardson, my son Alan Blake Richardson, and my daughter, Janet L. Richardson.

John Harold George grew up in Mantee, where he lived until his death on May 27, 1997. He completed gunnery school at Fort Myers, Florida, and radio school at Scott Field, Illinois. He served in the Mighty Eighth from December 6, 1944, to September 5, 1945. He was a radio operator and flew 29 combat missions, attaining the rank of T/Sgt. After the war, he went back to college and then returned to Mantee to self-employment as a merchant. He was married to the former Corinne Reeves, had two children, and two grandchildren.

PARIS – THE HARD WAY

By John L. Walker

John L. Walker was born in Memphis but moved to Jackson when he was eleven years old. He graduated from Jackson Central High School in 1939. After Pearl Harbor, John enlisted in the Army Air Corps and took basic training at Keesler Field in Biloxi. He attended armament school and then pilot training.

John married his wife, Helen, in August, 1942. He was sent to England in June, 1944, and assigned to the 95th Bomb Group. He flew 35 missions, then returned home. John was awarded the Distinguished Flying Cross, the Air Medal with four Oak Leaf Clusters, and the European Theater Ribbon with 2 battle stars. After coming back to the States, he was assigned to the Air Transport Command in which he served until he ended his military career in October, 1945.

John and Helen live in Brandon. They have two sons, the oldest born in March, 1944, just before he was sent to England.

Walker's crew; John L. Walker top left.

The morning of September 9, 1944, began as did most of our mornings when we were scheduled to fly a mission. This day when we went to briefing before the mission and they pulled the curtain back, we saw it was a long one to Stuttgart. There was a large patch of red around the target to indicate the area of danger from flak and several smaller patches to avoid going and coming back. When the briefing officer announced our target was the Spandau engine and tank factory, we knew it would be heavily defended. The weather was good, and we were supposed to have good visibility, which would help make accurate bombing. The take-off and climb to formation was uneventful, and we crossed the French coast at 20,000 feet. We saw

a few bursts of flak over the coastline as they let us know they were watching us. We continued on course, keeping a tight formation so that we could concentrate our fire if any fighters appeared. We could see our "little friends," P-51s, about 5,000 feet above us with their long-range tanks and felt more comfortable knowing they would be with us all the way. We knew we had to face the flak over the target, but with our fighter escort, at least we did not have to fight our way in and out. We climbed to 25,000 feet and continued on to the target.

The flak began before we reached the IP and made our turn for the bomb run, and the farther we went the heavier it became. They not only had their 88s but 105s and 155mm antiaircraft guns; and I believe they had been practicing, since they filled the sky with shrapnel. We could hear it hitting our plane as we dropped our bombs. We had a shell explode just in front of our left wing, and immediately a streak of black appeared on my left cockpit window. I could see it was oil coming from our #2 engine and knew we had a real problem. I called for the co-pilot to feather the propeller, and he hit the feathering button. The propeller feathered then immediately unfeathered; so I hit the button, and it repeated the action. I tried twice more without success and realized we would soon be out of oil which would cause the engine to over-heat and probably catch fire. To prevent fire, I shut off the fuel pump and fuel line to the engine and prepared for the worst. By this time we were out of formation since the problem required all of my attention. The propeller continued to turn until all the oil was gone and then froze with the blades in normal position, causing a tremendous drag on the left side. I was unable to regain my position in the formation due to reduced speed and gradually fell behind. I could then see that a piece of shrapnel about the size of my thumb had hit the nose of the propeller, where the feathering gears were, and caused us to lose all of the oil in that engine.

I notified our crew of our condition and asked them to keep a sharp eye out for enemy fighters who would be happy to find a lone straggler. I also asked the navigator to plot a course for England the shortest way avoiding any known flak areas. I called our base on VHF radio, hoping it would be relayed, that we were not down and for them not to consider us missing! I had cranked in all the trim tab I could and was holding right rudder to offset the drag of the dead engine so that I could hold a heading given to me by the navigator. I knew I must hold altitude of 20,000 feet to avoid fire from small arms of ground troops. We continued this way and decided we should get rid of as much weight as possible since we had a strong headwind slowing our ground speed, and the day was getting shorter. I decided to drop the ball turret and told the crew to do so as fast as possible. They watched it drop in a German farmer's back yard, and we laughed thinking about his reaction. This increased our speed a little, but I knew by now we would probably have to land before crossing the Channel since our fuel was getting low. My navigator informed me we would be passing not too far from Paris, and it had been liberated two weeks before; so we altered course and made a slight turn in that direction gradually losing altitude which increased our speed. I finally saw some air activity at a grass airfield and recognized the planes as P-47 fighters. I was

able to contact their control tower, a small moveable one, on my VHF radio. I told them who I was and received landing instructions. It was good to know we were among friends and on the ground.

After landing, I parked off to the side of the field and shut down the engines. About this time, a Jeep arrived with a captain driving. He was the Chaplain of the 9th Air Force fighter group on the field which, I found out, was Orly Airport. The Chaplain called for a truck to get our equipment and made arrangements for us to spend the night in one of the buildings. Since it was still daylight, he offered us a ride into the city; however, he said there were still a few snipers, and we would be limited in where we could go. We accepted and climbed in his Jeep. We drove down the Champs-Elysees, through the Arc de Triomphe, past Notre Dame Cathedral and finally had to head back to base. We thanked him for his hospitality and were happy things worked out for us as they did.

The next morning we boarded a C-47 transport and headed back to England and our base . All our belongings were still there for which we were most grateful and glad to be "HOME." Our plane was repaired and returned to fly again. This visit to Paris was better than not going at all and much better than what could have been a trip to a POW camp or worse! ! !

mustache and quonset hut

WE SUSTAINED THE WINGS

By William F. "Bill" Frizsell

Bill Frizsell grew up in prewar Jackson, graduating from Central High School. He was interested in athletics, especially football. He says that one of the toughest assignments he ever had was to block Bruiser Kinard; the second worst assignment he ever had was to block Bruiser's brother George.

After high school, Bill managed to get a very scarce job working for the State Highway Department. To get the job, he had to be willing to start out cutting bushes along the highway right of way. However, he soon moved up to the surveying crew, which was what he was doing when the war began.

Now retired, Bill and his wife, Frances, live in Ridgeland. His principle interest these days is in gardening; it is said that he keeps half of the housewives of old Ridgeland supplied with fresh tomatoes, squash, beans and okra.

Flags were flying, bands were playing and patriotism was at a fever pitch after the attack on Pearl Harbor that precipitated a declaration of war. I had previously registered for the draft and had been called to report for my physical examination. Due to poor vision in my left eye, I was classified 4-F. What could I do? My buddies were enlisting, and I felt I must answer my country's call *somehow*. I was 26½ years old, single and healthy except for the eye problem. One of my relatives had stayed out of World War I for some reason, and the family sort of considered him a "slacker." (That was before the term "draft dodger" was coined.)

I went to New Orleans to try for the Seabees, but upon arriving there, found the office closed. In a few days, an advertisement appeared in the *Jackson Daily News* for recruitment of semi-professionals in various fields, stating that it would take place at the Jackson Air Base. Since I had been working as a civil engineer with the Mississippi State Highway Department for five years, I decided to answer the ad. I was accepted on February 21, 1942, and entered active service that same date.

Young Bill Frizsell

413th Air Service Group

Fellows from all parts of the USA came together at the Jackson Air Base and became the 343rd Service Squadron. Those of us in that unit were privileged to stay together until the end of the war. Our designation was changed to 422nd Service Depot Squadron in November, 1943 and to 413th Air Service Group in early 1945. After the end of the War in Europe, when we had been moved to Belgium, we became the 732nd Air Materials Squadron. We were the same soldiers with virtually the same responsibilities, despite all the changes in unit designation. Our motto was "WE SUSTAIN THE WINGS." Our insignia pictured two hands with open palms under the B-17 bomber.

After about three months, our unit was moved out of the Jackson Air Base to allow some Dutch flyers from Java to come onto the field for training. We were sent to Columbia Air Base in South Carolina for about two months. From there we went on to Fort Dix, New Jersey for shipment overseas.

We crossed the Atlantic on the *USS West Point,* a passenger ship that had been converted to a troop transport ship after December 7, 1941. I do not know how many were on the ship at the time I was (from August 6, 1942, to August 17), but it was reported to be capable of carrying 10,000.

Two fellow Mississippians went overseas on the same ship at the same time I did. Charles Sanders and Carl Wilson, who did not know each other, were both sent to the 92nd Bomb Group. The three of us made the connection fifty years later, when we were comparing notes and experiences at one of the reunions of the Mississippi Chapter of the Eighth Air Force Historical Society.

The North Atlantic Ocean was stormy and rough for most of the trip over, but we counted it a blessing since German U-boats could not pose a threat in that kind of weather. On the way over, the military tried to educate us about customs, attitudes and language of the British. When we arrived in England, we were issued *A Short Guide to Great Britain,* a pocket-sized pamphlet. It included useful information about British life, such as pubs, sports, their currency and language differences. Problem terms listed were

vest/waistcoat, truck/lorry, cookie/biscuit, restroom/water closet, and others. It instructed us not to brag or get into arguments over politics or religion. The King and Queen were *never* to be criticized. They were held in high esteem as is our *Stars and Stripes.* The pamphlet included many other things: for instance, do not make a display of your money. It tried to say we were two democracies with more similarities than differences. I understood later that the British government was trying to help their people understand what was to them the strange ways of the Americans coming into Britain.

Our squadron landed in Liverpool and we were taken by train to Chelveston, where we were attached to the 301st Bomb Group. We stayed behind when the 301st was sent to Algeria during the North Africa campaign. A new service group was sent from the States to join them. The 305th Bomb Group was then deployed to Chelveston, and we were attached to the group that stayed at Chelveston until July, 1945; our service unit remained there until September, 1945, to turn the base back to the British military. It had been RAF Station 105 when our service squadron arrived.

My first assignment upon arrival was to the control tower. I slept there and monitored calls. The RAF distress call was "Darky." The American distress call was "Mayday." When these calls came in for permission to land, I responded. When the 305th Bomb Group arrived later, they brought with them trained air traffic controllers. I was relieved (I was only an untrained amateur), but somehow my southern drawl was understood by the RAF flyers! For the remainder of my tour of duty, I was in charge of procuring supplies from the RAF depots. Here, again, my southern/British accent was useful. There was a fringe benefit in this assignment; most of the people in charge of the RAF depots were young women!

Colonel Curtis Le May arrived with the 305th Bomb Group, as its commanding officer, in December, 1942. Six months later he was transferred to the 102nd Provisional Combat

Wing; later he became Commander of the Third Air Division in East Anglia. During his short term at Chelveston, he became known as an unusually strict disciplinarian; the tone he set carried over to subsequent commanders. Lieutenant Colonel Donald K Fargo followed as commander. Then in late October, 1943, Colonel Delmar Wilson took over command of the 305th.

On October 14, 1943, the 305th joined other groups in the infamous second Schweinfurt raid to hit the ball bearing plants there. Eighteen B-17s from our group started out, but three had to turn back because of mechanical difficulties. Fifteen bombers continued toward the intended target. Toward dusk that afternoon, all ground personnel waited and continued to wait in the darkness for the sound of engines; none were heard. Our spirits were as dark as the night! Actually, two of our planes had made it back to England but had to land at bases nearer the Coast, due to their damaged condition. Thirteen of our planes were shot down that day, and one hundred thirty good men lost their lives. In all, from those taking part from all groups, 60 crews failed to return from that mission. During that week, the Eighth Air Force lost 148 B-17s with crews of ten each. The outlook was truly dismal.

Ground crews didn't share the glamour of flight crews; neither did they face the dangers of the airmen. One of my most frightening experiences happened one night while I was on guard duty at the ammunition dump during an air raid over our base. It was the darkest of nights in deep woods. If I had decided to run, I would not have known in which direction to go.

Colonel Ernest H. Lawson took over command of our base from Colonel Wilson. General Anderson from Division Headquarters wrote a letter of commendation to our group and to Colonel Lawson. This was posted in every area, because all members of the group had helped earn it.

Colonel Anthony Q. Murtoe assumed command from Colonel Lawson, but his command was cut short when he was killed on a mission over the docks in Hamburg on June 18, 1944. Colonel Henry G. McDonald moved up from the operations desk to commander during the final months of the war.

The winter of 1944-45 was horrible weather-wise. We braved the cold and fought the mud. We wondered what had happened to turn the weather so ugly and made the mud so deep. They said it was the coldest January since 1890. The weather was certainly one of our worst enemies. If a lead plane dropped off the runway, there was no way to turn around; so all the following planes were held up.

Cyclist Bill Frizsell, right.

Bicycles became our chief means of transportation. As soon as we arrived in England, we began to try to acquire a secondhand bike. I had ridden one for years, but had to become accustomed to the lever brakes. Back in the States we braked by reversing the direction of the pedals. Also, we had to relearn traffic patterns since the English kept to the left side of the road when driving. Some of my group had to learn how to ride a bike, because they had not done so back in the States. We were in a rural setting; so it was walk or travel by bicycle. The only exceptions were when we went into the RAF supply depots to pick up supplies, and when one of our trucks took us into Northampton on a "Liberty Run" on Saturday night. The driver would drop us off and give us a designated time and place to meet him later, usually around 11 P.M. Often the "black outs" made our excursions not so delightful.

One memory I have of those days is of a visit to our base by King George VI and Queen Elizabeth, along with teenage daughters, Elizabeth and Margaret. The thing I remember most about their visit was having to stand in formation for two hours, dressed in Class A uniform, awaiting their arrival! I remember very vividly the rosy cheeks of the two young girls!

"Latrine-o-grams" had often swept the base to give us hope that the war was winding down to a finish. The comparative inactivity at Station 105 during the first days of May, 1945, supported the rumor.

On May 8, 1945, the station's complement was assembled in the main hangar at 9 o'clock, where the announcement of VE Day was made. Achievements were reviewed, and we were told we could have time off until Thursday to celebrate. The Chaplain said a prayer of thanksgiving, recalling the sacrifices of those who had been killed in action (around 750). The band played the National Anthem, and we quickly dispersed to prepare for our passes.

Two hours later a teletype brought a message from 8th AF headquarters that all were to be restricted to bases for VE Day! Colonel McDonald returned from the continent to the base with a huge Nazi flag - 15 feet long and 3 feet wide. All of us reassembled in the hangar and stared at the bloodied banner he displayed.

McDonald explained that this flag was flying over Schweinfurt when the "Rainbow" Division had captured the German ball bearing manufacturing center with only 60 casualties. Remembering the 305th's loss of 13 of 15 Fortresses sent out October 14, 1943, Major Collins of the 42nd Division sent the flag to General Spaatz, who selected the 305th Bomb Group as typical of 8th AF performance on crucial Schweinfurt missions. In the corner an inscription reads: "To the 8th AF - The "Rainbow" has avenged your losses at Schweinfurt."

Our group transferred to Europe and were assigned the task of mapping the continent. The entire unit became a photomapping outfit with no one originally trained for such work. Service groups began deactivation, and we began our wait for return to the USA. We were in Belgium at first; then we were sent to various camps in France to await processing. Those camps were given names of different brands of cigarettes. The one I was sent to was "Phillip Morris."

While we were awaiting orders sending us home, and since we were not doing very much of value, our commanding officer offered us an opportunity to go on "flak leave." That was a bit strange since no one in our unit had ever seen any flak, but we accepted his offer for a two week stay at a beautiful hotel at Annecy, in the French Alps. Since we were not needed, anyway, they must have forgotten about us; we stayed a month before they called us back to camp "Phillip Morris."

When my turn came (we were processed by points earned for service, such as time overseas, family responsibilities, etc.) I boarded a Liberty ship at Le Havre, on November 28, 1945, for the voyage to New York. Then I was transferred by train to Hattiesburg (Camp Shelby) for final discharge on December 12, 1945.

After being away from home and family for three straight Christmases, it was a very, very Merry Christmas, 1945, for me and my loved ones! My mother's eyesight was failing when I left in August, 1942, and during my absence, she became totally blind. That meant she did not "see" me again; nevertheless, she was happy for my safe return after 3 years, 8 months and 29 days.

In the Fall of 1983, I had the opportunity to return to RAF Station 105 at Chelveston. A couple of people were picking blackberries when we arrived and came to greet us. The man related his memories of being a young boy, about 10 years old, at the time we were there. He said, "I would slip through the fence and come over for a visit when 'me Mom' was not looking. The Air Corps fellows would let me climb into the planes and pretend I was flying." I asked him if he was one of those "gum-chum" youngsters. He said he was, and sometimes got a chocolate bar too!

Still standing on the base were an old hangar and a headquarters building of some sort. Also, you could see where the runways had been, though they had been removed. There were some old abandoned vehicles at the end of one runway. An air raid shelter in thick woods nearby was photographed last year by one of my fellow 413th Squadron friends. Recently an article from a local British paper was sent to us; it was entitled, "Farewell to Hangar." Despite efforts by the parish council to save it, the Ministry of Defense has begun demolition. It was one of three J-type hangars left in the country and the only one still to have working doors. The article concluded by stating, "It is a great pity as it was a local landmark and place of homage for visiting American servicemen."

We drove over to nearby St. John the Baptist Church where the 305th Bomb Group has restored the tower of the church and installed a memorial plaque to honor the 757 brave men who lost their lives from our Group.

The return visit to my old air base was so emotional that my lip became a solid fever blister. I had to grow a mustache because I couldn't shave my lip!

I am proud that I was able to serve my country in World War II! Although I was not a "hero," I was allowed to give support to many who were.

413th Air Service Group, Bill Frizsell, top left.

THE BOMB THAT WOULDN'T FALL

By William H. "Bill" Johnson

Bill Johnson, a resident of Decatur, is a retired attorney, having completed 50 years in the practice of law. He is a graduate of Mississippi College and the University of Mississippi School of Law. He is a former District Attorney for five counties (8th Circuit Court District), a Fellow in the Mississippi Bar Foundation, a former President of the Mississippi District Attorneys Association, and former President of the Mississippi State Exchange Clubs. He is the widower of the former Georgia Lizzie Butts and has two adult daughters, Nancy Rector of Petal, and Elizabeth Woodward of Pensacola, Florida. He has two teenage grandchildren. Bill is also a past President of the Mississippi Chapter, Eighth Air Force Historical Society.

After having gone through pre-flight training in Santa Ana, California, and advanced bombardier training in Victorville, California, I received my wings on January 2, 1943. I then attended Air Force Gunnery School in Las Vegas, Nevada, and upon completion, was sent to Gowen Field, Boise, Idaho, where I joined my original crew and took over my duties as bombardier on a B-17, "Flying Fortress." As a 2nd Lieutenant, bombardier, with my crew, I went through what was called "phase training," in Boise; Wendover, Utah; Sioux City, Iowa; Watertown, South Dakota; Kearney, Nebraska; and then Camp Kilmer, New Jersey for shipment overseas and assignment with the 8th U. S. Air Force - "The Mighty Eighth." After six weeks basic training in Bovington, England, we were assigned to the 381st Bomb Group stationed in Ridgewell, approximately 25 miles northeast of London, 35 miles southeast of Cambridge, and about 20 miles west of the English Channel. My crew joined the 381st Bomb Group as a replacement crew, since crews were being shot down on every mission in the early part of World War II. We were assigned to the 533rd Bomb Squadron, one of four squadrons in the group.

This story concerns my missions over Germany, France, Norway and Poland. Four of my early missions were to Bremen, Germany, a large city on the North Sea, where Nazi submarines were being built. On my 8th mission, December 13, 1943, my second mission to Bremen, everything went well until we started on the bomb run. This was a time when the German Air Force (Luftwaffe) was

extremely strong and potent. We began to have heavy fighter attacks from German fighters, and a number of our planes were shot down. At that time each of our planes, flying in formation, dropped (by salvo) its entire bomb load as soon as the lead bombardier in each squadron dropped his bombs. We were flying at an altitude of 25,000 feet in formation with the other bombers in the group. This was before we had electrically heated suits; and we had to depend on the heavy fur-lined leather jackets, pants, gloves and helmets for warmth to keep from freezing at that altitude.

On this occasion, at the end of the bomb run, the lead bombardier and all planes in the group dropped their bomb loads on the target. All planes in our group were carrying forty 100-pound incendiary bombs. As bombardier on our plane, I salvoed our bomb load at the proper time and in the proper manner. All of our bombs fell off the bomb rack, but one bomb lodged by the rim on the catwalk of the plane. By the bomb being in this condition, it was impossible to get the bomb bay doors closed, thus creating a drag, and other planes in our formation immediately began to leave us. We were "sitting ducks" with German fighters everywhere.

The rest of my crew began to yell for me, as bombardier, to get that damn bomb out. Of course, I had no choice but to try. We were having fighter attacks, and our other bombers had left us although we could still see them ahead in the distance. Being in the bombardier's compartment in the nose of the

50

airplane, I had to travel by the cockpit, by the navigator's desk, into the bomb bay; and I had to leave my oxygen supply behind. I clipped on a portable oxygen bottle onto my fur-lined jacket, with enough oxygen to last 2 or 3 minutes. I could then see the bomb on the catwalk but couldn't reach it because of the bomb racks which were upright. In attempting to squeeze through the bomb racks to reach the bomb, my portable oxygen bottle came off and fell through the open bomb bay doors. Finally, I gave myself a lunge and was able to reach the bomb with my right foot. With all my effort, I was able to squeeze the bomb off the catwalk, and it fell through the bomb bay doors (God knows where it hit).

I then started back to my bombardier's compartment, but didn't make it. I blacked out from lack of oxygen. I fell on the catwalk just before reaching the navigator's desk. Fortunately for me, my navigator, John Bruning, from Ohio, saw me and pulled me up and placed his oxygen supply on me. He got on mine in the nose of the plane. We were then able to get our bomb bay doors closed and, by the grace of God, were able to catch up with the other planes in our group. We were still having fighter attacks.

Back at the base that night, the ordnance people said there was no way that could have happened, but my crew (those still living) are proof that it did happen.

My navigator, John Bruning, now deceased, saved my life. We were each awarded a second Distinguished Flying Cross for this mission. "Thank you, Lord, for small favors."

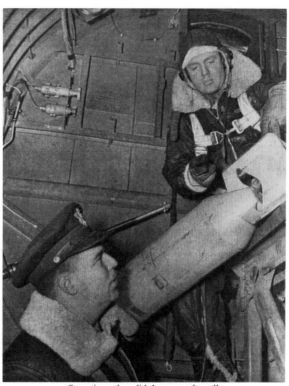

Sometimes they didn't answer the call,
:Bombs away!"

Luther Theodore Newman lives with his wife, Betty Simonton Newman, in the same house in Natchez where he was born in 1923 and grew up. He was a sophomore at Mississippi State College when Pearl Harbor was attacked; and, although he had never flown in an airplane and never wanted to, he says he was shocked and mad and wanted to fight; thus he joined the Army Air Corps as an aviation cadet. When he graduated from flying school as a pilot, he was assigned to the Eighth Air Force in England and as a pilot of a B-24 Liberator in the 446th BG at Flixton. Luther attained the rank of 1st Lieutenant, flew 30 missions from April to October, 1944, and was awarded the Distinguished Flying Cross and the Air Medal with three Oak Leaf Clusters. He says his worst mission was one to Munich and that he and his crew had about 9 hours with heavy flak.

FLYING IN THE MIGHTY EIGHTH

By Eugene Spearman

While some of our friends were already flying missions in 1942 and 1943, I was pulling a cotton sack on my father's farm in Scuna bottom, near Coffeeville. My hearing was good then, and I could hear the AT-6 trainers that were flying from Columbus Air Force Base to Pine Bluff, Arkansas. You can bet I stopped picking cotton long enough to follow the planes from horizon to horizon. I didn't realize that a few years later some German 88mm gunner would be following me as we flew over Bremen, Berlin, Dresden, Nuremburg and some thirty other targets in Germany.

With my two brothers already in service, I could hardly wait until I was eighteen years old so that I could go down to Greenwood and get in the Air Corps cadet program and fly.

My little high school at Coffeeville taught good courses in business and agriculture, but was shy on math and physics. Anyway, after basic training at Keesler and numerous aptitude tests, I was scheduled to go, first to Penn State, then Clemson, but as each training class embarked on the train, I was left waiting for the next class. Finally, I was sent to radio school at Sioux Falls, South Dakota. It was in the depth of winter, cold and damp, and with a smelly meat packing plant near the radio school. A lot of young dental students were there, on the same base, and they loved to drill without Novocain into young recruits' teeth. I kept a sore mouth part of the time I was there. I do remember the good bread and pastries in the stores and shops in the town.

In order to become a radio operator you had to pass certain levels of sending and receiving Morse code, in a given time, finally reaching a level of about 20 words per minute. A lot of my friends sometimes slammed the headset down on the table and walked out of the classes, and out of radio school.

Next came gunnery school at Yuma, Arizona, and then on to Avon Part, Florida, to meet my B-17 crew for operational training. We were a diversified bunch: from Rhode Island, New York, New Jersey, Pennsylvania, California, Nebraska, Oklahoma and Mississippi.

After a few months we picked up a new B-17 at Hunter Field, Georgia, and started overseas by way of Goose Bay, Labrador, Iceland, and on to Prestwick in Scotland. At Goose Bay the snow was so high along the runway that, as we took off, the wing tip hit the snow and we had to land again to check for structural damage. At Iceland, I had to help guard the plane at night, cold and wet with no trees on the island, just rocks. From Prestwick, we rode on an army truck down to Stone, England, a long, damp, dark ride. After a few days there our crew was assigned to the 384th Bomb Group, 544th Squadron, at Station 106, Grafton Underwood, near Kettering.

After just five months and with 34 missions flown and minus the tail gunner killed over Bremen, and the bombardier shot down over the English Channel with another crew, the pilot and I, having completed our tour took off for the United States with some others who had completed their tours. After we had flown for about eight hours, the plane suddenly went into a dive and then started climbing violently almost throwing me into the ceiling and against the floor. As soon as the plane settled down a little, I made my way to the pilot's compartment where I found out the pilot had sighted the good old USA and was celebrating by bounding the plane around. Boy, what a relief to know what was happening!

It was good to step off the plane at Westover Field, Massachusetts, in the USA.

A REMINDER OF STALAG 13A

By John M. Jones

John M. Jones was born and grew up in Macon. He graduated from the University of Mississippi and practiced as a CPA in Natchez. He was married to the former Mary Rogers Davis. During the war, he served as a bombardier in the 100th Bomb Group at Thorpe Abbots.

This article was written many years ago, for the author's children, and was taken from a diary which he kept while in a prisoner of war camp during World War II. John Jones died January 26, 1983.

It seems rather odd, as I read the newspaper today and find in an article on the front page that 1800 Nazi Prisoners of War were recently imprisoned in Stalag 13A near Nuremburg, Germany. Stalag 13A is now an American Prisoner of War camp for Germans. One year ago, I was being held in that same camp as a Prisoner of War of the Germans. The article brings back to my mind many memories. The thought that I was ever there is hard to conceive. As I sit here today, it seems as though it were a dream.

On the night of February 2, 1945, I was taken by train with twelve companions from a P.O.W. convalescent hospital at Meiningen, Germany to Nuremburg. This was during the period when Allied air power was beginning to show its strength against German transportation. Our train traveled only during the hours of darkness to avoid air attacks from the Americans. Every few miles we were side-tracked and stopped due to an air alarm caused by British night bombers flying overhead. Our train rolled into the giant marshaling yards near the city of Nuremburg forty-eight hours after we had steamed out of the station at Meiningen. We had traveled only sixty miles. Our German guards told us that we must sleep in our coach (incidentally an eight by four box car) until morning, as it was too dark for us to march to camp.

We were aroused early on the morning of February 5, 1945. The sun rose bright and clear

and sparkled upon the three inches of snow which had covered the ground during the night. Our small group was gathered together, and we began to walk toward Stalag 13A which was five miles away. That five miles seemed to be fifty, and time spent getting there seemed like days. I had been a prisoner for almost a year and had spent the entire time in the hospital recovering from a broken leg. This was actually the first time my leg had been used to any extent, and every step felt is if it would be the last. But the consequences of stopping forced us to march on.

The terrain near Nuremburg is very flat with a few trees to obstruct the view for some distance. The tall rusty barbed wire fence of our future home came into view some distance away. As we drew nearer, my dislike for the place grew stronger. Two large wire gates were swung open as we were herded into the first compound of the camp. All you could see for miles was wire and half-starved men huddled in every corner. We were taken by our guards to the small reception office and were assigned blocks and compounds. Again two wire gates were opened, and we were taken inside. This was Compound 13, and this was to be our home for the duration of the war.

Compound 13 was the size of a city block. There were four double barbed wire barriers on each side with a tall guard tower at each corner. Our party of thirteen brought the total men in this small area to 1006. I wish it were possible to describe my weakened, hopeless feeling as those two gates swung shut behind us. I was assigned a bed by the senior American officer in one of the fifteen blocks of the compound. Men were living and had been living here for months like rats. I was now among them and one of them. Life became miserable. The Germans gave us barely enough food to keep alive. The beds were infested with every sort of insect. The few hours which were spent in relaxation were interrupted continually by the parasites which thrived among us. We had no recreational facilities, no books to read, not even room enough for sufficient exercise. The situation was just as General George S. Patton said several months later when his 14th Armored Division came to liberate us, "men living like dogs."

I spent most of my time in deep thought. I often wished for pencil and paper to jot these thoughts down, but I was without both. The memories of how I wished to be from behind that wire and free will always be with me, even though they are not in writing. As I think back today, I can remember how I wished for food and to be home again; and how I wished for our armies to reach Nuremburg. As miserable as these days were, I think the happiest day of my life was also spent at Stalag 13A - the day of my liberation on April 29, 1945. This day is just as indescribable as the days during prison life, and I am sure that only a fellow prisoner is able to appreciate and understand the feeling of joy which was felt. It was hard to realize that all my wishes had been fulfilled - I was free again and on my way to America and home.

It is not very often that I think of those days. They seem so far in the past, and if I did not have evidence that I had been there, I would almost assume that I have only had a bad dream which I wish to forget. As I sit here comfortably at my desk, it seems that Stalag 13A has never existed or that it was ever a part of my life, and if I had not read this morning's paper, it would have probably been months before Stalag 13A entered my mind again.

A TASK FOR TRASK

By Roy E. Trask

Roy E. Trask was born and raised in New Orleans, Louisiana, and took the examination to join the Aviation Cadets in 1942. He was called to active duty in early 1943, sent to the West Coast Flying Training Command and received his Wings and 2nd Lieutenant's commission at Douglas, Arizona.

After going through phase training in the B-17 bomber at Hobbs, New Mexico, and crew training at Dyersburg, Tennessee, as a First Pilot, he was sent to Kearney, Nebraska to pick up a new B-17.

Trask and his crew of ten flew to Nuts Corner, Ireland, landing in Iceland on the way, for refueling.

He was assigned to the 369th Squadron of the 306th Bomb Group at Thurleigh, England, which was about six miles from Bedford and seventy miles north of London.

Roy and his crew flew 270 combat hours and completed 35 bombing missions over Germany. During these missions the plane was badly damaged on several, and managed to return to base despite having one or two engines out of service. On the 28th mission to Stuttgart, Germany, on December 9, 1944, with all controls shot out, except elevators, he had to make a forced landing at an emergency French field behind the front lines.

After two days the crew was ferried by plane back to their base. The plane was so badly damaged it was scrapped, and Roy's missions were completed in other planes. Only the tail gunner on the crew was wounded, losing partial vision in one eye.

Trask was awarded the Distinguished Flying Cross, the Air Medal with four Oak Leaf Clusters; he also is entitled to wear the Presidential Unit Citation ribbon and the ETO ribbon with three battle stars.

After the war, Roy Trask stayed in the Air Force Reserve and retired as a Lieutenant Colonel in 1964. He has been living in Jackson since January of 1949, and retired from South Central Bell in the beginning of 1984 with 47 years and 3 months service (war years bridged).

Roy Trask, standing, left

Lionel E. Gautreaux grew up in Louisiana but has now retired as a Mississippian at Gulfport. Lionel was a navigator in the 44th BG at Shipdam. His plane was shot up badly by enemy fighters on his fourth mission. Having lost two engines, his crew made an emergency landing in Sweden where they were interned. After the war, Lionel was recalled to active duty; served 16 more years in the Air Force and retired as a Lt. Colonel.

"FIVE BROTHERS SERVED – ONE KILLED IN ACTION"

By Jesse P. Phillips

The following story was first published in The Oxford Eagle *on April 8, 1994. It is reprinted here by permission of its author, the publisher of* The Oxford Eagle, *as the best account of the service and the untimely death of one of our "fine young men in World War II."*

There were seven boys and one girl in my family. Five of the seven boys served in World War II and I think without exception all volunteered. My oldest brother Paul was too old and I was too young.

Howard served in the Army/Infantry; Marvin, the Air Force; Ed, the Air Force; O.D., the Seabees/Navy; and Ralph, the Navy.

At the time we lived in Holcomb, a small town on Highway 7 between Grenada and Greenwood. Holcomb in the late 1930s and early 40s boasted of 8-10 stores, including a drug store, post office, blacksmith shop and grist mill where corn was ground into corn meal. Also, there was one doctor, Dr. Hill, who saw patients in a tiny small white building.

Early one morning the residents of the town awoke to the realization that some of the store buildings were on fire and about half of the business district was destroyed.

My family had moved "into town" from the farm located about two miles west of Holcomb on Cane Creek. This move took place around 1936-37 and my dad started operating a Shell service/filling station. He later ventured out into the business world and started running an ice route in Grenada and Carroll counties. He had a half-ton Chevrolet pickup and would go into Grenada real early each morning and pick up a load of block ice in 300-lb blocks and then would peddle it through the countryside.

While my dad was making the transition from a farmer to the "business world", our country was on the brink of war and this was escalated with the bombing of Pearl Harbor on Dec. 7, 1941.

With the declaration of war by President Roosevelt, things with my family unit started changing quickly. My brothers felt a sense of duty and wanted to be a part of defending their country.

I can remember on the front door of our modest rented home in Holcomb was a little banner/pennant which had a replica of the American Flag and around it five stars-each representing one of my brothers who was serving his country.

It is about the fifth born child of our family— Edward Lewis Phillips—that I write this in honor and memory to him. Ed was killed in action on April 11, 1944 -- 50 years ago on Monday of next week – as a tail gunner on a B-17 on a mission over Rostock, Germany.

His plane was named "Miss Raps-O-Dee," and the official military log states #2 engine damaged by flak, bombed TOP…

At 1218, 5415'N 1500'E, A/C winged over to the left and climbed slightly before the crew bailed out."

In the book, *B-17s over Berlin* by Ian L. Hawkins, intelligence officers stationed with Ed at Horham, England, state the initial target of

Ed's crew was Poznan, Poland; but at the last minute was changed to Rostock, Germany. It was here that his plane was hit, and the officers state that Miss Raps-O-Dee could not keep up with the formation.

Two engines were out, and somewhere over the Baltic Sea the crew bailed out and other crew members of planes in the formation saw all ten parachutes open. It is said with the temperature of the water that one can only survive 15-20 minutes.

I don't remember exactly the day we learned of Ed's fate, but I think it was like two days later—April 13. Fifty years ago there was no modern communication as we witnessed the actual bombing in the Persian Gulf.

The word about Ed being missing in action came by telegram, and the message was transmitted by Morse code to the little train station in Holcomb where Mr. Simpson was a station agent.

The railroad ran parallel to Highway 7 in front of our house. For some reason I was out in our front yard and can remember vividly Mr. Simpson walking down the railroad tracks toward our home with the telegram in his hand.

Dad was not at home at the time and he handed the telegram to my mother. The news was devastating!

Just days before the tragic news I can remember a florist in Grenada delivering several blooming potted plants to my mother for Easter—they were from Ed. It is almost like he had some reason to know that this might be the last Easter that he could show his love.

Our family lived in hope that word would come saying he was alive, but this never came. As far as we know, only one of the crew was ever found; this was Lt. David Janofsky, the co-pilot. A Danish fisherman recovered his body from the sea during the late evening of April 11.

Ed was attached to the 95th Bomb Group (H) the first unit to strike Berlin in a daylight raid. The legendary 95th was the only combat group in the 8th Air Force to win three presidential distinguished unit citations for courage and daring.

The 95th was activated on June 15, 1942, Barksdale Field, La. and departed for European theater of operations March 18, 1943. From May 13, 1943 to April 20, 1945, the group flew 321 combat missions utilizing a total of 359 B-17 Flying Fortresses while dropping 19,769 tons of bombs.

While performing this feat, 156 of the B-17s were lost in combat and 36 in other operations. Battle damaged planes totaled 1,362 with 61 planes force landing on the continent. As a result 425 enemy aircraft were destroyed, 117 probables and 231 damaged.

This was a costly engagement with the United States losing 569 men killed in action and with another 825 men as P.O.W.s and a total casualty count of 1,774.

At the time of Ed's death he was only 22 years of age and I was only 12 years old. In a way I "hardly knew him." I have listened to my brothers and parents talk about him, though; one of the things I have heard many times, "Ed was a fun person.. .everybody liked him."

One of my cousins, who lives in Tupelo, shared a special moment that she experienced with Ed during a summer revival in a Baptist Church in Holcomb as they were teenagers. She said at the time of invitation that Ed went forward and made a profession of faith in Jesus Christ and that it encouraged her to do the same.

Even though I do not remember a lot of experiences with him during our 12 years together, there is the hope and promise of a reunion with Ed in Heaven some day.

MY COUSIN ED
By Ethelda Phillips Nail

My cousin Jesse has written a story about his brother, Edward L. Phillips, but I would like to add some personal comments.

Even though Ed was three years older than I, we were together a lot while our families lived in Holcomb. Whenever Ed and I met each other, he would always say "Hi Cuz" with a big smile on his face. My family moved from Holcomb in 1939, and I don't recall ever seeing him again, but I shall always have special memories of him.

On October 10, 1990, my husband Kenneth and I drove to Bacton, Suffolk, England, to meet Ian Hawkins, Editor of *Courage, Honor, Victory,* an anthology of stories written by fellows in the 95th Bomb Group. The story, "A Fateful Day" by Jan Murray (Janofsky) brother of co-pilot David Janofsky, gives an account of their crash and death in the Baltic Sea. Ian went with us to Horham Airbase , home of the 95th, where Ed was stationed. Ian gave us a tour of the airbase, pointing out where various buildings had been. Inside the remains of the hospital building, a couple, who lived nearby, were growing mushrooms. Across the road were several apple trees. Ian said there were no apple trees there until the airmen came. They had stood there eating apples and threw the cores on the ground, and these trees came from the cores of fifty years ago.

In order to receive their mail-outs, I joined the 95th Bomb Group as an associate member. Through one of these I learned about a ceremony to dedicate memorial bricks to be laid around the base of the 95th Bomb Group's memorial monument on the grounds of the U. S. Air Force museum at Dayton, Ohio. I had ordered one for Ed, so Kenneth and I went to the ceremony May 7, 1995. Besides taking a picture of his brick, I also took pictures of the bricks given in memory of co-pilot David Janofsky and waist gunner Ralph Murray. Their brothers, Jan Murray

(Janofsky) and Max Murray were sent these pictures. Max sent me this crew picture and other information about them. Jan said, "In my heart and mind David is frozen in time forever— 22 years old, 6 ft. 4, good natured, happy and smiling." This is the way I think of Ed.

Ed, back row, right.

Their crew was carried as missing in action until August 24, 1949 when letters went to all the families, from Lt. Col. W. E. Campbell, Dept. of the Army, Memorial Division, stating their records were now closed, and all were declared deceased.

Ed's brother Howard said before Ed left the United States he called their mother and said, "Don't worry about me, because I'm a Christian—either way it goes, I'm O.K." She never accepted that he wouldn't come home again. When she sold her house in Grenada, she said to the buyer, "If you hear someone coming in during the night, don't shoot, because it will be my son."

S Sgt Edward L. Phillips' name is listed on The Wall of the Missing in the American Cemetery at Madingley, near Cambridge, England. A memorial plaque, furnished by the Veterans Administartion, was placed in the Woodland Memorial Cemetery, Grenada, Mississippi, in

April, 1988, for S Sgt Phillips—44 years after his death. This plaque is in the family plot where his parents, Mr. and Mrs. O. D. Phillips lie sleeping.

Howard, his brother, flies his flag every year on April 11 in memory of him.

95th Bomb Group memorial at Dayton.

Memorial brick.

Edwin W. Temple of Nettleton enlisted in the Air Corps in November, 1943, at Columbus Air Force Base. He was trained as a radio operator-gunner, and flew 35 missions with the 390th Bomb Group at Framlingham. On one of his missions there was a mid-air collision in his element (three planes in a vee formation). Edwin's plane was hit and knocked out of the formation losing two engines in the process. The pilot managed to restart both engines and return to the formation. On another mission, one of two to Merseburg, the formation was hit by a fighter attack and his plane was hit. The interphone to the tail gunner was out; the pilot sent Sgt Temple back to see about him. On the way he found that the ball turret had been damaged, and he had to crank the turret around by hand to the position that allowed the gunner to get out. Both the tail gunner and the ball turret gunner turned out to be unhurt. While Edwin was away from his position, either a piece of flak or a fragment from a 20 mm shell had hit the radio room shredding the radio operator's log book. If he had been at his station, he would have been hit himself. On another mission, Edwin's crew had to land in France after their plane had been damaged. On another occasion, they found Framlingham was socked in when they returned; they were diverted to a naval air station until the weather cleared. Edwin Temple was awarded the Air Medal with 4 Oak Leaf Clusters.

Sadly, Edwin passed away in May, 1987.

HOW LONG IS 60 SECONDS?

By William Tell Hewitt

William Tell Hewitt was born some 74 years ago, about two miles west of Cleveland, in what, at that time was a wide-open cotton field but is now covered with hundreds of new homes. He grew up chopping and picking cotton; he can tell you all about plowing up one side of a row of cotton and then down the other with a mule hooked to a "gee-whiz" or a "double shovel."

William Tell always wanted to operate heavy machinery. Because of that, he volunteered for the Seabees in 1943, but wound-up as an engineer-gunner on a B-17. This was after basic training in Greensboro, North Carolina; aircraft mechanics school at Amarillo, Texas; gunnery school at Kingman, Arizona; and crew training at El Paso, Texas.

He was discharged in 1945, worked for Mississippi Power & Light Co., owned and operated a couple of small businesses. He has been married (to the same lady) for fifty-four years, for which he claims he deserves a medal. (It could be that his bride is the one due a medal!)

March 3, 1945, was just like any other day in England - wet, cold and foggy. I got up early and stumbled around, took a shower and shaved, and then straddled my bike to head for the chow hall. The cooks had a good breakfast waiting, because it might be six to eight hours before we got another hot meal. (That is, if we were lucky enough to return.)

20 year old William Tell Hewitt
and his trusty steed

I got aboard my bike again and headed for the supply room. There I picked up my 'chute and two fifty-caliber machine guns, climbed in a jeep and headed for my B-17 bomber, "Aunt Callie's Baby," serial #429736. I got up in the plane, inserted the two fifties in the turret and placed the 'chute in position for quick access in case it was needed. I checked to see if my flak suit and helmet were in the proper place. Since I was a "horse trader," I had an extra flak suit. I wasn't too worried about being hit in the legs or arms, but there were certain parts of me that I always tried to protect, at all costs.

Stacy Tavis, our pilot; Chuck Ames, our co-pilot; Jack Noe, our navigator; Harvey Schneider, the bombardier; and Stanley Reed, the radio operator arrived from briefing with today's mission - Brunswick, Germany. The rest of the crew - William Kruger, ball turret gunner; Charles Luciano, waist gunner; Richard Slaven, our tail gunner; and I, engineer/top turret gunner - were ready to go.

Stacy hit the button to start #1 engine, then #2 and #3. Engine #4 coughed a few times before getting into rhythm with the other engines. As the engineer, I watched for any signs of malfunctions on the instrument panel or on the outside of the plane.

Everything was working like a Swiss watch. After a short warm-up, Aunt Callie's Baby began to taxi to the take-off position at 0615 hours. As she moved forward, Stacy did a zigzag in order not to run up another B-17's tail. When it came our turn at 0625 hours, Stacy eased all four throttles forward; Ames scanned the instrument panel, and I called out air speeds, "45 - 55 - 65" and on until Stacy signaled "wheels-up" to Ames. Aunt Callie's Baby zoomed into the "wild blue yonder." At this point it was hard to believe a war was in progress. All you could hear was the purr of four engines, and you could look down upon a beautiful countryside. It seemed impossible to have a killer instinct at that moment.

Aunt Callie's Baby was doing her job just the way she was built to do. She had on board nine men, twelve fifty caliber machine guns with ammunition for these, seven 500 pound general purpose bombs and six 450 pound incendiary bombs. With all this packed in her, she strained for higher altitude, round and round. Her buddies were waiting to get into formation. The time was 0640 hours; the altitude was 9,000 feet.

The flight plan called for Aunt Callie's Baby to be in the 95th Bomb Group high squadron, consisting of twelve planes. We were thankful for this, because the lower squadrons always caught hell from flak. We headed out over the North Sea, flying wing-tip to wing-tip. Stacy ordered all the gunners to test-fire their weapons. One fifty caliber gun in the top turret didn't sound just right, but with a minor adjustment, everything was fine.

In the top turret, I could see 360 degrees in one sweep. I have never seen such a sight. As far as I could see, there was nothing but B-17s. As we got closer to enemy territory, bandit territory, there they were, our "Little Brothers," the P-51s. (The time was 0942.) We saw them off in the distance as contrails and, in barely a minute, these contrails became fighter planes ready for a

fight. Aunt Callie's Baby was spurting out four perfect contrails, herself, which makes an ideal alley for ME-109s and FW-190s to creep up from behind. These were not bandits; however, but another danger was upon us before we knew it. Flak bursts began to appear all around us, flak bursts by the thousands. Some of these were low; some high; some, to the left; some, to the right; but on this mission we were spared a direct hit or even a near miss. One crew at 4 o'clock high, 3 miles out, got it in the bomb bay. All I could see were two wings floating to earth.

The flak gunners down below did not shoot at planes, but rather they threw up a "box," and we had to fly right through it. There was so much flak that it didn't seem possible any B-17 could go through it and still make it back home.

Then, at 1000 hours at 25,500 feet altitude, it came time for Harvey Schneider, the bombardier, to do his job. The pilot turned over control of the airplane to Harvey and his Nordin bomb sight. On the bomb run there was no such thing as evasive action, only straight and true, level flight. When the cross-hairs on the bomb sight came into line, our old lady spit out 3.5 tons of death and destruction. Very shortly after "bombs away" as we turned to leave the target area, our "Little Friends" appeared again. They had left us as we began the bomb run, but picked up again on the other side. Besides our own pilot and co-pilot, there was no one on earth we appreciated more sincerely than these fellows flying the P-51s.

After we left the target area, we began to relax and wait for a sight of the "White Cliffs of Dover." I spun my turret all the way around to watch other groups of B-17s come in on their bomb runs. All of a sudden I spotted two fighters at 8 o'clock high out of range. Since P-51s and ME-109s look similar at that distance, I kept a watchful eye on those two.

All at once there was a big "bang" and Aunt Callie's Baby fell off on her left wing. In just a fraction of a second, I saw another B-17 at 10 o'clock low about 2,000 feet out, missing a

61

complete tail section but with all four engines running and going into a spin. None of the nine men on board managed to bail out. Aunt Callie's Baby also went into a spin, and I couldn't get out of the turret because of the centrifugal force. After what seemed a lifetime (maybe 60 seconds), Stacy got Aunt Callie's Baby on an even keel. Somehow I managed then to get out of the turret and strap on my parachute. I was really scared and found out later that I had only strapped on one side.

Stacy was trying to raise the crew on the intercom, but no one answered. He asked me to check the nose section. I found Schneider and Noe to be all right, except for being in a state of shock like me. Next, I went to check the rear of the airplane, which I felt sure I would find full of blood and guts. I always thought the walk-way through the bomb bay was small, but I really had to struggle to get through it with an oxygen bottle and a strapped-on parachute. When I opened the radio room door, there were four "beautiful" men with all their arms and legs attached. Slaven, Luciano and Kruger were trying to help Reed find his 'chute.

After seeing that everything was all right in the waist, I returned forward and seated myself in the turret again. By the time everything was under control, we were headed for home. I looked out over the left wing and saw a pitiful sight; all the flaps were missing, up to the rear spar, and there was a big hole in the wing-tip. I could see dangling hoses and wires where the flaps had been. Aunt Callie's Baby was really struggling to get us back to England. But thanks to Stacy, our pilot, and to the Boeing Aircraft Company, it looked like nine men were going to live to fly another day.

We had dropped about 6,000 feet, and our plane was flying all alone. About this time an ME-109 spotted us and appeared to be just watching us, apparently trying to figure out why a B-17 was all alone, with four good engines and no trailing smoke. Fortunately, before he could attack, we heard a voice on the radio, "We see you, Big Friend, we see you. This is Little Friend; we've got you in sight," At that, two P-51s came from above, dove on the ME-109, and all three disappeared down toward the deck. Soon afterwards, one of the P-51s returned and stayed with us until we cleared enemy territory.

When the White Cliffs of Dover came into view, Noe, our navigator, gave Stacy a heading for a British emergency landing field. By the time Stacy could ask for landing instructions, there it was - about one mile wide and five miles long. What a sight! We had no flaps, and we didn't know whether the landing gear or the brakes would work. We certainly needed something in our favor.

Stacy ordered all the crew to prepare for a crash landing. Everyone, except the two pilots, moved to the rear and braced themselves against something solid. This was the second time within hours that I was scared beyond description. In a flash I visualized Aunt Callie's Baby cart-wheeling into a flaming mess. Under normal conditions our landing speed would be 80 - 90 MPH. With no flaps Stacy would have to land "hot" - 120 - 140 MPH.

Never, in all my flying days, have I seen such a smooth landing. Old Stacy "set that gal down" like she was loaded with TNT. If you had put a cup of tea on the floor, not a drop would have spilled.

After much discussion before a Board of Inquiry, a conclusion was reached on what had happened. Lt. Duncan's plane, No. 24501V, was hit by flak which blew off the tail section. The remainder of the fuselage crashed into Aunt Callie's Baby on its way down carrying its nine brave crewmen with it. I have been, and always will be, grateful to another brave man, Stacy Tavis, for bringing us home .

POEM

By William F. "Phil" McGuire

You lie awake and curse that fear,
Your constant companion of late,
For today you fly the enemy sky
And death could be your fate!

You know that soon you must prepare
To meet that formidable foe
Whose one great aim, and you're fair game,
Is to stop you as you go.

You mask your fears as do your men.
A bravado you display,

But your blood runs cold when you are told
The target for today.

Though long ago, the memories stay
That often chill your spine
Lest one was there one cannot share
Your feelings of that time.

So you look back with inner pride
When death was very near
But fiercest attack never turned you back
You faced the foe, you beat the fear.

GUNNER'S PRAYER

I sure was never a hero
Like some people think I was,
But just another good American
Fighting for a cause.

I always did my very best
Though I was really scared.
I wondered many, many times
Why I ever volunteered.

I'd crawl into that B-17;
I'd check my guns and gear;
I'd laugh and talk and do other
Things to cover up my fear.

There were fighters, flak and terrible
Cold and the constant engine roar.

I'd man my post and scan the sky
And say my prayers once more:

Oh Lord, if it could be thy will,
Let me live on through this day.
I need you Lord! Please hear me Lord!
Please hear me as I pray!

He must have heard, for here I am;
The years have hurried by.
Just my memories now live on
Of fighters, flak, men dying in the sky.

A hero, no, I never was;
No more than other men
Who faced the odds and risked their lives
Again and again and again.

63

BUILDING A DREAM

By Bettye Duke Jackson

The following account is excerpted from a feature by Matt Meyer's in *The Jackson Sun,* Jackson, Tennessee, with his permission. Bettye Duke Jackson has edited it to include in this anthology. The story features James Edward "Ed" Tyson, a Mississippian, a former B-17 radio operator in the 8th Air Force, and a man who has gone from building models to building the real thing. Bettye also interviewed Mr. Tyson by telephone.

It all started in 1937 at a Kuhn's Five and Dime Store in Corinth.

Ed Tyson, a 14 year old newspaper and *Collier's Magazine* salesman, saved his pennies to purchase a 35 cent plastic model of a Stearman biplane. He took it home, put it together and painted it: a blue fuselage, yellow wings and a red and white striped tail.

Sixty-two years later, Tyson, 75, is still putting together a Stearman. This time, however, he's restoring an authentic 1945 Boeing/Stearman PT-17. The plane, among the last of its kind, was used by the military to train World War II pilots.

Tyson has been saving and buying Stearman plane parts for the last 22 years. Behind his Jackson home, Tyson has even built a utility building - a 12 foot tall, 42 by 36 foot building - to hold all the parts and to build the plane. The place is filled with radios, tools, wings, propellers, rudders, two Stearman engines and semi-organized piles of other machinery and hardware. His co-pilot, Angie, a mannequin with a blond wig sits holding the throttle in the plane's steel frame.

Tyson speaks reverently of the plane. It's obvious that he is very determined to fulfill his dream. The challenge of restoring an old plane is not easy. Tyson had to repair part of the wings with dozens of pieces of wood, employing a friend to construct the intricate designs laid out in the plane's construction plans. The wings' covering is a thick yellow fabric.

Gathering the plane's parts has been a challenge, too. Tyson says he has been blessed by the many people who gave him various plane parts along the way - a rudder here, a cockpit seat there. They didn't ask for money; just a ride in the completed plane.

Tyson did have to spend a small fortune to collect the main parts. By his own estimation, he has invested a total of $50,000 in the project. He has all the parts minus about $2,500 worth of instruments. He says the plane will be completed in a year.

Tyson said restoring the old plane combines two of his passions: his zeal for airplanes and flight and the love of his country.

His love of flying began when he was a child when he dressed up and pretended he was Roscoe Turner, a World War I Colonel and aviation pioneer from his hometown of Corinth. His wife, Lorene, his high school sweetheart, also remembers Ed talking about wanting to be the first man on the moon.

The Stearman plane was designed in 1937 by Lloyd Stearman, a Californian who sold the design to the United States government. When Tyson joined the Air Force in 1943, the military was using the Stearmans to train pilots. He was amazed to see dozens of the biplanes on the training grounds in Gulfport.

Tyson flew over 22 missions as a radio operator on a B-17. He was with the 92nd Bomb Group based at Poddington near Northampton. Every other year, the 92nd meets in England for a reunion.

Tyson retired from TVA and has lived in Jackson, Tennessee since 1965. This very patriotic and energetic ex- 8th Afer claims to have done about everything he wanted to do in life - gospel singer, song writer, aviation researcher - now he's about to finalize the realization of building a dream.

Basil D. Red, Jr. was playing touch football in Meridian, where he grew up, when the Japanese attacked Pearl Harbor. He says he had never flown in an airplane at that time, but wanted to. His training in the Army Air Corps was in armament and gunnery schools. Basil was assigned to a B-24 Liberator crew and served as a gunner-radio operator in the 445th BG at Tibenham. He flew 25 missions before the end of the war cut short his tour of duty.
Basil describes his worst mission:

Magdeburg, Germany, March 3, 1945, 22,000 ft., Oil Refineries, Flak Intense, ME-109 and ME-262's.
In the target area the clouds were in broken patches; on starting the bomb run, the flak reached an intensity that I had never witnessed. Flak was exploding above, below and all around us. There were black, white and red shell bursts. Before we got to the target, I saw three B-24s going down in flames, men in parachutes were floating above and in the bomber stream in the barrage of flak. The flak was so bad, I don't see how any of them lived to reach the ground. The B-17s were above and behind us, and I could see ME-109s attacking them, then a group of P-51s came in and chased the 109s towards the ground. Several ME-262s flew through the formation firing their cannons. I don't know if they hit any of the planes or not. They came through so fast they were gone before I could swing my waist gun around to fire at them.

After the war he went to college and became a pharmacist. He now operates his own drug store in Ellisville where he lives with his wife Charmaine. Basil and Charmaine have five children and eight grandchildren.

FRIENDLY FIRE

By Bob Feloney

Roy F. Hodges

This story is included since it covers events that happened to the crew on which Roy F. Hodges served. Roy and his wife, Jean, live in Dumas, where he is retired from his career with the Mississippi Forestry Commission. He also continues to serve as a part-time Tippah County fire coordinator. During the war, Roy served as a waist gunner in the 389th Bomb Group at Hethel. He flew 33 combat missions between August, 1944 and May, 1945, and was awarded the Air Medal with four Oak Leaf Clusters. This story, written by the navigator on Roy's crew is an example of an age-old problem of war.

The term "friendly fire" is relatively new and seems to have gained notoriety from some unfortunate incidents during the Gulf War when allied forces accidentally became responsible for killing one another while thinking they were attacking the enemy. In actuality, friendly fire and the accidental killing of one's own forces probably has been going on since the first war involving man where confusion led to errors and errors led to unnecessary and accidental death. At the time it lacked the day to day coverage of every development now made possible through sophisticated media exposure.

The first time I witnessed friendly fire taking its toll was while I was on my thirty-third bombing mission during WW2. I was a navigator attached to the 389th Bomb Group with the 567th Squadron, part of the 8th Air Force. We were flying out of Hethel, England, and our target was a pocket of substantial German resistance on the French coast just north of Bordeaux. The location had been by-passed during the invasion, and later reports confirmed the presence of 122,000 Germans at the site.

The position of what was known as Target 24 involved gun batteries situated midway between Royan and Pointe de la Coubre. These strongholds denied the Allies the use of Bordeaux as a port, and these emplacements had to be eliminated prior to any further ground offensive by the French. It was April 14, 1945; and I was twenty-two at the time.

As a veteran crew we swapped Tom Ryan, our co-pilot, with the pilot of another crew who were flying their first mission. This was standard procedure and meant to give better balance to both crews. At the briefing we were told that we had drawn a milk run with little likelihood of encountering enemy fighters and the probability of minimal flak.

Our takeoff was delayed nearly an hour by a runway crash at another base where other planes were scheduled to join us in formation. Finally, the problem was resolved; and the formation headed for France. Over Orleans, we altered course for the target.

We headed for the IP from which the bomb run was to be made. We were at 20,000 feet and on an 8° heading, almost due North. The weather was clear and we were only experiencing some light flak well below us.

I was in frequent intercom contact with Horomanski, our pilot. I informed him that we were all clear for the bomb run.

Moments later to the West, I saw a formation of B-17s coming in over the Atlantic, higher than us and flying due East. I could not see if their bomb bay doors were open, but I assumed that they were headed for another target. This was unusual because the rule was that all targets were bombed from the same Initial Point on the same heading at the same altitude in order to avoid dropping on one another.

Below us was the target. The bombardier released his load of 2,000 pounders, and soon the explosions being caused by all the B-24s created so much smoke that it blocked our view of the ground. It appeared that the saturation bombing had to be taking out many of the battery emplacements in the area.

A few moments later I heard a loud explosion and felt the plane shudder from a direct hit. Because all B-24s carried gas tanks in the wings it was imperative to check each wing. If one was gone, you only had a few seconds to get out before the plane started to spiral downward. Fortunately, both wings were intact so that bailing out was not an immediate concern.

Another B-24 in the formation was not as fortunate. It also had been hit and it was going down trailing smoke. One of its propellers had been blown off and it spiraled by in front of our plane. Only one parachute was visible drifting below us. I did not know at the time that it was my friend and fellow navigator Paul Robbins.

Refocusing on our own problems, I discovered that our #3 engine had serious damage and that the fire was spreading along the wing. The flap was gone and we were being pulled into a steep dive to the right. Despite the flap problem Horomanski gradually seemed to regain control of the plane though he seemed unsure of a proper compass heading as the plane leveled off.

#3 engine had serious damage and the flap was gone

I tried to communicate with Horomanski on the intercom but the electrical circuits seemed to have been blown out. I climbed up on two ammunition boxes housing 50 caliber belts which were fed into the nose turret. Now, with my head in the celestial dome, I pointed to Horomanski the general direction I wanted him to head.

Meanwhile, in the waist section at the rear of the plane, shrapnel had ignited flares which in turn had set fire to blankets which we carried for wounded. Waist gunner and armorer, Roy Hodges, and tail gunner, Jim Allman, opened the escape hatch in order to throw out the burning material. Seeing the escape hatch thrown open and assuming that the bail-out order had been given, waist gunner, Joe Wolchanski, bailed out.

Horomanski sent our flight engineer to summon me to the flight deck. He informed me that Joe Wolchanski had bailed out, probably thinking the plane was going down and being unable to confirm it over the intercom. I agreed that I should go forward to the flight deck because I couldn't navigate from my station with a gyrating compass and no intercom contact.

I managed my way through the crawl space to the flight deck. On the way I found our radio operator, Forrest Cornett, propped upright and bleeding from a piece of flak lodged in his face beneath the right eye which was protruding. He seemed only semi-conscious and probably unable to open his chute if we had to bail out.

After reaching the flight deck we decided to return by way of Orleans. Fortunately, I had taken my maps with me when I left my station and could now reference ground points for him along the way.

Tom Ryan piloting another B-24 had left formation when he saw we were having serious problems controlling our plane. He was trying to lead us back, but we didn't follow because his navigator was new and on his first mission. We felt we were better off on our own.

We were losing altitude at a serious rate and therefore decided to lighten our load by throwing everything we could overboard, including machine guns and parachutes. When Ryan realized we were headed for a possible crash landing in Orleans he radioed ahead to clear the runway and to alert the fire and medical equipment.

We headed in on the runway as fast as we could because of the possibility of a stall due to the damage to the right wing and the loss of the #3 engine. Lacking hydraulic power, we had to lower the landing gear by hand and hope that it was secure enough to withstand the impact when touching down.

We touched down very fast and with much less control than normal because we had no brakes and a missing flap on one wing. The plane just kept going until there was no runway left. It finally stopped in the rough beyond the runway near the edge of a ravine.

A few days later, when we returned to our base at Hethel, it was confirmed that our plane and four others had been hit either by eighteen pound

fragmentation bombs or napalm bombs dropped by the B-17s flying overhead. The medics had taken good care of Cornett but were unable to save his eye. However, we were pleased to learn that Joe Wolchanski, who had bailed out of our plane, had been released following his initial capture by the Germans and their subsequent surrender following the bombing and the ground assault by the French. Paul Robbins, who had evaded capture after bailing out of one of the downed B-24s, also found his way back safely after a few close encounters with the Germans before locating other allied troops.

In the end, friendly fire claimed two of the five B-24s which had been hit by the bombs dropped by the B-17s and twelve crewmen who went down with their planes. Two of the remaining damaged planes made it back to England and ours made a forced landing in Orleans.

We accomplished our mission but through an unfortunate set of circumstances we inflicted a heavy price upon one another in the process.

The crew; Hodges, front row, second from right.

Roy Hodges' missions were flown largely over the heartland of Germany. Targets were mostly oil refineries, factories, air fields and railroad yards. Another difficult mission Roy participated in was on March 24, 1945, at Wessel, Germany. During the crossing of the Rhine, his crew flew a low-level mission dropping supplies to Allied paratroopers who had landed in the area. One plane in Roy's Squadron didn't return.

ENTER THE SANCTUM SANCTORUM OF MY LIFE

By James C. Tyler

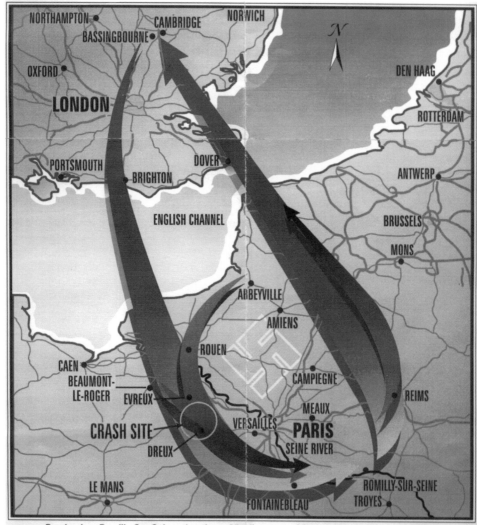

Destination: Romilly-Sur-Seine, shot down 35 miles west of Paris, between Evreux and Dreux

On December 20, 1942, a cold, gray, foggy day in Bassingbourn, after four consecutive briefings for the same target, the 91st Bomb Group of Flying Fortresses, together with all other Groups stationed in England, managed to get seventy-five bombers airborne. The target, Romney Sur Seine, was a refueling airdrome in France where enemy planes were refueled on their North Africa missions. Even though a black cat crossed the path of crew members as they hurried to their craft, no one was superstitious, for being the invincible young American airmen that we were, soon all would be well and another mission accomplished. Little did we know, or even suspect, that after each "briefing" an American Intelligence Officer, with the cooperation of a British pub owner, was giving the target location to the Germans. This particular target was no exception, for as we approached the target there were fully 500 Folke-Wulf 190s that intelligence told us we would encounter, plus the flak from the many anti-aircraft guns. The casualties were very heavy as the 190s started picking off, one by one, the bombers from the rear of the formation. The plane flying next in formation to our craft was singled out and the 20 millimeter shells from the guns of the FW-190s were so heavy that the tail section was soon sheared off and ten friends plunged headfirst to the ground to their deaths. Salvatore Dalterio, a crew member who was the tail gunner was one of the lucky ones, for as the tail section plummeted to the ground, he was thrown out, pulled his parachute ripcord and floated down to captivity to become a fellow war prisoner.

Next in formation to receive the brutality of war, which America was not yet prepared for, was the invincible crew of which I was a member, flying the position of radio-gunner, a "sitting duck" right in the top middle of the craft just above and behind the engines. With machine guns flaming bullets, one by one the fighters came so close that one could actually see the color of the Jerry pilot's eyes, scoring numerous hits with each pass made.

Three of the four engines were hit and set aflame. The pilot was killed with a direct hit. The engineer-top turret gunner was mortally wounded and was knocked down to the floor. The tail gunner was also mortally wounded. Both waist gunners and the ball turret gunner caught bullets and a 20 millimeter cannon shell had exploded in the radio compartment, piercing my lung and other parts of my body with bits of shrapnel. The order was given to bail out and those who were able to drag their mangled bodies to the door responded, even though we had never had drills in this procedure, nor had the parachutes ever been adjusted to fit, for the "invincible men" always thought that such could not happen to them. As we were flying high altitude and wore padded jump suits for such, my parachute would not strap around the upper portion of my thighs, but by exhaling I was successful in buckling it at the breast bone. One can imagine the loose dental work when the improperly fitted chute snapped open, hitting me under the chin, leaving my body dangling without leg support, and pulling the wound in my lung even wider while I floated to earth to become the first air corps prisoner of war from Mississippi. I landed in a pasture, frightening a herd of cows as my parachute folded down, narrowly missing the horns of one. I am grateful I missed, for I could have been injured even more had I been drug for any distance. Since I was unable to walk and was bleeding profusely, my only alternative was to await being picked up by the Gestapo to be carried to the "American Hospital" in Paris for treatment. Soon the German guards arrived in a closed van and the fear of my unknown destiny enveloped me - a genuine case of being in the wrong place at the wrong time.

Little did I know at this point that our co-pilot, Chuck Mendel, being the humanitarian that he is, did not depart the aircraft but chose to crash-land the craft in an open field, despite the fact that the bomb pins were pulled and the plane was in imminent danger of explosion. He chose to land the plane in an open field in order to assist the two mortally wounded crew members who were unable to bail out. His conspicuous courage and selfless devotion to his fellowman was again demonstrated at the hospital when he refused treatment until after all crew members received medical attention, even though he had sustained a broken leg in the melee.

Here is where the nightmare begins: Anesthetics were very scarce and ineffective, causing every suture, or stitch, to become a vivid, everlasting, memory; lapsing between consciousness and unconsciousness for a period of several weeks;

being unable to speak German and hearing no English whatsoever spoken; hearing carols being sung in German by the staff in their native tongue on Christmas Eve, still lapsing between consciousness and unconsciousness, thinking these songs were sung by a heavenly choir; knowing how seriously wounded the two crew members were and hearing their delirious screams from down the hall for what seemed like an eternity - then silence that was so deafening that it pierced your ear drums; no one being able to tell you why the screaming had stopped.   When I tried to inquire as to their welfare, a German nurse would only utter "tote." It was many months before I learned the definition of the word to be "dead." Being tied to the bed unable to move (of course, this was for my own good and finally I became reconciled to this fact, although most frustrating at the time); and after nine weeks the news that it was time to go to Frankfurt, Germany to "solitary confinement," and the additional news that before leaving the fluid collected in my lung would have to be drained - no Novocain, legs strapped to a table; body in sitting position with arms being held by two huge German orderlies, and a needle plunged through the chest wall to start the flow. Another example of being in the wrong place at the wrong time.

Under heavy guard, I was escorted to Dulag Luft (solitary) at Frankfurt, which was to be my home for the next two weeks and was in a room, with no windows, just large enough to accommodate a single size make-shift bed, constructed of brick corners with wooden slats across, topped with a "palaise" (burlap feed sacks stuffed with wood shavings). A single light bulb burned from the center of the room as the interrogation began. Of course, as we had been trained, to each question asked, I repeated my   name, rank and serial number. The questioning went on repeatedly, and repeatedly, and repeatedly, and the answers of name, rank and serial number remained the same. Finally, just before leaving for my first Kriegegefanner Camp (prisoner of war), the interrogation officer, in sarcasm and disgust, blurted out more information about my outfit than I knew myself.

I looked forward to leaving for, at least, I would be with some of my people and thought that I would be leaving behind the "bill of fare" ... soup, made with inferior grains and meats, three small potatoes and a sixth loaf of black bread once a day but, boy, was I in for a surprise for this was the standard rations for prisoners.

My next stop was Stalag VIII-B, a prisoner of war camp near the Czechoslovakian border, which housed all British subjects who were taken prisoner earlier in the war when fighting in North Africa, Italy and from the Battle of Dieppe.

From Dulag Luft (solitary) I was accompanied to VIII-B by a fellow crew member, who had also been wounded and was with me in the hospital in Paris. Of course we were under heavy guard during our train trip, and upon arrival were escorted through the de-louser where we lost our hair for the first time, and our underarms and genital area were powdered with something to control lice. We were given bunk assignments. The bunks were in three tiers, with twelve prisoners to a bunk section. Two by fours and one by ten planks nailed together formed the main structure, and each prisoner was allotted eight small boards to hold him up. The general rule to follow in placing these boards so a man could sleep in some comfort, was to put one under his head, another beneath the shoulders, one at the small of his back, another under the buttocks, thighs, calves and one under the ankles or heels as preferred. The burlap sack of excelsior (wood shavings), which served as a mattress and called a "palaise", or "pally-ass" was laid across them. There was an important use for the eighth board, but it had nothing to do with sleeping.   The Jerrys furnished little, if any, firewood and the extra piece of wood, whittled up, was splendid for building a hot, fast-cooking little fire. Consequently, there were many bed boards stolen, especially if a man slept on a middle or upper tier.

The Germans did not allow nails in camp, and because the bed boards were not fastened down, a prisoner who was restless during his sleep, was a menace to those below.   The nights were continually interrupted with the crash of falling bodies and splintering wood. Naturally, the whole barracks would awaken and begin laughing and swearing. Such happened to me the first night in camp as I lay sleeping in the middle tier of bunks, favoring my wounded left side that had caught the shrapnel, when my fellow crew member who was sleeping on the top bunk came crashing down, all 200 pounds of him, bed boards, palaise and all. It goes without saying, I was carted off to the prison hospital to recuperate.

Fluid had again collected in my lung and I owe a debt of gratitude to a British "masseur" who had been taken prisoner on Dieppe and was working in the Lazaret (prison hospital), for it was by massage and deep breathing exercises over a great period of time that my lung was restored to normal. In England, masseurs are recognized as doctors and practice in the hospitals and perform services comparable to our chiropractors.

Being the only American from the South in the camp was quite a novelty to the British subjects, and other nationalities, and everyone ganged around just to hear the accent. I made many friends whom I hated to leave when word came that we were being shipped out to join our American comrades.

The fear of the unknown constantly remained with me, and this segment of my prison journey was no different. Stalag VII-A was backed up against a group of pine trees. On the East side was a small creek and a meadow. On the far side of the meadow was a group of leafy trees, hiding the small town of Mooseberg, Germany. A church tower stood, like a sentinel, above the roof tops, and over the roofs of the barracks and barbed wire fences, the hills rolled in the distance and looked very green and smooth. We were marched from the railroad track and through the front entrance, and I noticed a huge gate of barbed wire which was overlooked by a tall guard tower. One main street stretched for at least a quarter of a mile south from the main gate, and on each side stood long-roofed barracks of gray stucco. Black tar paper covered the roofs. Every fourth building was separated from the next by a barbed wire fence, making an area called a compound.

The standard rations of soup, potatoes and black bread continued to repulse one's appetite because of the inferior ingredients. Rumors were floating that the International Red Cross would send food parcels to us, but because of the bombed railroads and terminals, the International Red Cross had a hard time arranging for food parcels to be sent into the camps. As the Allies piled victory on victory, and drove the Nazi's from Africa, the island of Sicily and on into Italy, the food came a little more often and trading reached a fever pitch.

The food had a trading value which was based on the German mark, which like the American dollar, was divided into one hundred parts called pfennings. An American chocolate bar, or D-bar, sold for fifteen marks, and a block of cheese had the same value. A small bar of American soap was worth one mark, and a package of cigarettes was worth two and a half marks, or two marks and fifty pfennings. One Red Cross parcel contained the following articles and was supposed to be a week's supply (but never once did I ever receive two packages in succeeding weeks during my entire confinement of 21 months) : five packages of cigarettes; two small bars of face soap; one pound box of cubed or diced sugar; a one pound tin of what we called butter, but was animal or vegetable fat; one box of twelve crackers, called C-rations; two D-bars; one twelve ounce cake of American cheese; one can of sardines or salmon; a small can of jam or jelly; and a one pound can of the GI's favorite meat...SPAM! Two of the most valuable articles were a one pound can of powdered milk, and a twelve ounce can of powdered coffee. Another food was a six ounce can of orange paste, which when mixed with water and sugar, was a pretty good tasting beverage. A six ounce can of liver paste at times took the place of the orange. (All tins were punctured at the time of issue by the Germans to keep one from storing up food for an escape attempt. With all tins being punctured, one would have to eat the food quickly before spoilage.) It is a shame that we didn't get a parcel every week as we were supposed to. I often wonder what the Germans did with the parcels we did not get that were sent.

The German rations were not enough to live on very long and we were certainly grateful to the Red Cross for the parcels that did get through to us, as this is what kept us alive.

Every morning a Jerry guard came through our barracks blowing his whistle to awaken the group whose turn it was to go to the kitchen for our breakfast…hot water. The men fortunate enough to have some powdered coffee left from a parcel made a "cup of brew." The rest drank it straight. One man in each barrack was chosen to be the "Chow King" and it was his job to dip the water out evenly. For lunch or dinner, we had a couple of potatoes or maybe a watery soup, which we called "bed board soup." It got that name because we could sometimes find pieces of wood in it. At supper time, we had the same conglomeration, with maybe a few pieces of rotten horse meat thrown in for flavor. I even found a cat's claw once, not to mention other pieces of strange meat with hair on it.

Several boys in the camp were liked and admired for their unfailing good humor and ability to entertain. Marty and Mertz played together quite often and during an evening; the boys would crowd into the barracks to listen to Marty"s beautiful tenor voice accompanied by the two guitars. One of the favorite songs of the prisoners was "Paper Doll." After each song, the boys would cheer and bang their tin cups against the bunks. During the entertainment, which took place on a group of tables forming a stage, the boys listened avidly and cheered and clapped lustily. When the shows ended, everyone heated cans of water and sat around drinking brew 'til sleep claimed them. Many nights, after all was quiet, I lay awake thinking of my life and would wonder what I could have done differently during the first twenty-one years of my life. I would dream of the things that I would like to accomplish when I got home. I would dream of my folks and feel their concern for me, not yet knowing whether I was dead or alive. I'd think how heart broken they would be if I were killed while a prisoner. Then, I'd get to feeling sorry for them and, more so, sorry for myself and a lump would swell in my throat and I would nearly cry. Other times, sounds from the darkness would

penetrate my thoughts as muffled weeping, trying to keep others from hearing, drifted across the barracks from the bunk of the most recent prisoner. This weird sound of a grown man crying filled me with compassion. Later, I would seek that person out and try to explain the sterling quality of "living one day at a time"---that's the only way I made it.

Every day there would be new rumors, or old ones revived. No one knew their exact origin, but the latrine was the assembly point and dispersal area. Men coming in to sit and chew the fat told whatever news they had gotten from the "wire." The "wire" was the barbed wire fence separating our compound and the Main Street. The news off the wire came from boys who spoke French, Polish, German or some other foreign language. These men stood by the fence and called to the POWs passing by. Anyone coming back from the latrine and handing out the latest news, or hot rumor, would be asked what hole he had gotten it from, the "Number One Hole" or the "BBC Hole." Most of the news that seeped into us via the wire was from the British Broadcasting Company. The official German news given to us was always a month or so old and we got the best news from the small crystal sets the GIs traded the guards for. Nearly every day, the Germans searched for them, but very few were ever found.

Late in September a rumor went around that the Air Corps boys were going to be taken to a new prison camp built just for airmen. By the first of October, there were over one thousand air corps prisoners in the American compound, and the Germans didn't like them being mixed with Army infantry privates. The air corps boys refused to salute the German officers, if they could avoid seeing them, and infantry men, who were used to rigid discipline, behaved better toward the Germans and did as they were told. If we could influence them, we would, by doing just the opposite.

The rumor of our moving became stronger as the first days of October passed and many didn't like the idea of moving because they figured the War would be over and we would be home by Thanksgiving. The feeling became stronger when Italy capitulated and the Allies began the invasion of Italy. Incoming prisoners told stories that knocked our dream of being home for Thanksgiving into a cocked hat and, as time passed, the air corps men began to talk with more enthusiasm about the new Luftwaffe camp. It was rumored to be in Austria, near Vienna, and to have been especially built for us. The day of departure finally came and by four o'clock we were over loaded into the old familiar forty and eight French box cars and then another wait of an hour before the train began to move. Most of the men had been on train trips before and were prepared for the crowding and shoving, but men who had been wounded and brought into the camp from a hospital, and had traveled first class, were not prepared for the discomforts of a box car, and consequently suffered severely. In fact, it was so crowded that all could not sit down or sleep at the same time. Turns were taken by some sitting, some standing and some sleeping.

The train moved slowly through the green, hilly country around Munich, and at about five o'clock we were passing through the yards of the famous Beer Hall town. We passed fire and bomb-gutted factories and when the train halted in a large marshaling yard, we could not help but worry about our being bombed while sitting there trapped in the box cars. We watched the many activities, trains passing through the yards, some carrying Jerry troops, some civilians, heading out across Germany to whatever destination or fateful career.

A train slowly ground to a halt on the track beside our prison train. Four Jerry soldiers were just opposite the window of our box car. A friend raised up on his toes to look out when one of them saw him. Getting up, he let down his window and said something in German and we assumed he was asking who we were. My friend told him we were "American Luftwaffe Kriegegefangenen." As he spoke, other boys got up to see who he was talking with and one of them didn't like his talking with the Germans.

After the troops left, my friend explained why it was important to get every scrap of news possible and he told him that he had just been released from a hospital and didn't realize how important every

bit of news was. Then came the question, Where were you wounded?" He laughed, "Well, if I said that I couldn't do a woman any good any more, that would explain itself, wouldn't it?" and, yes, he did have a beautiful wife back home. He was repatriated in July of 1944 and during the time we knew him, there was never a moment that his morale wasn't at a high.

Just before dark, the train began moving out of the yards and we were on our way. One could raise up on his toes and by clutching the barbed wire at the window, watch the scenery pass by. Bavaria was a beautiful country. Every tree and blade of grass seemed to be in place. The forests of pine atop each hill looked well kept, and every field had a cared-for look.

The train crossed a large river and the guard pointed to it and told one of the prisoners that it was the famous Blue Danube. Word passed around that we were near Linz, Austria.

By twelve o'clock, October 13, 1943, the train had pulled into the yards of Krems, Austria and the train ride was over. We had been in the cars for twenty-four hours without a break and everyone had to relieve themselves very badly. The Germans had put a large can in the car which was soon filled and was running over, so no one wanted to make a worse mess and stink than was already made.

We were unloaded immediately and the Jerry officer in command ordered an interpreter to warn us not to laugh or speak as we marched through the town. We formed into ranks of five and started marching. For the first time in days, the sun shone brightly and we were soon wet with perspiration, and cursing the day the first German was born -- under our breaths.

The town of Krems was very old and the buildings had been built against the edge of the road, which was very winding, up-hill all the time. The people stared from the windows with interest, but said nothing, and naturally, we didn't care to have bayonets stuck in our butts, so we kept our mouths shut.

The four-mile march to the prison camp, up a continuous ascent, nearly killed us and many dropped exhausted by the side of the road. In my weakened condition, with aching body and feet burning with pain, I was in agony as were the rest of the airmen. Looking back, I could see about a mile down the hill. The prisoners wound in and out around the bend of the road. The farthest ones were like tiny ants, laboring under heavy loads as each person carried all of his worldly possessions. All were crouched forward, straining and panting toward the top of the hill.

At last, the crest was reached and the Germans let us sit down to rest for about ten minutes. After the break I wished I hadn't bothered to sit down, for my legs had tightened into hard, painful knots and I could hardly move.

Across the fields that lay on top of the hill, we could see a group of white buildings with a barbed wire fence around them. Four guard towers stood at the corners. Surely this was the new camp we had heard so much about and we were all looking forward to the new accommodations, just dreaming of a hot shower and clean sheets.

Off to the left another group of buildings appeared, and when we came to the road that went in among them, the German at the head of the column turned into it and we started worrying for we didn't understand why we were not being taken immediately to the new camp. The first two buildings were long and high, looking like a huge garage, because of the big doors. We marched in between them and the Germans set up machine guns and barbed wire entanglement barricades at each end of the building. I couldn't help but think that the Germans had brought us all the way to Austria to do something terrible to us.

Our fears were allayed by the announcement that we would be processed and searched and later taken to camp. The first group of men to finish would go to the de-lousers before being given barracks assignments.

A little while later, a rumor went around that the white buildings we thought would be our new air force camp, was a French hospital and that our camp was down the hill to the North of us. An hour later, we were lined up and marched north through the rest of the buildings and barracks that housed the guards for our "new" camp, Stalag XVII-B. We approached the administrative area at the brow of a slight hill and the camp slowly appeared. First the roofs, which didn't look new, and then the barracks which definitely were not new. All around, the drab, the dead, brown hills of the lower Alps stretched, and our morale sank.

We settled in to await the duration and the first duty was to elect one of our own men as an "intelligence man" to represent us with the Germans so that all directives would be passed through him to us. The Red Cross learned of our move from VII-A and the food parcels started dribbling in, but never in such quantity that we could be issued one twelve pound parcel per man per week. We formed combines among ourselves and pooled what food we had and took turns being the cook. A little sporting goods equipment was sent in by the Red Cross and soon those who were interested were engaged in sports in a limited way.

Our barracks was designated for a gymnasium; but after a few months as an escape attempt, a tunnel was dug beneath it and the Germans tore the barracks down. Likewise, a barracks was set aside and used for a Chapel but when a tunnel was found, this barracks was also destroyed.

The "many-holed" latrine was just outside the group of barracks in my compound and it was not uncommon for it to become filled. When such occurred, the Germans would use pumps to fill the "honey wagons" and haul its contents off and put it on their vegetable gardens. At one time, the "flow" was so great that the Jerrys pumped the latrine out, letting it flow down the hill in a ditch behind our barracks. This was a "stinking mess" for months. It is a real wonder that we survived.

Each night we would be barricaded in our barracks and were not privileged to go to the latrine. On a cold, snowy night, during our first winter at XVII-B, two Americans slipped out of the barracks after midnight and made their way to the latrine. Then in an escape attempt they started crawling for the wire, only to be caught by the guard tower's spot light. We were awakened by machine gun fire and the sound of whistling bullets as the guards opened fire, not only on the men attempting the escape, but randomly throughout the camp. At the first burst of bullets, we dived for the wash room between each end of the barracks for protection since the side walls were made of brick and stucco. The next day we learned that a boy who was in his bunk caught a bullet through his bladder and, after surgery, lay critically ill at the prisoner hospital for a long time.

Early in the Spring of 1944 it was rumored, and finally came to pass, that a Swiss board of doctors serving under the Geneva convention came to camp to examine the severely wounded who needed to be sent back to the States on a three-for-one prisoner of war swap – three Germans for one American. When the day arrived, we were given a number and marched over the hill to the Lazaret (prison hospital) to appear before the team of doctors who examined and reviewed our medical records. The lucky number around my neck was "85." All who were examined did not make it.

Every few days new prisoners arrived, were processed and given barracks assignments. We were eager to examine the registration books to see where the new prisoners hailed from. We had forty-eight notebooks nailed to a wall, one for each state, and each prisoner would sign in his respective state's book. Then I would spend some time looking up the ones from my home state, asking the latest news, and trying to impart my knowledge of the importance of "living one day at a time," since there's nothing more heart-breaking than seeing a comrade go "stir-crazy," or "wire-happy" – just walking continuously around the inside of the barbed wire fence, all day long, around and around, not uttering a word to any one. Then there were other types of degeneration equally as heart-breaking.

In July of 1944, word finally came that the time had come for repatriation and I was exuberant to be among the number of 244. The afternoon before we were to leave for home, we heard someone call attention at the far end of the barracks. Our combine's bunks were the tier at the opposite end of the barracks from the approaching guards. My friend, suspecting that a search was in progress, snatched our crystal radio off the end of the bunk, slipped out the adjacent back door and made his way over to the adjoining compound. I am reasonably sure that had the crystal set been found on my bunk, my trip home would have been canceled.

Through the years of mutual hardships and suffering, the bond of comradeship had grown and our leaving camp, even though we were coming home, was an emotional experience. My friends had given me the names and addresses of their loved ones that I was to contact on arriving in the States. I did my best to fulfill each obligation and people came from miles around just to see me and learn first-hand about the welfare of their sons.

We thought when we left XVII-B that we would be home within a few weeks, but soon learned after a train ride from Krems, Austria to the northern part of Germany, near Annahoff, that we would be housed in an old castle for two months. The rations we were given were a little better and in larger quantity, and after a few weeks we started to put on a little weight. I don't suppose the Germans would really want the Americans to know just how scarce food really was. Day in and day out, we sat around thinking that any day we would leave. One of the boys who was "stir crazy" wandered away from camp. We told the Jerrys about his condition, but they shot him anyway. Then they gave him a "propaganda funeral" and took pictures of the casket being carried by the pall bearers and gave us each a set of pictures to bring home. This is the only casket I saw being used during my entire 21 months in Germany. I did witness the Germans, on numerous occasions, carrying stretchers by our compound loaded with several naked Russian bodies, arms and legs dangling, and taking them around the curve, dumping them in a mass grave, returning with the stretcher and the brown paper that was placed over the bodies. The Russians occupied the compound next to ours and died like flies during a typhus epidemic.

We, at last, made our way across the Baltic Sea to Goteborg, Sweden, where we boarded the Gripsholm and set sail for New York. Before leaving, I had been singled out to write an intelligence report and have it ready when we docked in New York. I was assigned a typewriter aboard ship and started immediately to struggle laboriously with how I would put such information on paper. The second day out, while still in German controlled waters, I heard the ship's whistle blow as we came to a halt. In looking out the port hole, I saw German guards boarding and, naturally, I thought they were coming for me. At any rate, I ate, literally chewed and swallowed, the report I was working on. Then I went up on deck to mingle with the crowd and saw them bodily remove a member of the ship's crew.

After this, the report was re-written and we headed to Halloran General Hospital in New York.

Thus, ends the war prisoner chapter in the life of ......

Jim Tyler, ASN 14600957
POW No. 27624
(James C. Tyler)
8th Air Force - 91st Bomb Group
401 Bomb Squadron

A TAIL GUNNER'S TALE

By Malcolm Holcombe

(Note: This piece was originally published in the newsletter of the 389th Bomb Group, Spring 1994. It is reprinted here by permission of the author.)

Among senior (senile?) citizens a lapse of memory is common, but since I recall certain events vividly, I'll claim 37% sanity. As the tail gunner, I am proud of having served with Bentley Kern's crew.

We arrived at the 565th Squadron, 389th BG in May, 1944. During our first days, the other crews in our billet had little to say. We assumed this was due to the loss of the men whose bunks we were occupying. Not so! They were guarding us by stifling any comments that might be demoralizing. They knew that our baptism by flak and fighters would come soon enough.

On June 10, we accomplished our first mission. This was uneventful as were several no-balls, milk runs, or whatever. Then we went to war!

Boredom was not on our menu over Hamburg, Berlin, Kothern, and Halle.

Between July 25 and August 5 we were stood down except our nose gunner, John Danneker, who flew with another crew and was lost in a mid air collision near Stade, Germany. Ed Rake became our nose gunner. Shortly thereafter we were transferred to the 564th and designated as a lead crew.

Strausbourg France, August 11, 1944. This mission accorded meager but accurate flak and presented our crew with three pieces. It became a keepsake. In 1952, I finally got around to examining it with a magnifying glass, and I found the Wehrmacht marking: WaAA52, with a swastika directly above it. I have had an enlarged picture made of it.

Madgeburg, January 16, 1945, a most impressive mission. Ramsay Potts was command pilot of our airplane. Solid overcast until bomb release. Then, accurate and intense flak. Our #3 engine was knocked out and the smoke bomb ruptured. All oxygen behind the bomb bay was lost and the intercom was inoperative. Visibility in the waist area was 10%. I don't remember leaving the turret! Roy Duffey was at the hatch and prevented a premature bail out. He knew that fire was not imminent and advised all to get auxiliary oxygen. We learned later that most crews, having witnessed our fast descent in a trail of thick smoke, felt sure that we would not leave Germany.

After dropping to a reasonable altitude, we limped back to England, throwing out non-essentials to reduce weight. The engineer cranked down the landing gear when in the proximity of an emergency base, a RAF field with the longest and widest runways imaginable. Landing could be made from any point of the compass.

Colonel Potts commended the pilot and the crew members, all of whom appeared pale and drained. Since the CO was a blonde it was difficult to know whether he too was pale.

After our tour several of the crew volunteered to stay and perform duties relating to Group functions. Ed Rake at the skeet range, I checked our turret gunners, and Hugh Martin worked with newly arriving radio operators.

Enjoying what others have written provided me with the impetus to submit my small bit. Every input regarding our memories stimulates our camaraderie. Those of us remaining shall always remember the great 389th and realize our blessing with ground crews whose work was superb.

Max Juchheim graduated from Grenada High School in 1940, a class of 46 graduates of whom 20 were male. Every one of those young men served his country in the armed services during World War II, almost half of those in the Army Air Corps. At least six served in *The Mighty Eighth*.

Max was the only fighter pilot in the class; and what a fighter pilot he was! He flew a P-47 Thunderbolt with the 78th Fighter Group out of Duxford. Two incidents are recorded about Max in *The 78th Fighter Group in World War II* by Garry L. Fry:

"Max Juchheim followed two ME109s to the deck, hitting one steadily with a pair of two second bursts at 200 yards. The Messerschmitt's canopy came off and the plane crashed in a field. Pulling up on the second one, Max chased him over a little town where he streamed black smoke and rolling inverted, crashed in a small woods."

And regarding another occasion:

"Captain Juchheim got behind a Focke Wulf and scored hits, also causing the pilot to hit the silk. Spotting another FW attacking a squadron mate, Juchheim did a head-on pass causing the German to abort the attack. Reefing into a reversal, Max gained the 6 o'clock shot spot on another 190 and then ran out of ammunition before he could finish him off properly. By then the two fighters were tearing along just off the deck, and never a man to quit the advantage, Juchheim put his P-47 on top of the FW and dropped his nose a bit. This caused the German to clip the ground with his propeller, and in panic, he tried to turn away. Digging a wingtip into the ground, the plane crashed and exploded."

Max recorded 14 enemy planes destroyed before he himself was shot down and became a P.O.W. for the rest of the war.

Max still lives in Grenada where he has continued his father's business in an automobile specialty shop. I'm sure Max remembers very vividly the days he spent as a "Kriegie" in a German prison camp. I hope he recalls just as vividly the days when he flew his Thunderbolt across the skies of Europe, making those of us who flew in the bombers mighty proud to refer to him as "Little Friend."

A CAP TO REMEMBER;
AN OXYGEN HOSE NEVER FORGOTTEN!

By Ethelda and Kenneth Nail

Our good friend, Billy F. Shumpert celebrated his 19th birthday two days after he enlisted in the Army Air corps on November 17, 1943. Within a month he was on his way to Miami Beach for basic training. Knowing Billy as we did, we are absolutely sure that what he gained fame for there was completely without malice or evil intent. What he did was perfectly innocent; how was a young man from Tupelo, with no experience whatsoever with military rules and regulations, dress codes and protocol, to know the differences in hats and caps worn in the Air Corps?

Billy Shumpert on Collins Avenue

What happened was this: Billy and a friend were strolling about seeing the sights on Collins Avenue. How interesting it all was! Not only was the scenery very different from that back home, with palm trees and sandy beaches, and very beautiful, but all the architecture of hotels, restaurants, homes was unusually striking. Shops offered unusual attractions: clothing and other things. What caught Billy's eye particularly, was the snappy uniforms some of the young airmen one met were wearing. Some had what appeared to be tailored uniforms while his and his friend's were ill-fitting and shapeless. And the hats! Some military figures

had caps which rose to a peak in front and had a gold eagle on the front. They were made of expensive looking twill. The crown of the caps were not stiff and round on top, but had a gently *crushed* look. How softly this twill dipped and fitted down close to the head! The caps Billy and his friend wore were very simple. They looked to be made of a single piece of cloth, folded over and sewn so that they fitted over the head, more like an envelope than anything else.

It didn't take our friend, Billy Shumpert, long to begin to want a better hat. And, right there on Collins Avenue, was a shop that sold all sorts of military headgear. In a few minutes a transaction was concluded and Billy walked out with an Air Force officer's cap with a fifty-mission crush. I can just see him proudly exhibiting that splendid chapeau! And the next thing he did was to walk into a photo shop and have his picture made in that hat, plus an A-2 leather jacket and a white silk scarf.

The Cap

Well, Billy got into some difficulty with his superiors about that hat; not terrible trouble, not like desertion or being AWOL, but trouble. They called it "impersonating an officer." He didn't have to go the guardhouse or anything like that. What they did to him was to make him scrub the floor of his quarters *with a toothbrush!*

Sadly, our friend Billy Shumpert died on January 8, 1990, after a massive heart attack. We feel that if he were still here he would laugh again with us at the telling of this story, as he used to do about that cap to remember!

Billy went on from basic training to gunnery school and training as a B-24 Liberator gunner. After his crew was assembled and trained together, they were given a new B-24 to fly to England, which they did with stopovers in Greenland and Iceland. When they arrived in England, their plane was taken from them; and they were transported by truck to the 489th Bomb Group base at Halesworth. There they learned that the 489th had been converted to B-17 Flying Fortresses; they flew their first mission on a B-17. Billy and his crew flew only three combat missions before they were reassigned back to the States for training in B-29s and combat in the Pacific.

On their first mission over Germany, Billy was flying as right waist gunner; Henry "Slim" Bethke was the left waist gunner. In *A History of the 489th Bomb Group,* Slim wrote of turning on the bomb run and seeing "the lead squadron had turned into a wall of flak!" He goes on to tell of the occasion:

"Ships were being tossed all over the sky. Suddenly, without any warning, we were up on one wing tip, then the other, then almost upside down. If Pitts and Gardner (the pilots) hadn't been on their toes, I wouldn't be here to write this, nor would any of the others on the crew....

"In our mad gyrations in those brief seconds, I was thrown against the top of the plane, then flat on my back on the floor. My oxygen line was disconnected, and I was too numb to fasten it.

By this time the plane was under control and out of the flak area. Shumpert was right on the ball. He slipped my connections back together and turned on the emergency oxygen supply. His own hose connection came apart; so he left me for a second to fix it but was right back and held me for a minute or two until I was once again functional. A little thing you may think, but something that has given me these extra years, for which I will always be grateful.

"Well, we had dropped our bombs and were on the way home. It didn't seem possible, yet there we were... We had just made our second turn after Bombs Away, when all of a sudden, WHAT! -- number one engine cowling was blown to bits. Lieutenant Pitts quickly feathered the engine...and slowly but surely we lost our place in the formation.

"We finally reached the English coast and were sweating out the time as we kept dropping farther behind the other planes...We were almost home...I felt like singing 'Coming in on a Wing and a Prayer,'" when #3 engine suddenly started throwing oil and just quit.

"With only two engines running, we began losing altitude fast. Pitts told us to throw things out, and believe me, we did! Everything we could get through the hatch! Stevenson quickly plotted our position and gave it to Ed Pavolich, who contacted Air-Sea Rescue. It looked as though some of our ditching practice might come in handy. All this time, guns, ammunition, flak suits, oxygen bottles, etc., were going out of the rear hatch. We were working like beavers, and I think each of us was silently praying, too. Pitts didn't hear any interphone talk; so he called to see if we had all bailed out.

"Stevenson's plot was right on the ball and brought us in only a few degrees off course; so we were safe for the moment - well over land. Now it was up to the pilot to set us safely down with only two engines going...Pavlovich was firing red flares to warn other planes of our emergency landing. We had confidence in Pitts, but we were still sweating. First toward one side of the runway, then straight for the center. Shumpert, Penke and Yelton were near the half deck. I stood near the left waist window. The crash wagons and ambulances were waiting. We leveled off, and the wheels hit. We'd made it!

"When we stopped rolling there were ten very humble men on that ship… We found out later that there was only a pint of oil in #4 engine; another few minutes and we'd have lost that one too. If that had happened on final, probably none of us would be here now. That was our first mission…and today, Sunday, we gave our thanks to God."

Well, there you have two sides of Billy Shumpert: a very young, very fun-loving young lad who could get himself into some scrapes, and a very serious, mature, heroic young man who grew up quickly in a combat situation and bore himself with great presence of mind and fortitude when the going got rough. There were other sides to Billy which we also remember. He was very devout and showed his Christian character by spending some of his leisure time in the Air Corps serving as an assistant to the Chaplain. He was gifted musically (he was to receive a musical scholarship to Tulane University if war had not intervened); he played in the high school band; he sang in the church choir. He was a sturdy family man; he and his much-loved wife, Gwen, have one daughter, two granddaughters, two great-grandchildren and two step-great-grandchildren. He was a successful business man. And, among many other sides to Billy Shumpert which we saw, to us Billy was a friend, a special friend; and we remember him constantly with the greatest affection.

Billy Shumpert: fun to be with, serious, devoutly religious, a patriot who served his country at a very young age, a great companion. We hope he has a really sharp hat to wear where he is.

Chaplain's Assistant

Billy Shumpert, front row right, and his crew.

IN MEMORY OF CLAYTON M. JUNKIN

By Roger F. Smith

The following story is written in memory of Clayton M. Junkin, the author's uncle. Mr. Junkin passed away on March 4, 1983.

Clayton M. Junkin was born on January 18, 1921. After graduating from high school, he planned on attending Auburn University and studying architecture. However, war changed his plans and he volunteered for the Army Air Force and was inducted August 22, 1942, at Ft. McClellan, Alabama. From there, he was sent to Keesler Air Field, on the Mississippi Gulf Coast, for an airplane mechanics course. Next, Clayton attended an aerial gunnery course at Harlingen, Texas, which he finished on February 13, 1943.

Clayton arrived in England on July 18, 1943, as a flight maintenance gunner after being assigned to the 388th Bomb Group, 562nd Bomb Squadron.

He flew his first mission aboard the B-17 "Wolf Pack" on July 25, 1943. Pilot of the "Wolf Pack" was 2nd Lt. Edward A. Wick who told the author, "The name 'Wolf Pack' was chosen by the crew either because they thought they were a pack of real fighters or because of the way they talked about their adventures after a night in town or both."

Clayton's fifth mission was the historic double strike against Schweinfurt and Regensburg on August 17, 1943. The 388th struck Regensburg. Lt. Wick described the mission:

"Our group was second in the combat wing formation. We encountered only a small number of fighters. However, the groups behind us came under heavy attack. Losses this day on the two missions were the greatest thus far in the war. Sixty aircraft and 600 men were lost. Strike photos showed that the entire Messerschmitt plant was destroyed. After bombing the target, the Group turned south, crossed the Alps, Northern Italy, the Mediterranean Sea to the west of Italy and made landfall at Bone. From there we proceeded for another half hour and landed at Telergma Field in North Africa, as briefed. We ran out of gas on the two outboard engines as we came over the field and had to make an emergency landing. Only three planes from our group of 23 made it all the way to the assigned

base. One airplane ditched and the rest had to land at emergency fields because of the shortage of gas. I had red warning lights on all four gas tanks for about one hour before reaching Africa. We spent the next week pumping fuel in the airplane from 50 gallon barrels with a hand pump, loading bombs and waiting for the weather to clear in England."

The crew's ninth mission against Stuttgart was on September 6, 1943, and would be their last. Again, Pilot Wick gives the details:

"We had a little trouble getting our crew together that morning and as a result took off late with a substitute radio operator and waist gunner. The number three supercharger ran away during the takeoff roll. The co-pilot brought the supercharger under control and the takeoff was otherwise normal. We gained altitude, found the group and joined up. Things were rather normal until we were over Germany. Our group then came under heavy fighter attack which continued all the way to the target. At the IP, things started turning bad fast. The number three supercharger froze up and the manifold pressure dropped to the point where we didn't have enough power to keep up. Almost immediately we took some hits from the fighters. I could see some rather large holes in the left wing which increased the drag. About this time the top turret was hit. A 20mm shell exploded in the gun sight and sent the top gunner, Clayton Junkin, tumbling forward and down through the hatch between me and the co-pilot into the lower passageway to the nose. I was about to call the navigator and have him check on Clayton, when Clayton popped up between me and the co-pilot and looked at me with a questioning look on his face. His helmet and oxygen mask were gone and the lenses of the sunglasses he was wearing were missing. Otherwise, he looked OK; so I nodded and he went back up into the top turret. He kept on fighting, and, as far as I know, without oxygen.

"We were behind the group formation and under heavy attack by this time and the gunners were calling fighters' locations and firing steadily. About this time I discovered that the Group hadn't dropped on our first pass over target, so we had to salvo our bomb load in hopes of catching up. As I looked back, I saw an ME-110 twin engine fighter at the seven o'clock in almost formation position. As I watched, he turned his nose toward us and opened fire at close range. One or two hundred rounds of 20mm were pouring into our aircraft. I didn't expect to survive. I noticed that Clayton was firing burst after measured burst into the right wing and engine of the 110. I thought this was pretty cool under the circumstances. I saw the wing fold upward on the 110, and he went down. By this time we were flying from one heavy flak area to another to keep the fighters away. Fighters were more to be feared than flak in the summer of '43.

"We were now on a southern heading and had run out of flak to hide in. At about this time a fighter came in from high up and delivered the fatal blow. Hits were taken in the tail section and the tail wheel assembly was either torn loose or blown away. A gang pulley for control cables was mounted on this assembly. When that went, all the control cables in the plane went slack. I had no rudder, no elevators, no aileron and no trim tab control. We always flew with the auto pilot turned on but disengaged. I even tried to use that but with no control cables it was useless.

"By this time the aircraft had slowly turned to the right and was in a vertical bank. There was no way to recover. I turned on the bailout bell and gave the order to bail out on the intercom. We were still above twenty thousand feet. The aircraft went into a spin to the right. The co-pilot and I went through the hatch between our seats. All the front crew went out through the forward hatch. A spin is a more gentle maneuver than most people think. I could, however, feel and hear the structure of the aircraft bending and twisting. I had no trouble moving forward to the hatch and went out headfirst. I had mixed feelings. I was relieved to get out of the aircraft before it blew up or trapped us but felt very lost. I later found out that Clayton was lying unconscious in the right rear corner of the flight deck. Neither the co-pilot or I saw him as we turned and dropped down through the hatch. He

regained consciousness at the last moment, saw the ground coming up fast, snapped the chest pack chute on with only one snap, fastened one leg strap and out he went. He was lucky the chute didn't pull off. He landed only a moment after the chute opened. I wanted to free fall for a ways to get to the ground in a hurry in order to have a better chance of evading capture and waited until I was very close to the ground and pulled the ripcord. The aircraft crashed directly beneath me. I slid to the side and hit the ground. I could hear people shouting. I turned to the west and was looking right down a village street. There were people on that street, and they were coming my way. They were still a ways off, and I had at least some small chance of evading them. I was in the west edge of an apple orchard. The ground and orchard sloped up to the east until it met the edge of a forest which went on up and over a long ridge that ran north and south. I dropped the gun belt and pistol I was wearing but kept the sheath knife. I ran around the aircraft that was burning furiously and headed up through the orchard. I heard a shout and turned to see Clayton taking off his chute harness and heavy flying clothes. He had several small scalp wounds and streaks of blood down his face. These wounds turned out to be little more than scratches and of no consequence, but he had sprained his ankle on landing and that made movement painful and difficult. We slowly worked our way up the hill and into the forest. I expected to be overtaken and stopped at any moment, but apparently the people from the town stopped to watch the plane burn. We found an open area thick with small bushes only about a foot and a half high. It looked like an unlikely place to hide; so we went to the center and lay down. It turned out to be a good choice. About an hour later a line of German soldiers moved through the area searching for us. I saw one pass by below us on the edge of the clearing about sixty feet away and heard another pass by above and much closer. Our hiding place must have looked so unlikely to them that they didn't look. We stayed put that night and the next day. The following evening we started moving south through the forest. Clayton was having a difficult time because of his sprained ankle. We found a garden during the night and dug up some potatoes which we ate raw. Early the next morning, we came to a village that filled the valley and blocked our way. As it got light, we started working our way up the hill in hopes of finding a place to hide for the day. The forest was very open at this point, and we were soon spotted by three men who were walking to the village. Our attempt at evading was over. We were taken into the town and to the town hall. We were probably the first enemy seen by the city officials who didn't seem to know exactly what to do with us. Later that day we were taken to a nearby airfield and were interrogated. It was then I learned that three of my crew had been killed and had been found in the aircraft. The next day we were taken by train to Frankfurt Am Main and from there by truck to nearby Dulag Luft, the Luftwaffe interrogation center and transit camp. When they were through with me, I was taken to an adjacent holding compound where prisoners were held until there were enough to make up a shipment. I saw Clayton here for the last time during the war. I was taken to the railroad yard and loaded into a boxcar. These were the famed 40 & 8 cars of World War One. After a rugged two day trip we arrived at Sagan, Germany and Stalag Luft III. I was put in Center Compound."

The author wishes to thank Edward A. Wick who answered many questions about the author's uncle, Clayton Junkin. Wick and Junkin remained lifelong friends. Wick retired from the Air Force in 1968 with the rank of Lt. Colonel. After twenty months in a German P.O.W. camp, Clayton Junkin settled in Columbus, Mississippi, and married Willadean Smith in 1947. They had no children. Clayton served as Chancery Clerk of Lowndes County, Mississippi, between 1968 and 1972. Before his death, he was a farm loan officer for Merchants and Farmers Bank.

The first member of the Eighth Air Force to shoot down a German plane was Sam Junkin, a young man from Natchez, who, at the time, was flying a Spitfire borrowed from the RAF. This victory occurred on a fighter sweep over Dieppe, which was about as far as a Spitfire could fly, engage in combat, and still have enough fuel to return to its base.

Sam Junkin was also among the earliest fliers in the Eighth to be shot down. This, too, occurred over the Channel; Junkin bailed out over the Channel and was rescued by British Air Sea Rescue. He was wounded, too, in this engagement and was taken to a Canadian hospital where he was attended by a most attractive Canadian nurse. These two allies, the young flier from Natchez and the young nurse from Canada, fell in love with each other and later married and lived happily as leading citizens back in Natchez until Sam's untimely death in 1967.

A footnote to this Mississippi first and the subsequent Allied romance is that fifty years after Sam's service in England, two children were playing in their back yard, which was on the site of the war time RAF base at Biggan Hill; they must have been using a metal detector, a favorite piece of equipment for British youth, for they uncovered a set of American dog tags. These dog tags bore the name of Sam Junkin, Natchez, Mississippi. A letter to the editor of the newspaper in Natchez soon put the children in touch with Evelyn, Mrs. Sam Junkin.

Sam Junkin's memorabilia: The flag which draped his coffin, a large war time portrait of Lt. Junkin, his medals and citations, and his war time uniform, were graciously given to the Mighty Eighth Heritage Museum by his widow, shortly before her own death in 1997.

AN ABBREVIATED CAREER
IN THE MIGHTY EIGHTH

(Note: This account was written by the editorial staff of this anthology, based on an account furnished by Leon C. McWilliams, Jr.)

Leon Clayton McWilliams, Jr. embarked on his military career on August 2, 1940, as a private in the Mississippi National Guard. His squadron, the 153rd Observation Squadron, was activated October 15, 1940.   The squadron aircraft consisted of O-38Es with fabric covered bi-wings, and 0-47s which were all-metal planes, carrying a pilot, an observer and an aerial gunner manning a 30 caliber machine gun. McWilliams was placed on flying status as an aerial gunner but was later moved to headquarters section as an administrative clerk.

Following the bombing of Pearl Harbor, the squadron was joined by observation squadrons from Minnesota, Indiana and Michigan and moved to Wilmington, North Carolina. From there, these former National Guard units flew anti-submarine patrol over the Atlantic Ocean.

In June of 1942, the 153rd Observation Squadron was assigned overseas and departed for England on the Queen Elizabeth. They were based at Membury where they were reconstituted as the 67th Reconnaissance Group, an arm of the Eighth Air Force. This service in the Mighty Eighth was short-lived, however, as they were shortly relocated to Keerid in Wiltshire, and became a part of the newly formed Ninth Air Force.

From this Wiltshire base, the air crews flew raids into France. The 153rd was notified in early June that it would be involved in the D-Day landing. Part of the squadron left England on June 18 for Omaha Beach, and the second group left June 23, 1944 for Utah Beach. They saw action across France, Belgium, the Netherlands and Germany.

Leon McWilliams was discharged from the Mississippi National Guard and joined the U. S. Reserve Army Air Force on his return home in 1945.

Leon and Ann McWilliams live in Starkville, where they recently celebrated their 52nd wedding anniversary.

This, then, is the story of another Mississippian who, though his time in the Mighty Eighth was short, served his country honorably and well there, before going on to service with one of our closest allies.

Robert Lamar Gray grew up in New Albany but now lives in Greenville with his wife, Juanita. He is the father of three children and has four grandchildren and four great grandchildren. Having grown up always wanting to fly, Robert joined the Army Air Corps and attended aircraft mechanics school and aerial gunnery school. When he arrived in England in 1944, he went to Mendlesham to fly 35 missions as a flight engineer with the 34th BG. His worst mission was his 35th; the 34th had 24 planes that day on a mission to Kiel; 12 were lost over the target. Robert attained the rank of T Sgt and was awarded the Distinguished Flying Cross and the Air Medal with 3 Oak Leaf Clusters.   In civilian life, Robert is a retired manufacturing plant manager. After retirement he got his private pilot's license and is still current with that and in good physical condition in his mid-seventies. His bomber crew (The Mischief, B-24) still has reunions every 4-5 years, though only four are still able to attend. Robert and Juanita are in their second half-century of marriage; they have a motor home, travel extensively and enjoy their lives as Mississippians.

FROM HEYDEKRUG TO HELL,
AND THEN SOME

By William D. Henderson

William D. Henderson was born in Senatobia, grew up and attended school at various locations in North Mississippi and graduated at Independence. He served in the Civilian Conservation Corps for two years and went into the Army in January, 1943.

He first met his combat crew, on which he was the tail-gunner, in September, 1943. The crew flew a new B-17G to England where they were assigned to the 95th Bomb Group at Horham. They flew a couple of easy, uneventful missions and then, on March 4, 1944, they were on the first raid on Berlin flown by the Mighty Eighth. As it turned out, Bill and his crew had engine trouble and had to abort the mission. However, two days later, they were assigned to fly on the next mission to Berlin again. They were given a battle-weary B-17, named "Situation Normal." Just before boarding the aircraft, the bombardier told the pilot that anyone flying that battle-worn aircraft to Berlin and back should receive the Medal of Honor. As it turned out, that was a fateful comment, as the plane was shot down just inside Germany on the way to Berlin. Five crew members were killed. Bill and four other crew members survived to suffer over a year in German POW camps. They interned first in a camp near the village of Heydekrug, where they remained for about four months.

The following is an account of a terrible time during their move to their next place of incarceration.

About the second week in July, the rumor mills really cranked up. The most prevalent one was that we were to be evacuated. Anxiety continued to mount, and we began to squirrel away what little food we could spare.

In the late afternoon of July 15, evacuation of the camp began. We were issued extra food and marched to the nearby village of Hydekrug and crowded into box cars. We were then transported to the port of Memel on the Baltic Sea (just inside the southern border of Lithuania). We unloaded, marched to a dock and loaded on a tramp freighter, the *Mausern*. We later learned it was a captured Russian coal ship. There were about one thousand Americans and some British loaded on this ship.

Everyone was packed in the hold of the ship which had a semi-V bottom. This made it extremely difficult to sit, stand, lie down or assume any comfortable position. When the ship got under way, the crowd gradually slid to the center of the ship, creating more discomfort. There were no bathroom facilities except a bucket lowered by rope from the deck. The only water supply was a few buckets bargained for by trade of cigarettes with the ship's crew. It was lowered in buckets which were probably the same ones used for latrine purposes. (Fresh water coming down and used water going up!) It was totally impossible for everyone to relieve themselves in the buckets and before long the stench in the hold was unbearable.

The weather was extremely hot, and to add to the heat problem the Germans stretched a tarp over the hold of the ship. It was impossible to sit in a comfortable position, reach water, or move about in any way. It would have been impossible to escape the hold of this ragged vessel in the case of any accident.

We proceeded on this tramp steamer through the mine-infested waters of the Baltic Sea to the port of Schweinemunde near Stettin, Germany. All during this trip we were under the constant threat of American or British bombers. Many times we heard scraping alongside the ship. Fear of being sunk by a mine was constant.

One prisoner was allowed topside to go to the latrine and jumped overboard. It had to be a case of suicide because he surely knew he could not swim several hundred miles to Sweden. In addition to his almost certain death from drowning, the German guards fired many rounds at him in an attempt to kill him in the water. They were probably successful.

After slightly more than two days, we arrived at Schweinemunde and were unloaded from the ship and placed in box cars. Even though we were extremely crowded in the box cars, it was a great relief to be out of the horrible conditions of the ship's hold. It was impossible for us to foresee the barbaric treatment to which we would be subjected in the near future. Many prisoners were handcuffed by twos prior to being crowded into the box cars. The supply of handcuffs was exhausted before they reached my group, and this proved to be extremely fortunate for us on the next day.

Shortly after we were loaded in the cars, sirens began to wail and flak guns opened up. We felt sure someone was attacking the German light cruiser that was tied up in the harbor. Fortunately for us, this was not the target; and before long when the all-clear sounded, we breathed a sigh of relief. We had been spared one more time. We departed the area shortly thereafter and after a very slow train ride, we pulled off on a spur track in a small village. We later learned it was Keifheide. We spent the night locked in the box cars.

Early the next morning we were awakened by many loud noises, much shouting and screaming, and wondered what all the clamor was about. We soon saw a strange new red-headed German Captain who was raving and ranting about the American Luft Gangsters, baby killers, murderers, and any other vile name he could conjure up. In addition to the regular guards we had on the ship and a new group of Wermacht soldiers, we were faced by a group of young Kreigsmarines. The conduct of the Captain was similar to that seen in the movies where the bad guys attempt to incite a crowd to conduct a lynching party.

We were soon unloaded from the train and ordered to fall into ranks of two. Many of us had packs we had made from shirts, blankets, etc. In these we had stored what precious supplies of food, cigarettes, toilet articles and any other possessions we had.

Still screaming and shouting, the Captain gave the order for us to start marching out of the village and up a narrow road through a forest. As soon as we started up the road, orders were given for us to increase our pace, and the Kreigsmarines began to hit some of the prisoners with the butts of their rifles and to prick us with bayonets. They continued to yell at us to run faster. They then turned dogs loose on the column. One of their objectives seemed to be to get all of us to drop our packs. Early on, using their bayonets, they began to cut the packs off the backs of those not dropping them automatically.

As we entered the forest, we became aware of machine gun emplacements on each side of the road with each gun manned by two soldiers. This was the first time I felt I was about to be executed and buried in some mass grave in the forest.

Everyone ran as fast as he could. Those of us who were not handcuffed were able to avoid the Kreigsmarines much better than those poor unfortunate souls handcuffed in twos. Many fell and were bitten by the dogs and/or bayoneted by the Kreigsmarines. Some were still suffering from wounds received when captured. Others were sick from the boat ride. Many heroes were created that day. When a prisoner stumbled or fell, he was picked up and carried by his comrades for the remainder of the four kilometers.

At last we broke out of the forest and saw a prison camp in front of us. We had arrived at Stalag Luft IV. It would seem at this juncture that our group had suffered the worst possible treatment at the hands of the enemy. Not true!
We were evacuated from Stalag Luft IV on February 6, 1945, and forced to march for a period of eighty-three days. During this march, the weather was terrible (snow, sleet, rain and

Ice). We slept in open fields, woods, barns, abandoned factories or at any spot we happened to be at days end or whenever the Germans wanted to stop for the night.

There was barely enough food to survive on and no medical attention. We were allowed to bathe for the first time in the Elbe River in early April (very cold). We were sick, lousy, dirty and totally exhausted. Most in my group had reached the limit of their endurance.

Upon liberation by the 104th Division on April 26, 1945, we felt the Devil had finally lost control, and we had returned from HELL!

****

(Bill married Ruby Carolyn Dix of Coldwater in 1946, and they have two children, three grandchildren and three great-grandchildren.

He was employed by the Navy Department at the U. S. Naval Air Station, San Diego, from October, 1946, until June, 1956; transferred to the Navy Department in Washington, D.C. and retired from the Office of the Chief of Naval Materiel on June 30, 1972.

He and Ruby have resided in Batesville for the past twenty-three years.)

Denver, CO, June 1943

Moses Lake, WA, Sep. 1943

A few days after liberation, April, 1945

William D. and Ruby C., 1998

A SOJOURN IN FRANCE

By N. Kenneth Nail

Victor Byrd flew as a waist gunner on a B-24 Liberator, out of the 466th Bomb Group at Attlebridge, near Norfolk. During part of their tour, Victor and his crew flew air sea rescue. Their job was to patrol the Channel and the North Sea, helping to spot crews who had ditched on their way home from missions. When they spotted downed airmen, they circled the area and reported the position to surface rescue craft.

On April 1, 1944, Victor and his crew were on a bombing mission to Brunswick. They had eleven people on board: the crew of ten plus a photographer. They were flying low so that the photographer could get some good pictures. When they ran into some intense flak, they were badly crippled and the order was given to bail out. There were three survivors; the remaining eight on the flight lost their lives. Victor Byrd, one of the three survivors evaded capture by the Germans and was picked up by a French family. They kept him hidden several months until the Allied armies reached the area and liberated him.

Victor never forgot this heroic French family who risked their own lives to save him from the Germans. He kept up with them after the war, always grateful for their sacrifices and risks in his behalf.

One of the other survivors of the crew reported that Victor Byrd was a very quiet and likable young man. And so he was when I knew him in later life. The crew member said that Victor always refused the medicinal whiskey given to air crews after missions, giving his ration, instead, to another crew member.

Victor passed away in 1974; he left his wife, Mary, and two daughters, Laura and Suzanne. There are now four grandchildren, Lee, Steven and Emily Porter and Will Poynor.

The Crew, Victor L. Byrd, front row, left

Byrd receives French commendation.

Victor Byrd, back row left, and his French family

MANNA / CHOWHOUND MISSIONS
Flights of the RAF and the 8th USAAF, May 1945

By Harold E. Province

The author of this story was born in Kent, Ohio, and entered kindergarten on the Kent State campus in 1930, and took a BS in Geology in 1950 after serving two years in the U.S. Army Air Corps. He flew 19 combat missions against Germany as an enlisted bombardier in a B-17, out of Mendlesham in Suffolk.

Harold married Janice Folkman in 1949 the day after finishing his course work at Kent State. He went to graduate school at the University of Cincinnati receiving a Master of Science degree in Geology in 1952.

He began work for the California Company in June, 1952 and worked in Louisiana, Mississippi, Alabama and Florida until retirement from Chevron in 1986. He later retired as a Staff Geologist working in Computer Applications to Geology.

Harold enjoys living now in the Picayune area and attending the First United Methodist Church. He has three sons who live in Louisiana with his 6 grandchildren. He is currently Corresponding Secretary and Treasurer of the 34th Bomb Group Association. He is a life member of that Association, the 8th Air Force Historical Society and the Mississippi Chapter.

This is a story of events which are seldom, if ever, reported in the histories or accounts about WWII. During the period of May 1 through May 7, 1945, the 34th Bomb Group as a part of the 3rd Bomb Division of the 8th USAAF, took part in some relief flights into western Holland at low levels. Where we had been dropping bombs from altitudes of 18,000 feet and higher, we flew into Holland at less than 400 feet above sea level. At the start of the CHOWHOUND missions, as the 8th AF called them, (the RAF called theirs MANNA missions) the Germans were still there with their anti-aircraft and machine guns pointed at us. We had to remove the innards of our guns before we took off! The Germans insisted upon this as a condition before allowing the flights to proceed. And we had to fly within the lanes or corridors which had been prescribed along with time restraints. Quite naturally we were a little tense not knowing if the Germans would keep the truce or begin to fire upon our unarmed aircraft.

In western Holland the average daily caloric intake at than time (late 1944 and early 1945) was less that the amount of calories (550) now contained in

a MacDonald BIG MAC! Without the MANNA and CHOWHOUND flights of the RAF and the 8th USAAF, western Holland was doomed to starvation, and we might have then liberated a nation of corpses.

In mid-January, 1945, after the Battle of the Bulge and after a very severe winter in western Holland (in England, too, as many of us remember), the mounting crisis was such that Queen Wilhelmina addressed identical notes to King George VI, President Roosevelt, and Winston Churchill. In her letter Her Majesty wrote with great anxiety:

"Conditions have at present become so desperate that it is abundantly clear that if a major catastrophe, the like of which has not been seen in western Europe since the Middle Ages, is to be avoided in Holland something has to be done now, that is to say before and not after the liberation of the country."

Hans Onderwater, 1985, page 19, OPERATION MANNA / CHOWHOUND. It was to this need that the RAF and the 8th USAAF began to fly

A 390th BG B-17, 44-6954 LIQUID 8 OR, drops it's load of 10-in-1 rations over Valkenburg Air Field during one of the
CHOWHOUND MISSIONS.

missions of mercy to Holland. The RAF began their food droppings on April 29, 1944, two days before the 8th AAF started dropping rations. The final drop for the 8th USAAF was on May 7, 1945 and for the RAF on May 8, 1945 (VE Day, as many will recall). A total of 25,058,576 pounds of food was dropped by the 5,343 flights of Lancasters and B-17s used to make the drops. (The British reported long tons of food dropped [2,240 lb/ton] while the 8th USAAF reported short tons [2,000 lb/ton] hence the total in pounds.)

It was my nervous privilege to fly on my first Chowhound mission on May 2, 1945, when we went to Utrecht to drop our "ten-in-one rations." False floors of plywood had been installed in the bomb-bay hinged at the edge nearest the skin of the aircraft and supported by aircraft cable hooked to the highest bomb shackle on the inboard bomb racks. Later, on the return of the aircraft to the USA, these floors were to hold the baggage of the 20 men who were flying back in each aircraft.

As we approached the target or drop areas we dropped our wheels and used partial flaps in order

to slow our speed when we dropped the 10-in-1 rations. On subsequent missions we dropped tins of British food wrapped in burlap cement bags, again with our wheels down and under partial flaps. It has been reported that many of the aircraft, after dropping the food, had to take evasive action in order to avoid hitting church steeples!

On the May 2, 1945 mission, the Germans were still in command in the towns and villages of Holland. As we flew over the towns, there was very little activity in the streets. Perhaps the Germans had warned the populace to stay indoors. The greatest activity was in the pastures between the canals where the horses, cows, and sheep were frightened by the noise of the B-17s flying so low. We saw German flags flying from the offices in the small towns and German soldiers standing guard in sentry huts at drawbridges over the canals and other installations. One German cyclist was so surprised that he pedaled right into a nearby canal! In Utrecht at the drop site, the Dutch people were around the drop zone, a delta shaped area between railroad spurs where cars and engines could be turned around. Fortunately, the Dutch did not

93

intrude on the drop zone where the cartons of ten-in-one rations were falling.

On my second mission, May 6, 1945, it was a different story. The Germans had left and, instead of seeing the swastikas flying, we saw flags of the Netherlands flying from every window. People were in the streets waving their hats, or hands or small flags. At one pasture a message had been spelled out in pillowcases and sheets - "Thank you, Boys!" Many of the airmen who had been on previous missions had made parachutes of some material and dropped candy, gum, cookies with a message - "for the children." Some had even packaged their cigarette rations and dropped them to the Dutch.

There were many on later missions who were not crew members. The ground personnel had heard of the flights, and many were taken along to give them a chance to see what was going on in Holland.

We reportedly had been told that we were not to take any cameras on these flights, although I don't recall hearing such orders. One cameraman from the 34th Bomb Group was TOLD to take some pictures but he was to sit discreetly in the radio room with the door to the bomb bay open so that he could use his camera but not be seen by the Germans. On the way to the drop zone the aircraft he was riding in happened to get out of the lane in which it was supposed to fly. Tracers from a machine gun on the ground quickly got the attention of the pilot and he took some rather violent maneuvers to get back where he was supposed to be flying. The maneuvers so bounced the camera man around that he became air sick for the first time in his career and he upchucked. Unfortunately, he managed to coat the camera and lens with his breakfast which rendered the camera useless. I heard that he then tossed the camera through the bomb-bay!

I was fortunate to be invited by the Dutch in 1985, 1990 and 1995 to help them celebrate the 40th, 45th and 50th anniversaries of the food drops. My wife and I were able to attend the 1985 and 1995 celebrations; and, believe me, it was very emotional to walk among, greet and talk with some people we helped save from starvation by our food drops. Walking in downtown Rotterdam in 1995, a young man asked me if I "was one of the FOODDROPPERS?" I told him I was and he said, "my Grandfather told me I wouldn't be here if it hadn't been for the food which you dropped. We were slowly starving to death until the food came."

This is a story that very few 8th AF veterans know about unless they were involved with the food drops. Roger Freeman, in his book *The Mighty Eighth War Diary* documents the missions, the bomb groups which participated and even the amount of food each group dropped. Of all that I am proud of regarding my participation in WWII, the food drops are that of which I am most proud.

There are two books, written by a Dutchman, born post-war, which describe the conditions extant in Holland during 1944-45. The first was written in connection with the 40th anniversary of the food drops and was published separately in both English and Dutch text. The book is *Operation Manna/Chowhound* and the author is Hans Onderwater. The second book is entitled *Memories of a Miracle Operation, Manna/Chowhound*, also by Hans Onderwater and written for the 50th anniversary. This book was published with both English and Dutch text on adjacent pages. I wonder what Hans will write for the 55th Anniversary in 2000?

In May, 1998, a contingent of Chowhound veterans visited the Mighty Eighth Heritage Museum to present a PLAQUE OF APPRECIATION, signed by the patron of the Manna/Chowhound Brotherhood, HRH Prince Bernard of the Netherlands, and other members of the Dutch FOOD AND FREEDOM FOUNDATION, to the Heritage Museum. There was an account of the presentation on page 26 of the December, 1998, *8th AF News*. The plaque will be hung in the Museum. The bomb groups participating in Operation Chowhound were: 34th BG, 95th BG, 100th BG, 385th BG, 388th BG, 390th BG, 452nd BG, 490th BG, 493rd BG, and the 3rd Scouting Force. The Group Patches surround the proclamation.

The following photograph of a B-17 dropping 10-in-one rations over Valkenburg Air Field has been enlarged to wall-size and is mounted in the Special Events section of the Heritage Museum.

The cover of the 1985 40th anniversary
publication by Hans Onerwater.

Four of the William H. Wilcox crew, 34th BG 391st BS, Mendlesham, Suffolk, England, 1945.
Rear: Hal Province, toggleer; Donald Plank, waist gunner; Anthony Coutros, engineer.
Front: Jan Province, Millie Plank, Clyde Willis (dec) co-pilot, Mary Coutros.

SPAM WHAT AM !

By J. Paul Duke

Paul Duke and Ilene live in Tupelo, where he is very active in his church and in the Tupelo section of the Mississippi Chapter, 8th AFHS. Paul is retired after many years with Standard Coffee Company.

I was in the 8th Air Force in England, in the 388th Bomb Group, in 1945, serving in the European Theater of Operations. I was an engineer/gunner on a B-17.

One of our beauties from the 388th BG

Many things happened over there on different occasions. All of these things we did were strictly voluntary. You had to volunteer to get into this and wherever they sent you this is where you went. As we went through all these places there were many things that happened. Sometimes, as we look back they are humorous, but they were not humorous at that time.

One thing I remember, before the war was over, was that the German soldiers had broken the dikes around Holland and flooded the land. The people had nothing to eat. They were starving to death. A deal was made between the Allied forces and the German forces so that the people could be relieved of their starvation.

We were commissioned to carry food to these people. We were to fly over the airfields and we were to drop foodstuff to the Dutch people. I remember on one such mission (I don't remember how many of these missions we flew), I looked down at the Germans and they were standing by their guns. If we had made any kind of an effort to fire on them, they would have fired back. We would have been sitting duck targets, because we were flying only about 200 feet off the ground.

On the way over, I decided that I would see what they were going to have to eat, or what we were carrying to them. I expected it to be very basic stuff, because in those days we didn't see a lot of filet mignon steaks or T-bones. Anyway, I wanted to see what we were feeding the Dutch people. So, on the way over I found a carton that said "spiced ham." Of course, we hadn't been eating much ham lately, so I opened the carton and got out a 5 pound can of spiced ham. I thought that was really going to be something when we got back to England. I was going to get a loaf of good sliced bread from the mess hall. My wife had sent me a 2 pound can of coffee from the U.S. I thought I was going to be "fixed up."

After dropping the food over Holland, we made our way back to England without incident. I could just taste that good old ham. After we landed back at our base I got back to my barracks just as soon as I could. I told the fellows, "Listen, I have just come into some good spiced ham here, and I've got bread and coffee." We were going to have a feast on something we hadn't had in a long, long time!

The Barringer crew, with Paul Duke standing at left.

Well, we gathered around the stove and set to work to put our feast together. You know what was in that can? **SPAM ! ! !** They just called it "spiced ham."

I look back on those times now, and that's just a funny happening. But at the time, I can tell you, that was serious business. We did, though, gather around and eat spam sandwiches and drink our good coffee. We had a good time, as good a time as the times would allow.

When the war ended shortly after that, we all knew that we would be coming home soon. I wasn't over there very long, but my hat's off to some of our folks who were over there two or three years. Some served in ground jobs, some in the air, but the important thing to all of us was getting to come back home.

I was in the 388th Bomb Group, and many of our crews got shot down. My crew was shot-up a few times, but we always managed to get back to our base. We were all very thankful that we made it through our missions and got to come home; many were not so fortunate. We saw many of our planes go down. On one raid I saw seven B-17s blow up in one short period of time, just one after the other.

As I look back over my time in England, I think of some of these dreadful happenings. Some times were humorous, but most of the time what we were

doing was very serious business. All of us together, ground forces, air crews, all the Allied forces put Hitler where he belonged. Then those of us who survived were able to come home and enjoy the great freedom for which we had fought. I'm thankful for the small part I had to play in our great endeavor, and I'm truly grateful to those heroes who gave so much more than I did so that we can all enjoy this wonderful freedom that we have in the United States of America.

Paul Duke with his brother, one of our Allies.

B-17s over the Alps

Strike photo - Deitz

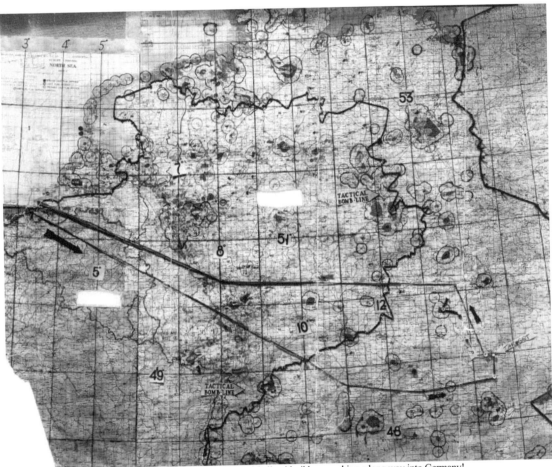

Mission board at Knettishall, with ribbon reaching a long way into Germany!

ON-THE-JOB TRAINING

by Craig Harris

Craig Harris (Cecil C. Harris to the Army), of Raymond Mississippi, enlisted in the Air Corps Enlisted Reserve in Jackson, in January 1943. Entering the aviation cadet program at Keesler Field, in April, 1943, he graduated from twin-engine flying school at Freeman Field, Seymour, Indiana as a 2nd Lt in Class 44-E. He underwent operational training as a B-17 co-pilot for at Gulfport, and in February, 1945, Harris's crew arrived at Glatton, England to join the 748th Squadron of the 457th Bomb Group. Here Harris flew 32 combat missions between February 20 and April 17, 1945.

Harris received BS and MS degrees in electrical engineering at the University of Tennessee in 1949 and 1951, and after a year as an instructor of electrical engineering at what was then Mississippi State College, joined Oak Ridge National Laboratory in Oak Ridge , Tennessee. In 1967 he joined the clinical faculty at Duke University Medical Center in Durham, North Carolina as a medical imaging physicist. He was active in the USAF Reserve, and was separated from the reserve in 1969 at the rank of major. Harris retired from Duke in 1992 as Associate Professor Emeritus of Radiology. He and his wife, Bobbie, also retired from a long Duke career, continue to live in Durham. Harris is active in the affairs of the 457th Bomb Group Association and is a member of the Board of Directors of the Eighth Air Force Historical Society.

All of us who were in the 8th Air Force encountered situations for which we had not been trained, and combat had a way of handing us, unexpectedly, "on-the-job training." Here is how one person received some of his.

The day was March 12, 1945, and the 457th Bomb Group was to join in an attack on the port city of Swinemunde, Germany, at the mouth of the Swine River, 40 miles from Stettin. It was to be a long mission for all, but even longer for the B-17 crew of Lt Marion K. Burk attempting its 14th mission. I, as co-pilot on that crew, was trying for my 13th, and later in the mission had good reason to reflect upon the numerology involved.

The background story is interesting, but irrelevant to the main theme of this story. The target was nominally an oil depot at the port, but everyone was distracted by the large number of merchant ships and warships in the port. It was covertly decided for the group to swing one squadron wide to the left in an attempt to hit the German pocket battleship, *Admiral Scheer,* which intelligence indicated was moored in the port east of the oil depot.

The mission route led up over the North Sea, and after a double-90-degree turn to get in behind the 3rd Air Division, we crossed Denmark north of the Kiel Canal and just south of Flensburg. Over the Baltic Sea, two double-drifts were made to avoid overrunning preceding groups, causing the group to be approximately 20 miles north of the briefed IP. Despite these maneuvers, bombing was successfully done with PFF equipment through the 1010 undercast, with each squadron doing its own sighting operation.

For most of the group the operation went smoothly; flak at the target was minimal and ineffective. The group returned to base approximately as briefed, successfully rejoining the division column.

However, it was on the bomb run that I got some unexpected on-the-job training. Burk was flying his 15-minute shift (we swapped every 15 minutes). The bomb bay doors were open, which always aggravates problems of holding good formation. Suddenly Burk realized that we had slid back behind our proper place and made the mistake of trying to regain all of it at once. He got a bit too aggressive with the throttles, and all four engines' RPM's surged, dangerously high. He realized his mistake and backed off with engines #1 and #4

settling back down. However, #2 and #3 wound up even higher. I was suddenly confronted with something that surely had happened to others, but which no one had ever mentioned in operational training (OTU), even in pre-combat training in England.

Fortunately, I recognized the runaway situation in #2, feathered the prop to get the RPM's back down to normal, then unfeathered the prop, and - to my great relief - #2 came under normal control. However, while that was going on, I made a huge mistake in not paying enough attention to #3 before applying the same treatment to it. When I finally realized that the other runaway was #3, it was feathered, but my delay gave the engine RPM's time to wind up to where the dump valve in the propeller governor unseated; while the prop responded to feathering, it could not resume normal control operation. For a split second I didn't know what to do, but with #3 winding up again, I realized that I could get us through the bomb run by alternately feathering and un-feathering #3's prop.

So, we continued down the bomb run with 4 engines running, but with #3 operating back-and-forth between 2400 and 3200 RPM as I pushed and pulled on the feathering button. Burk was too busy holding us in formation to notice what I was doing; all he knew was that he had 4 fans turning and that was good. We both were too busy to talk about it.

When the bombs were dropped, and the bomb bay doors closed, I signaled to Burk that I was shutting #3 down. He nodded OK and began to re-trim the ship but was clearly mystified at just what was going on. Here we had an additional complication. One of our crew members was very shaky after a bad night with nightmares, and we didn't want to unnecessarily upset him, so we couldn't use interphone to communicate. This was a problem, because in the thin air of 23,000 feet direct speech was useless. However, by using double-talk and gibberish on the interphone, and by hand signals, I finally got Burk to understand our situation, and we agreed to drop out of formation, but to stay near the bomber stream.

Our situation, a long way from home - all the way across Germany - and 3 engines running, was not desperate by any means; but it wasn't comforting either. We had adequate fuel, the 3 operating engines were running fine, and the ship trimmed up OK. We counted on our proximity to the division formation to keep us from blundering into a hot flak area, and no enemy fighters had been reported. (Ironically, the B-17G we were flying, 43-38203, would be shot down 6 days later over Berlin in an attack by ME-262s, but this day we saw no enemy fighters.) While we were not "out there all by our lonesomes," it would have been clear to any one that our ship was a straggler, and despite the fact that we were well north of known concentrations of enemy fighter bases, we couldn't help but sweat a bit until we were back over the North Sea.

On the long flight home, I had time to reflect on what had happened and had good feelings and bad feelings. The good feelings were about having a sudden emergency for which I had had no training, reacting instinctively in restoring the #2 engine to normal operation and in saving the bomb run. (We were very fortunate that the #2 propeller governor's dump valve reseated itself, allowing normal control.) The bad feelings came from the realization that the same could have

been accomplished for #3, if only I had been smarter and quicker in assessing the situation. However, not to have done anything soon enough could have been an instant disaster. It was a mess of our own making, and we were truly lucky to have survived our mistakes. That luck was to hold for the rest of our missions for which we were grateful.

Intelligence later told that, while the group had hit the oil depot, only a few 100-pound bombs fell near the *Admiral Scheer*.

For me, that very long 13th mission was finally over.

"Big Gas Bird"

A FORTRESS

By William F. McGuire

William F. "Phil" McGuire was born and grew up in Macon, where he still lives with his wife, Virginia. Phil is a graduate of Mississippi State University, and he has been in the jewelry business in Macon since college. Phil has served on the Board of Directors of the Mississippi Chapter for the last several years and has been very active in all its projects, especially in the production of this anthology. During the war, Phil was a ball turret gunner on a B-17 in the 388th Bomb Group where he was a Staff Sergeant.

Phil has written the following five essays which are unique in that, rather than relating scary stories from his experiences (although I'm sure he has some from flying missions in the very difficult period leading up to D-Day), these essays tell some of the day-to-day procedures which he and his crew followed in their service in the Eighth Air Force. We as editors believe that they represent an invaluable part of the story which this anthology attempts to tell.

Phil did tell one story, a mystery which has never been solved. The story tells about a crew flying nearby in formation with Phil's crew. They were a new crew, on their first mission. They had been led to believe that crews were usually given a "milk run" for their first mission and, therefore, should not expect heavy flak or fighter attacks. As it turned out, they had both on the way to the target. As the Group left the target area and were, at that time encountering no enemy flak or fighters, this plane with its new crew suddenly veered off from the formation and the crew bailed out. One of Phil's crew members says that the first man jumped without a parachute, but that was not confirmed by others. Phil's crew kept watching for something to happen to the plane; they thought it would go into a spin or blow up. Nothing happened. The plane just gradually separated itself from the main body of the formation and slowly flew out of sight in the distance. The crews on the mission never heard from this ghost ship or its crew again. Perhaps it is still up there in the contrails and propwash over Germany, doomed to fly forever in the flak of our imagination!

Here is Phil's first essay telling us details he remembers about that plane many of us loved so well - the B-17, Flying Fortress.

Here I am, a twenty year old from "Small Town," Mississippi, standing by this big old airplane called a B-17. Today I've decided to really look it over.

You see, I've already flown in one of these while I was training in the States for many hours; and to date I've spent over fifty hours in this one on my five combat missions I've already completed. Now they've given me three days off to do as I please, and one thing I've wanted to do is to really look this plane over.

The first thing I notice is that it's big, real big. It measures about one hundred feet from wing tip to wing tip and it's almost that long. Where the wings are attached to the body of the plane, they must be seven or eight feet wide, narrowing out at the end to about three feet. The wings at the tail are much smaller but still big, and the tail sticks high into the air. My plane's tail has a large square "H" painted on it so that other planes in the air with us will know what bomb group we belong to.

I'm standing here by the waist door which measures, I guess, about three feet wide and four feet tall. This is where all the enlisted men enter the plane. You see, we are all positioned generally toward the rear so we can get to our stations more easily through this door. This is no set rule; it is just the way it works.

Looking just to the right of this door and up just above the center of the fuselage is the waist window. Sticking out this window is a fifty caliber machine gun. This gun is operated by the right waist gunner. Then going toward the front for five or six feet there, under the center of the body of the plane, hangs the ball turret. It actually is a ball and hangs from a yoke from inside. About sixty-five percent of this ball can be seen from where I stand. This turret has two fifty calibers, and the ball gunner rides inside. Moving on several more feet and looking up, I can see the small window on the side of the radio room. Now, up on top, I can see the radio gunner's machine gun sticking out the top of his room. Next, I approach the wings. However, just before I reach them, I can look at the top of the plane and see the top turret. It looks as though it is all Plexiglas. While the ball gunner has to rotate his turret to see all around him, the top gunner can see just by turning his head. His turret will also turn 360 degrees like the ball. The top turret gunner also operates two fifties.

I have to stoop slightly to walk under the wing. These wings have three main functions. First, they are designed so they give this big plane maximum lift. Second, they house several gas tanks which are supposed to be self-sealing when bullets or flak puncture them. Third, they each support two huge engines, four in all. The propellers on the front of the engines look as though they are at least ten feet from tip to tip. Toward the front of these wings there are two huge wheels supporting the main weight of this B-17. These planes are designed with a tricycle landing gear arrangement: two wheels up front and one under the tail. These front tires are very large, bigger than any truck tires I've seen. In flight all the wheels are retracted so that the bottom of the plane seems smooth.

Up high just to the front of the wings on top of the plane and reaching across are the windshields for the two pilots. The fuselage at this point is contoured so that these pilots have a great field of vision. Then at the nose there is a lot of Plexiglas. There is a fifty caliber sticking out of each side of the nose, and just below the nose is a remote controlled turret that has two more fifties in it. Both the navigator and the bombardier fly in this section, and they must be able to see well. I circle and start down the other side. There, under the pilot's compartment, is a small door about two feet square. This is where the officers enter the plane. This door is rather high off the ground and these men have to muscle themselves up through this opening.

I find the other side just like the first except there is no waist door. After I circle the tail section and am at the back, there are two more fifties sticking out the tail. These belong to the tail gunner who sits cramped in the back of the plane. From his shoulders to the top of his head, he has glass on both sides and in front so that he can see all that is going on behind the plane.

Now I go through the waist door and on inside. To my left is the tail wheel assembly which is right in the center and goes up to the top. When the tail gunner goes back to his position, he has to climb around this contraption. You more or less have to crawl back to the tail position. Back there is a bicycle seat which is tall enough for him to kneel on his knees and sit back on this seat. He flies in this position. Right in front of him are his guns side by side. Since it would be very difficult to crawl back to the waist door and bail-out, he is provided a bail out exit to his left. Once the lever is pulled this door falls away from the plane.

Back in the waist, on each side, there are the waist windows, and each has a fifty caliber mounted in it. The waist gunners stand back to back when they are firing. Just beyond the waist is the ball turret mechanism. I step around it and go into the radio room. As you may suspect, there is a lot of radio equipment in several cabinets. There is a chair and a small desk. Unless we are under attack, the radio gunner is busy with his radio duties most of the time.

Just beyond the radio room, the bomb-bay is located. There is a narrow catwalk going through this area, and space on each side houses the paraphernalia for holding the bombs and then releasing them. On missions, both sides are full of bombs. Instead of a floor below this area, there are actually doors that open so that the bombs can fall freely.

When I step out of the bomb bay, I have to move around the top turret. It reaches all the way from the floor and out the top of the plane. At the bottom there is a small platform that the top gunner stands on as his head is up in the Plexiglas dome. There is a small space between this turret and where the pilots sit. The top turret gunner is also the engineer, and he has to stand behind the pilots on take-offs and landings, calling out valuable info to them. I slip into the pilot's seat. There are two seats. The pilot usually sits in the one on the left while the co-pilot sits on the right. There, in front of me, is an array of instruments, dozens of them. Right in front of each seat is the stick used for steering. In the center, between the pilots, are the throttles, one for each of the four big engines. There is a lot of other stuff that I don't understand.

I crawl down into the nose where the bombardier and navigator fly. The most important equipment that the bombardier has is his bomb sight. This is a very complicated piece of equipment. When he sights through it and aims at the target this sight compensates for air speed, wind speed, and other factors that affect where the bombs land. During the bomb run, the plane is actually guided by this bomb sight. This is a much better system than with the bombardier trying go give the pilot instructions as to where to go. The navigator has all sorts of measuring instruments and maps that he uses to tell us where we are. He also uses these instruments to tell the pilots what headings to take to reach our destination, which could be the target area, our base back in England or you name it.

From nose to tail, I've checked it all out. Now, I have a better concept of this plane. I wanted to

know all about it since I"ll have to trust it with my life for the rest of my missions.

COMBAT AIRMAN

By William F. McGuire

I am a combat airman stationed in England. My home is in Mississippi, a place that, right now, seems a million miles from here. Nine other men and I compose the crew of a heavy bomber. All of these men have been thoroughly trained to do their respective jobs well. The one major drawback to this training was that none of our instructors had been in combat so there was no way that they could prepare us for this phase of our activities over here.

Once we got to our bases here, there was a short period of intensive training which was the transition between flying the very peaceful skies over the States and flying over occupied Europe. When we are flying over the continent, there is a concerted effort on the part of the Germans to shoot us down. We all know that there are three possible results of being shot down: first, we could die in our plane; next, we could bail out and upon landing safely, be killed by angry Germans, or be captured and placed in a P. O. W. camp; or, the best scenario, escape capture and get back to England. (By the way, bailing out of a tumbling airplane is virtually impossible most of the time.)

Our living quarters, considering the times, are OK, not great, but adequate. Some of us complain, but when you consider what England has gone through and the problems the USA is encountering getting supplies, men, planes, bombs, ammo, food and everything else that we need to us, there is little justification in complaining. We all have commodes and wash basins with running water. Some even have a bath tub (this is rare), but most are taking sponge baths. I occasionally hear that someone has improvised a shower. Quite frankly, I even find the food to be pretty good, again considering the situation.

Our equipment is very good, and we are sure that it is the best in the world. Another thing that gives us assurance is that our planes, bomb sights, guns, turrets are maintained by very dedicated and super-well-trained men. There could be no missions flown without them. While we are only here until we finish our missions, (that is, if we finish our missions, and from the statistics I've heard, our chances are very slim), these men are here for the duration.

The mental conditions that I'm going to describe now, come slowly for some, possibly beginning in the States when the realization hits us that we are actually going into the war. With others it might be when they are under fighter attack, or flak is heavy, or when they see planes going down; anyway, it is a part of our lives twenty-four hours a day. Now we may keep up the front that things are great; we may laugh, joke or whatever; but ominous reality is always there. Dying is a part of war, and we could be next. We go to sleep, we wake up, we go about our chores and all the time this thing eats at our innards. This is stronger than ever on the days that we fly. Our every move could be bringing us closer to death. Breakfast, usually very early in the morning, the briefings (briefings introduce us to the target for the day, the purpose of the mission, where the flak areas are and what we can expect in the way of enemy opposition), going out to the plane, checking out our equipment - all are bringing us closer to our fate.

After all this, the signal is given that we're ready for takeoff.

Taking off is, at best, always hairy. Our plane is loaded with high explosive bombs which, even though they are not fully armed yet, they still could explode in case of a crash. Also, our tanks are full of very volatile gasoline. There is always a struggle to get a very heavily loaded plane airborne, and we always feel some relief when takeoff is behind us. Once we are in the air we head for the rendezvous with our own group. We recognize them by their markings, usually a large letter on the tail. There is a designated time for departure; the proper flare is fired from the control tower and we are on our way.

There are always other groups of bombers around us, some distance from us but usually headed for the same target we are. Our own bomb group usually has twenty-one planes in the air. There are three squadrons of seven planes each, a high squadron, a low and a lead squadron. The crew that flies the lead plane in the lead squadron is the best. They actually lead us in, and we drop our bombs when they drop theirs. There is always a second lead and a third in case there is a loss of the first or second leads.

I am always amazed at how peaceful the countryside is as we fly over occupied Europe. This could be, with little change, anywhere in the States. How deceiving! At this moment we know that there are German fighter pilots preparing to take-off and intercept us. Then they will try to shoot us down. Some will even strafe the men who

have managed to bail out. There are also spotters with their radar or whatever notifying the pilots and anti-aircraft gunners of the things they need to know about us.

Our own fighter cover goes with us as far as their gas will allow. After they have to turn back we are on our own. Some missions are real rough with fighters all over the sky, it seems. Flak over the target, and in other areas, for that matter, can be very accurate and very, very thick. We pray and sweat and then wonder how we lived through it. Then there are the milk runs where no fighters show up, and flak is not bad at all. I wish they were all like that ! ! ! !

The Germans do all they can to discourage us. One thing is that they know that the Americans love good music and knowing that the British broadcast what I would call chamber music, they beam good modern music toward England. That's fine, but their announcers spout all sorts of stuff like putting doubts about what our wives and sweethearts are doing back home with all the men who are stateside. One girl announcer has a very sweet voice and sounds really convincing. Then some dude will come on and tell us how stupid we are. We put up with it to hear the good music.

Another thing they do is that when we fly near a flak area and, especially when we approach the target, they throw up heavy barrages of flak that sometimes darkens the sky. We know that each burst means that hundreds of pieces of shrapnel are flying in all directions and that one piece hitting the plane in the right spot can bring it down, not always, but it is possible. Now, we've got to fly through that stuff in order to drop our bombs on the target. It is frightening. When we are hit by fighters, we have eleven guns on the plane to protect us, but for flak there seems to be no defense. We just pray and sweat it out.

The missions, themselves, are long and tiresome. We've gotten up very early, and even after takeoff it seems that it takes a long time to get with the rest of our own group and get ready to leave England. I have my job to do, but it is generally routine;

so the best way for me to describe a lot of the mission is that it is boring. Of course, there is also that gnawing fear that something is about to happen. So, we are there, waiting, hoping, praying and thinking. It has been rightly said *at this time the plane is your universe and each moment is an eternity.* It is always very cold even though it may be warm on the ground. The roar of the four big engines is constant. We communicate by using an interphone system and each man has a button that he pushes when he needs to talk. Ever so often the pilot asks for an interphone check. When things are peaceful, this is to be sure that all crew members are OK, especially that oxygen equipment is working properly. (One can die quickly if he loses his oxygen supply.) Then, right after a fighter attack or heavy flak there is always this type of checking by the pilot, just to see that no crew member is in any kind of distress.

Until we reach the target we can take evasive action to avoid the bad flak areas. However, when we are a few minutes from the spot we have to bomb, we must fly straight and level so that the trajectory of the bombs will put them right on the target. The Germans know this and fire very accurately during this bomb run. When the bombs are released, the plane bounces up because of the weight of the bombs leaving the ship. Now we can take evasive action again, and we get out of the heavy flak as quickly as we can. The German fighters never attack us in their own flak. However, they sometimes attack us just as we leave the flak area.

Now we are homeward bound. Sometimes this part of the trip is without incident; other times it's pretty rough. When we get back to the base, if we have wounded aboard, we fire a red flare and this gets us permission to land first. Since there is always a possibility that the landing gear has been damaged in a way that we can't detect, which means that the wheels would fold up and we would belly in, it is always a good feeling when everything works as it should. We then taxi to our revetment, and the mission is over!

We have our own plane which we have affectionately named. We call it *our plane*, but we surely don't get to fly it on every mission since it takes some pretty good hits and can't be repaired quickly enough. Sometimes that takes several days.

Once we are on the ground we have one more duty, and that is to go to interrogation. Each crew sits at one table, and an officer listens and asks questions as to everything we did and saw. All the information from all the returning crews is then compiled so that the powers that be will have a pretty good picture as to what happened this day. During the questioning, we are given whiskey. This, I guess, is to relax us, for even on a milk run we are pretty tense. Also, there is a really good chance that we've seen planes going down and we know there are men dying, perhaps friends of ours. We could also find empty bunks in our barracks, bunks of boys who didn't make it back. So we need to relax if it is at all possible. Such is the air war over Europe. Whiskey helps, but even if we get drunk as a skunk, when we sober up the war is still there. After all this we are free to eat, get drunk, or whatever. We realize we are very hungry.

The darkness is coming on, and we haven't eaten since very, very early this morning. The chow is good. The cooks seem to know we've had a rough day, and they do their part to make it better for us. We then go to the barracks or to the club. We write home; we sit and shoot the bull; we do almost as we please. Our job is through for the day. Another mission is under our belt. Tomorrow is another day . . . another mission . . . . or a day just to do nothing. Later we will try to sleep. Sometimes we are so dog-tired that we fall asleep quickly. Other times, sleep just won't come, we roll and tumble. When we are asleep, we jump at sounds, fearing that they are here to call us out for another mission. The war goes on.

BRIEFING FOR ENLISTED MEN

By William F. McGuire

Should you have been fortunate enough to have had a good night's sleep thus far, things change abruptly with the sound of a voice calling out, "Jones' crew briefing at four o'clock, Smith's crew briefing is at four o'clock" and so on. This disturbing voice is that of the non-com whose duty it is to get us up and going.

Normally, you aren't sleeping too soundly when this occurs, simply because you are all too aware of what the next day could bring. I can't help thinking that this non-com is also very aware that he is actually telling some of these men that today is the day that they won't make it. At least we are all surely aware of this.

Then, there is the getting dressed, going to the latrine, grumbling, hoping for the milk run (an easy mission) and envying the crews who are not called out. Then you go outside and wait for the trucks to carry you to the mess hall for breakfast. The food is usually pretty good, and you really need to eat since your next meal will more than likely be very late in the evening when the mission is over.

After this you move over to the briefing room. This room is large enough to accommodate all the enlisted men who are flying that day. There are rows of benches like in an improvised theater, all facing to the stage up front. At first the stage is empty except for a large map which shows England but with the continent covered. There is a line of ribbon originating at our base and stretched out, then disappearing behind the curtain. You wonder and speculate as to which target it extends.

Then someone yells, "ATTENTION!" and you all rise and stand at attention as the briefing officers come into the room. Each is carrying brief cases and materials pertaining to today's mission. They stand near to or on the stage.

One of them starts by giving a pep talk as to how important our effort is and how important this mission is. Then he raises the curtain; and, as usual, it seems the ribbon stretches out to a rough target. He tells where the flak areas are located (where the Germans have a concentration of anti-aircraft guns) and where there will be the greatest likelihood of fighter attack, also, where our fighter escort will have to leave us. (Later in the war, fighters will be developed that can go all the way to the target with the bombers.) A weather officer then tells what kind of weather you can expect. After this, actual photos of the target area are projected on the screen so that you can recognize the target when you get there. You are also shown the direction from which you will approach the target as well as where the IP is. (The IP is the "initial point," a location a few minutes from the actual target. From this point on to the target all the planes have to fly at an exact speed, an exact height, and straight and level so that the released bombs will have the proper trajectory and hit the assigned target.)

Finally, you are again called to attention and the briefing officers leave the room. You are then dismissed so that you can go out to your planes and begin your day.

FLYING THE BALL

By William F. McGuire

When I compare the seven gun positions on a B-17, I think the ball turret was the most fascinating. I am sure that any ex-ball operator would give you about the same details as I do here, as we all manned the same station, but this reflects my memories and my feelings about the ball.

The ball turret was the only protection for the underside of the plane. Its guns could point any of 360 degrees horizontally and 90 degrees vertically. They could fire in all of these directions except when any part of the B-17 came into the line of fire. Protection for the plane was afforded by automatic switches which cut the circuit to the firing mechanism when the guns pointed toward parts of the plane (more on this later).

The turret itself was a masterpiece of design. It was, as the name implies, a complete ball. It was 36 inches in diameter. Within this small space were two fifty caliber machine guns with ample ammunition. Too, there was a computing sight, a 10 to 12 inch cube, that, if used correctly would give you maximum accuracy. There were drive mechanisms that moved the turret in its various ways. Add to this oxygen and interphone equipment, and you can see how there was hardly room for the gunner, so he had to forget about the luxury of a parachute or anything else. The turret was supported by a yoke that went around the top like two of your fingers half way around a softball. At the center of this yoke there was a pipe attached which went to the top of the plane and supported the weight of the ball.

Since there was not enough clearance between the bottom of the plane and the ground, the turret had to be rolled up with the guns next to the fuselage and pointing back when the plane was on the ground. To enter or leave the turret while in flight the guns had to be pointed down since this was the only position that would allow the access door to open. After manually rotating the ball to the right position, you could open the door and engage the gear train. You were then ready to climb in; but, first, you needed to secure your parachute. I had a special place where I tied mine. I used a very tight bow knot (so that it would be secure and yet could be quickly untied). Then I tied a handkerchief to the end of the rope so that I could find it more easily. Imagine what it would be like to be in a plane tumbling from the sky and not being able to locate your chute. If I were able to get out of the ball, I wanted my chute to be there.

The next move was to step down into the ball, place the right foot next to the intercom switch and the left on the sighting controls. Next you would make the proper intercom and oxygen connections and lean forward in order to close the door which is locked with two latches, one over each shoulder. There was a safety strap immediately behind your back, but I never fastened this as it might slow me down when I tried to get out in a hurry. It is rather uncomfortable in this position, so you roll the turret until most of your weight is on your lower back. In the turret you are in what has been described as a fetal position. You are sitting following the contour of the ball and looking out from between your knees. Once the turret is moved the door can't be opened and, I guess, this is the chief

reason that the ball turret had such a bad reputation.

When flying combat, my clothing consisted of my flying suit worn over my coveralls, my aviator's cap which buckled under my chin (my earphones were part of the cap), my oxygen mask and gloves. I wore an improvised saddle bag around my neck. On one side I carried a couple of candy bars and on the other side the "escape kit" which was issued on each mission. This kit contained a silk map of the area, a shaving kit, sewing kit, pills to purify waster, foreign money, possibly some food, etc. I always wore a heavy towel around my neck, too, since it got so cold at the altitudes we flew (like 50 degrees below). My parachute harness was worn over my flying suit. This harness had two loops on the front which connected to two on the chute.

A few weeks after starting my overseas training stint, my original crew was disbanded (I never did find out why); so I was placed in a gunners pool. A few days later, I was interviewed by Lts. Brunk and Cory and was assigned to their crew. Lt. Cory was the co-pilot. I joined the crew as a ball turret gunner. It seems that there was a waist gunner on this original crew that Lt. Brunk did not care for; so he had him removed from the crew. When this happened, the ball turret operator asked to be moved to the waist; thus the open ball position.

We finished our training and were assigned to the 388th Bomb Group at Knettishall, England. When we got into combat, I developed a routine that I followed on all twenty-five missions. I had heard stories about attacks when assembling in formation; so I always got into my turret as quickly as I could. After a struggling take-off due to the weight of full gas tanks and a full bomb load, when I knew we were airborne, I would go through the radio room into the bomb bay to remove a pin from each bomb. These pins prevented the bombs being detonated prematurely. Now they were ready to be dropped even though the release point may be hours away. Then I would go back to the waist and secure my chute and get into the turret. This, I would imagine, took possibly fifteen minutes. As a safety precaution I never charged my guns until we neared the enemy coast. I followed this procedure religiously on all my missions; then I would leave my turret when we got into the landing pattern at the end of the mission.

Charging the guns was a neat procedure: to charge the right gun you would reach down to your left foot and grasp a handle. This handle was attached to a cable which went through a series of pulleys to the carriage on your right gun. You pulled this handle briskly, and a shell was loaded in your right gun. To charge the left gun you pulled the handle by your right foot.

Just above your head when you leaned over the sight there were two handles which moved in unison and controlled the turret. They resembled two short round pieces of wood. At the end of these were firing buttons which were operated with your thumbs.

On our first mission I was in my turret and ready long before we reached enemy territory. Of course, there was fear, apprehension and mixed emotions at this time. I really believed that we would be met by a hoard of enemy fighters just as soon as our "Little Friends" turned back because of lack of fuel. ("Little Friends" were the P47s and P38s that flew cover for us as long as their fuel lasted.) But, there were no enemy fighters.

The landscape looked much like any other landscape. There was no sign of war. Was this what war was to be like? Where had all these stories come from? Then we reached the IP (the initial point of the bomb run). Until now we had been flying a somewhat zig-zag course for protection, but from the IP on our flight had to be straight and level so that the bombs would hit the target. Up ahead I could see the airport that was our target and I could see puffs of smoke over it. In my mind they resembled skyrockets we had shot off back home. It still did not look like war to me.

Then, the first group of planes went over and two of them went plummeting down, one with a wing blown off that was flipping like a leaf; the other went down in a steep dive. There were only two chutes. At this instant I knew what war was. Some of the crew members said they saw a third

plane go down. I didn't see it. My mind was racing. If this is a "milk run" (we had been promised an easy mission, a "milk run"), what will a tough one be like? I soon found out but that's another story.

I must admit that as a ball turret gunner I never was able to get off a good shot at an enemy plane. I had one come so close under me that I heard either his guns firing or his engine over the roar of the B-17. Another time I could easily see the silhouette of the pilot (this may have happened more than once, but I can't remember). At these times I was trying very hard to get my sights on them; but as they zoomed under me, the good shots that I had envisioned just didn't happen.

There were two times that I remember well, that I could have or should have got results: one was an FW-190 that dived through in front of my plane. I could see him in plenty of time and had my sight on him, but smoke was pouring out and he was obviously going down; so why should I waste ammo on him. Just as I moved my sight off him, he cut the smoke off and away he went. I (and maybe other gunners) had been suckered. The other time was very frustrating. ME-109s were coming in on our tail. Here was my chance. When I pressed my firing buttons, nothing happened; the cut-off switches that I mentioned earlier prevented me from firing. I held the buttons down and kept aiming, thinking that perhaps my plane would move up a little or that they would drop a little and that my guns would fire automatically. It never happened. Knowing my tail gunner, I knew he was firing away.

Twenty-five times I pulled the pins; twenty-five times I got into the ball; twenty-five times I stayed in the ball for as many hours as the mission was long, and I never got a good shot.

I've been asked what it was like to fly missions and the best way I can describe it is that it was being very bored but also being very scared. Being bored in that you would fly for hours and hours with little to occupy your time but your thoughts and whatever you could see and you were always filled with fear that fighters would hit you or that you might fly through a flak area.

Flak was worse than fighters. With fighters at least you could try to fight back but with flak all you could do was to sweat it out. Flak hitting the plane sounded like someone was flogging the fuselage with a length of chain. Sometimes it would explode so near that you could feel the concussion.

When the mission was almost over and you were ready to exit the ball, you first had to remove the rounds from your guns. This was a rather tricky maneuver. To unload the right gun, you pulled the handle by your left foot just far enough for the round to be exposed but not far enough to insert a new round into the chamber (remember the loading procedure). Then with your left hand you could reach across and push the live round out the chute that the spent cases fell out of. Then you repeated the procedure in reverse for the left gun. After this you turned your turret to the back of the plane and rolled it so that the guns were pointing down. You locked the ball in place and opened the door. You crawled out, closed the door and rolled the turret so that the guns were up next to the plane, facing backward.

Since you were never sure that your landing gear was going to work (because of possible battle damage), you got into landing position with your back against the radio room wall with your head between your knees and hands clasped behind your neck. You sat there until you were on the runway. The pilot taxied to the parking area and cut the engines. Just as the props stopped turning, the plane gave a shudder which to me was a great feeling. Your mission was over!

Once interrogation was over you were free to do whatever you wished. I guess that is why it has been called a "gentleman's war" since you went out and did your thing, then came back to the relative tranquillity of the base. The worst experience on the ground to me was trying to sleep when you were up tight about the possibility of flying the next day, and you could hear the sounds of the engines being revved up in preparation for the next day's mission.

It was always tough to see the planes go down, but the worst single sight in my opinion was the day the ME-109s got our right wingman. The plane was immediately engulfed in flames from the nose to the tail. It went into a shallow dive as though the pilot was trying to keep it under control so the crew could possibly bail out. There was no way. This, to me, seemed to be worst possible way to die in a B-17. You can't get over memories like that.

INTERROGATION

By William F. McGuire

Even though your plane was on the ground and your mission was over, there was still interrogation. As soon as you and your crew members could, after checking in equipment, picking up your valuables (things you didn't want to carry on the mission with you) from the crew chief, and performing a few other chores, you headed for the interrogation room.

Each crew would sit together with an officer whose job was to find out all he could from you as to what happened on the mission.

The information he got did two things. First, the things we told him, along with the recollections of the other crews, gave the "powers that be" a pretty good picture as to what the mission was like. Next, all this information helped in planning the forthcoming missions.

We would gather around the table and wait for the whiskey to be served. (Was this to relax us or was it a reward?) We didn't worry why it was served, we were just glad to get it.

Then the questions would come. Where did we catch flak? Was it an area where we expected it? How heavy? How accurate? How many planes were lost to these various areas of flak? How many chutes were seen?

Then Fighters? Where did they first attack? How many were there? How many planes were lost? How many chutes? How many did we shoot down? Who thought they had gotten one? If you were one of the gunners who thought you had shot one down,

what position did you fly? Why did you think it was you that got him? How long did the attack last? How many fighters were there? What kind were they? How many times did they attack? Were any on your plane wounded? Thus the questions went.

Did we hit the target? Did we notice anything different that we would like to report? There were many other questions that might be of interest.

A fascinating thing about interrogation was the different opinions that the crew members had. One would say that we were hit by about a dozen ME-109s. Another would counter with the statement that there had to have been at least twenty. Then it would come out that he was thinking of the second attack when there were many FW-190s instead of ME-109s. And so it went.

We tried to tell it like we saw it, but in the excitement of the moment, very often we saw things differently. The top turret gunner did not see what the ball turret gunner saw. The left waist's view was different from that of the right waist. This was true of the tail gunner and the men in the nose. We all saw it differently and tried to report what we remembered.

So, you see it was a good thing that these officers were trained to sift out the needed information from these varying reports.

After interrogation we were free.

George L. Garst grew up in Clarksdale where he still lives. He arrived in England toward the end of the war in the ETO and flew four missions in the 351st Bomb Group at Polebrook. He attained the rank of S Sgt.

A RADIO OPERATOR IN THE MIGHTY EIGHTH

By Kenneth Wilburn

Kenneth Wilburn was discharged on November 25, 1945, and came home to the family farm in the Ozark community. He married Hazel Young of the Centerville community on December 1. They had two sons and one daughter.

Kenneth was appointed a rural mail carrier of the Marietta rural route in 1948. The couple moved to Marietta and made it their family home, where he still lives today. He retired in 1956 after 33 years of serving his rural route in northern Itawamba and southern Prentiss Counties. After 49 years together Hazel passed away May 31, 1994. Kenneth and Hazel have nine grandchildren, and he feels that God has really blessed them.

Kenneth has enough hobbies to keep him pretty well occupied, especially in spring through fall, such as vegetable gardening, yard work, fishing, hunting and operating his ham radio. He stays in contact with his World War II crew members; he says he has a lot of good memories!

How do you get from the cotton patch to thirty thousand feet over Europe as a radio operator on a B-17? Well, it's a pretty long story, but here goes.

I was a Class of 1943 student at Itawamba Agricultural High School at Fulton, where I thought I was a student of a little better than average grades. The war was raging in Europe, but I hadn't given it too much thought. In my senior year I had the opportunity to take a semester class in Pre-Flight Aeronautics, which was about the airplane and how it flew. We learned about thrust and drag, lift and gravity, and other things about how planes were controlled. I don't know if this was the reason I wound up in the Army Air Corps; but after I was drafted into the Army in September, 1943, and made a score of 80 on the test at Camp Shelby, I was told that I qualified for aviation cadet training.

There were about twelve of us out of the two bus loads from Itawamba county put on a bus to Keesler Field, down at Biloxi, to begin our training. I'm sure I caused my family some grief when I wrote and told them that I was going to be flying in an airplane. Flying wasn't just an everyday, ordinary thing in those days.

After going through basic training almost two times, due to a delay in getting a certified copy of my birth certificate, we were called out one day in late December and told that the cadet corps was overcrowded, and we were to be reclassified. We would be assigned to Air Corps tech schools. I, along with others, would go to radio school; some went to mechanic school; and some to gunnery school. This ended my career in aviation cadets.

Next was a long train ride to the Army Air Force base at Sioux Falls, South Dakota, one of the coldest places I was ever stationed; however, it was a nice town with very friendly citizens. The radio school was sort of like basic training in that there were a lot of spit and polish inspections in a strictly controlled environment. In twenty-four weeks we were to learn to send and receive the Morse code at a minimum rate of twelve words per minute and learn elementary radio theory and operating procedures. In the code class we sat at tables with headsets and listened to the code with an instructor identifying each character until we learned them. After that we copied the code and moved to different speeds as we gained in proficiency.

In the theory classes, we learned how radios worked and how to build small radios on bread boards. When we saw that they really worked, we were pleasantly surprised. Later in the theory classes we began to learn about the radio equipment on a bomber, including the liaison equipment which is used by the radio operator, the command and the VHF equipment which is used in the cockpit, the radio compass, the intercom, the IFF, the marker beacon and the Gibson Girl radio located in the emergency life raft. Later in classes on operating procedures we began to tune and operate the equipment which was mostly used in sending and receiving Morse code. Radio operators didn't usually use voice communication. This, then, was the final phase of radio school.

Before we left the base at Sioux Falls, we were called out and told that the school needed fifteen volunteers to remain to receive further training to become instructors. After a long silence with no one volunteering, they put all the names in a hat and drew the fifteen names. We were all sweating that one out - my name was not drawn.

When we left radio school we were shipped by train to Yuma, Arizona, for gunnery school. The first thing we did was take an orientation flight in a B-17. Before we got on board, we were given two brown paper bags, told to put one inside the other and advised that we would know why later. I was standing by the waist window looking out at the Arizona desert, turned my head for just a moment and then turned back to the window. Now, instead of the land being down below us, it was standing up beside us. That is when I knew what the two brown bags were for. I wasn't the only sick person on board.

I liked the gunnery school. It was exciting to do all the firing of guns. We learned to detail strip the fifty-caliber machine gun, put it back together and make adjustments on it while blindfolded. We practiced ground-to-air firing, ground-to-ground, air-to-ground and air-to-air firing. At the end of our training at gunnery school, we were presented our wings which I still have, over fifty years later.

We were finally given a furlough (fourteen days, I think), a delay en route before reporting to Plant City in Tampa, Florida, which had been a zoo

before the War. Naturally we called it the "monkey cages." Here we were formed into nine-man crews. When this was done we were sent to Gulfport Air Base to begin our flight training as a crew.

It is time now that I explain the duties of the radio operator. In addition to his duties in the radio room, the radio operator also served as the right waist gunner. Thus, he was officially designated as ROM Gunner, Spec. #757. His equipment consisted of a 75 watt transmitter and matching receiver. The cockpit radios were short-range and reached out only about 50 miles. These were used for take-off and landing communications by the pilot and co-pilot. The radio operator's equipment was much more powerful. I think that under good conditions at high altitude you could communicate half way around the world using Morse code. The radio operator was never out of contact with his home base. I was asked once why a radio operator was necessary. The obvious answer to that was so that he could always be in contact. In an emergency, this could be very important. For instance, in case we became hopelessly lost, the radio operator had access to the Air Force direction finder stations. The DF system could plot a fix on the lost plane and give us our exact location. In addition, they could give you a compass heading to your intended destination. The heading could be updated as often as necessary to get you there.

After finishing our advanced training at Gulfport, we were shipped to Hunter Field at Savannah, Georgia, where we were issued flying equipment and a brand-new B-17, loaded with K-rations and mail sacks. After a few orientation flights we headed for England by way of the North Atlantic. We were told that in case of an emergency en route we could land on the Greenland ice cap or could ditch in the cold waters of the Atlantic! Personally, I didn't much like the idea of doing either. We radio operators were given a station frequency to monitor as we flew across. I took the precaution of tuning my transmitter to the emergency frequency and writing down all the dial numbers; so that I could get back on it really quick if necessary. After stops at Goose Bay, Labrador, Greenland and Iceland, on a long flight, we landed at Valley,

Wales. We left our new plane in Valley and went by train to Lavenham, in Eastern England, the location of the 487th Bomb Group. There we were placed in a pool of crews waiting to be assigned to a squadron. While in the pool we flew several training and orientation flights. After about a month we were assigned to the 837th Squadron, finally to begin doing what we had trained for over such a long time.

We first appeared on the alert list for the mission of March 11, 1945. I didn't sleep much the night before thinking about what it would be like. I thought about home and family and the fact that I could have volunteered to stay at the radio school and become an instructor. There I would have been safe, and my Dad and Mom and brothers wouldn't have been worried. However, to me to be a crewman on a B-17 seemed lots more exciting.

We were awakened in the wee hours of the morning (2:00 or 3:00 AM) and went to the mess hall for a breakfast of one fresh egg, pancakes, powdered eggs, cereal and powdered milk. After breakfast we were trucked to the briefing room. This was sort of like a movie theater with a curtain over the screen. When the briefing officer opened the screen, we saw a red string running through big-headed pins to the target, which today was Hamburg. After the general briefing we divided into separate groups, with the radio operators going to their special briefing. We were given something called a flimsy which contained the bomber code for that day, a pencil and a writing pad. Duties of radio operators varied according to position in the squadron formation. We were assigned to position number 4; this meant that I would be in contact with the 4th Combat Wing station with call sign 08T. After the briefing was over, we got our equipment and headed out to our plane. The one we were to fly looked as if it should have been in the junk yard. We had brought a new plane across the Atlantic, but now we were given this old olive-drab model, named "Fearless Fosdick." My checklist included the oxygen supply, the radios and the intercom system. Thus began our first mission!

I tuned the transmitter to the 08T frequency and settled down to monitor it. We were to observe radio silence until we got to the target after which I was to send the strike report back to base. When we were over the Channel, the bombardier came on the intercom to tell us to test our guns. I went to the right waist position to do my test firing. We then closed up in formation with the rest of our group. The radio operator in the squadron lead plane was on a different frequency than I, base station call letters ITL, which was the 3rd Division frequency. I had to tune to his frequency in order to hear his transmission. As we reached each check point, he sent a coded message. I'm sure someone back at our base was charting our progress as we proceeded toward our target, the submarine construction yards at Hamburg. As we neared the target, I saw my first flak. It just looked like black puffs of smoke floating in the air. After we dropped our bombs, the bombardier called on the intercom to give me the strike report. First, I translated it into our bomber code, then turned on my transmitter and called 08T to tell them I had a message. It was a good feeling when they came right back to me with a go-ahead. I sent my message and received their acknowledgment. I felt very proud of having sent my first strike report.

On the way home, I continued to monitor 08T. As we got nearer to base we received a transmission of weather conditions at the base, and I passed this information on to the pilot. Once I received a message that there were enemy fighters in the vicinity of our base, but we never saw them. This first mission had not been too bad, and I felt better that night when I went to bed.

One thing about the radio operator's position is that he can't see too much that's going on outside the plane. The small window limits his vision to a very small area. On our third mission, after we had dropped our bombs at Oranienburg and headed back, all at once shells started bursting all around us. They were very loud and were bouncing the plane around. I looked out my small window and could see the red flashes as the shells burst. Just as I was looking at a B-17 off to our left, it exploded and everything from the wing forward just disappeared. I think this is the first time that I knew real fear. Other crew members saw three members of the doomed plane's crew escape as it went down. I don't remember whether other planes in our formation were lost that day, but it was one of our rough missions.

Once I was watching a dog fight up above us when I saw an ME-109 coming down, out of control and with his wheels down. He was coming straight toward our squadron. He crashed into the tail of our wing man and knocked a lot of yellow tail off it, but the B-17 could take it and still get its crew back home.

After our 18th mission, the Germans finally gave it up, and the war was over. What a great feeling! We were allowed to go on flak leave, but after three days were ordered back to base. We were going home!

As I write this, a lot of memories have come back that were pretty dim after more than 50 years. One of the things I remember is the sight of smiling young faces as the crews boarded their planes. Many of these fellows were still in their 'teens. They knew the danger, but it didn't seem to deter them at all. They knew that it was their duty to their country to fly these missions and that the home front was behind them 100 percent. I think our country was at her greatest in World War II.

There was no running off to Canada to avoid the draft. There were no demonstrations by long-haired hippies. There were no Hanoi Janes or Moscow Bills. Everyone was patriotic and willing to endure the hardships brought on by the War.

This radio operator feels honored to have served his country in such a great organization as *The Mighty Eighth Air Force*. It did its job well and we will always be proud. GOD BLESS AMERICA! !

"The best crew in the ETO, ask Hitler." Wilburn standing center

A GI IN AN APPLE TREE

By Janine Dardenne Adams

Editor's note: To those of us who served in THE MIGHTY EIGHTH, some of the greatest heroes of the war had to be those men and women, and sometimes even children, who worked underground in the occupied countries helping unfortunate Allied airmen who were shot down. They gave these airmen, many of them from Mississippi, food, shelter and protection from the Germans. They hid them in cellars, attics, and barns, and often set them upon their way back to England to fly again. This story is about a young girl, of junior college age, who was called upon to help in this great effort.

Janine married an American soldier shortly after the end of the war in Europe, and came to live in Brookhaven, where she worked as a service representative for South Central Bell Telephone Company.. Janine's husband died a few years ago; she continues to live in Brookhaven and considers herself a Mississippian by choice! She is now a very special member of our Chapter, where she is greatly loved and appreciated by one and all.

On August 17, 1943, two crippled B-17s shattered the peace and quiet of the Belgian village where I lived. They flew low and erratically, trailing smoke, and, thank God, parachutes, and eventually crashed in the fields above the valley. We found out later they had been hit by antiaircraft fire on their way back from a mission to Schweinfurt.

Joseph Walters, the rear gunner in Captain Loren Disbrow's crew, landed in an apple tree behind the box factory run by the Tilkins, father and son.

118

Albert, the son, active in the underground, immediately set out to rescue the American; cutting branches to set him free and removing the 'chute to be burned in the stove that the shop kept going at all times. With the help of Lambert, the father, they helped Joseph into the kitchen of their house next to the factory. One of the employees grabbed a camera and took a picture of the rescuers and rescuee. In the picture, Joseph looks as if he thinks he is headed for the gallows! The poor man was in shock, had a broken arm, and several large bruises. By the small dictionary he carried, he understood he was in friendly hands and opted to try to get back to England rather than surrender. That fact established, he was given a shot of the local white lightning, which took care of the shock, made him forget the broken arm and assorted bruises, and probably forever cauterized his digestive system. (That stuff is potent!) He was hidden behind some crates in the factory, the camera with the film in it was confiscated by Lambert and hidden (the film was developed after the liberation) and when the Germans came to search, there was nothing to be found.

Later that evening, Joseph was taken to a safe house where I saw him for the first time. I was in my second year of English in junior college and I was asked by the underground to tell him a truck would pick him up at 4:00 the next morning, and that dressed as a construction worker, with pick and shovel, he would be taken to the next stop on his long way back.

He gave me his K-ration chocolate, a compass and some chewing gum, which I kept for months! (When I talked to him a few months ago, he said the 8th wanted the chocolate back!) It took Joseph about four months to get back to England, through Belgium and France and Spain. The famous picture, he tells me, hangs, life-size, at the 8th Air Force Heritage Museum in Savannah. Now 86 years old, Joseph is still going great guns. All of us in Belgium will be eternally grateful to him and to all American servicemen, just ordinary people required to do extraordinary things and doing them so well!

Thanks y'all,

Janine Dardenne Adams

TWO VERY ENGLISH MISSISSIPPIANS

Our Chapter feels very fortunate, for a number of reasons, to have two veterans of the Royal Air Force as members. John and Marie Carrington, both British citizens, now live in Oxford where they settled in 1982.

Marie served in the Women's Auxiliary Air Force from April, 1941, to February, 1946. Her duties were with both Balloon Command and Bomber Command. She married John on March 16, 1946; they have one daughter, Angela, who married Captain F. Wiebe of the U. S. Air Force. He is now a professor in the Business School at Ole Miss.

John remained in the RAF, serving from February, 1937 to April, 1971. During World War II he served in India and in Aden in Bomber Command. He was commissioned in 1956, serving after that date in Home Command, Coastal Command, Special Duties List in Lebanon, in Malta, in Germany and other assignments.

These two add a very special flavor to our reunions and are a vital part of our Chapter. In retirement, John has spent some of his time writing poetry. One of his poems is included below.

The Remembering Chair

Oft I wonder sitting here
about those who, from year to year,
passed my way but didn't stay.

My first recall are friends at school
with whom I studied many a rule
and met at play. They moved away.

The workshop and the common meal,
the bickering that friendships seal.
Togetherness? More or less.

Comrades in arms who, one by one,
were here today tomorrow gone
to foreign shores. To fight in wars?

The brotherhood of many races
encountered in so many places
with feeling. So appealing.

Where are they now these passers by
who touched my life, evoked a sigh.
Could it be they think of me?

John Carrington

120

THE DIARY OF
CHARLES W. MORRIS

By Bill Morris

Charles W. Morris of Jackson kept a mission diary while pilot of the "Lucky Rebel," a B-17 of the 410th Squadron, 94th Bomb Group at Rougham Air Base in England. He flew from May, 1944 until March, 1945. His entries are short and to the point but still convey the tension and occasional terror experienced by most airmen of the 8th Air Force. The following are some excerpts:

First Mission, June 11, 1944

Target was a hotel in northern France, "Paris Hotel" to be exact. There supposedly were high-ranking German officials residing at this place. Went as co-pilot for Lt. Burns in "Spirit of Valley Forge." Made tow runs…clouds apparently had the P.F.F. boys worried. We let go the second time and I guess the brass had taken shelter by this time. Saw a couple of bursts of flak, very low and inaccurate.

Third Mission, June 19, 1944

Target: an airfield near St. Jean D'Angely, nor far from Bordeaux, France. Went as co-pilot for Lt. Graves. Made two runs and still didn't drop. Had an awful time in clouds that day. Had P-38s to escort - beautiful sights, those babies!

Fourth Mission, June 21, 1944

BERLIN!! A so-called "retaliation raid" for the flying bombs that rained on London from Pas de Calais, M.P.I. was the "Madison Square Garden" of Berlin. First raid as a crew. Made one run, needless to say. Bomb doors stuck down, flaps froze in ½ down position. We had our moments of anxiety today. Wow! My God! Look at the flak! We lucked out, but Morningstar disappeared on this raid. Saw Moreman in London later. He told me the bad news.

Eleventh Mission, July 13, 1944

Target: Munich again. It's getting to be a habit. All the crew goes again for the second time. Continent still completely covered with low clouds. Contrails break up formation near "bombs away." Flak more accurate and tracking. Got hit in right horizontal stabilizer. We wer "Tail-end Charlie" which proved luck for us because we were attacked by ME 109s and FW 190s on way back. And No.'s 1 and 2 had seriously-injured men aboard upon return. Fighter escort was not as planned and was broadcast over VHF by group lead…this merely told the Luftwaffe to "Come after us, boys, the woods are full of game." A 20mm exploded in left wing panel, rendering ship useless until repaired.

Twelfth Mission, July 16, 1944

Target: Stuttgart, Germany. We were going after Munich again but the clouds kept us away. Whole crew went. We get to Munich IP and do a 180 and head out and back for Stuttgart. Flak bursts close as hell and one little stray piece knocks out our hydraulic system. We land without brakes - do a quick 180 at the end of the runway and roll to a stop on the grass.

Thirteenth Mission, July 20, 1944

Target: Synthetic oil plant at Merseburg, Germany. Entire crew plus a radar man. Turbos on engines 3 and 4 cut out, leaving only two engines doing any good. We drop the bombs on the run before hitting the flak area and head for the rally point. Out there alone, we were spotted by fighters who swooped in on us. We figured our number was up! But they were "Little Friends," P-51s! One stayed with us until his oxygen ran out, and a second Little Friend picked us up a few minutes later. I talked with them It was a wonderful experience. Later the formations catch up with us; so we crawl under and make it home safely.

Twenty-sixth Mission, August 27, 1944
Target: Berlin. We were recalled after hitting solid cloud cover at Danish peninsula. It turned out to be the biggest "head-up" trick I'd ever seen. We were icing up---couldn't see our lead ship, nor wingmen. Only an act of God kept us from collision. Brought the bombs back.

Recalling this incident, he wrote in 1992: "Flying into those icy clouds, then turning around inside them, was the most hair-raising experience I had during my entire tour! The recall (to return to base) came after what seemed like an eternity (in the clouds) and we started a slow left turn. Ant that's when I got vertigo! I remember feeling like I was continuing to steepen the bank. Confusion set in. I told my co-pilot, Willie Moulton, to take over. I remember thinking our end was just a midair-collision away and was bound to happen any second. Moulton hung on until we reached the reciprocal heading and leveled the wings. Where the other planes were in those thick clouds we had no idea. Then, we broke out into the clear, and I was able to reorient myself..."

Twenty-ninth Mission, September 11, 1944
Target: Jet-propelled plane plant at Zuchkow, near Leipzig, Germany. A midair collision at the target ruined what would have been a good mission. One ME 109 busted right through our wing formation but apparently got through scratchless. Can you imagine?!

Thirty-fourth Mission, October 6, 1944
Target: Berlin. Fausnaugh and Brashers went down today. And my original bombardier, Norbert A. Emery of Brooklyn, went down with Fausnaugh. Fighters shot their tail assembly off and reports have it that they spun down, obviously out of control.

Thirty-fifth –and LAST! October 15, 1944

Target: Marshaling yards at Cologne, Germany. Dunham overstayed his pass in London and missed this raid of raids! Flak was intense and accurate but behind us. We got one small hole in the left wing near the fuselage. We dropped our wheels and left the formation near the Dover coast…and Callan, Kern, Summers, and Hanselman began firing flares as we split the mouth of the Thames River and put up a continuous barrage all the way up to the base! Providence, luck, and self-confidence brought us through intact.

Charles was awarded his "Lucky Bastard" certificate upon completion of his 35th mission. He made a career of the Air Force and retired in 1970. He died at age 72, in August, 1994, in Jackson.

Aviation cadet, 1942, age 20

Combat veteran, 1945

THE MEMOIRS OF CHARLES SANDERS

I finished my junior year at Mississippi State in the spring of 1941. I could not get a job, and on September 18, I enlisted in the Army Air Corps in Jackson. They sent me and other enlistees by train to Camp Shelby Indoctrination Center.

A few days later about 200 of us were told to put on our Class "A" wool uniforms to board a train for Keesler Field. Upon our arrival at Keesler we were lined up and marched in groups of forty or so to a barracks. The next week was spent getting shots, taking tests, going to lectures and two hours of drilling. If anyone ever asks you, it is hot in Biloxi in September. An interviewing officer asked me if I wanted to go to aircraft mechanics school while I was waiting, and it was not a hard decision to make.

I moved down the street to the 3505th School Squadron. I attended class five hours a day, five days a week where I learned about generators, motors, propellers, airplane structure and hydraulic systems. Propellers were very complicated and I was selected to attend a special course after finishing my training at Keesler. On December 7th, 1941, I was writing a letter to my mother when I heard the announcement that Pearl Harbor had been bombed by the Japanese. The next week we were informed there would be no Christmas leave, and we could no longer wear civilian clothing. I finished school on March 10; and on March 13, a warm spring day, two hundred of us packed our "B" bags with our wool clothes and shipped out to Chanute Field, Illinois, where we arrived with six inches of snow on the ground. I was assigned to a barracks and told that I would be attending a propeller course for eight weeks. School at Chanute was quite interesting. We started with the constant speed props and worked our way up to the hydraulic props, which are the types used on B-17s and B-24s. Balancing a prop was intricate and precision work at its best.

Three days following graduation, five of us got our orders to ship to McDill Field, Florida. Upon arriving, my buddy Clyde Pitchford and I were immediately assigned to KP as no one there knew what we were supposed to do. The First Sergeant looked into the matter, and a Jeep showed up the next day and moved us to a new barracks. After getting settled, we went out to a hanger where a Sergeant directed us to the mess hall for more KP duty. A line chief took me out on line and told me to help the crew chief work on an airplane which I did. That was all I ever heard about KP while at McDill for two weeks before moving thirty miles farther South to Sarasota, Bradenton Air Field where I became a line mechanic.

I was in Sarasota one evening when I heard a civilian say, "I hear your group is not going to the South Pacific." I said "Well, where are we going?" He replied, "Near London." I got a chance to volunteer for guard duty on our equipment train going from Sarasota to New York, our port of embarkation. We left the base in the cab of a big truck on a flat car with our bags and everything we owned. The next six days and nights were spent on this flat car. After six days of traveling, we pulled into New York and spent the night visiting saloons. I also had my first ride on a subway. In the morning we were loaded onto army trucks and went to Fort Dix, New Jersey. There we joined the rest of our buddies and were issued rifles and passports. In a few days we rode the same Army trucks back to New York and P.O.E. There we boarded a ferry, sailed past the Statue of Liberty and boarded a big liner, *USS America.* The date was August 6, 1942.

After sweating out long lines aboard, we were issued a blanket and told, "You can sleep here tonight. We will assign you to a room tomorrow." In the morning we were assigned rooms originally built for three persons, but we had twenty-two in ours and there were only eleven hammocks. Half of us were given blue cards and the rest white.

Those with white cards were supposed to sleep during the day, and blue card owners were to sleep at night. On the way to breakfast, we discovered that the line began next to our room and went through seven flights of stairs and what seemed like miles of halls before we reached the mess hall. Once there, we were served cold beans and toast. I noticed they had Army KP's and assumed they were recruited from the passengers. On the way back following breakfast, I found a big round pin-on button with the letters "KP" on it. From then on we just ate in the room; and if supplies were short, someone would pin on the button, go to the mess hall and liberate food for sandwiches. Two days out we noted many ships in the convoy; one of them was the *Queen Mary*, but I don't think it was as big as our *USS America*. After twelve days at sea, on a boat crammed with soldiers, we landed in Liverpool, England. It was a long ride before we reached our destination of Bovington Air Field, very close to London. It was so close that when they bombed London, we had an alert. We were restricted to the base, but it was rather hard to enforce since hard stands and dispersal sites were across main roads from the main part of the base. After a few days, the restriction was lifted and passes could be picked up at the orderly room.

About this time I got on permanent KP. It was permanent as long as we had the same Engineering Officer. It was the easiest work I had during my Air Force career, and it was not long before I was firing boilers at the mess hall, working eight hour shifts.

It was now September, 1942, and I had been in this man's army for one year. In that time I had been to school for six months learning how to work on airplanes, two months studying propellers and then overseas, where I landed on permanent KP. I did manage to make PFC, however.

****

On September 6, 1942, our station, the 92nd Bomb Group, went on its first mission. Our planes got shot up losing one plane; however, no one was seriously injured. On the second mission, we did not lose any planes but had a lot of plane damage

and wounded. During this time, ground and air crews occupied the same barracks, and the empty cots became stark reminders of the missing fliers. Later, combat crews were placed in separate barracks and it worked better.

On pass in Cromer.

Chesham was my favorite town to visit, and we could ride in on our bicycles or catch a cab. Pubs in town were open from 10 A.M. until 2 P.M. and 6 P.M. until 10 P.M., which was universal throughout England. The favorite drink was "half & half" beer and most guys cultivated a taste for it. In November, 1942, our cigarette rations were cut to seven packs a week. I remember that on Christmas of that year we had some English children on the base. We had turkey with all the trimmings, hot rolls and bread. The bread was brought to the base on a horse drawn cart, and it had no wrapper on it. A lot of English people grew potatoes and ate these as a substitute for bread. In January of 1943, the weather became horrible. Sometimes the fog was so thick you could not see two feet in front of you.

It was about an hour ride from the base to downtown London. We usually stayed at a Red Cross place where bed for the night cost half a crown (50 cents). Everyone wanted to visit Madame Tousaud's Wax Museum with its life-like figures of famous people. Other things I remember were the Tower Bridge, Westminster Abbey and the changing of the guard at the Tower of London. An incident I recall was the breaking of my watch crystal. A jeweler said he could send it off for a replacement but it would take a month or two. This was too long; so I proceeded to take a piece of plexiglass from the broken nose of a B-17 and sawed out a two inch square piece. I made it concave by softening it under steam and then molding it over a ladle I got from the Mess Hall. When it cooled I filed it to fit the watch. It lasted over two years.

We changed Engineering Officers and I asked to get out of KP and back on the line. The new officer arranged a swap and assigned me to a ground crew of two men making me assistant crew chief. They eventually gave me an airplane and my own tool box. The shortage of engine mechanics meant I had to work long hours but I was glad I made the switch. In May, 1943, my plane developed a slight oil leak around a retaining nut. The only wrench to fit this nut belonged to a service squadron, and they would not lend it, causing me to be quite unhappy. I flew out of the hanger smack into an army truck and was thrown over the right front fender.

The driver of the army truck inquired whether I was hurt, and I didn't think I was; so I proceeded to the engineering office. When I arrived, I squeezed the hand brake and felt a pain in my shoulder; so I went to the dispensary where a doctor examined it and sent me to a hospital at Oxford. They put a figure eight brace on me and said I had to stay there. They would not release me so I could return to Bovingdon; so I stayed until June, when the ward started filling up. They released us to Chorley Replacement Center. After some vigorous therapy and exercise, they reclassified us but would not ship us back to our outfits. We appealed to the orderly room where a corporal got us an interview with a classification sergeant who listened to our request. He started the paper work resulting in our being shipped back to our old groups.

We arrived back at the base and were informed there had been a big shake-up. Part of the 92nd had moved to Alconbury. I was given a choice to stay or move to Alconbury, which I did. I thought things would be back to normal, but such was not the case. The engineering department was very short of mechanics, and we had to work long hours,

but no one seemed to mind. We were in combat again, and we felt this was the reason we were sent to England.

On the Line.

It was now August, 1943, and I had been in England for a year. Two things happened about this time that I remember quite well. I got a helper fresh from the States. He was a buck sergeant who completed two mechanics schools. He came out to the plane when I was washing my wool ODs in gasoline and asked if I knew who the other Sanders was in the squadron. He then informed me that I had made corporal! Strange having a buck sergeant working under a corporal. I got a new airplane fresh from the States, and we made modifications and readied it for combat. It made seventeen missions in sixteen days, and on the last mission it was shot up so bad that it could not lower the landing gear, forcing it to make a belly landing.

Sander's Crew

In September, 1943, they moved the 92nd Bomb Group to Podington; and the base began making raids quite regularly. I was sent to another school; this time it was hydraulics. I was the only Yank; the rest were English. As winter approached, the missions began to slack off a little, and many were scrubbed due to bad weather. One of my planes returned with holes in the main rib spar of the wing creating a problem that base engineering had not encountered and did not know how to fix it. We contacted England's best authority on the matter and they informed us to "patch it." We got a section just like it from a junked plane and literally bolted it to the damaged part with a triangle type connection to better take the stress. We had no trouble with the patched area.

Sanders in his winter "work suit"

It was January 18, 1944, when another mechanic, Johnny Harkins and I got orders to move to Station 105 at Sculthorpe for thirty days. I served under a Master Sergeant Howton, a line chief, and worked with a U. S. Air Crew. We were to teach the RAF how to maintain and fly the B-17. I noticed an RAF crew trying to start an engine with little success. The prop would turn over, but the engine would not fire causing the batteries to completely discharge. I then suggested a remedy that was contrary to the "book;" but since this was an emergency, we proceeded to turn off all the gauges and other essentials used in the starting process. We then used the power from an idling engine by idling it back as slow as I dared, then turned on everything that was supposed to be on and watched the pilot start the dead engine from the idling one. The next day the RAF Squadron Leader and Post Commander sent for me. He was aware of the starting problem and in a nice manner said he knew there was more to be known than what was printed in the books and that was the reason he wanted the Yanks to help them. I was assigned a B-17 C plane from two planes that the RAF used for coastal patrol. They were "antiques" and Lt. Keating, our co-pilot asked us to get one of them in shape to fly. We borrowed and patched until we got one checked out. I preflighted it and was invited to go along for a trial run, but I declined.

Our thirty days temporary duty was extended for sixty days. The RAF preferred the B-17 to their own Sterling bombers for coastal patrol because it could carry more fuel and stay out longer. They stripped the bomb racks and installed radar equipment. We figured these modifications were hush-hush when we took out the Norden bomb sight. Our temporary duty was extended indefinitely, and by March we were getting more planes and personnel. We were officially called part of the 803rd Bomb Squadron (H) (Provisional), and we were the 8th AF RCM (Radar Counter Measures Detachment).

The English stored a lot of gliders at Sculthorpe and started to move them out in March or early April. They towed gliders out for days, stopping only long enough for our planes to land.

The detachment continued to fly practice missions, and we were told that our first maximum effort would be the invasion of Europe. They then moved us to an RAF base at Oulton, about ten miles from the North Sea coast. Major Scott, (later Colonel) became our new commanding officer and Captain Paris became Operations Officer. This was mentioned in the book *Secret Squadrons of the*

Eighth. Orders were issued to carry firearms with us at all times.

The fifth of June, 1944, started out as a routine day. A new B-17 landed at the base, and we were supposed to equip it for night flying; however, it arrived so late that we waited to do it the following morning. During evening chow, Captain Preuss came in our mess hall announcing that he wanted everyone at the engineering office when we finished eating. Since the line chief, Sgt. Howton, was in the hospital, I went to see what was up. He informed us that the Base CO had told him that many lives depended on getting our planes in the air as soon as possible. As I recall, we had four planes that took off between 6:30 and 7:00 P.M. and the B-17 awaiting modification took off shortly after 9:00 P.M. We had put flame suppressers on all four engines and completed the rest of the modifications in about three hours, a feat of accomplishment.

We all knew this must be the big night and for the first time since leaving the 92nd BG at Podington, I really "sweated out" our planes. Each plane was flying alone in an assigned area; and if German fighters spotted any of them, they stood little chance of returning. We had heard that the zero hour was 0300 hours. All night long planes thundered in the skies going over, and I don't think I ever heard that sound before. They were ordered to stay out until fuel forced their return. In the morning we accounted for four of the five, but the fifth had to go in at Bovingdon because of the shortage of fuel. D-Day was on, and there was action everywhere. It was now nine in the morning of June 6, 1944; and I had been up for twenty-six hours; so I "sacked out" for four hours. I awoke and found that we were alerted for flying that night; so I went for lunch and the afternoon rush.

On June 7th, our Colonel told us that our squadrons had saved hundreds of lives. They had expected up to forty percent loss of airborne troops, but due to the radar screen put up by our planes they had less than two percent loss. Our special radar kept the Germans from picking up the movements in England.

In July, someone decided the B-24 would be better suited for radar counter measures, and we sent out our first B-24 on the twelfth. By the end of the month we had all B-24s. I asked Sergeant Howton about reverting back to crew chief, since we now had two master sergeants; and I didn't feel right about being assistant line chief. This job gave me more free time and less work; plus I got the chance to go into town and do some loafing. Captain Pruess arranged the transfer.

The middle of August we were ordered to Cheddington, Station 113, about 15 miles north of Bovingdon. We merged with the 803rd Bomb Squadron and became known as the 36th Bomb Squadron (H) (RCM). We were back on an American base, although we continued to make missions in the evening for the RAF; and in addition to the Mandrel sorties, we started using some new radar equipment known as "Elint" (Electrical Intelligence) which was used to locate radar used by the enemy. In October we began using Mandrel screens for 8th Air Force planes returning from leaflet drops, and this changed our mission objectives. RAF missions were cut from six or eight to two or three planes. In support of the 8th AF missions we increased to six or eight. Our planes began taking off between 4:00 and 5:00 A.M. so there would be a Mandrel screen in place before the heavy bombers started taking off and assembling. In December, 1944, we even sent three planes to Belgium to jam in the Battle of the Bulge. We had grown from a very small detachment to a full size squadron. We had been a part of research, refining, testing and operation of special radar equipment for which we received letters of commendation from both the RAF and 8th Air Force for our jamming effectiveness.

In January of 1945, it was bad weather, but we still managed to get in about 25 missions. Some of these were of the "spoof" variety where we would get the Germans to pull their fighters in to a certain area while our bombers went to another area. In February we lost our third plane and part of the crew, and then later in the month we moved back to Alconbury where I had been nearly two years before. This time there were three of us working on the plane, and in a short time we had thirty-two missions on it without an abortion (turn back). On the 33rd mission it was gone only fifteen minutes when it returned because the pilot had a checklist of things to do before take-off which he performed but accidentally turned on both magnetos at the same time instead of only one. This caused the plane to back-fire, bursting the ducts leading to the carburetor. We were disgusted.

One day the Engineering Officer told me we were getting in three P-38 fighters and asked if I would be crew chief on one of them. I thought "what the heck, I started over again with the B-24, why not." So we agreed to that on condition I would be among the personnel selected to fly home when the war was over. I became a P-38 crew chief. These planes were not armed, but an observer with Elint equipment took the place of the guns and ammunition. One of the pilots came out to the ship I was assigned to and invited me to take a trip to his home base with him. On take off, I thought I felt the wheels retract, and as we reached the end of the runway he flipped it upside down and completed the takeoff this way. This was my first and last ride in a P-38.

While the middle of March, 1945, was one of our busiest times, our last mission was flown on April 25. After this we would go out to our plane, crank it up and almost hope to find something wrong. In other words, it was "goof-off" time and well earned. On May 7, we heard that it was over, so we celebrated a night early. We had to wait until nearly midnight for it to get dark enough as the nights were very short at this time of the year. We fired the flares until there were none left. May 7th report of the war's end was rumor but not the 8th: it was the real thing ! ! What a feeling to be in the real world again ! !

I made a trip to Europe and saw a lot of bombed out places and flew around the Eiffel Tower. Our pilot flew so low that we had to look up to see most of it.

We were alerted to go home. We finished our work, packed and took off with the plane circling the field one last time. A few hours later we landed in Iceland for refueling. We ate lunch and then found out the weather ahead was bad, and we would have to stay until it cleared. We departed for Greenland and stayed that night. The next morning it was off for Bradley Field, Connecticut. We landed in the good old USA about 8:00 A.M., Friday, July 13, 1945, nearly three years after I had departed the country on the liner *USS America*.

Maurice J. Herman, who is a native of Connecticut, now lives in Ocean Springs, with his wife, Bettina. He became an airplane buff early on when, at eight years of age, his father gave him a model airplane. He experienced his first flights in 1929 in a Travelair and in 1930 in a Spartan biplane.

Maurice entered the Army Air Corps early and received his wings as a navigator in 1942. In England, he served in the 91st Bomb Group at Bassingbourn, attained the rank of 1st Lt., and was awarded the Air Medal with one Oak Leaf Cluster. He was credited with shooting down one German plane, over Wilhelmshaven on April 5, 1943. His career as a navigator was cut short on June 22, 1943, when he was shot down on his 9th mission. He evaded capture for about 10 hours before Germans picked him up. He was a P.O.W. for 21 months in Stalag Luft III and Stalag Luft XIII-D. On March 4, 1945, Maurice escaped from the latter and managed to escape recapture until April 28.

IT'S NOT EASY REMEMBERING

This story is based on an interview with Russell Gilbert Kahl, by Bettye Duke Jackson.

Lt. Russell Kahl

This is the story of Russell Gilbert Kahl. Russell was a 1st Lt. in the 306th Bomb Group, a pilot on a B-17, stationed at Thurleigh. His home is in Aberdeen, where his wife, two children, and two granddaughters live. Russell is a resident of the Oxford Veterans Home. He has lost both legs, but he is filled with the humor, determination, and fight that so characterizes the men of *The Mighty Eighth.*

Russell was going through his pre-flight training when the Japanese bombed Pearl Harbor. He was graduated and commissioned at Bakersfield.

On his second mission, Russell's Fortress, the "Woody Woodpecker," was attacked by heavy flak and German planes. He witnessed two B-17s colliding in mid-air. This was in the early stages of

the war when crews were told that if they survived the first six missions, they had beat the odds. On Friday, January 13th, 1943 over Lille, France, Russell's plane, under heavy fire, blew up. He was blown out of the cockpit. A piece of Plexiglas covered his upper body, and he had to dig the Plexiglas off to get to the ripcord of his parachute. Less than half of the crew got out of the plane. Russell landed on a German air base and was immediately taken prisoner. There were no American P.O.W. camps at that time; so he was placed in a British camp. By the end of the war, Russell had been in four P.O.W. camps: Subin, 21-B, Stalag III, and Mooseburg. He was a prisoner for 29 months. Russell recalls the lonesome feeling he had when he knew planes from *The Mighty Eighth* were flying over. All of the prisoners would be ordered inside when the bombers were sighted.

129

Russell was one of the prisoners, along with British prisoners, who dug the escape tunnel which was the plot of the movie, *The Great Escape*. The prisoners drew straws to decide who would be the ones out of the tunnel. Just two days before "the great escape," Russell was transferred to an American prisoner camp. The escape was not successful, and approximately 50 British prisoners were captured and shot. There were many tunnels dug, and the Germans were aware of most of them.

Another incident Russell recalls with laughter is the time he and five of his fellow prisoners saved their raisins and sugar from the Red Cross packages and made home brew. They got pretty drunk and decided to go over the barbed wire fence and visit their British friends. They made it over the fence but they were soon caught and spent two weeks in the "cooler" with only bread and water. The hangover was worse than having no food.

Russell remembers life at P.O.W. camps to be pretty bad. He looked forward to Red Cross packages. The prisoners could play baseball on a make-do field and had a track to run on which bordered the barbed wire fence.

The long march from Stalag III to Mooseburg took about two weeks in weather often below zero. "We lost a lot of lives on that march," Russell remembers. "Food, even for the Germans, was scarce - we all suffered."

Russell Gilbert Kahl was discharged on February 22, 1946, at San Antonio, Texas. He returned to Aberdeen where he had extensive farm lands and raised cattle.

Russell Kahl has had both legs amputated; he now lives at the Veteran's Home in Oxford. Shown above with friends, Kahl, in center.

CLARKSDALE GUNNER

Ellis Q. Mitchell, E.Q. to his friends, is a native and lifelong resident of Clarksdale. He first enlisted in the Armed Forces as a high school student in the Mississippi National Guard. He served for three years in the 31ˢᵗ Infantry Division, better known to many as the famed "Dixie Division."

He would later enlist in the Naval Air Corps at the outbreak of World War II for flight training, but a tendency to become dizzy during spinouts meant that serving as a pilot was not an option for the young soldier.

So, it was off to the U. S. Army Air Corps with still a burning desire to fly. His patience and year long training in flight gunnery and armament schools led to the possibility of flying once again as a crew member on heavy bombers.

After the completion of a series of schools training in gunnery and armaments, he was assigned to a crew, and with the crew flew a new B-17 to England. He was instrumental in the naming of the plane, "Super Wabbit." He says that the crew was eager to get into the action. "We had trained for the war, and in 1944 we were taking the battle to Germany. In June, the Eighth Air Force was part of the largest invasion force in the history of the world as we began to cross the English Channel to the Normandy beaches.

"We know it now as D-Day – June 6, 1944. I'll never forget it. We were flying support for the ships and the men landing on the beaches. Man, from the air you could see so many ships at once, it looked as if we could have walked across the water on them."

Mitchell was in England for only six months. During that time, he served as a waist gunner and had the additional duty of pulling the bomb pins after take-off on each mission. His bombing missions included raids on oil refineries around Paris, ball-bearing plants at Schweinfurt, shipyards at Bremen, factories at Kiel, plants at Posen in Poland and, finally, Berlin. His group (the 96ᵗʰ Bomb Group) was awarded a Distinguished Unit Citation for a bombing mission on the Sablon Locomotive Depot at Metz.

All this was at a terrible price. "The skies were not as friendly as I thought they might be," he remembers. "Over Paris, we had to fly low for one particular mission. Cloud cover put us under 16,000 feet. We were hammered over the site by flak, and on the return trip, German Messerschmits came out of the clouds and picked us off. We lost half of our bomber group in one mission. We were lucky to get back ourselves. When I saw those famous white cliffs of Dover, I was never so grateful for home, such as it was."

On later missions, the crew was not at all lucky. Flak from anti-aircraft guns killed his pilot on their third mission, the navigator on another. The flak punched holes in the bomber and he and others saw sights they never forgot.

Mitchell said, "While flying in formation, planes would be stacked on top of one another. When the Germans attacked, they would cut in and out of us, shooting at whatever was there. And then over the target, you could see hundreds of flak shells exploding all around you. Men were bailing out of their aircraft and landing on craft underneath them. It was horrible."

After 30 missions, the crew was rotated back to the States. Mitchell said, "Man, you really needed it. By the time most of us flew 30 missions, we were a bundle of nerves. Back home we took some needed time off. When our turn came up to go back, we all met in Atlantic city to get ready. But we learned they were rotating stateside training crews to Europe for a tour.

"Instead, I was sent out west to train as a central fire controller on a B-29, Superfortress. That plane was loaded with guns, all of them controlled by one person. I was getting ready to go to the Pacific when the war ended in August."

Ellis Mitchell was awarded the Distinguished Flying Cross and the Air Medal with three Oak Leaf Clusters. His Bomb Group was awarded a Distinguished Unit Citation.

The above account was, for the most part, taken from an interview with Ellis Q. Mitchell by John Mayo, which was published in the CLARKSDALE PRESS REGISTER, on November 10,1995

Mitchell, standing, left

EVADING THE HUNS

By William T. Blaylock

William T. Blaylock lives in Grenada, where he grew up and finished high school. After the war ended, Bill served on for a few years. When he was discharged in 1948, he enlisted in the National Guard. He served a tour of active duty during the Korean War. He retired as a CWO 4, in 1984.

August 26, 1944. The ramp at Flixton Air Field was a scene of activity, big four engine bombers stretching far down the field. Pilots, ground and air crews were engaged in loading ammunition, bombs, preflighting engines and equipment and making sure all was in readiness for the mission ahead. As ball turret gunner, I checked my guns and ammunition, and stowed my escape kit and candy, and awaited orders. When all was in readiness, we climbed aboard and listened while final warm-up of engines was done. At intervals, each B-24 wheeled into position, taxied to the starting point on the runway, and roared off down the field. At the appropriate speed the landing gear was pulled up, the airplane settling for a moment, and then climbing, turning and fading in the clouds.

We broke out of the clouds with the silver planes near and far shining in the early sunlight, converged in flights and took a heading for the battle zone. At an early briefing, we were told our target this day would be the vicinity of Ludwigshafen, Germany, far down the Rhine Valley, where 147 antiaircraft guns would be waiting for us.

Our unit was the 706th Bomb Squadron, 446th Bomb Group, 8th Army Air Force, home station, Flixton Air Base, Bungay, England (U.K.). Our bomber was a B-24 Liberator. The flight crew numbered eleven this date: Pilot - Second Lieutenant Dean M. Peppmeir, Truro, Iowa; Co-Pilot - Second Lieutenant Walter Meihle, Chicago, Illinois; "Bombigator" (Bombardier/Navigator) - Second Lieutenant Rubin, New York; Radio-Gunner - Staff Sergeant John P. (Jack) Strain, Forest Hills, New York; Engineer Gunner - Staff

Sergeant Richard W. Dawson, Brookline, Massachusetts; Top Turret Gunner - Staff Sergeant Thomas Peevley, Pennsylvania; Nose-Turret Gunner - Sergeant Robert Algee, Byhalia, Mississippi; Right Waist Gunner - Sergeant Sylvester M. Novak, Pittsburgh, Pennsylvania; Left Waist Gunner - Sergeant Frederick O'Dell, Ohio; Tail Gunner - Sergeant Carl R. (Andy) Anderson, Bridgeport, Connecticut; and me, Ball Turret (or Belly) Gunner - Corporal William T. Blaylock, Grenada Mississippi. S Sgt Peevley was an extra from another crew. He was making his twenty-fifth mission and would be going home.

We were a crew with high regard for each other, most having been through months of training and preparation for our combat roles; and though fearful of combat, I felt a strong pride to be one of them.

Crossing the enemy coast over Belgium and Holland, we took some "flak" from enemy antiaircraft, mostly inaccurate. Several hours later, flying at approximately 23,500 feet altitude, with escort fighters, P-51 Mustangs, we crossed over the target near Ludwigshafen, Germany. We dropped our bombs, as did the other ships in our formation, while flak burst fearfully close. As the bombardier yelled "bombs away," the hail storm of flying shrapnel struck with fierce intensity, and exploding shells rocked our plane. The hail of flak was riddling our plane from front to rear. Many times the big bomber which was our hope for return home shivered, groaned and roared like a prehistoric animal.

An excited voice came over the intercom, "Open the door, Lieutenant! Open the door! My oxygen mask is cut in two!"

"Who has the oxygen mask cut?" asked Lt. Peppmeier.

"It's me, Algee."

"Use the broken end of the oxygen hose." said the pilot calmly. "Dick," to the engineer gunner, "get an extra mask to him with a portable oxygen bottle."

"Wilco, skipper," came from S Sgt Dawson.

****

I sat in the ball turret wearing a flak helmet, no flak suit on, parachute harness and "Mae West" on, parachute outside the turret in a ready area. One waist gunner was throwing out "chaff" (metallic bits of foil used to confuse the enemy radar.) The other waist gunner was watching the combat action from his window. Suddenly I leaped up with a cry of alarm and pain. Shrapnel had come through my turret striking the armor plating of my seat, radiating outward, and hitting my legs. As I opened the hatch and stood up, Sgt Novak came over to check and found that the shrapnel had cut open my suit and left several large bruises on my left leg but no real injury. I sat down in my turret, relieved. The barrage of enemy antiaircraft explosions continued.

As we rode out of the cloud of smoke and exploding shells, still in formation behind the "pathfinder" ships, flying along with the green country of Germany below us visible through rifts in the clouds; we were on our way home, congratulating ourselves on our good fortune that no one was injured. Algee was still using the large oxygen bottle; S Sgt Peevley had a dent in his flak helmet but was unharmed. We were out of the target zone with all engines going.

Oxygen was running low at all stations, but we felt we had enough to last by careful use. Then sometime later one of the crewmen called on the intercom to report seeing a gas or oil leak coming from one of the engines. S Sgt Dawson was told to check it, and his report was bad. There was a fuel leak on an inboard engine. The inboard engine could not be shut off without also stopping the outboard one. We rode on with orders to watch for fire.

Some time later the pilot called S Sgt Dawson to check the fuel supply, and the report was approximately forty-five minutes fuel left. A check with our navigator confirmed that we were about forty-five minutes from the coast of England.

I listened to the conversation over the intercom and thought "forty-five minutes from England and maybe enough gas to get there, but a fuel leak would make it most doubtful we would." We were out of normal range of fighter aircraft, but this situation was bad, and we still had to cross the coastline defenses.

The oxygen was getting lower, and Jack was getting ready to send the "SOS;" but before he could send the message, there was a terrible explosion. The plane heaved and plunged.

The pilot's bell rang, "BAIL OUT."

THE PLANE WAS ON FIRE!

I climbed out of my turret; Fred O'Dell was lying on the floor, the left waist window having struck him, smoke was pouring through the open window. I picked up my parachute, strapped it on watching as Mike Novak reached to lift the escape hatch door. He got it partially open when the plane plunged and yawed throwing him across the hatch and the door across him and me on top of all. My mind whirled with desperation, being trapped; but as we struggled, the plane righted itself; and we got the door open. Mike fell through, and I followed him out into the cold, whistling wind. Sgt Anderson, our tail gunner, and Sgt O'Dell, the left waist gunner, I saw no more.

Back of the flight deck, Jack Strain and Peevley abandoned their stations, grabbed their chutes, Peevley going out a front hatch. Reaching for the door to the bomb bay, Jack burned his hand and the hair on his forehead. He plunged into the bomb bay catwalk and made his way to the rear. As he stood up in front of the escape hatch, he discovered to his horror that his rip cord had been pulled. He hesitated, thinking of the danger with his chute coming out. Then the plane lurched tossing him through the open hatch; his parachute opened and snatched him away. It caught on the tail of the plane but pulled loose, and Jack went down OK.

(This part of the story is from Jack's statements to me.)

By later report of Lt Peppmeier, a near direct hit of antiaircraft fire took out the lower front of the plane, and in this we lost our nose gunner and bombardier. It also critically damaged and set the plane on fire. Lt Meile, S Sgt Dawson, Sgt O'Dell and Sgt Anderson stayed in the plane. Lt Peppmeier, after the bail-out warning, bailed out himself. Further reports indicated that Lt Meile, survived the plane crash but with injuries to legs and back. Lt Peppmeier, S Sgt Peevley, and Lt Meile were captured by the Germans. Sgt Novak was reported to have been shot.

My first feeling after I left the plane was immense relief that I would not be killed in a fiery crash. Having been taught to delay pulling the ripcord, would give me a better chance to escape, I did so but started a violent body spin. I tried holding out my arms and then other body positions to stop the spin, but nothing worked, and the spin became increasingly violent. I delayed, watching the ground, and then could see clearly no longer, and pulled the ripcord.

I looked at the ground far below, the plane above with its nose in a downward glide, and near and far the dark figures hanging beneath their parachutes, drifting down.

Then the ground came up, and I hit with a fierce thump. Rolling over, I stood up as a Dutchman came toward me with a book in his hand asking, "Are you hurt?" I told him "no" and started to go to the plane which had crashed about fifty - sixty yards away. The Dutchman called me and urgently suggested that I " Cache! Cache!" Realizing the need for immediate action, I gave him my parachute (at his request), and ran toward the woods nearby. As I ran, I pulled off my "Mae West" and throat mike, tossing them aside. Reaching the woods and looking for a hiding place, I cut sharply into a small opening in the pine trees where hopefully the grass was tall enough to conceal me from all except a close search. The Dutchman saw where I was going and told me he would be back.

I lay there all afternoon from 12:10 by my watch until about 9:00 P.M., strained and fearful that I would be discovered. Searches were made all around and through the woods between me and the downed plane; but as I had hoped, they did not look in the point of woods where I lay. Patrols also were operating along a nearby trail, and I could often hear the talking. The ammunition in the plane was exploding as it burned.

At late dusk, I heard a sound and raising on an elbow; I could see a figure stealthily moving from bush to bush and toward me. He called in a muted voice and I recognized him as the Dutchman. He led me away across the trail and to a place where Jack Strain was hiding. He gave us something to eat and drink and gave each of us a pair of shoes. (I had lost one of my boots on the way down.) By our maps he showed us where we were; and with many thanks, we slipped away into the dark woods and fields.

We traveled mostly by night and slept during the day, hiding in bushes, and once in a haystack where we were discovered by a farmer, who called his family to meet us. They also gave us food. On the third day, we became desperate, needing shelter from rain and the cooling days and lacking enough to eat. Once we approached a man and boy who were doing early milking of cows, and they fearfully allowed us to drink the fresh milk from a pail. In a garden with a house nearby I had found some mature green corn and with a stick plucked some apples from a tree, but it was certain we needed help to continue. Getting good water was also a problem. We took water from a cistern one night, used our Halazone tablets to sterilize it, but discovered the next morning it contained mosquito larvae.

On the fourth day, after having slept in an open grotto (or shrine), we entered a town at early dawn and made our way toward a ringing church bell, went in, and Jack approached the "Cure" (or Father). We found out later he thought we were thieves. He called the police. To our great fortune, the policeman who came was the police chief and a member of the ""underground""(resistance forces). He led us out and hid us in a field at the edge of town, gave us some ""ersatz" coffee, raw eggs and bread, introduced us to a friend of his who would help, and both left us, promising to return later.

Later in the day, the friend came back and moved us to a barn where we hid in the hayloft. At dusk, he came again and led us several miles to a house on the highway. There we met a Frenchman and his wife who would be our caretakers, we would sleep upstairs, and a Belgian commander of the resistance army would see us later. The couple showed us our room, suggested we would like to bathe and get some rest. *In a bed!* It seemed weeks since we had such comfort. We were given food. Common food in this time and place was "pop", any type of oatmeal or pudding fare; but under the circumstances, it was very, very good.

****

We slept so soundly that night that it was noon before we awoke. Our hosts came knocking on our door and brought the Chief Marquis, a tall, distinguished man about thirty to thirty-five years old (by guess) who spoke English very well. He asked us questions, and we enjoyed a good conversation. We discussed options and plans for us to further evade capture and return to allied control. Methods and obstacles included bicycling or walking, crossing the Albert Canal near Antwerp, and evading the movement and mass of German soldiers on the roads. There was a beginning of a mass exodus from the war zone toward their homeland. Then he said goodbye and left with plans incomplete.

We stayed in the home for three days, the war reaching us as more and more Germans streamed along the road in front of our hiding place. Once a flight of fighters, P-47s, attacked the railroad station about two blocks away striking a locomotive and exciting all in the area. A short distance away a number of vehicles (wagons, etc.) with supplies and possible ammunition was attacked and badly damaged. The docks at Antwerp were set ablaze, and we could see the heavy smoke from our window. The enemy became a threat because of their presence and our possible discovery, and it was decided we would be moved to a large chateau in the woods not too far away.

There we met a most interesting lady, Mme. V. Van Mons, who could speak English. She had been a refugee to England during WW I and always spoke of the Germans as "Boche" with a deep feeling of hate. Her estate included a tract of possibly 15 or 20 acres, heavily wooded; and the home was set back off the road and bordered by fences. As time progressed, it seemed most reasonable we would spend time waiting on the war and developments for evasion and escape.

During the approximately five weeks we stayed with her, we had many visitors, friendly and generous, who always made known their fierce loyalty to home and purpose of helping in driving the invaders out of their land. Our friend, the chief of police, came often; the Dutchman (my first contact at landing) came once. Outside of Mme. Van Mons, our most important friends were the family of Standaert: mother, daughter Marie Therese, Florient, Felix and Stanny. The boys were really young men of purpose and valor. On one of their visits, Marie Therese brought us a "tart" in a pie pan which we enjoyed, and on other occasions they brought other things. We also met an elderly gentleman, a jolly fellow, red-nosed and a source of inexhaustible tales and jokes. He had served during WW I and had been exposed to poison gas while serving as an interpreter for the Canadian forces. He brought us books and magazines to pass the time.

136

Early during this stay in the chateau in the woods, a couple of young ladies came to see us. I assumed this was an effort on the part of our hosts to make our time pleasant. If so, they succeeded. Early on, our Mme. Van Mons insisted we have no "hanky-panky." We recognized her resolve, and to the credit of these two ladies, we enjoyed the freedom to pass much time in their company. My friend was Annette Rose, a round-limbed young girl of eighteen, pretty, and always with a happy smile.

During one period we, our host, Mme. Van Mons, and our young ladies took walks along a looping trail around the estate, enjoyed the freedom and activity, little fearing discovery, and just enjoying the company of friends.

The Germans were reported to be setting up guns nearby, between us and the Canadian forces, and their occasional "Boom! Boom!" jarred the silence of the autumn days. We could also hear airplanes, always "ours," as they searched and attacked the Germans.

As time went by the war came closer. Often motorcycles and other vehicles came near, and we could hear small caliber weapons firing (probably test firing). Then we heard that the allied forces were advancing, and the artillery "booming" grew ever closer. We realized plans for us could change any day.

About the first of October Canadian shells began falling near us, and although our host and others feared for our safety, we chose to stay in our comfortable rooms.

Many stories of the local fighting were brought to us, many from our jolly red-nosed friend, who rode his bicycle everywhere.

****

On the fourth of October, German activity began to increase in the woods and nearby town. In the afternoon, the policeman came and told us that everybody would have to evacuate within an hour or be shot. The Germans wanted the civilians out of the way.

Jack and I wondered aloud about where we would be taken, hoping it would not be farther from the friendly battle lines. That we did not want. Of course, we would do as our friends wanted. They were to be considered because they were under more danger every day.

We packed our few belongings; and with some apples and canned sardines, we made preparation to leave. Ma'm'selle helped us and with crying and much ado said she was sad because she would never see us again. We promised to see her again if possible and to get in touch with her when the war was over.

At about five o'clock, the policeman and two of the Standaert boys came for us. With the policeman leading, we went down the road, crossed by the Frenchman's house, crossed the railroad tracks, and then went through the small village. As we entered the main street, we saw two German soldiers, one walking and one riding a bicycle. One soldier appeared to be very young, on foot and armed with a pistol, rifle and hand grenades hanging from his belt. The other was older and similarly armed. The young soldier looked us over curiously, and Stanny asked him, "Is this the way to go?" "Ja," he answered and walked on his way. The other soldier just looked at us as he rode by.

At the next cross street, we turned away from the direction given by the German, and an old man tried to talk to me. All I could do was shake my head. Stanny noticed and shouted to him, "He cannot understand you. He's deaf and dumb." And so I was to their language.

We hurried on down a little traveled roadway, a country lane, then turned aside, and hid in a small covered pen or shed, and waited, watching to see if we were followed. Some of our guides were dropping out at different points; and then we proceeded further into the woods. Our guide at this point was the Belgian Marquis who led us to a thatch covered foxhole, just big enough for an entrance and a small room where a bunk bed was set up. He showed us the cache of canned foods and other useful items. He explained that we were to await the Canadian army. In the meantime we could hide, biding our time, and they would bring us food and news from time to time. We assured him we were well pleased, and thanked him.

After shaking hands with us, he left. Jack and I unrolled our blankets on the bunk; and stowing our gear, we lay down to rest. We discovered that sleeping two in a bunk was not easy, but we were thankful for the security of our abode.

The next day the Germans and Canadians were firing artillery over us, back and forth; the screech of their shells gave a weird sound. That day and the next, the fifth and sixth of October, the shelling continued. The Chief Marquis, his little son, and the Chief's uncle came bringing food, information and friendship. His little son was a handsome little lad who immediately wanted to shake hands. During the three days there, Jack and I dug into our store of sardines and other "goodies" and passed the time talking little, thinking much and listening to the war outside.

On the seventh of October, a middle-aged man, a member of the secret army, came calling the password and crawled into the tunnel. He was there to lead us to safety, to meet an advance patrol of the First Canadian Army. Our trip was short, furtively dashing quietly from places of hiding, and then going out to meet a huge dark Canadian soldier who, along with others, waited for us near a farm house. Jack was overcome, ran and embraced the soldier. Although more restrained, I was having much the same feeling of joy and deliverance.

After some questions about our events, assuring that we were genuinely American, he took us into the house where we were fed (mortar rounds landing often, sometimes too close even for their sense of safety). Then we were on our way, riding a jeep to the rear area for more interrogation, care and return to the proper military control.

The next day we had the opportunity and honor to meet the Chief Marquis, who appeared in his military uniform, a colonel, neat and impressive, and this was a poignant farewell to a brave and patriotic man.

We were given Canadian uniforms, and sent to Antwerp, to Brussels, to Ghent, and back to Antwerp, where we were to rest and await further orders. On the 17th of October, we were put on a C-47 cargo plane bound for Paris. For five days we saw the sights of Paris (ravaged by war) then hitched a ride on a B-17 bound for London. We were allowed freedom there for fifteen days, exchanged our uniforms for those of the U. S. A., returned for a brief visit to Flixton Air Base, where we met one of the air crews we had left behind. Then our orders brought us home.

EPILOG

Those we left behind in Belgium and Holland have remained a warm memory of brave and patriotic men and women without whose help our time in their country surely would have been most unpleasant. They deserve much praise and admiration.

The Dutchman, Mr Koopmanchap, is still living and doing well, in his eighties. Mme. V. Van Mons, has been deceased for a number of years, as has the Mr. Franz Roop, the chief of police, and certainly though unconfirmed, has the jolly red-nosed friend. Of Annette Rose and her friend, I have not heard, nor have I heard from the Chief Marquis. (I never knew his name.)

Of the Standaert family, Mrs. Standaert is still living, at 103 years young, with Florient, her eldest son, a retired banker (and unmarried). Felix who lives in Brussells is a retired foreign diplomat. The family lost the youngest son, Stanny, in a tragic swimming accident within a few years after we were there. Marie Therese is married with a daughter who lives in California. At the time of this writing she and her husband and daughter have plans, of which my wife Earline and I happily approve, to visit us here in Grenada.

Jack Strain and I went our separate ways, corresponded several times, and then lost contact.

As of the date of this writing, all of my crew are now lost to me, some killed in battle, some died at home. I think of them often and treasure the comradeship, the time we shared, and pridefully believe that I belonged with those brave men. The years have not dimmed my deep sense of loss.

Many of our heroes are never acknowledged, and many more have been sacrificed in the cause of God and country, leaving us with freedom to inherit and hopefully to build a brighter future for our most treasured ones. We must give those who follow us the opportunity to enjoy life in a strong nation, in a society free from fear and threat of war.

One of our greatest American heroes has said, we should: "HERE HIGHLY RESOLVE THAT THESE DEAD SHALL NOT HAVE DIED IN VAIN." So let it be.

Alfred H. "Bill" Freeny grew up in the Freeny community near Carthage. When the Japanese attacked Pearl Harbor, Bill was working at a sawmill at Thomastown hauling logs. His service in the Eighth was in the 490th BG at Eye where he was a heavy equipment operator. In his words: "My job was hauling airplane engines, wings and oxygen, and sweating missions out at the end of the runway with a crash truck. I saw quite a few planes come in bad shape and some that didn't get off the runway. All in all, it was a memorable experience, and I am proud to have been a part of it."

Henry Park Hiter was a sophomore at Ole Miss when the Japanese attacked Pearl Harbor. He felt he would not be able to complete college at that time, and he did not. Instead he volunteered for the Air Corps as an aviation cadet and was sent to a College Training Detachment at Shippery Rock College in Pennsylvania. His flying schools were at Chester, Illinois; Malden, Missouri; and Stuttgart, Arkansas where he received his pilot's wings. He met his crew at Colorado Springs and learned that he would serve as co-pilot with Dave Bridgers of Vicksburg as his pilot. They flew a new B-24 Liberator to England, and were assigned to the 466th Bomb Group at Attlebridge. Henry and his crew flew 25 missions from September, 1944, until the end of the war in May, 1945. He says his worst mission was his first one, which was to Magdeburg. When the crew returned to base, he counted 153 holes in his plane made by flak, though no one was injured. However, the bomb load did not release, and they had to release them one by one with a screwdriver on the way home.

A TYPICAL MISSION

By Eugene Spearman

In 1944 and 1945, my parents were very concerned because their three boys were in combat in WWII. The eldest was in the south Pacific on Leyte and later on Okinawa; the middle son was already wounded just after D-Day in France; and the youngest was flying missions over Germany. I was the baby of the family, and my mother wrote so many letters, or V-mail, to me that I decided to write her describing a typical mission. I knew as soon as I finished the letter that it would never get by the censors, so I put it in my duffel bag thinking that if the worst happened, she might still get to read the letter. A few years ago while going through some of my old belongings, I found the letter. It was called:

A TYPICAL MISSION

The morning of February 15, 1945, started early for me when the sergeant shook the small bunk I was sleeping in and said, "Wake up, Spearman. You are flying today in Nichols' crew, in B-17 No. 242. Be down at briefing at 4:45." I, along with several other sleepy crewmen, struggled out of bed and hurriedly pulled on my clothes. The place was Grafton Underwood, near Kettering, England, in the Midlands, home of the 544th Bomb Squadron, 384th Bomb Group, 2nd Wing, 8th Air Force. Outside the small Quonset hut, I picked up the little English bike and pedaled down toward the mess hall, or chow hall. I had often wondered before on similar trips to the "Ptomaine Tavern" (as the chow hall was known) just how many flight crewmen had owned the little bike I was riding. It was never necessary to buy a bike, nor did we have to wait any time after reaching the base before acquiring one. All we had to do was go down to the flight line and pick up one that Bill, or Pete, or Joe rode down yesterday or the day before, but did not get back across the Channel to make the return trip to the little Quonset huts.

After chow I rode on down to the flight line and entered the briefing room. Our briefing was conducted by several operational officers. First, the group commander told us the target for the day. If it was a well-known place like Berlin, Hamburg, Schweinfurt or Leipzig, a low "Ah-h-h" mingled with a few moans usually echoed around the room.

Today, it is Dresden. After giving us a description of the target, the type target, and other pertinent data, he listed the first and second alternate targets. The intelligence officer then took charge and pointed out the probable locations of flak and fighter concentration we would encounter. The weather officer told us the cloud conditions over the target and the expected weather conditions back at the base at our estimated time of arrival back at Grafton Underwood.

A navigational officer pointed out our route in, the time of "Bombs Away," and the return route. With a wave of the hand and a "Good luck, Boys" we would rush in and put on the heated suits, wobble out to the small jeeps that carried us to the dispersed planes. I always thought everyone else looked like stuffed toad frogs in those suits. After reaching the planes, I noted that on this particular mission, our plane, #242, was christened, "Stardust." The fact that she had 29 small bombs painted on the fuselage did not impress me that she would make #30 round trip any easier. In fact, I shuddered to think what some German civilians would do to anyone who rode her down on German soil.

Our cargo consisted of several magnesium incendiary bombs and six 300-pound demolition type bombs. In a few minutes we had pulled into the line of traffic of about forty B-17s awaiting our turn to pull on to the end of the runway. The roar of engines as they struggled to lift the heavy load of fuel and bombs was enough to awake all the residents of the Midlands. It was an impressive sight for this country boy.

Standing just beside the end of the runway where we made that final check of instruments before releasing the brakes was a minister. I don't know what denomination he represented, but it was an inspiration to me to see him there. And then we were on our way.

All whom I knew who flew missions were superstitious. My superstition was a candy bar. At briefing they always gave us a candy bar, usually a Milky Way or Snickers. I always placed the candy bar on the small table in front of me and ate it just before we touched down at home on the return. On this particular mission, the ball turret gunner came by my position, and, before I could stop him, ate my candy just after takeoff. To me that was a major disaster. It was as if all my luck had run out. He resembled one of these ostriches with that candy bar going down his throat, and I would have shot him if we had not needed the belly gun to protect our plane underneath.

It was a long flight in with considerable flak, but few fighters sighted. A diversionary flight by B-24s up the North Sea toward Hamburg had caused Herr Goering to use up much precious fuel to try to keep the submarine pens at Bremen and Hamburg from being attacked, while some one thousand B-17s struck straight across Germany to Dresden.

The Germans used two types of flak. First, pattern flak is when they just shoot the 88mm guns into the air over the area they wish to protect; another is the tracking flak, where they use their radar to stay on the target as it moves above them. Oddly enough, the pattern flak was the most effective. At the end of the 20th century, when they vote on the man of the century, I will cast my vote, not for Einstein, Anderson or Von Braun, but for the man who invented this - chaff! On a radar scope, it looked just like a B-17, and it saved a lot of country boys from having to get out and walk at 30,000 feet altitude.

It was a long flight back, but 11½ hours after takeoff we were back at the base. This mission was not one of the most important of the 8th Air Force, nor was it our worst. It was just one of the many that broke the back of the German nation, and convinced the German people as well as their leaders that they lost the war due to the strategic air power of the allies.

T Sgt Eugene Spearman

It got us back every time.

141

FLOYD H. METTS

(Floyd H. Metts was interviewed by Bettye Duke Jackson and Charles H. Walker. The interview with this veteran of The Mighty Eighth, is presented here just as it was recorded.)

Interviewer: What is your name and where were you born?

Mr. Metts: My name is Floyd H. Metts, and I was born in Lafayette County about 4½ miles southeast of Oxford.

Interviewer: In what branch of service did you serve during World War II?

Mr. Metts: I served in the United States Army Air Corps.

Interviewer: What was the date of your induction into service?

Mr. Metts: Well, I was in the enlisted reserve from May, 1942 until October of 1942, when I was appointed an aviation cadet.

Aviation Cadet Floyd H. Metts

Interviewer: What was the highest rank you achieved while you were in the military?

Mr. Metts: 1st Lieutenant.

Interviewer: What overseas service did you see?

Mr. Metts: I was in the 8th Air Force, stationed in England.

Interviewer: Where did you take your training in this country before going to England?

Mr. Metts: When I first went into service, I was sent to Nashville for classification to see if I would be a pilot, bombardier, or navigator. From there, I went to Maxwell Field, Alabama, and then to Camden, Arkansas, for primary pilot training. From Camden, I went to Greenville, Mississippi, and then to Columbus, Mississippi Air Base. From Columbus, I went to Florida for B-17 training with my crew. We left Florida, picked up our B-17 in Georgia, and flew it overseas.

Interviewer: How many hours did you fly before being commissioned as a pilot?

Mr. Metts: It's been a long time, but I think around 100. After we picked up our B-17 at Hunter Air Force Base in Georgia, we had orders to go to Bangor, Maine, then to Newfoundland, and then to Ireland where we left our B-17. We were called a replacement crew when I went overseas. That was in May of 1944. Instead of going as a unit, our crew was the only crew I knew that was assigned to the 381st Bomb Group.

Interviewer: What was the marking on your aircraft?

Mr. Metts: It was a triangle with an "L" on the tail.

Interviewer: Did you have the same crew the entire seven months you were in England?

Mr. Metts: You had a choice. The bombardier, pilot and navigator could try out for lead navigator, pilot or bombardier. If you were accepted, you could fly 30 missions as a lead navigator, pilot or bombardier and be entitled to one extra rank. Both my navigator and bombardier chose to do this. After 25 missions, my co-pilot was checked out as 1st pilot and flew 10 missions with another crew.

Interviewer: Were there any Mississippians in your crew?
Mr. Metts: My radio operator, Claude A. Curtis, was from Iuka.

Interviewer: What was the name of your plane?
Mr. Metts: We flew several aircraft, but the one we flew 13 missions was "Hell's Angel."

"We flew 13 missions in "Hell's Angel"

Interviewer: Did you have fighter escort on your missions?
Mr. Metts: When we flew, it was late in the war and they had formed what was called a "bomber stream." It was like a river flowing with airplanes from England all the way through to the target or maybe several targets, and fighters were briefed on this stream and how it would run and they more or less flew cover over the whole "flowing river." They flew above and out in front of us, and they kind of flew a "stream" of their own.

Interviewer: What kind of planes flew in this stream?
Mr. Metts: Most of our missions were covered by P-51s; earlier, the P-38s. We were escorted home several times by P-38s. I saw very few P-47s.

Interviewer: What was the longest mission you flew?

Mr. Metts: About eleven hours. That's about all the fuel a B-17 had.

Interviewer: How long would it take you to get into formation to head out to your target?
Mr. Metts: To do our pre-flight check took approximately 15 minutes from the time we started the first engine 'til we took off. Getting with the formation would vary some because of cloud cover and weather, and the old B-17 didn't climb too fast. If you figure 500 feet climb per minute and you were going to form at 10,000 feet you can figure how long that would take. Sometimes we formed at 20,000. We would bomb about as high as we could go; usually 25,000 to 30,000 feet.

Interviewer: Were your targets strictly military targets?
Mr. Metts: To my knowledge we never bombed any civilian targets. There were secondary targets, but they were of military value. Sometimes we had incendiary raids on towns, and probably there were civilians but it was not intended against the civilian population.

Interviewer: On a typical bomb run, when you reached your initial point, how long a period of time would you be locked in formation, straight and level, so that you couldn't undertake any evasive action?
Mr. Metts: We tried to keep it to 30 seconds; never wanted it to be more than a minute at the most.

Interviewer: Did you see much of the Luftwaffe?
Mr. Metts: The German Air Force was about shot down before I flew my 35 missions. What was left would hit this "stream" I spoke of earlier. They never hit the formation I was in.

Interviewer: How would you describe the flak on raids that you made?
Mr. Metts: They had perfected the flak, and this was one thing that we most feared. They had two kinds of flak. One was known as "barrage." They did their best to measure the height you were flying, and they put up the barrage over the target. Then

143

they had flak that was known as "tracking." The radar men tracked you, and they controlled the guns with radar; sometimes they were very accurate. We had different means that were supposed to help prevent their accuracy, but sometimes they didn't work too well. We had aluminum foil that we threw out when we got to flak areas, and this was supposed to throw their radar off. Sometimes it worked pretty well. The heavy flak area was over targets the British bombed at night. Munich had a lot of flak. Our crew bombed Munich twice.

Interviewer: Were any of your crew wounded?
Mr. Metts: We lost our bombardier/navigator (he held both assignments). After bombs away, some bombs hung up in the bomb bay of the B-17 and killed Lt. Drummond from Birmingham. I had a shell that burst and knocked the turret out right behind me. A piece went through my flak vest and hit the parachute buckle on the left side, broke the latch on my parachute harness. I still have that piece of flak and that piece of parachute harness.

Interviewer: Where did you go after completing your tour in England?
Mr. Metts: I came back to the States by way of New York on December 31, 1944. I had a few days at home; then I went to Miami and on to Hobbs, New Mexico. They told us at Hobbs we could either fly B-29s or train as instructors for B-17s. I chose instructor training. In the fall of 1945, I married. My wife lacked one semester finishing pharmacy school, and I knew her parents would never forgive me if she didn't finish. So I got out of the Air Force; we came back to Oxford, and my wife finished Pharmacy at Ole Miss, and I went into Metts Hardware on the Square.

Interviewer: How many hours did you log in the B-17?
Mr. Metts: My records show over 1,000. About 200 of these would be combat hours.

Interviewer: Did you receive any decorations?
Mr. Metts: I have the Air Medal with 3 Oak Leaf Clusters and the Distinguished Flying Cross.

Interviewer: Mr. Metts, it has been a privilege to conduct this interview with a veteran of THE MIGHTY EIGHTH AIR FORCE.

Floyd Metts retired from the Air Corps in the fall of 1945 and entered the hardware business on the square in Oxford. He remained in this business until 1986 - 41 years. He and his wife, Luna Cook "Cookie" Mayfield Metts have been married 54 years. They have five children, nine grandchildren and one great-grandchild. Floyd is very active in his church and community. He believes that "freedom did not come cheaply; we must always be prepared."

The crew's navigator on a recent trip back to the base.

I REMEMBER JOHN VICKERY

By N. Kenneth Nail

I remember John Vickery as rather quiet but very amiable, seriously studious but fun-loving, freckled but a handsome and clean-cut young man. John was my friend: we were in high school together and graduated from Grenada High School together in 1940. We were on the basketball team together, John a fine athlete and I with minimal ability spending most of my time on the bench watching him play.

After graduation from high school, John joined the Navy and served for almost two years. In July, 1942, he was allowed to join the aviation cadet program in the Army Air Corps. After primary flight training, he was sent to bombardier school in which he had an excellent record serving as cadet squadron bombardier. It was May, 1943, before John arrived in England, and was assigned to fly with the 91st Bomb Group at Bassingbourn. Here, again, John compiled an excellent record, winning promotion to Captain and the job of Squadron Bombardier.

I remember a lot about John Vickery from our high school days together, but one thing I didn't know about him was that he was superstitious! Perhaps he acquired this facet of his personality later when the missions began to get tough; and get tough they did. Anyway, John began flying with a pair of green pajamas under his flying clothes and began wearing the same old, grease-stained officer's cap on every mission. He would not leave the ground without this very special attire. It seems to have worked, as John flew some of the toughest missions of the War and at a time when missions were really tough. He flew on the mission to Wilhelmshaven on May 21, 1943; he flew to Bremen in June, to St. Nazaire, to Hamburg, to Kiel, to Gelsenkirchen, to Hanover, Kassel, Frankfort; worst of all he flew on the first Schweinfurt raid on which 60 of our heavy bombers were lost. The formation was attacked by over 250 enemy fighters and the flak was extremely heavy. On another mission, to Nantes, in France, John's crew limped home in their Flying Fortress with two of their four engines out. They barely made it home from the St. Nazaire mission as their gas was running low. They had to throw out guns, ammunition and other loose equipment to lighten the load. On another mission, 20 mm shells from enemy fighters left gaping holes in their aircraft. In June, 16 feet of their horizontal stabilizer was sheared off. The two pilots had to fight with all they had to control the aircraft. From his position in the nose of the plane, John was tossed about while he stayed at his gun firing at German fighter planes. The pilots finally got the plane under control and brought the crew safely home.

For his service in *The Mighty Eighth* during the war, John was awarded the Distinguished Flying Cross and the Air Medal with three Oak Leaf Clusters.

Captain Vickery served in the post-war U. S. Air Force, retiring with the rank of Colonel after nearly 20 years service. Before retiring,

however, he went to college on a part-time basis, receiving his B. S. degree from Florida Southern College. Then, while serving as an instructor-officer with the ROTC unit at the University of Alabama, he worked on and earned his M.A. degree in education.

After retiring from the Air Force, John taught at Grenada High School and flew as a crop duster in the summer with Grenada Flying Service. Sadly, he was killed in his Pawnee in a crop dusting accident on August 24, 1960, near Cadaretta.

John Vickery loved flying. He had taught his son, Mike, to fly the Aeronica and the Cessna before his untimely death. But John also loved recalling the days when he served so valiantly in *The Mighty Eighth,* as a bombardier on a B-17 Flying Fortress, as evidenced by the following poem which was found in his wallet when he died; it was battered and worn and torn from much reading:

NIGHT OF THE BOMBER'S MOON

By Thomas V. Calkins

This is a night of the bomber's moon
And the planes are out again.
The moon is high in a purple sky
And shadows race the plain.
The earth is stark and vast and dark,
And her people cringe in fear,
This is a night of the bomber's moon,
And her king is the bombardier.

Great-engined bats against the moon
And the bomber's sights are set.
A plane and a score and more and more
In a widespread silhouette.
Now death is loose, for the golden goose
Is speeding toward her prey,
For this is a night with the bomber's moon
And the bombs are on their way.

This was a night of the bomber's moon
And the planes were out again.
The sun rose red from a fire-red bed
And a city died in pain.
The planes went out in a roaring shout,
With a mighty-throated din,
Four score went out with the bomber's moon
But three score came back in.

Yet evermore great planes shall roar
From set to rise of sun,
And men shall sleep in slumber deep
Because of missions done.
Great wraithlike bombers, dim and thin,
Shall soar – the ones who came not in.
Sleep well, Earth, free of war and fear,
And thank the God of the bombardier.

John left his widow, the former Loraine Fisher, his son John Michael and his daughter Patricia Ann. Everyone in the Grenada High School Class of 1940, remembers John Vickery. We all loved him, too. He was one of our finest.

146

A P. O. W. RETURNS

By John M. Jones

This article was taken from a talk given by John M. Jones in 1972, to the Kiwanis Club in Natchez. He tells about a trip which he and his wife, Mary Rogers Jones, made to Europe in May, 1970.

Lt. John M. Jones

Jones waves from far down the old runway

During World War II, I was an Air Force bombardier with the Eighth Air Force stationed in England, some 100 miles north of London, near the small village of Diss. I completed twelve combat missions over Germany and German occupied countries. My stay in England was really for a rather short time, but I did get to visit London several times and had much fun visiting the nearby villages and English people and pubs near our base.

This was in April, 1944, and during this period of the war, the Allies were busy preparing for the invasion of Europe which was to come on June 6, 1944. The Germans had the Normandy Coast of France very strongly fortified; and on April 27, 1944, our bomb group which, incidentally, was the 100th bomb Group (which anyone of the 8th Air Force will tell you had a rather famous reputation, that of having every plane shot down by the Germans on two different occasions, without a single plane returning to base).

The 100th BG was based near the English village of Diss

The crew, trained and ready for combat

Anyway, on April 27, we had been scheduled to fly two bombing missions over German occupied France. When flying two missions a day, we would be briefed at midnight, takeoff in the dark, get in formation by daylight and take off across the Channel for France. We would return to base by noon, eat lunch, attend a second briefing and take-off again, bomb and return to base and land by dark. These were pretty full days.

On April 28, we were again scheduled for two missions. But on our first mission of that day, we had our new Group Commanding Officer flying in formation with us. As we passed over our target of rocket installations on the Cherbourg Peninsula near the French town of Cherbourg, we were flying at 22,000 feet; but a low cloud cover was over our target area. The usual procedure was to drop your bombs in the English Channel and head for base. But Col. Kelly, on this mission, ordered us to make a 360 degree turn and bomb. During the second bomb run, I looked up and Col. Kelly's plane disappeared in a cloud of flak dust. I dropped our bombs and my last word to my crew was "bombs away;" "bomb bays closed." At that moment we had reached the spot where our lead plane had blown up. We began to get direct hits. This happened to be my 13th mission; and after all my many experiences with the number 13, I was flying with my parachute, the first combat mission I had ever flown with a chute. The next moment I realized I was sailing through space. Our plane had received a direct flak hit and had exploded. As I fell, I wondered what had happened to the rest of my crew. I could hear the Germans screaming at me. When I hit the ground, my leg was broken in two places; and I was promptly captured. I learned later in the day that two other members of my crew had survived; the other seven , including my pilot, had died.

The Germans took me to a hospital in Paris. Then, as the invasion came in June, I was moved to Frankfurt and on to Meinningen to a hospital compound where I stayed until February the next year. I was then taken to a prison camp at Nuremberg. General Patton made his break-through in early April and, rather than see us liberated, the Germans moved some 10,000 Air Force officers and men out on the highway and forced us to march to Mooseberg, near Munich. This march took us 17 days; and then on April 29, 1945, one year and one day after capture, we were overtaken by General Patton's 3rd Army and its 14th Armored Division and liberated. That was really the greatest day of my life! Up until that time, at least.

For many years, I had had a really burning desire to return to those places in Europe and especially to visit the graves of my crew members and friends who died on April 28, 1944. On May 4, 1970, my wife, Mary Rogers, and I finally set out on a trip to Europe. We drove to New Orleans and caught a flight connecting us with a 747 jet direct to London. We landed there at 7 A.M. the next morning and got checked into our hotel. We began to move around that afternoon and began our sightseeing of the many beautiful sights in London which I had remembered so well. We visited Westminster Abby, the Tower of London, St. Paul's Cathedral, saw Big Ben, walked across Westminster Bridge and did all those things that you do in London. It was great fun.

Before leaving the States, I had ordered road maps of all the countries we were to visit as all our travel was to be by car. The maps were excellent! But after watching London traffic, Mary Rogers got cold feet about my driving. They drive like mad and on the left side of the road, you know. Mary Rogers made several real sharp remarks on this trip; one was in London when she said, "These cars over here need only two wheels, both on the same side." Anyway, when our car was delivered to the hotel, it was with driver, for which we were both very thankful.

We left London early and set out for my old air base near Diss. Upon arriving at Diss, we found the railroad station at which I had arrived 28 years before. There was an old man shoveling coal at the station, and I asked him whether he was there during the War. He said he was and remembered so well the planes taking off every morning and landing every afternoon. I asked him directions to get to the base. He said it had been completely dismantled, but the main gate was up the road

148

about one-half mile. We drove there, and I recognized the gate. I asked the driver to go on in and drive down the narrow walkway. When we had driven about 200 yards, I looked each way; and, as far as we could see , there was a concrete runway right in the middle of a beautiful wheat field. This was the runway we had left on our 13th mission on April 24, 1944, and this was one of the great thrills I would experience on our trip.

The next morning early we took a jet from London to Paris, where we spent several delightful days visiting Notre Dame, the Louvre, the Eiffel Tower and the Folies Bergere. That was great!

A toast to old times and lost comrades

Our car was delivered to our hotel. Being well prepared with road maps, we took off for the Normandy Coast. We arrived at the French Coast where we were to spend three days at Caen. Here we were to begin to see the effects of World War II. Caen was nearly leveled, but it had been rebuilt block by block so that a stranger could hardly know that it had ever been disturbed for centuries. We had found this in London and were to find cities such as St. Lo in France, Frankfurt, Nuremberg, and Munich in Germany, and many other cities which had been almost completely destroyed during the war and had been rebuilt so that you could hardly tell the damage which had been done. Much of the rebuilding had been done

through the United States Marshall Plan with U. S. funds, equipment and labor. A great job of rebuilding has been done. It was almost unbelievable, especially if you had seen those cities and countries during and immediately after World War II.

The Normandy countryside is beautiful. We were there just as the millions of apple trees were in full bloom. The farm land is also beautiful. Every inch is in use and not a weed is to be seen anywhere. We traveled on rural roads as much as possible, and the small villages in France and throughout Europe were most interesting. All farm families live in these villages. Their farm land is outside the village, and they go there each day either by walking or by small tractor or bicycle. Their homestead in the village usually has a large barn attached to their dwelling where all their cows and other livestock are kept. There is not enough land for cows to graze year round; so green grass is cut each day and taken inside to the stock. One thing most distinct about most European farm villages is the smell of manure. We smelled it as we came in and smelled it going out. Each house usually has a manure pile well fenced-in neatly at the front door. It must be a sign of wealth or prestige, because the larger the house the larger the manure pile.

On our second day at Caen, we set out to find the spot where I was shot down and captured. We think we did, but I am not sure, for every hedgerow there looks like every other. Anyway, we did get back to the invasion beach and visited the British Museum at Omaha Beach.

At Omaha Beach

Before we left the States, Senator Stennis' office had obtained for me through his Armed Services' Committee, the exact location of the graves of my crew members. So, from Omaha Beach we drove along Highway 13 to the Normandy American Cemetery. This cemetery overlooks Omaha Beach and is one of the most beautiful spots I've ever seen.

Jones at the grave of his pilot at the cemetery at Omaha Beach

The grounds are more beautiful than any golf green. There are 9,386 American boys buried there, most of them killed in the invasion on June 6, 1944. From the description which Senator Stennis had given me, I walked straight to the graves that I had come to see. I had wondered if the Germans had recorded the correct dates of death and other information about my crew members, but I found myself looking at the beautiful white cross on the grave of my pilot, Lt. James W. McGuire, Colorado, April 28, 1944. This was a great thrill for me to return to this spot which held such a great friend of many years ago, whose friendship had ended so suddenly.

After taking some good pictures, we walked back to the Superintendent's office which we had passed on the way in. I learned that this was the third grave for my crew. On April 28, 1944, they had been buried by the German Army in a French civilian cemetery, near Cherbourg. Later, after the invasion, they were all moved to a military cemetery near Omaha Beach. Then in 1952, this

Normandy American Cemetery was established, covering some 172 acres overlooking the English Channel at Omaha Beach. At that time some 45,000 next of kin were notified and given the choice of having their bodies returned to the United States at government expense or else having them reinterred, *forever,* here. Of the 45,000, all but 9,386 families chose to have their boys returned. Those are the ones now there, and my pilot, Lt. James W. McGuire is among them.

I asked the attendant the number of visitors they had, and I was surprised to learn that this cemetery (and you must know there are many other American cemeteries in England, France, Belgium and Germany) has some 900,000 visitors annually. Upon talking further, I learned that only 5% of the visitors are Americans, and only a very few are next-of-kin of the boys buried there. But what really amazed me was that about 80% of the visitors to this cemetery are French. I was told, and I believe since my trip there, that the French people do have a great and warm feeling of gratitude toward these Americans who gave their lives in the liberation of France in 1944. I believe this in spite of what you read in the press and hear elsewhere.

I was really so moved by this experience that I had forgotten about the weather. Going back to our car, I learned it was zero degrees centigrade, it was raining and I was almost frozen. Before we left the States, Mary Rogers had assured me that I would need neither an overcoat nor hat. At this moment, I looked over at her; and she had on a big heavy coat and rain hat - I had brought neither.

We made our way, then, through the lovely Normandy countryside to St. Lo. My first order of business was to buy myself a hat and an overcoat. We found no one who spoke English, but we did find a hat shop and did purchase a real sharp-billed French cap. A coat shop was across the street, and I found the coat I wanted, but not having enough money to pay for it, I was sent off to the bank to cash some American Express checks. On the way we heard the town clock strike twelve noon. We got to the bank, and it was closed tight with a sign, "France closes everything from noon until 2 P.M."

We hurried back to the coat store, and it too was closed with the same sign. Thus I was still without a coat.

From St. Lo, we drove down to Mont St. Michel, a beautiful castle fortification built out in the sea. You can only get to it at low tide.

We returned to Paris, and I had one other mission which I wished to complete. I wanted to return to the hospital where the Germans had held me as a P.O.W. in Paris. This was still another thrill for me to return to this spot.

The next morning we boarded a German airliner at Paris and flew to Frankfurt. This was another place where I was held prisoner; and it was not long after we checked in our hotel that I visited the rail station which I remembered so well both from the air and from the ground.

We had planned to visit the small town of Meinningen but learned that it was in East Germany to which we couldn't travel.

We got our car in Frankfurt and headed for Nuremburg. Upon arrival and still freezing, I announced that I was going shopping for an overcoat. I found a nice store and coat almost like the one I had picked out at St. Lo. I noticed the German man waiting on me could speak very good English, and I asked him where he learned his English. He hesitated a moment and then said, " I was an American prisoner of war in Denver during World War II." He was a nice person, and we became quite friendly after I told him I had been a German P.O.W. here in Nuremberg.

Nuremberg is a beautiful old city. It, too, was about ¾ destroyed during the war but has been beautifully rebuilt. We had a great guide here to drive us over the city; his name was Richard. He spoke perfect English. He told me that during the war he was stationed on the Cherbourg Peninsula and that he was an anti-aircraft gunner. I said, "Richard, you may have shot me down." He agreed that he could have done so. He was a great fellow, a great guide; and I would like to

recommend him to anyone going to Nuremberg. He was a good shot too!

We saw many very old buildings in Nuremberg, some built before the discovery of America. We saw the Hall of Justice where German war criminals were tried, and the prison where they were held and executed. Richard told us the story of their bodies being cremated and dumped out as ashes at 20,000 feet.

We first learned here that the Germans do not wish for their unrepaired war damages to be seen. I asked Richard several times to show us the great outdoor stadium where Hitler made his great wartime speeches. Each time I mentioned it, he put us off, but finally he said, "I haven't forgotten the stadium, but we go there last." The stadium was a sight to see; there were acres of concrete. It would hold 200,000 people, 100,000 seated and 100,000 standing. Richard said the Americans, upon arriving in Nuremberg in 1945, had blown up the speakers platform and all the Nazi symbols there. There were weeds growing in the seats and the place was, in general, a wreck. Our prison camp was not too far from this spot; and, during our stay there, I could imagine the activities that must have taken place here.

During the last stages of the war, the Germans were without transportation, fuel, and many of the other necessities of life; but they chose to fight on. As General Patton broke through the German lines in early 1945, to prevent the liberation of prisoners, the Germans forced many prisoners to march to distant new prison camps. In April, 1945, such a march was forced on the prisoners at Nuremberg.

On our trip, it was my wish to drive back down the route of the forced march. We left Nuremberg and were able to follow the same back roads and pass through the same small farm towns. On the march the Germans gave us nothing to eat and no cover. We ate what we could find and slept, when lucky, in barns along the way. As we drove this route again, I recalled to Mary Rogers that here we found a sack of chicken feed, which we boiled for supper, or here we found a potato, or in this town we learned of President Roosevelt's death. We crossed the Danube at the same spot and then drove on into Mooseberg where I had been liberated in 1945 after a 17 day march, which now took us only four hours to drive. This was another of the many thrills I experienced on this trip - to return here to this spot, where I had experienced one of the greatest days of life on April 29, 1945 - LIBERATION DAY!

This trip was certainly a "once-in-a-lifetime" experience for both of us. But for me, returning to those places and especially to the graves of my crew members has given me a kind of relief and a feeling of having completed a final mission; it has fulfilled for me a great desire that had been with me all these many years past.

Old Glory finally seen on April 29, 1945

Sgt. Harvey K. Tillman, Jr. of Tillatoba, was a tail-gunner on a B-24 Liberator, flying out of Bungay, near the coast in East Auglia. On December 31, 1943, his Group, the 446th Bomb Group, had as their target the Laleu Airfield in LaRochelle, France. They were unable to hit this primary target, however, due to poor visibility. Instead they moved on to hit their secondary target, Chateau Bernard Airfield at Cognac, a French airfield being used by the Germans.

On this mission, Tillman's plane, "Buzz Buggy," made it to the target but did not survive to return to England. No one saw the plane get hit, but it was seen to leave the formation heading out in the direction of Spain. It was assumed that the plane went down in the sea; all 10 crew members were reported as Killed in Action. Harvey Tillman's body was found in the waves of the Atlantic, about two months later by Austrian, Dr. Hans Grabner. Dr. Grabner later wrote to the Tillman family telling them exactly where the body was found. It was interred in a military cemetery at Biarritz.

Fifty-four years later, Phillip Tillman, the airman's younger brother, who was only 11 years old in 1943, went to France and scattered a bouquet of large, yellow sunflowers at the spot where Harvey's body was found.

This is just a little bit of information that is known concerning the fate of one Mississippian in the Mighty Eighth.

SHUTTLE MISSION,
AUGUST 6, 1944

By John L. Walker

Pilot, Lt. John L. Walker

August 6, 1944, was our crew's 12th mission; however, it was different in several ways. Our navigator, Saul Cohen, became sick before we left and was admitted to the hospital for appendicitis and surgery. Lt. James Heard, from another crew, was assigned to our crew temporarily as our navigator. We were told August 5 that we were to fly the next mission and should take along a change of clothing, toilet articles and a Class A uniform to wear after landing. We did not understand these unusual orders until the briefing on the morning of August 6, when we found out we were going to Russia, then Italy and back to England; we would be gone 5 - 6 days. This was the second shuttle mission the 8th Air Force made, and I think it was more to prove to the Germans that we had complete air superiority and could go where we pleased than anything else. Of course, we did hit some important targets!

The first leg of this mission was a target at Rahmel, Poland, near East Prussia. This was an aircraft and engine assembly plant and was heavily defended by flak and fighters. We had three fighters pass through our formation with guns blazing and two of our P-51s hot on their tail. We never found out the results of that attack, but believe the P-51s were the victors; and our gunners got in a few shots, also. We bombed the target with good results, then turned southeast toward Russia. After 12 hours flying, we landed at Poltava, Russia, in the Ukraine. This was the longest of our 35 missions, and we were tired. Flying formation can be tiring even with a co-pilot to help! Most of our missions were 6 - 10 hours; so this was an exception in more ways than one.

We landed on steel mats in an open field and were met by GI trucks driven by Russian women soldiers. When we parked, they took us to our tents where we changed clothes. We were given strong coffee and our evening meal in mess kits, not very tasty. We then assembled in an old building for entertainment. The building had been bombed before this. One of our friends, Lt. Paul Feiss, was flying an old B-17 with many bombs painted on the fuselage and "B" on several of the bombs, indicating missions to Berlin, even though his crew did not fly all of them. Pilots had been designated aircraft commanders; and when the Russians were told Paul was a "commander," they assumed he was a General and had made several missions to Berlin. They gave him a seat with our brass and theirs. This gave them and our Colonel some embarrassment but no "serious" problems.

The next day, August 6, was Helen's and my second anniversary! What a way to spend it. Unusual, to say the least!

Our planes had been refueled and loaded with bombs, and we flew to an oil refinery target near

Krakow, Poland. Oil was critical and a target of high priority; so we destroyed this one and were happy with our results. We then returned to Poltava for another night and more Russian food which gave most of us diarrhea to different degrees! We were glad to leave Russia the next morning to fly to Italy. Enroute we bombed an airfield and assembly plant in Romania and then proceeded to Foggia, Italy. This was an area of Italy which had several airfields with B-17s and B-24s. We were told we would be off a day or two; so we could relax.

I have a younger brother who was a ground crew mechanic with a B-24 outfit near Foggia; so when we landed and parked our planes, I found out where he was stationed and used the field telephone to locate him and advise him where I was. We had a mini-reunion, and he showed me around a small town. We had our picture made together to send home and just enjoyed ourselves as much as we could in a small town in war-time!

On August 12, our planes were loaded with bombs and gas and took off on the final leg of our shuttle mission. We took a route home through southern France and bombed an airfield near Toulouse. This was an easy mission with little flak and no fighters, and we were happy to get back to our home base.

This was an unusual mission, and I am glad I was able to participate since we made it safely and have memories to share with friends.

The Crew; John L. Walker, standing, left

AIRCRAFT NAMED D'NIF

By Willard F. Nester

I have been asked many times how the crew of B-24J, aircraft 44-40100, of which I was pilot, got the name, "D'NIF." It came as a result of an incident that happened to the crew while in training at Pueblo, Colorado.

About a month before we were to begin our deployment, in May, 1944, we began getting new airplanes, and I was assigned one of them. The custom was to give the airplane a name, a logo, or some visible identification and have it painted on the nose, most commonly referred to as "Nose Art." The ten members of our crew could not agree on any suggestion for a name or logo and had to depart Pueblo without naming our plane.

Two or three weeks before we were to depart for overseas assignment, the entire crew was given the weekend off. Friday afternoon most of the crew began making plans for the weekend party they had looked forward to for so long. But, to my surprise, Operations had scheduled us to fly the next morning. This was to be a maximum effort to allow a visiting VIP to observe the 491st in formation flying.

The Flight Surgeon had me "grounded" at the time while treating me for blocked sinuses. I reminded the Operations Officer that he had already given the crew the entire weekend off, and my boys had begun the party at a downtown hotel and would not be able to fly the next day. He seemed to understand but ordered me to have the crew report to the Flight Surgeon for a physical check.

When I told the crew they were scheduled to fly the next morning, some of them took the news as a big joke. They weren't about to go back to the base the next morning. A couple of the guys, however, realized the seriousness of not reporting as ordered and assured me they would all be there.

When they returned to the base, I heard them about a block away, whooping and hollering; and I knew then they were in no condition to fly. That meant the entire crew would be "grounded" and classified D-N-I-F (Duty Not Involving Flying). That made the crew very happy, and they considered that they had achieved a "first." Never before had they heard of an entire crew being "grounded" at the same time.

We were in West Palm Beach, Florida, getting our final check before leaving the USA when someone suggested we make a word or name using the letters D-N-I-F. By putting the apostrophe between the D and N it became; by unanimous approval, the name of the airplane.

A commercial artist was located, and he painted the name and used the World War II character, "Sad Sack," as the logo for our "Nose Art." Sad Sack was to appear as though he was nursing a big hangover and carrying the D'NIF slip.

After flying nine missions in D'NIF with the 491st BG(H) during the first twelve days of their combat operations, we were given a three-day pass (which we spent in London) and then were transferred to the 93rd BG(H), leaving D"NIF behind.

There she is, D'NIF

155

THE TRAGEDY OF
THE "IRON DUKE" AND ITS PILOT,
LT. WILLIAM A. DUKE

By Bettye Duke Jackson

In foreign lands far beyond an ocean, the Mighty Eighth Air Force fought the enemy from June, 1942 to April, 1945. This is the story of one pilot of the 458th Bomb Group and his crew. The permission to use exact excerpts from the accounts of the fate of the "Iron Duke" was given to Bettye Duke Jackson, sister of Lt. Billy Duke, by George A. Reynolds, author of *The Iron Duke and Its Crew*. Mr. Reynolds' research was published by Challenge Publications, Inc. in *Air War*.

The experiences in the story are based on a collection of official documents and accounts of persons involved or observers that were compiled by Richard M. Eselgroth, Sr., navigator on the "Iron Duke." Recognition is also given to Herr Eugene Lux, author and historian from Offenback, Germany; 8th Air Force historian and author, Roger A. Freeman; and Herr Hubert Blasi, author, historian and translator from Heilbroun, Germany. Herr Lux has corresponded with Bettye Duke Jackson and graciously given her pictures, documents, maps and records pertaining to Lt. Duke and the story of the "Iron Duke." Herr Lux had researched and recorded the "Iron Duke" story from the German point of view.

…"And now, the rest of the story."

In the early hours of February 22, 1945, about 2500 bombers and fighters of the U. S. Eighth, Ninth, Twelfth and Fifteenth Air Forces and the R.A.F. were preparing for Operation Clarion - a maximum effort to deliver a coup de grace to the Nazi rail and communications systems. This was the largest combined air campaign since D-Day over central and southern Germany and the Mediterranean area. Weather was to be favorable.

The 458th Bombardment Group, based in East Anglia near Norwich, was preparing to launch its B-24 Liberator elements. Their objective was railroad marshaling yards at Peine and Hildersheim in Central Germany.

At dawn a heavy overcast verified the local weather was not as forecast. A reconnaissance P-51 reported clearing conditions over the continent and at 0900 hours thirty-eight B-24s of the 458th left on its most unusual mission in eleven months of combat. Instead of the normal 25,000 foot flight level, bombing altitude was to be 10,000 feet. There would be no clouds to screen the bombers from flak batteries.

The Liberators climbed over Alkmaar, Holland and Zuider Zee to 22,000 feet before breaking out for assembly into combat structure. To avoid midair collisions in the clouds, the planes had scattered but eventually formed into two boxed forces of sixteen and eighteen ships. During the climb, four of the planes aborted with mechanical trouble. The sixteen plane element headed for Peine, the other to Hildesheim.

After large breaks appeared in the undercast over Germany, the sixteen B-24s descended to 10,000 feet and headed southeasterly. Dortmund slipped by to the left, and crewmen remarked at how plainly they could see enemy territory today after flying over it "blind" in the past. Cologne passed to the right. Ahead the initial point, Elsenach, loomed on the horizon. Here, the armada would turn northward with their bombsights on Peine, but a smaller town had to be crossed first.

It was clear over Hersfeld when flak crumped under the formation where planes number 51215-

The "Iron Duke, " named for Pilot Billy Duke

B and 10491-1 brought up the rear. Suddenly, 215-B received a disintegrating blast in its bomb bay. One wing rolled away as though in slow motion, and a parachute emerged from the waist section. That lone crewman was drawn back into the inferno as a fiery mass plunged all ten men earthward.

Aboard the 491-1, named "Iron Duke," were the pilot, Lt William A. Duke, recently turned 21 years old, from Oxford, Mississippi; Co-pilot, Lt Archibald A. "Bubba" Monroe, the pilot's high school and college close friend from Batesville, Mississippi; Flight Officer Richard M. "Dick" Eselgroth, navigator; Flight Officer Al Miller, bombardier; and Sgt "Luke" Lucas, radioman. Other crew members included flight engineer Sgt Garcia, and gunnery sergeants, Chuck Frazer, Carl Johnson, Charles Gretz, and "Pan" Panarese. "Pan" called his sighting on 215-B, as required, by intercom to Eselgroth for entry in 491's logbook. Just moments later, Iron Duke was slammed upward by three bursts of flak. Billy felt the controls go slack in his hands and knew they could

not remain in formation. Practically all of the ship's left rudder had been torn away, a wing's aileron vanished, holes appeared in the fuselage and severed control cables dangled in the waist compartment. Lt. Duke made a jagged right turn, then ordered Miller to salvo the bomb load.

Their twelve highly explosive cylinders were screaming earthward immediately, and soon began bursting in the village of Meckbach. Five homes were hit with one documented fatality. Above, the pilots struggled to keep Iron Duke airborne while asking the navigator for a heading to the nearest friendly forces lines. Billy did not want to risk going back toward heavy flak areas along the Rhine with limited control and at such a low altitude.

The Iron Duke maneuvered easier without the bombs' weight, but it was impossible to hold a fixed heading with only the autopilot's few cables intact. They were flying with a 30-degree yaw to the right, airspeed of 110 knots and with 20 degrees of flaps and were able to maintain 7000 feet of altitude.

157

With a heading of 210 degrees called by the navigator, Billy could get them closer to advancing American ground forces south of Frankfurt. The Iron Duke moved slowly on; and although the crew was on alert to jump, they felt good about reaching allied lines before having to leave the ship. At 1315 hours, the 491-1 was north of Gelnhausen, and Billy tried to turn southward to avoid flak batteries around Frankfurt. The German commander of a railroad battery, Lt Erich Bauder, saw the four-engine bomber approaching and posted his crew. They had four 128mm and two 20mm guns mounted on a flatcar at Muhlheim Station near Offenbach. Bauder reported he felt pity for the men inside the aircraft. He knew at their speed and altitude they could not escape from his deadly radar controlled firepower.

A shot exploded in front of and below the "Iron Duke." Then three quick bursts put the Liberator out of control, and it began descending immediately. Eruptions under the left wing had ripped out a five foot section of fuselage and started a hot fire in the waist compartment. The Iron Duke could not escape. Billy ordered his crew to bail out while some measure of control remained. Seven of the crew bailed out just before the Iron Duke dropped its nose and fell earthward. Billy juggled the auto-pilot while centrifugal force glued him and his copilot to their seats. Sgt Gretz was still in the top turret. Slowly the plane responded to his coaxing and leveled off at 3000 feet. Billy sent Gretz out the open bomb bay, and Bubba, his copilot, right behind him as puffs of flak continued to burst about the Iron Duke.

People on the ground had heard the flak barrage begin, and they started to watch the course of events. Many saw chutes blossoming and a burning bomber bobbing its nose while slowly losing altitude. Southeast of Frankfurt, near the village of Hainhausen, Iron Duke dropped one wing just before it struck ground, nosed over on her back and exploded with an intense rumble.

Seven of the crew, each uncertain of their fate, landed within a close radius of each other. One tragically crashed through a skylight on the roof of a large warehouse and, not allowed treatment, bled to death; one was taken to a sports field and shot. Six of the crew were eventually interned in Stalag 3 near Nuremburg. Lt. Duke and Lt. Monroe were captured near Bieber. Lt. Duke was taken to the police station. He asked for and was given something to drink. Offenbach police director arrived and strongly rebuked those present for allowing Billy any privileges. More conversation followed and Billy was sent to an army post in Offenbach to be held as a P.O.W. On the way there, Herman Moler, Bieber police, shot Billy "while trying to escape" . . . in his heavy flying suit and fur-lined boots. Tragic details reveal a similar fate befell Lt. Monroe.

On March 6, 1946, Lt Duke's and Lt Monroe's graves were discovered in a small cemetery at Muhlheim. Their remains were exhumed and sent to an allied cemetery in St. Avold, France, the next day. After family notification, Graves Registration officials conducted a thorough examination on the bodies. It was obvious they had not died from wounds consistent with the known facts – statements from fellow crew members that they had all reached the ground safely except the crewman who fell through the skylight.

The decisions of the Dachau court convicted those police responsible for Lt Billy Duke's, Lt Monroe's and Sgt Frazer's deaths. On October 15, they were hanged. Others involved received 15 year sentences, but most were paroled before the sentences were fully served or granted clemency.

War crimes investigators entered into the inquiry, and a more intensive investigation began. Meanwhile, Lt Duke and Lt Monroe were returned to Oxford and to Batesville respectively for burial in their hometowns. The body of Lt. Duke's brother, Lt Kendall Duke, a P-38 pilot killed in the Pacific, was returned and a double military funeral was held for two young Oxford pilots.

The crew of "Iron Duke." Pilot, Lt. Billy Duke kneeling, left.

The Superior Orders War Crime Case (The United States of America v. Jurgen Stroop et al) was held in Dachau, Germany, from January 10 to March 21, 1947, in which twenty-two individuals were tried under a general charge of violation of the Laws of War . . . criminal acts against allied airmen. Lt General Jurgen Stroop was accused of receiving and transmitting orders from Heinrich Himmler and Ernst Haltenbrunner down to local police levels to shoot any flier parachuting from a damaged aircraft over Germany. He was also charged with following the principles of Joseph Goebbels and Martin Bormann to incite the German people to lynch airmen. The police were instructed not to interfere when civilians assaulted the defenseless fliers. Jurgen Stroop was convicted by the Polish government for crimes against the Polish people. He was executed May 6, 1952. His compatriots, all those known to have been involved in the deaths of Lt Duke and his two crew members were prosecuted. The trial revealed the last

agonizing hours of life of Lt. Duke, Lt. Monroe, and Sgt Frazer. In 1973, the Iron Duke's navigator, FO Eselgroth, returned to the scene where the Iron Duke and its crew met their fate. Eselgroth, Herr Lux, Herr Blasi, and Herr Girbig, a historian on crashed German aircraft, went to the site of Iron Duke's tomb. Using Girbig's metal detector, they dug up twenty-five pounds of debris such as switches, ammunition, hoses, and the like. Farmers had plowed up various fragments and tossed them into a clump of trees nearby. At least part of the Iron Duke would finally rotate back to the United States. Its pilots, Billy Duke and Bubba Monroe, would have loved to come home . . . to have danced; looked at the sun, the moon, the sky; and felt the joy of living. They are gone, only to remain in the hearts and memories of those who knew and loved them . . . borne away in the prime of their young lives fighting to preserve a way of life they never fully lived.

A FINE ROMANCE

By Joan Wilson

In October, 1942, the War in England had been going on, it seemed, forever. My father, who worked in the War Office, had long since been evacuated out of London and was living near Liverpool and came home only sporadically. I was an only child; this left my mother and me coping with the blackout, the rationing and a series of evacuees, since we lived in Buckinghamshire, about thirty miles out of London, which was considered a "safe" area, far out of the bombing raids on London.

I was a teenager; and, of course, all the local young men had vanished into the various branches of the service, and a lot of my girl friends had also joined up. I worked for a doctor and was considered to be in an "essential" job. To add a little spice to my life, I worked at a local canteen for servicemen on Sunday evenings. The canteen was run by one of the local churches, and we served tea and coffee and easily prepared items such as Baked Beans on Toast or Welsh Rarebit and an assortment of cakes and cookies. Each time we worked we rotated duties. Sometimes we took care of the teapots and the coffee urn; some evenings we washed the dishes and gossiped in the kitchen; sometimes we waited on the troops at the counter, which was the favored position, of course.

One Sunday evening I was serving at the counter, and we had been steadily busy with an assortment of customers, one of whom was an American, decked out in a very spiffy uniform and sitting with some men from the R.A.F. After a while he came up to the counter, and I asked him what he would like to eat. He asked me what was available, and I said that his best choice would be either Baked Beans on Toast or the Welsh Rarebit. He chose the latter; and, when I gave him his order, he looked puzzled and asked where the rabbit was. We had a brief conversation about Welsh Rarebit being a savory cheese dish and nothing to do with rabbits! He returned to his R.A.F. cronies and I got busy with other people.

As I was to discover many weeks later the conversation between the American and the R.A.F. men had gone something like this: "What's wrong Yank - can't get a girl friend?" The American, leaping to the bait, "Shoot, I can get a date with any girl in this place." For reasons known only to himself, one of the R.A.F. men pointed me out saying, "I bet you five pounds you can't get a date with that brunette behind the counter." Shortly before we closed up that evening, the American of the Rarebit incident showed up again and started talking to me. I was fascinated by his accent since I had just finished reading *Gone with the Wind* and had become totally enamored of anything Southern. He told me his name was Carl Wilson and asked if he could see me home. I was highly intrigued by the whole episode, especially since my last name was also Wilson; so off we went.

Incidentally, I was told much later that the R.A.F. guy never did pay up!

I also had no idea that this odd meeting would end up by changing my life forever and that it would be the beginning of a fine romance!

"FLAK LEAVE"

By Craig Harris

A full set of memories of any fifty-one-year-old event is hard to come by, but "going on flak leave" was an event sufficiently significant to many members of the 8th Air Force that at least parts of it will never be forgotten.

The tale that we were told - in the 457th Bomb Group at Glatton - was that " the-powers-that-be," showing Infinite Compassion, would note when hard-flown crews were becoming "flak happy" and send them away for R&R (Rest and Rehabilitation). It is difficult to know if that tale is the correct rationale for flak leave, but it could have been true for our crew. While we had flown most missions (February-April, 1945) against minimal opposition, there had been a few moments of sheer terror; and the frequency of missions (33 in 58 days - even with serious time-outs for weather) was beginning to take a toll on our crew.

This was especially true for the enlisted crew members when a distinctly non-compassionate squadron operations cadre would roust them out of bed at 3:00 A.M. to put out flak armor for the day's mission, after they had flown 3 or even 4 missions in a row. Our pilot and I (the co-pilot) would protest this practice vigorously, but all that we gained by our protests was the animosity of the Squadron Operations Officer and reputations for being trouble makers.

So, its obvious why we might have had trouble believing the oft-told-tale when, after flying 4 missions in a row up through April 17, 1945, and before another flak-armor confrontation could take place, we were all sent on flak leave, beginning the next day. It was about time. Of course, some of us were so erratic that we could have qualified much sooner, but some squirrelly behavior was normal in those days for a lot of us. I was OK, but the others were really acting strangely, especially the navigator.

It would have been great for all the crew to go away and relax together; but while we all flew together and got shot at together, we couldn't do R&R together. For to do so, would be to commit the evil sin of fraternization. So the enlisted crew were sent to some place over near Southampton. The pilot, navigator and I were sent to a place called "Furzedown House" which, we were told, was "some place down near Salisbury."

Some memories do remain, fortunately. Such as - catching the train at Holme (just south of Peterborough in Cambridgeshire), getting off at Kings Cross station in London, making our way by the underground over to Waterloo Station. There we caught a train down Salisbury way, and there remains a memory of leaving the train at a tiny station with the name "Horsebridge" on it. There is a faint recollection of being transported a very few miles (by Jeep, maybe?) to a large house. Definitely out in the boondocks by itself, Furzedown House turned out to be a country mansion taken over by the American Red Cross and operated as a rest and recuperation facility. There were a few other similar places nearby, the names of which were known then, but which have now faded out of memory.

There are mixed memories, some strong, some faint, of the experience at Furzedown. Lodging was in warm, comfortable quarters in the mansion, which had a large living room with a huge fireplace around which we sat in the evenings. For sleeping we had real beds (we actually had sheets!). Food was excellent, including fresh eggs for breakfast, sometimes good steaks for dinner; all of this was served by our very own butler. We dressed in civilian clothes for the week, ill-fitting old sweaters and slacks. We must have really caused a sensation when we met local people on the lanes as we cycled the area nearby!

I have strong recollections of the layout of the grounds - reinforced by a contemporary photograph, and of playing on the spacious grounds in a softball game against some guys from another "flak house." Also prominent are memories of seeing the sun, real honest-to-God sunshine, which was an experience our January-to-April tenure at Glatton had all but denied us. There were plenty of things to do: archery, horseback riding, sight-seeing, golf. Then I remember being able to relax when there was nothing we had to do. There was a visit to Salisbury, not far away, for shopping and to see the magnificent Salisbury Cathedral One of the flight surgeons from the 457th was in residence with us, ready to take care of any signs of disability or squirrelly behavior and , also, to dole out our ration of medicinal spirits every evening.

One other vivid memory remains. Late on the afternoon of a beautiful day, while we were enjoying refreshments under some magnificent trees on the estate, someone suddenly noticed a B-17 approaching us. This aircraft was so near the ground that the tips of the props seemed to be ticking the heads off the tall grass stalks as it thundered across a field, heading directly for us. When the B-17 pulled up over the large trees, very few of us were still in its path , having fled well to either side. The pilots of the aircraft clearly knew well where and what Furzedown was, and undoubtedly were former flak leave visitors. What we did not know at the time was that the 8th Air Force had virtually shut down operations and that our war was over. The B-17 crew was probably out joy riding celebrating the fact.

Indeed, when we returned to Glatton (I don't remember the trip at all), we discovered that the 457th Bomb Group had, in our absence, flown its last mission against Germany. There would be no completed tour for our crew; but, frankly, we didn't mind at all. Our minds began to fill with thoughts of going home. But, in retrospect, it was probably a good thing that we spent the last days of our combat tour – not in the air – but on flak leave.

Can you "go home again?" Not really. In 1994, my wife, Bobbie, our daughter, Becky Harris Moore and I had hired a car for a week's tour of southeastern and southern England. As both Winchester and Salisbury (east and west of

Furzedown House, respectively) were directly on our route, an attempt to find Furzedown House would be made. With the help of detailed instructions from Ken Nail, a former navigator in our group, we made our way to King's Somborne, a few miles south of Stockbridge which is about halfway between Winchester and Salisbury. There we sojourned, partaking of food and spirits in the local public house, and getting final directions to Furzedown House from a most interested proprietor. Even with all the help, it still took a bit of doing to find the house, but we did.

We had been prepared for a changed situation for Furzedown House, now cut up into several apartments in the main and outer buildings. Ken Nail had sent me copies of modern photos. What caught me, the only one of our party ever to have seen it before, by complete surprise, were the immense changes in the landscape! The beautiful, extensive lawn, backed by tall trees, was gone, along with the trees. Instead, there were tall hedges and small trees up close to the house, and none of them were anything like 50 years old. Despite all this, and despite failing to meet the gracious lady who is now the host, we thoroughly enjoyed the visit. But, we decided that you really can't go home again.

Then, leaving Furzedown, proceeding back through King's Somborne to Salisbury, our destination for the evening, we passed through - of all things - Horsebridge, less than a mile from King's Somborne! We had about decided that it was a false memory, for it had appeared on no map we could find. However, it was clearly shown on the large Landranger map we now had. The station was gone, as was the rail line it served, but its location was distinct. Also, still there was the River Test, the stream where Isaak Walton, of *The Compleat Angler,* did his thing. Our finding Horsebridge, and realizing that the memory of leaving the train there was real, led us to believe that maybe you can go home again, a little bit, after all.

MY DEAR OLD PARACHUTE!

By Jourdan L. Browning

(Note: Much of the following story was based on stories printed earlier in Northeast Mississippi Daily Journal *and in* New Albany Gazette. *Some phrases or sentences may be direct quotes from those accounts.)*

With the reputation of the 100th Bomb Group as "The Bloody Hundredth," the Group the Germans hated, the Group that had lost so many of its crews in combat, it was no wonder that I felt fate was against me when I was assigned to it. I soon understood that the title "The Bloody Hundredth" was well deserved. The Group lost 200 aircraft and 86% of its original crews by war's end. One day, only one plane out of eighteen came back from its mission of the day.

I was 26, older than many other volunteers when I joined the service in 1944. I figured I was about to be drafted. I had just gone back to school after working for 10 years and had married my wife Eva, a few months before being sent overseas.

My basic training was at Miami Beach, from which I next went to Indianapolis to school. I blistered in Miami and then nearly froze in Indianapolis. Then came a stint in Nashville for classification. They wanted pilots, but I wanted to be a navigator. I got my wish; Out of 100 candidates, I was one of only two selected for navigator training.

When I got to England, I was assigned to the 100th Bomb Group at Thorpe Abbots, in East Anglia. I flew missions to Munster, Bremen, Cologne, Dresden, Nuremberg, Hanover and Weimar. And then there was a mission to Berlin toward the end.

I was very proud to be a navigator; the navigator is an important part of the crew, since he tells the plane where to go. When I graduated, I felt very proud to have reached my goal. When I started flying as a navigator, I did my best to do a really

good job. I must have succeeded, because I was soon picked to be a lead navigator. This meant that I would be guiding the entire Group. The crew that I was flying with would be staffed with the best men at all positions from the pilot on down. Our plane would be out front, leading large formations of planes. There I was, a boy from Tishomingo, leading all those planes on bombing missions over Germany. Sometimes the formations were so large they would reach as far as from New Albany to Jackson. This was quite an experience.

We flew a lot of ten and twelve hour missions, with temperatures up to fifty-five degrees below zero. This was bad enough, but to fly with "The Bloody Hundredth," put terror in my heart. We had a lot of men killed. I was lucky in that I was the only one of four from my navigation school to survive.

When my plane did go down, it was not from enemy action, but from plain old fatigue and wear and tear. It was in early February of 1945 that my plane became a statistic that added to the record of the 100th. It was on fire when I bailed out, and I watched it crash after my chute opened. Although it had been riddled with flak and 20mm shells many times, on this day it was a leaking oil line that caused the fire. This, however, did not mean that it was not a casualty of the war just as though it had been shot down.

I really didn't want to jump. I think my flight engineer really had to give me a shove out of the hatch! As I told Eva later, "I quickly grabbed my dear old parachute that I had petted like a baby all these months, and I snapped it on my harness at the chest.

I seemed to be hanging in space lying on my back as the plane moved out of sight. Then I saw 65 yards of the most beautiful silk I ever laid eyes on blossomed out like an umbrella, and I thanked God as I had never thanked Him before. Frankly, I had never trusted a parachute very much in the past."

I landed a few miles behind the American Lines; but when I hit the ground, I found myself facing rifle barrels aimed by three Free French who wanted to make sure that my other surviving crew members and I were Americans.

Since the pilot had set the plane on automatic pilot before he bailed out, the crashing did comparatively little damage when it plowed into the ground. In fact, I was able to recover some of my possessions from the wreckage. I felt that I was very fortunate to retrieve some of my navigation maps. They were charred, but I still have them.

Soon after this I was able to return to my base and fly seventeen more missions

Today, I am mostly retired. I still harbor vivid memories of combat experiences; I know my life was changed forever because of them. I would never want to go through this again, but I am very proud that I did my part to the best of my ability to serve my country.

Joe E. Davis grew up in Ludlow but lived in Jackson when the war began. He completed training as an armorer and a gunner. He flew as a ball turret gunner in the 91st Bomb Group at Bassingbourn. He shot down 6 German aircraft and had joint victories with his tail gunner on others. He flew 35 combat missions between March 15 and December 31, 1944. He was awarded the Distinguished Flying Cross and the Air Medal with 4 Oak Leaf Clusters. His group was awarded a Presidential Citation.

Arthur H. Moss grew up in Water Valley but was working for E. L. Bruce Co. in Memphis when World War II began. He says he never cared about or wished to fly. However, there was a place for him in the Air Corps; after training at Chanute Field in Illinois, the Boeing School in Seattle and Muroc Field in California, he was well qualified to help keep them flying in the Mighty Eighth. Arthur served as a crew chief and then as an inspector from January, 1942, to October, 1945, about as long as anybody in the Eighth stayed in England. His service was in the 305th Bomb Group at Chelveston. He attained the rank of M Sgt After his discharge in October, 1945, Arthur returned to Memphis and the E. L. Bruce Co. He then operated his own mercantile business until his retirement. He now lives, with his wife Margie, in Bruce. They are the parents of two and the grandparents of five.

FROM CLARKSDALE TO
CAMP LUCKY STRIKE

By Barton W. MacNeill

Bart MacNeill retired from the U. S. Air Force after 23 years service in 1963. He taught in public schools and later, upon receiving his PhD in Education Psychology from Mississippi State University, taught there for 15 years until he retired in 1985. He lives with his wife Kathryn on their cattle and tree farm in Sturgis. His USAF and civilian travel has taken him to 32 foreign countries and all 50 States.

My first flying experience

A brand-new Lieutenant, with pilot's wings!

My first ride in an airplane was at Fletcher Field in Clarksdale, Mississippi. I was an aviation cadet trainee riding with my instructor. I finished my

pilot training in the Southeast Training Command and was assigned to a B-17 Replacement Training Unit at MacDill Field, Florida. There I was assigned to a crew and after completing RTU training and additional radar bombing training at Langley Field, Virginia, we proceeded to Gander Field, Newfoundland. On our way to Gander, we had the opportunity to buzz my hometown. We made two low passes over the small community of Penns Grove, New Jersey. I saw my parents clearly, waving as we flew over. I wouldn't see them again until the end of the war.

At Gander Field, we prepared for our flight to the United Kingdom. The flight from Gander to Nutts Corner, Ireland, was a great experience. We couldn't help but recall Lindbergh's flight in 1927, which was somewhat the same course as we flew. During the flight we thought of the difference between his flight and ours and how much more courageous his effort was.

After arriving in the UK, we delivered our airplane to Alconbury Airbase and proceeded to report to the 95th Bomb Group at Horham, where we were assigned to the 334th Bomb Squadron. We were sent to Bovington, near London, for "combat school." A notable event, while there, was a fly-over by a V-1 flying bomb! We all climbed on top of the bomb shelter to get a good look while our English friends crawled inside! Crazy Americans!

Back at the 95th, we started flying missions on September 8th (my Father's birthday). Our first mission was to Maintz near Frankfort. We thought it was a milk run until we landed back in England

and discovered almost 200 flak holes in the aircraft. After that we had a higher respect for our targets and the 88 mm anti-aircraft guns of the Germans!

On a shuttle mission to Poltava, Russia, in september,

Our mission on September 18, 1944, was quite different. The 13th Combat Wing of the Eighth Air Force, composed of the 100th Bomb Group, the 390th Bomb Group and the 95th Bomb Group was assigned to drop supplies to the Polish Freedom Fighters in Warsaw, who were positioned between the Russians on the East side of Warsaw and the Germans on the West. We completed the mission, which was one of our roughest, having to fly in at 12,000 feet, drop our para-packs and hope they landed where we intended. Fifty years later, on September 18, 1994, at a ceremony at the USS Intrepid Museum in New York harbor, I was awarded the Polish Freedom Cross, along with about 50 fliers from the 13th Combat Wing for our efforts.

On November 2, 1944, we flew our 17th and last mission to Merseberg oil refineries which, we found out later, was one of the biggest air battles of the war. The Germans, who had been absent in the air with their fighters due to lack of fuel, chose to made a significant showing that day. Later we found out that our fighters had a field day, and more German fighters were shot down than on any other mission of the war.

We made our bomb run without incident; but as we turned away from the target, we were hit hard by flak. Our tail gunner was killed instantly, and we lost two engines. No. 1 engine was the only one with full power, and No. 3 retained about 15" of manifold pressure (about one-half power). We threw out flak suits, guns, ammunition - even unbolted the ball turret and let it go. We maintained flight at about 3,000 feet at about 110 MPH and were making good progress toward friendly territory until a Folke -Wulf 190 jumped us and started a wing fire. We all bailed out at about 1000 feet. While we were still in the air, our aircraft exploded before it hit the ground! We believe a Higher Power was looking after us!

We were all captured immediately, and I was taken to a separate location because I had broken my ankle upon landing on some uneven ground. I didn't see any of my crew after that day until the war ended, because I was taken away immediately, I suppose because I was injured. My transportation was a motorcycle and side car! I was accompanied by no less than *four* German soldiers *on* the motorcycle with me! Half way to our destination the motorcycle ran out of gas; and while the Germans seemed to be arguing as to what to do, a German Officer in a staff car drove up. He apparently severely reprimanded the NCO in charge but gave him enough gas to deliver me to the destination intended. Looking back on the incident today, it reminds me of a Keystone Cops comedy; but at the time I didn't find it humorous!

I was taken to a rural house a few miles away from the crash site, which was a sub-post for the local SS unit. A crew from another bomb group was being held at this same location. One of the officers from that crew, a bombardier named Wietzman, was being questioned enthusiastically by the SS officers. They questioned him about his Jewish name and also about the list of missions he had flown which they found in his wallet, a foolish mistake on his part and against security practices. He was removed from the room and taken outside. We heard two shots, and Lt. Weitzman did not leave with us when we were later moved.

During my interrogation an SS officer took a liking to my B-15 flight jacket and my Air Force issue watch and relieved me of both. The Germans had fashioned a makeshift splint for my leg which was bandaged heavily. Otherwise I might have lost my B-15 flying trousers! I was furnished crutches for the rest of my journey to Dulag Luft.

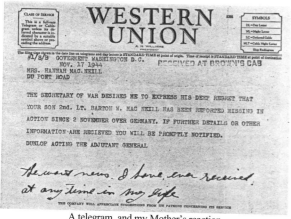

A telegram, and my Mother's reaction

That night we were loaded on a truck to start our trip to Frankfurt, the location of the main interrogation and processing center for most P.O.W.s. A young German corporal was our guard in the rear of the truck. He surprised us by singing, in English, an American song of the '30s called, "The Music Goes Down and Around." He explained that he had lived in Chicago until age 14, when his father moved the family back to Germany in the late '30s. I thought later that since he understood the English language his presence there was not a coincidence!

Interrogation at Dulag Luft took about 3 days during which time we were held in solitary confinement. After interrogation I was transferred to the hospital at Hoe Mark, a Red Cross hospital which was supervised by Germans but staffed primarily by captured British and U. S. medics. This I found to be the case in two other hospitals in which I stayed later. Hoe Mark was located about 16 KM northwest of Frankfurt. There I received the first real medical attention for my fractured ankle during the 2 1/2 weeks travel from our crash site to Dulag Luft. I received good medical treatment at the three hospitals in which I stayed. The last one was in Meinegan, Germany. The prisoners along with the German supervisors and the hospital staff celebrated Christmas, 1944, together. Our Christmas dinner was something

special with the best food served out of the Red Cross parcels, plus one glass of beer provided by the German contingent for each prisoner.

Shortly after that I was transferred from the hospital in western Germany to Stalag Luft III in Sagan, Poland. I was placed in the North Compound which was composed of about 1,700 British airmen and 500 U. S. airmen. This compound was the one from which *The Great Escape* was made some 9 months before, in March of 1944.

My stay at Stalag Luft III was cut short when the Russians made their January, 1945, offensive starting their drive to Berlin. To prevent our being relieved by the Russians, our captors chose to march all prisoners at Stalag Luft III to a railhead some 150 KM west at Spremberg.

At 1:00 A.M. on Sunday, January 28, the North Compound started evacuation. The last man cleared the gates at 3:45 A.M. It was snowing and I have read that the temperature was about 12 degrees below zero. It didn't seem that cold, but perhaps marching kept us somewhat warm. Each man was afforded the opportunity to carry any food he was able to, which we obtained from the Red Cross storage building. I made a blanket roll and managed to carry enough food for the 3 day march and the 4 day train trip. During the march, one of our guards was an older man who had lost an eye on the eastern front fighting the Russians. (Most guards were either very young or very old.) We had nicknamed him "Popeye," and he was one of the more friendly guards. He was visibly having a difficult time marching and carrying his pack and rifle. I jokingly offered to carry his rifle for him. To my surprise he handed it over to me! I carried it for some distance until a German officer rode by and *immediately* corrected the situation!

When we reached Spremberg at the end of the third day, we spent the night in a French labor camp. It was good to sleep in a shelter after having to rest only in woods and barn yards during the march.

We were placed aboard "40 or 8" (40 men or 8 horses) box cars, approximately 55 men to each car, and we departed Spremberg traveling west to Chemnitz, then south to Stalag VII-A at Mooseberg, approximately 20 KM northeast of Munich. We arrived there on or about February 6th after spending 4 almost sleepless days and nights on the train. The Germans gave us no food during the trip, but we shared among ourselves the food we had brought with us.

Conditions were crowded and food scarce at our new camp. We endured for 3 more months until we were liberated by Gen. Patton's 3rd Armored Division and the 99th Infantry Division on April 29, 1945. Americans took over as gate guards and a friend of mine Bob Stone from Kansas City talked a guard into letting us go to town the next day. Arriving in Mooseberg, a couple of KMs away, we found an army field kitchen and the GI food never tasted so good. We spent the night there. The next day we strolled uptown where a U. S. tank column was passing through. We asked the tank commander for a ride, and he obliged us to our surprise. When the tank on which we were riding reached the Isor River east of town, it was halted to open the single lane bridge to allow a jeep to cross from the other side. When the vehicle was half-way across the bridge, the tank commander said, "Boys, pop-to. Here comes the 'old man'!" When the jeep approached, we all saluted. Gen. George Patton returned our salute, standing in his jeep, wearing those famous ivory handled pistols. Quite a thrill!

Shortly after we crossed the bridge, gunfire was heard and exploding shells could be seen farther ahead. The tank commander explained that "the Germans are trying to get our range." With those words, Bob and I quickly made our departure and made our way back to Mooseberg!

The next day while walking in town, we decided to visit a German family. We knocked on the door of a house which evidently was the home of a miller with a water wheel on the side of his house by a stream. The head of the house answered the door and immediately asked if we were Americans or Russians. When we answered "Americans" he practically pulled us into the house! The housewife insisted that we sit and eat, which we did. The husband asked if we would stay a few days with them, explaining that the Russian prisoners who were liberated at Mooseberg and turned loose, were not obligated to fall under "Allied Control." They had raided and burned a German winery and had committed a number of rapes. The husband feared for the safety of his wife and 8 children, therefore we agreed to stay a few days. Later that afternoon two Russian prisoners knocked on the door. The husband asked me to intercede and answer the door, which I gladly did. I told the Russians who we (Bob and I) were and that this was "our place" and for them to "rausmittern." They left without incident, much to the relief of the household.

We enjoyed three weeks of VIP treatment with the family of Herr Heintz in exchange for furnishing protection for the family and the house. During that time, on May 8, 1945, the news of the German surrender came over the radio! We were in the kitchen having lunch and Herr Heintz and his wife seemed quite relieved and glad the war was over. Frau Heintz had been awarded a Deutschen-Mutter medal by the German government for having given birth to eight pure Aryan children!

Bob and I decided that we had better go back to the camp and prepare for our journey home. Upon returning to the prison camp we found it deserted! What to do? We went back and stayed another week with Herr Heintz and family before hitch-hiking from Munich to Le Havre, France, to Camp Lucky Strike, the processing center. While there, we cleaned up from our journey, drew some back pay and uniforms and talked the C. O. into letting us go to Paris for 4 days while waiting our turn to ship out to the U.S.

We managed to survive our Paris visit, returned *on time,* boarded our boat and arrived in the U. S. on June 27th, 1945, about 2 months after we had been liberated. We felt this was time well spent, which I'll never forget!

SHUFFLING THE DECK

By Craig Harris

Three elderly "fireballers" from the 748th Squadron. Harris, right.

Crews who survived flying in the close formations of the US Army 8th Air Force over Germany in World War II will tell you - almost without exception - that one of the most frightening experiences was that of "shuffling the deck." In this situation, two formations of aircraft, usually squadrons or "boxes," collided at angles ranging from ninety degrees to head-on and slithered between each other as best they could. It was harrowing, terrifying, unforgettable; and people died in collisions that it caused. And it happened with greater frequency than anyone would have liked.

In recall of WW II experiences in the 8th AF, personal memories usually must give way to official mission narratives where there is a conflict. However, the mission narratives often have errors ranging from trivial to some really serious omissions. Thus it is that this author's memory insists that it is correct despite the lack of corroboration in the mission narrative for the

457th Bomb Group's mission to Merseberg on March 31, 1945.

The mission narrative states that the assigned target was the Leuna oil refinery at Merseberg, but that the target bombed was the marshaling yards at Halle "… in policy with keeping Hitler's transportation system as completely disrupted as possible." This is technically correct, but conspicuous by their absence are, how that really came about, and what really happened in the process.

For example, neither the mission narrative nor the track chart reflect the fact that the Group, bedeviled with very bad weather - clouds and contrails - had difficulty finding the primary target, Merseberg. Failing to pick up the target in time to make a proper bomb run, the Group overflew Merseberg without dropping its bombs, but drew - not surprisingly - heavy flak from the target. The Group then proceeded to make a left turn to get set up for a bomb run on Halle, the secondary target. However, the eastward heading carried the Group on toward Leipzig, where heavy flak was also encountered. So far, two targets overflown, two sets of flak, and two no-drops.

As Halle was approached, the cloud cover - already heavy - thickened to a full 10/10ths, above and below, aggravated by heavy, persistent contrails. But the radar bombing equipment functioned well, allowing a bomb drop on the marshaling yards at Halle, although results were, of course, not observed.

After the drop on Halle, with the Group still heading about 280 degrees, crew members in the high squadron breathed a huge collective sigh of relief and sat back in their positions. They had been delivered from the incredible stress of runs on or over three heavily defended targets in really terrible weather. The relief was short-lived as, out of nowhere (except the dense contrails) came a squadron of red-tailed B-17s only slightly above our altitude and heading about 80 degrees, almost head-on! Those red-tails seemed to be everywhere, above, below and on each side as we did what we could to dodge them. Aircraft were shuffled just as if they were playing cards in a

deck. Mercifully the incident was over in a few seconds; and, miraculously, there were no collisions. That there were no collisions was most likely due to Providence, rather than any action taken by pilots, because there was really no time to respond with anything but frantic prayer (and a few anguished epithets).

In the aftermath, there were no atheists, only a couple of dozen badly shaken pilots and co-pilots, and a score of other crew members who had happened to see what had taken place. Interphones rattled with conversations, "What the h… was THAT?", "MY God, did you see THAT?", and other remarks far less printable. After what had to be Divine intervention, the Group was further blessed with the same abominable weather on withdrawal, so that after crossing enemy lines the Group was allowed to disperse, eliminating the stress of formation flying. Now all the crews had to do was find the way home and avoid hitting some other aircraft.

Back on the ground at the 457th Bomb Group's base at Glatton, several crew members who normally passed up their post-mission whiskey ration were seen reaching for today's ration with shaking hands. Among them was this author, who now realized that among the things that could really command one's attention - such as flak, fighters and flying cartridge cases - was that phenomenon know as "shuffling the deck."

The outfit with the "big red tails?" Memory and recorded fact come together with the best fit if the "big red tails" represent the 34th Bomb Group, a B-17 group that formerly flew B-24s, in the 3rd Division, at Mendlesham, north of Ipswich. This author wonders if somewhere, someone from the 34th Bomb Group is writing about "Shuffling the Deck" with those B-17s with the diagonal blue stripes and the "triangle U."

HOLMAN REMEMBERS

By Ralph Holman

By way of introduction, I am formerly Lt. Ralph Holman, Pilot, 568th Squadron, having arrived at the 390th Bomb Group, Framlingham, December, 1944. I flew my first seven missions with the Victor Proffatt crew, then flew the rest of my missions, with the exception of four missions, with new crews to the ETO with Ernest Yeager as co-pilot, until the end of the War in May, 1945.

It was my pleasure to take a European trip in May of 1995. The trip had two purposes, first to celebrate the 50th wedding anniversary of my wife, Yvonne, and myself, and to once again stroll down memory lane and visit Framlingham and Station 153 where I had so many years ago lived and flown combat against Hitler's hotshots.

We were in England at the celebration of the end of World War II with ceremonies at Hyde Park in London with all the gala activities. It was interesting to see the Lancasters, Halifaxes and Spitfires once again flying overhead. After visiting many historical sights in London, we motored to Dover and crossed the Channel to Calais, France and on to Brussels, Belgium. I remember a mission in January, 1945, after a deep penetration bombing mission in Germany, we ran out of gas and landed at a fighter base just outside Brussels. The crew spent the night in Brussels and I must confess that as I again visited Brussels in 1995 it was hard to recognize. One of Brussel's most famous landmarks, the little naked boy at the fountain, had been removed from the main street to a side street and someone had clothed him.

Continuing our journey, I was quite anxious to arrive at The Hague, Holland. At the end of the war Yeager and I flew a number of food missions at low level to The Hague where people were starving. I remember our first mission to The Hague. We came in at low level and as we passed over the city, the streets, roof-tops, everywhere people were waving bed sheets, towels, whatever they could find, welcoming us as a means of thanks for coming to the aid of their plight. I also remember, just as we dropped our food, we ran into a flock of geese and Yeager and I thought the Germans were shooting at us. Talking to a few of the townspeople in The Hague, I could find no one who remembered the food drops. Well, fellow crew members and crews who participated in the food drops, we remembered.

Yeager and I also flew several missions, at the end of the War, to Linz, Austria, where we ferried French prisoners who had been in concentration camps, back to Paris, France. Those missions I will never forget. As we landed at the Linz airport and taxied up to the hangers we could see row after row of cots filled with French prisoners that were sick or too weak to stand. We picked up 25 ambulatory French soldiers and flew them to Paris. There were two French soldiers standing behind the cockpit and as we crossed over into France, I pointed ahead and said, "France." They looked at me with blank stares and I reasoned they probably thought we were taking them to another concentration camp. When we arrived in Paris, we put the left wing on the Eiffel Tower and circled Paris, and when they saw and recognized the Eiffel Tower and saw Paris, I have never seen such a transformation of expression on their faces. They headed to the back of the plane where the other liberated prisoners were located and then there was a roaring sound of whooping and hollering. They at last realized they were free and they were home. Whatever small part I had played in the bombing missions I had flown, the constant knowledge of death all around me day after day, all of that was justified by the transformation of death on the faces of the French soldiers to that of life and freedom, and home.

Back to my story. The trip through Germany was quite interesting. We visited a lot of cities that I had bombed during the War, including the remains of the Remagen bridge where so many of us hold battle stars. Of course, Germany has been totally rebuilt and very few scars remain. After several delightful days in Paris where we indulged ourselves in sightseeing and fine food, we returned to London.

Sunday, May 14. Our intention was to rent a car and drive to Ipswich, but observing the driving around London, we decided it would be safer if we took the train. We boarded a train at Liverpool station and it was my wife's first train ride. They were working on the tracks at Ipswich, so we stopped at Witham and rode a bus to Ipswich. Being Sunday, most transportation is closed but we managed to hire a gentleman to take us to Framlingham who had been a taxi driver since WW2 and knew the base quite well.

As we approached Station 153, you come on it suddenly. It stands on top of a gently sloped hill, and all of a sudden all the memories of what we did, where we lived, the runways, the roar of engines as they broke the stillness of the early morning, the bicycles, the briefing where the curtain is slowly opened to reveal our target for the day, the take off, the landing, the officers' club, the comradeship of the crews, it all came rushing back and it brings a tear to your eye. The control tower stands alone in the middle of a field of wheat and it seems somehow out of place there.

The control tower, now a museum.

To those members that have not been back, they have erected a Quonset hut next to the tower and inside the Quonset hut one corner is glass enclosed and kept under lock and a returning member may go in and sign the book and write his name, squadron and rank on the wall. And I must say the wall has quite a few names on it.

Inside the quonset hut, a glass enclosed wall
with hundreds of signatures

The tower is now a museum and it is full of memorabilia. I guess what caught my eye more than anything else was an electric heated suit we wore on high altitude bombing.

Ugly but warm at 30,000 ft.

The taxi driver then asked if I would like to see the remains of the officers' club. We drove down a small road overgrown on each side with scrub trees and underbrush and we pulled up to what used to

172

be the officers' club where so many years ago we hung out and made our home away from home. The right end of the building when we were there had a Quonset hut attached to it and that was our famous Bermuda Room where lived "Milly the Mermaid." This part of the building has been torn down. The officers' club through the years has been ravaged by time and weather. Trees are growing out of the paneless windows, underbrush is all around the building and it was a disheartening sight to behold. Opposite the officers' club still standing is a brick building with a large front opening, if everyone remembers, and I believe between the two buildings were concrete trenches we could get into in case of a bombing attack. We had a number of raids but I don't recall anyone leaving their drinking duty at the Bermuda room to run out and get in the trenches.

We then toured Framlingham castle and before leaving we visited the site of Parham Hall which had been torn down 35 years ago. Where Parham Hall once stood is now a beautiful flower garden. To those of us that were at Station 153 at the end of the War, the base was closed and we were billeted at Parham Hall before returning to the States. I think it would be wonderful if some organization would take it upon themselves to restore the officers' club and make it part of the tower museum. In fact, the museum is a tourist attraction that draws quite a few visitors. It was full the day we were there.

In closing, if I may, I would like to recall a mission I participated in as co-pilot on the Victor Proffatt crew flying with the 568th Squadron. This mission has been retold many times and may I yet give another version of it. The mission, January 14, 1945, the oil storage tanks, Derben, Germany, the Berlin area. Proffatt and I lost power on Number 3 engine at the end of our takeoff roll. Increasing power on the other three engines, retracting the wheels, we barely maintained flying speed. Number 3 engine would only give us 22 inches of mercury. It was apparent we had a malfunction in the turbo supercharger. Overburdening the other three engines, we managed to get into squadron formation. As the bomber stream headed out over the North Sea and climbing to bombing altitude we

found we could no longer stay with the squadron. The group engineer had us pull out of formation and feather #3 engine, hoping the cooling of the engine would activate the supercharger to working. After restarting the engine, it still would not maintain over 22 inches of mercury. After working with the group engineer for a long length of time we were about 2,000 feet below the group and several miles behind. We were ordered by the group commander to abort the mission and return to base. As we all know, the 390th Bomb Group suffered its greatest casualties that mission, losing all 8 of C squadron and one from B squadron. The fighting as we know was not one sided because the 390th accounted for 24 German fighters confirmed and a lot more unconfirmed from downed B-17s.

It has always been a mystery to me why some of us survived combat when we daily were subjected to death all around us and I truly believe the real heroes of World War II are those who did not have the chance to come home and open the front door and call out, "MOM, I'M HOME."

The Yeager crew, with the exception of Russell Stoner (deceased), waist gunner, Harrisburg, PA, hold a yearly reunion somewhere in the United States. Over the years the wives of the crew have become a close-knit group and we all look forward each year to the reunion. Although the crew members live far apart, during the year we sometimes visit each others home. This comradeship that the crew has shared with each other over the years has indeed blessed all our hearts and the War, if nothing else, has shown it was at least good for something.

We are now senior citizens, enjoying the golden years of our life. We recall with fond memories of a yesteryear, long ago, when we were so young, so full of life, our energy was boundless and we believed we were indestructible, and to those of who flew the "BIG BIRD," we knew without a doubt that we were really "SOMETHING ELSE."

A STORMY JOURNEY FROM MARRAKECH TO LANDS END

By Willard F. Nester

(Note: This story by Mississippian, Willard F. "Faye" Nester, first appeared in, Second Air Division *Journal, Winter, 1994, edition. Used by permission of the author.)*

The Willard F. Nester Crew. Nester is standing second from left.

I was a member of the 491st Bomb Group (H) that was formed and stationed at Pueblo, Colorado. Most of my crew phase training was accomplished at Blythe, California, prior to transfer to Pueblo. I was in the 852nd Bomb Squadron of the 491st and was one of the lucky ones to be assigned a new B-24 J aircraft. Its number was 44-40100, and we gave it the most unusual name of "D'NIF."

Our training continued until we were ready to deploy as a group for service overseas. We took the southern route from West Palm Beach, Florida, via Puerto Rico, Trinidad, Belem, Fortalaza, Dakar, Marrakech, Lands End, and on to home base at Metfield, England, arriving there May 11, 1944.

We flew with the 491st on their first mission to Bretigny, France, on June 2, 1944. On June 14, 1944 I had completed nine combat missions. We were given a three day pass and went to London, where on the first night we experienced a heavy buzz-bomb attack on the city. Upon returning to our base at Metfield, we had orders waiting to transfer the crew to the 93rd Bomb Group (H) located at Hardwick.

The crew trained in GH instrument bombing procedures; and when we had completed our training, the 93rd made us a lead crew. We flew the GH lead with other groups in the 2nd Air Division until completing my tour of thirty missions, which I finished on December 25, 1944.

I have many memories of some of my combat missions, but the time I remember most was on our trip overseas on the flight from Marrakech to Lands End.

We left Marrakech on May 10, 1944 on a night flight that was mostly over water. Weather was forecast to be good most of way with scattered to broken clouds. A short time later we were forced to climb to an altitude of 12,500 feet to be on top of the clouds. Soon we were approaching a bank of dark clouds that towered above the altitude we were flying. We were using the auto pilot, cruising at 165 mph indicated airspeed at 12,500 feet. In my opinion, to avoid getting into the clouds would have been very dangerous because of getting lost over the ocean or too close to the coast of France and possible enemy fighters. There was no other choice but to go on instruments, hoping to fly through the clouds in a very short time.

The first indication we got of things to come was an upward lift of the airplane and a drop in airspeed. A small correction in the auto pilot to pick up speed had no results. Still losing airspeed, another adjustment was made; and when the airspeed dropped below 160 mph, the auto pilot was turned off; and I began flying the plane manually. At this time, more power was added, but we continued to lose airspeed. The control column was moved forward almost against the instrument panel. My last visual check of the airspeed indicator was 90 mph. My estimate was that the airplane quit flying between 70 and 75 mph, at which time the plane went into a spin.

All of our gyro-controlled flight instruments were inoperative; it was night; we were out of control and going down very fast. My primary flying school instructor taught that "when all flight instruments are out – go to needle-ball-airspeed," which we did. The co-pilot helped on rudder control while I handled the aileron controls. In a matter of seconds it felt like someone was on the controls with me, and the plane was suddenly nose down and picking up airspeed at a very high rate. Power was reduced and back pressure applied to the elevator controls. To recover the downward movement too quickly could have very easily caused the loss of a wing; so we took our chances that we had sufficient altitude to recover slowly before we would crash into the ocean. The airspeed indicator and altimeter were changing so fast that my mind went blank. Their readings on the instruments are unknown to me at this time.

Soon the airspeed began to decrease; and after two or three ups and downs and by increasing power back to cruise settings, we leveled off at approximately 7,000 feet and were heading about 270 degrees. We were at the base of the cloud cover; and after resetting our flight instruments and lowering our altitude to 5,000, feet we proceeded to Lands End. After landing we checked the airplane for damage and the crew members for injuries. The crew was OK and so was the airplane. The airplane had some small wrinkles in the skin of the wings near the fuselage, and a few rivet heads were raised, but none of them had "popped" or pulled through. The rear section of the airplane showed signs that loose items had been tossed about, but no significant damage was found.

After a short delay at Lands End, we joined an escort plane that took us to Metfield. They relayed landing information to us form the control tower, and the green light from the tower was our clearance to land.

As for the incident we experienced in the thunderstorm cloud, it was truly a miracle. The Lord must have had other things He wanted us to accomplish in our lives, and He sent a guardian angel to save us that we might have the opportunity to fulfill His will. I will always remember that experience.

****

Biographical Sketch
by David D. Nester

Until he wrote his stories included in this book a few years ago, I don't recall my father ever relating any personal accounts of his involvement in WW II.

What I recall of Dad during more than twenty years as an Air National Guardsman was a half-Colonel / half-farmer." And as anyone who knew him will tell, he performed the duties of both these vocations beyond what would be expected of any two individuals.

During the war, he was a decorated B-24 pilot and later, as a small-farm cattleman, he bred championship polled herefords – it's hard to say which made him proudest.

In the twenty-plus years following retirement, he worked the farm like a man 30 years his junior, scarcely breaking stride until late 1997 when he sold his herefords and began dedicating his time to making, arguably, the best peanut brittle in Decatur.

On January 24, 1998, at the age of 81, while putting up a fence row in the garden, he set down the axe he was using and lay down and died – with his work gloves on.

Harold Jernigan, who grew up in Blue Mountain, flew with the 381st Bomb Group at Sudbury. Although he had a private pilot's license before entering the Air Corps, he flew as a gunner. As such, he shot down 4 ME109s and 2 FW 190s. On the Berlin mission of March 6, 1944, five crew members were killed; Harold flew the plane back to England. For this heroic performance he was given a battlefield promotion to 2nd Lieutenant. On another mission, Harold's crew was shot down and had to ditch in the North Sea. The crew all survived and were picked up by the British Air-Sea Rescue. He was awarded the Silver Star, the Distinguished Flying Cross, the Air Medal with 7 Oak Leaf Clusters and the Purple Heart. Harold passed away in 1998. His widow Lucille lives in Tupelo.

Thomas R. Culpepper lives in State Line with his wife Mary. During the war he completed Aircraft Mechanics School and gunnery school before meeting and teaming up with his vrew at Casper, Wyoming. He and his crew were sent to England to serve in the 448th Bomb Group at Seething. He flew 18 missions as flight engineer. He was shot down on his 18th mission, his third to Berlin, in April, 1944. He was captured, spent almost a year as a P.O.W., chiefly at Krems, Austria. After the war he worked for the State of Alabama and later Scott Paper Co. in forestry positions.

IT WAS MY WAR, TOO

By Ethelda Phillips Nail

No, I didn't fly a B-17, a B-24 or one of the fighters. I was not a navigator, a bombardier, a pilot or a gunner; **BUT,** it was my war, too!

In October, 1942, Kenneth enlisted in the aviation cadet program and was told he would not be called to active duty for a year. So, we were married the following month on the 19th in Grenada, fully expecting to have at least eleven months together before he would be called into service, as he had been promised. That was not the case, as we soon learned.

At the end of November we went to Pinehurst, North Carolina, where both of us worked for J. A. Jones Construction Company. They were building an army base near Hoffman. Our first home was a garage apartment in nearby Pinehurst. Later we moved into an apartment in beautiful Boxwood Court in which other J. A. Jones employees lived.

We were very happy with this arrangement, and we thought we were settled down, at last. On January 31, 1943, we walked down into the village to see a movie. We decided to go by the Post Office first to check our mail. There in our box was a long white envelope: greetings from Uncle Sam. Kenneth was to report to Miami Beach the next day, February l.

The movie was forgotten; and as we returned to our apartment, my tears started to flow. A friend, Woodrow Rush, and Kenneth did our packing while I cried. A telephone call was made the next day to Miami Beach explaining our situation, and Kenneth was given a week to take me home to Grenada before reporting for duty.

After basic training, he was sent to Ouachita College in Arkadelphia, Arkansas, where I joined him. There was a reservation for me at the Caddo Hotel when I arrived. Soon after I went to my room, I heard: "Hup, hup, hup" and the sound of marching feet coming down the street. I flew to the window, raised it and got my first glimpse of my husband in uniform somewhere in that formation. (Actually, in the front rank as he was one of the tallest in the outfit.)

Our home there was a room with kitchen privileges. Two other Mississippi couples, the Paul Tardys and the Alvin Words, had rooms there also. The fellows could only come "home" on week-ends, not an ideal arrangement for newlyweds, but certainly better than being separated.

Half the men in the detachment at Ouachita College were from Mississippi and Alabama; the other half were "Yankees" from Missouri and Kansas and a few other states. Several of the young men from Mississippi and Alabama had illustrious careers after the war; some were outstanding attorneys; at least two were CPAs; one was a famous newspaper editor; one was a noted orthopedic surgeon; and one, George Wallace, became Governor of Alabama for several terms, got his wife elected after his term, and ran for President of the United States.

The men were divided into three groups. Kenneth was in the first group to leave. Knowing their departure date, I went to the train station to buy my ticket. I was standing in line behind an officer and heard him say, "fifty tickets to Nashville, Tennessee." I rushed back to the house and told the other wives where our fellows were going. I left Arkadelphia on the same train, not in the same car with my husband, of course.

Nashville was the classification center. From there Kenneth went to Maxwell Field in Montgomery, Alabama, for pre-flight. Wives could not be with their husbands there for a month; so I worked in Lickfold's Jewelry Store in Grenada until I could join him again.

From Maxwell Field we went to Arcadia, Florida, for Primary training at Dorr Field. I rode down on a Greyhound bus with Ve Ve Hay from Colorado, and Marge Huebner from Iowa. Marge and I found a room together with kitchen privileges. One weekend when the fellows came home, the Nails had the room to live in while the Huebners went to the hotel. The next weekend we switched places.

Some of the wives worked in an ant poison plant, and others worked in a brassiere factory. No job was too menial in order to earn a few dollars which would enable us to stay with our husbands. We were not there long enough for me to find work.

Kenneth "washed out" of pilot training and was sent to Selman Field in Monroe, Louisiana, where he entered navigation school. Again, I had just a room with kitchen privileges. A "Toddle House" restaurant was just two doors down; so I didn't use the kitchen a lot of the time. That was when they sold their hamburgers for a dime.

I was qualified to do clerical work; but no one would hire a cadet wife, since she could not be with them on a permanent basis. Therefore, I worked at F. W. Woolworth, five and dime store, while I was in Monroe. Kenneth was sent to Fort Myers, Florida for six weeks gunnery training, but I stayed in Monroe while he was gone, since he would be returning to Selman Field.

A new set of gold bars and a pair of navigator's wings

Graduation time finally came, and my navigator became a 2nd Lieutenant. Part of the fellows were granted leaves, but we weren't in that group. Instead we were sent to Lincoln, Nebraska. It was around Easter and I had bought a yellow light-- weight wool coat. When we arrived in Lincoln, it was snowing; and, of course, the coat was not warm enough. So, I went to a ten cent store and bought a heavy blue sweater to wear under it.

Again, I found a room for the short time we were there. Payday came for Kenneth, and he called me to meet him at the train station at midnight so that he could give me some money, as they would be leaving by train for Pyote, Texas, very shortly. I tucked the $200.00 in my bosom and caught a city bus that came within two blocks of my house. I ran those two blocks as I was afraid of being robbed. Surely, God watched over the wives while we were bumming around alone. We couldn't do that these days.

I caught a train the next day, a Thursday, and rode until after midnight on Sunday, sitting up all the way to Pyote. My ankles were so swollen they were hanging over my shoe tops. As we neared our destination, I struck up a conversation with an officer who was going to Pyote, also. I told him my husband was supposed to meet me at the depot. He said there would be someone meeting him; and if Kenneth was not there I could ride to the airbase with them. When the train stopped, there wasn't a light to be seen, nor a husband. So, I crawled way up into the Army truck, glad to have a ride. When we arrived at the airbase, we stopped at the gate; and the guard on duty called Kenneth. He was sound asleep, but he soon came to meet me. We got out on the highway and flagged a Greyhound bus at 2:00 A.M., which took us to Pecos, 20 miles away, where we had a room reserved at the Brandon Hotel.

It was at Pyote that the crews were formed and went on training flights together. Too soon for us all, we left on the train for Herrington, Kansas, where we spent our last night with our husbands before they left for England the next day. I cried so hard that night that Kenneth said, "if you'll stop crying, I'll turn a somersault for you." What a sight that was seeing my 6'3" husband doing just that. I'm sure every room in that hotel had a crying woman in them.

At Herrington, Kansas, just before leaving for overseas duty

And so, my navigator left the next day to join the 8th Air Force. He was in the 457th Bomb Group, based at Glatton, near Peterborough. From there he flew thirty missions over Germany and occupied Europe.

While Kenneth was gone, I worked as Price Clerk in the Office of Price Administration (OPA) in Grenada. It was my duty to check stores to see if they were complying with the price regulations.

Grenada County Price Clerk, far right.

To be able to live in Tillatoba with my sister, Frances Frizsell, I needed a car. I bought a 1939 Dodge with recapped tires for $650.00. On those fifteen mile drives each day I sang those beautiful songs of the forties, many times with tears trickling down my cheeks.

Every night I wrote to my B-17 navigator and prayed that God would protect him while he was flying his missions and bring him home safely to me. When the newspaper headlines would report hundreds of B-17s shot down over Germany, and I didn't get a letter from him for a week, I became very anxious. The next day seven letters would come. I lined them up and read them in the order they were written.

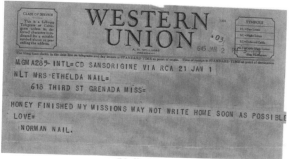

'Nuff said!

On January 21, 1945, I received a telegram from him saying he had finished his missions and would be home as soon as possible. After he came home we were in Miami Beach for two wonderful weeks. Then he was sent to Ellington Field, near Houston, Texas. From my upstairs room I heard little children out on the lawn saying our wartime President, Franklin D. Roosevelt, had died. This was April 12, 1945.

From Houston we went to Memphis, Tennessee, where Kenneth was assigned to the Air Transport Command. He was discharged from active duty October 10, 1945.

My war ended when my husband came home from England.

"ALL THE KIN GATHERED TO WELCOME ME HOME"

By Bettye Duke Jackson

A. T. Bunch left his hometown of Oxford on October 22, 1942, and reported to Camp Shelby in Hattiesburg, where he was inducted into the United States Army. There were 72 boys from Lafayette County who left in two buses for Camp Shelby that day.

A. T. received his basic training in St. Petersburg, Florida. He remembers being quartered in room 610 in a very "swank hotel" for approximately six weeks. Then off to Sheppard Field, Texas where those whose names began with the letters between A - L went to the Air force. A. T. was sent to California where he was assigned to a B-25 factory. From California, he was sent to Rapid City, South Dakota where he trained and was assigned to a B-17. A.T. went overseas in January, 1944 and was stationed at Glatton, in England.

My crew. Standing, left center, myself. On the right my bombardier, co-pilot, pilot.

Assigned as a bombardier/gunner with the 457th Bomb Group, S/Sgt. A.T. Bunch was shot down on his 13th mission. The date was April 9, 1944. He had been hit in the left thigh by shrapnel. All of the crew got out of the plane, but no one landed near A.T. He was unable to walk because of his wound; but he made his way to a nearby road and waited for the Germans to find him.

Germans came along in an old Jeep, picked up A.T. and took him to a hospital. After surgery was performed on his leg, A.T. was transported to jail. The next morning, he was taken in a buggy to a depot and moved by train to near Frankfort to be assigned to a P.O.W. camp. A.T. remembers that the train had civilians on it, and they were "not too friendly." His guard told his two companions, Andy Kauffman and Jon Roberts and him to ignore the civilians. The guards administered first aid to A.T.'s wound while he was on the train.

A.T. was assigned to Stalag 17-B where he met another Oxford 8th AF airman, Leenard Ragland. (Leenard passed away in August, 1997.) He stayed in a make-shift hospital until late July because his wound just would not heal. Finally, after using self-transfusion, his wound healed.

For the next 13 months, the prisoners passed the time playing bridge. When there was an air raid, they all ran inside, but the camp was never hit.

Around the first of April, the Germans moved soldiers overland to make the march from Krems, Austria, to Brueno, which was 278 long suffering miles. Farmers along the way felt the sting. Each soldier would take a few potatoes and demolish their planting potatoes. They caught live chickens, raided pantries or whatever it took to survive. They had to sleep on the ground during the march.

When liberated (May 3, 1945), they slept in a big factory until planes came in and flew them to La Havre, France (Camp Lucky Strike). After about 25 days, transportation arrived to take them back to the States. From New York, A.T. traveled by train to Camp Shelby - the circle was complete.

"Home at last, and all the kin gathered to welcome me home."

THOUGHTS OF ENGLAND
1943 - 1945

By James Barron Caulfield

ON GUARD

While on guard duty
At a heavy USA bomber base in England
I could feel security in the vast fact of American
power.
As I looked at the countryside from the dispersal
area,
I found peace and security from the fields,
homes, oaks
That had been "the same" for times far past
through stormy days and ordinary days,
With the close of the daylight hours, I would
become a part of this intense secure darkness.

SHIPDHAM CHURCH

As old as the Tudors, with lofty tower
This ancient church on sacred ground
Stares at us with pride and power.
Unselfish loneliness is not found;
It breathes a spirit of its day
When people were eager to stop and pray.

181

SOMETHING BORROWED, SOMETHING BLUE

By Craig Harris

The 12 flak holes that 42-97190, an aircraft of the 748th Bomb Squadron of the 457th Bomb Group, sustained at Munich on February 25, 1945 seemed only light damage, especially compared with other aircraft in the squadron. However, that was sufficient to ground the aircraft for repairs. So, we, the crew of Lt. M.K. Burk, having flown only two missions in 190, that very fine aircraft in which we were to fly seventeen more, were sent over to the 749th Squadron to borrow an airplane for the mission to Berlin on this day, February 26, 1945.

We found our bird for the day, 44-6518, call letter R, innocently piled aboard, and cranked up for the trip to Berlin. It wasn't long, on the climbout, to be precise, that the crew's education into the real world took a quantum leap. We learned first hand that when a crew goes to another squadron to borrow an aircraft, that crew does not get the best one the squadron has. *Au contraire,* that crew is most likely to get the **worst** one the squadron has. The aircraft 44-6518, a Douglas-built B-17G, block 55, was arguably the worst B-17G we ever flew, but we joined up with the Group and headed for Berlin. The R stood for "Raunchy," we said later.

The manner in which the aircraft flew reminded us of a boat trying to make headway with a sea anchor out, or a big truck with several flat tires; it just felt heavy and slow. Its tendency to guzzle fuel was made worse by all the on-course maneuvering the Group found necessary to stay in the bomber stream. We were still 150 miles from the target, inbound, when I, the co-pilot, checked the fuel status and calculated that we had a very high probability of running out of fuel on the way home.

We stayed in formation for the bomb run and for the flight home until it was clear that, at that altitude with 105 knot headwinds, we would exhaust our fuel long before we reached England.

At a position south of Hamburg and SE of Bremen, we dropped out of formation and slowed down to reduce fuel consumption.

No fighter opposition had been noted that day, but with none of our fighters in sight, we felt quite lonely. We let down to about 19,000 feet in the hope of finding diminished head winds and began to make better headway. However, it seemed to us that we hovered for a very long time over the Dummer Lake region, a known hotbed of German fighter bases (Diepholz, Vechta, Vorden, Hesepe, and Hopsten-Achmer), and were very fearful of fighters coming up to attack a lone straggler. None appeared, however; and we gradually departed the region letting down to 17,500 feet. It did occur to us that - unseen by us - there might be some Allied fighters above us using us for bait; but that did not make us feel any better. The airplane was something borrowed, and we were something blue.

After crossing the Zuider Zee, and over the North Sea, we began to let down and to throw overboard anything that we could - guns, ammunition, flak armor, anything that was not essential to our flight home. The ball turret was not jettisoned, because of the real possibility we would have to ditch the aircraft in the North Sea. Fred McDuffie, the AEG, and the co-pilot tried to keep the dwindling fuel balanced among the tanks to keep all engines running, but that was not easy.

Finally, the coast of England came into view; and for the first time in a while, we began to believe we would make it. We circled Halesworth, a former 489th Bomb Group, 2nd Division base, then operated by the 5th ERS Group, calling on 6440 kilocycles, "Hello, Darky!" according to our emergency instructions, but to no avail. After one circle, we said, "To hell with this, we're coming in." At last, "Darky" answered, "Do you have wounded aboard?" We responded, "No, but we don't have any fuel, either!"

The No. 2 engine died on final approach, and No. 3 died before we could taxi in, but we had managed to keep enough fuel in the outboard engine tanks to taxi into the flight line. A refueler stuck his stick into the No. 3 tank and asked the co-pilot, still in his seat, "Lieutenant, what were you flying on? There's no gas in this tank at all!" There were a few gallons of fuel in the outboard engines' tanks, enough, actually, for some more flying.

Base personnel refueled our aircraft. They fed us a good meal, and we returned to the home of the 457th Bomb Group at Glatton that same evening. We were thankful for our good fortune in reaching the English coast, even though it turned out not to be as close a call as we had feared at one time. We also were very firmly resolved that if 44-6518, R for Raunchy, were ever again offered to us, we would find some way to decline the honor and find another aircraft. We had by then a very dim view of borrowing airplanes.

Mission board at Glatton.

Glatton Contrails

The aircraft in the foreground of the above photograph was a B-17G - 55 - DL, (Block 55, Douglas, 44-6518, belonging to the 749th Squadron (call letter R), 457th Bomb Group, Station 130, Glatton. It was in my humble opinion, the worst excuse for a B-17 that ever flew. 457th BG records show that it was salvaged on May 13, 1945, not a moment too soon, for this person. Craig *Harris*

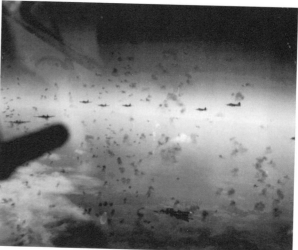

September, 1944 Flak

TWO LANDINGS OF NOTE

By N. Kenneth Nail

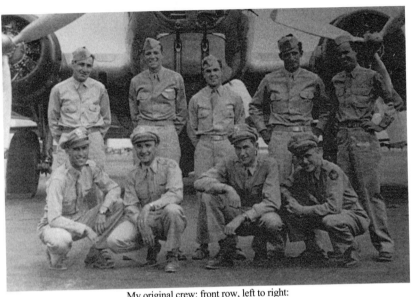

My original crew: front row, left to right:
Gamboa, Rossner, Nail, Braverman,
back row: Zocks, Black, Elliot, Bennett, Westhoff

My crew, along with several other crews who wound up in the 457th Bomb Group, 748th Squadron, didn't get to ferry a plane to England, but took two weeks to go by ship in a convoy. None of us came close to getting seasick, but we did lose our appetites with very little exercise on board the *Dominican Monarch* and with three meals per day of British cooking. We couldn't believe, nor could we stomach, a fish course served at all three meals!

When we got to our base, Glatton, near Peterborough, in August, 1944, we still had some training to do. We had to be oriented to the English landscape, we had to get introduced to navigational aids such as the "Gee" box, and the pilots had to get in some formation flying. We all had to be introduced to assembling with the Group after taking off in what was often very poor weather.

I don't remember being at all afraid of flying in combat beforehand. I think we all rather looked forward to it. Crazy boys! If we had been a few

years older, we probably would have had at least enough sense to be scared.

For this reason, we were somewhat surprised when Gamboa came in from flying a combat mission. He was our first pilot; and, as was customary, Gamboa flew one mission as co-pilot before he was to introduce his crew to combat. We weren't so much worried about him that day as we were curious. We were eager to hear from him, from one we knew and could trust; we wanted to hear his first-hand account of what it was like. We wanted to hear how exhilarating it was, how thrilling, how satisfying to get "into the action." We talked about it all day, those of us who were left behind, and we made it down to the flight line when the crews were coming in to meet him and find out, at last, all about it.

As I said, we were surprised; this wasn't the jolly Gamboa who was joking with us the day before. When he got out of the plane, he wasn't laughing or making jokes; he looked harrowed, he looked tired, he looked like a man who's been through a sausage-grinder. To our questions, "How was it?", "Did you see any fighters?", "How was the flak?", he didn't even answer us; he just sort of grimaced.

But, the next day we all went. The target was Munich: a long way to go, heavy flak expected at the target, almost sure to see some ME-109s or FW-190s, going in and coming out. We didn't talk much about it, but I'm sure we all were thinking about Cisco's demeanor when he came in the afternoon before.

Assembly was rather routine. We climbed to altitude as we crossed the Channel, all the guns were test-fired, the pins were removed from the bombs, thus arming them for their later drop. Everything we did, all our procedures, clicked along normally for all of us as we kept a good, tight formation, moving across the coast and into Belgium.

Then, one of our engines started acting up; it had to be shut down, the prop feathered. A B-17 will fly pretty well on three engines out of four; but with a full load of fuel and a full load of bombs, it couldn't fly well enough that day to keep up with the formation. We had to turn back. We wondered whether we would get credit for a mission when we had only gone as far as Belgium and hadn't delivered our bomb load to the target in Munich. The pilot, Gamboa, asked over the intercom if anyone had seen any flak. He said that he believed if we encountered flak we'd get credit for a mission. About that time, we not only saw some flak, but felt it as well, though we had no particular damage to our plane or ourselves. Everyone reported flak. We did get credit for the mission.

The mission was not over yet, not over by any means. As we crossed the Channel, we could have salvoed the bombs; that was the usual procedure on aborted missions like this one. However, I heard the two pilots discussing the fact that "we owe it to the Group to take the bombs back, at least, since we didn't get them dropped on the target." How's that for being conscientious? Of course, we only had a load of incendiaries, which could go off prematurely or with the slightest mishap, but we took them back to Glatton.

By the time we were in mid-Channel we didn't have to start letting down. About then we lost another engine and began to lose altitude pretty rapidly, anyway. When we got about halfway from the coast of England to our base, our bombardier suddenly realized he had forgotten to put the pins back in the bombs. Without pins being replaced, the incendiary bombs were really a danger.

Needless to say, old Milt, the bombardier, went to the bomb bay at once and, feverishly, began to put the pins back in the bombs. The trouble was, there was practically no time. Gamboa announced that we were losing altitude so fast, we would do well to make it to the field; we wouldn't have time to circle the field but would have to go straight in. As Milt was still in the bomb bay with only about half the pins replaced, we had to land!

I don't know how high Gamboa would have had to bounce our dear old B-17 to make those incendiaries explode - perhaps a foot, maybe only six inches. He didn't. I've never seen, I've never experienced, I've never heard of a smoother landing. Gamboa was a mighty good pilot, but I seriously doubt that he had ever made a better landing or ever did thereafter - just like setting it down on velvet. And, we all survived to start on the remaining 34 missions.

After I had flown with my crew for 13 missions, I was taken off the crew to fly as a "lead navigator." Among other things, this meant that I was to fly with a different crew just about every mission. Sometimes I hardly knew the personnel I was flying with. Gone was the togetherness of a crew, the camaraderie of ten men who had trained together and flown into combat a number of times together. (What I was offered, was a limit of 30 missions in my tour rather than 35.) Certain crews were considered better than average at their job of hauling bombs to

Germany and dropping them. These were the lead crews; they alternated on flying lead in the Squadron or the Group. Whoever the lead crew was, if it was my turn to do so, I served as their navigator.

Just before Christmas of 1944, I had almost completed flying my required 30 missions. The weather had been so bad that even on days when we could take off from Glatton, we never knew whether the field would be open when we returned. We would be diverted to a field in some other part of England. We had been for a week down in Cornwall, near Lands End, because we could not get in at Glatton. Then, when we finally got home, we flew another mission but couldn't get in to our base when we returned and were diverted to a base over near the Channel.

Christmas Eve found us at that East Anglia base. The weather turned out to be good, and General Doolittle put up his record of over 2,000 heavy bombers and over 1,000 fighters on a mission to Germany. Our lead crew, even though we were on a strange base, was ordered to fly with the Group stationed there. The weather was pretty good over the target, but when we got back to England and tried to get home to Glatton, the weather was closed in and we were sent to a fighter base down near Bury St. Edmunds.

By the time we got to Bury, the weather was closing in fast. The pilots could see patches of runway (a metal mat, really); they thought they could perhaps get the plane in, but they had to hurry. With swirling fog around them, seeing the landing strip, then not seeing it, they did get down. But, both pilots fought the controls all the way down.

Both pilots were concentrating so hard on seeing the landing strip, they were fighting the controls so fiercely, they both forgot something - something pretty important. They forgot to put

the wheels down. They landed our brand-new B-17, a B-17 especially equipped with a "Mickey Set" (a radar set used for navigation and bombing), on a metal landing strip, with wheels up.

The bombardier and I had both flown a lot of missions before this one. Early on, we used to go to the radio room and sit with our backs to the bulkhead for landings. Now we were much too sophisticated, too long on the job for such foolishness; that was far too much trouble. We were in the nose, surrounded by Plexiglas, for the landing.

When the belly of the plane hit the metal mat, the props tried to keep on turning, but they couldn't because they hit the mat. The props must have gone through a few turns, though, for a terrible clanking and banging was taking place just outside all that Plexiglas for an eternity. I don't know - I've always wondered - why the gas tanks on that B-17 didn't explode with all the sparks that were flying from props hitting the metal mat. We may have been practically out of gas (we had been flying around up there trying to find a place to land for quite a while), but it probably wouldn't have taken much gas to explode fairly violently. I think the reason we didn't blow up was because we were going so fast down that metal mat runway we outran the sparks.

Whatever! It was Christmas Eve in MERRY OLD ENGLAND! We were on the ground, the plane was a ruin, but none of the crew was hurt, just scared absolutely to death.

I flew 30 combat missions. Thus, I came back to England from those missions 30 times and landed. Twenty-eight were not memorable; I don't remember a single one of them, though I'm sure I was always mighty glad to be back home. But I do remember two landings: the one on our first mission and the one on Christmas Eve of 1944.

HOME BY THE GRACE OF GOD

By Webb Pruitt Lee

Webb Pruitt Lee was born in Oklahoma but grew up in Winston County where he still lives with his wife Lucille. Pruitt was awarded the Distinguished Flying Cross, the Air Medal with 3 Oak Leaf Clusters, and the Purple Heart. The following story is based on an interview with The Winston County Journal, *and has been personalized by converting it to first person. It is used here with specific permission by* The Winston County Journal.

I was called to service in August, 1942. I would normally have been sent down to Camp Shelby for induction, but my father's cousin was head of the Draft Board of Mississippi, and he saw that I went to the Air Corps instead. I already had my private pilot's license, which made pilot training a natural for me.

Pruitt Lee, third from left, in primary flight school, with Stearman

When I was in primary flight training, I got a telegram from Dr. Pearson back home in Louisville saying Lucille was seriously ill, and I should come home right away. I knew that the chances of getting leave during training were extremely limited, even in the case of a death in the family. I went to my commanding officer and told him I was leaving, and they would just have to shoot me as I jumped the fence. I really didn't know how serious my wife's condition was. Finally, he told me I could have a three-day pass but to report to him on my return. When I got home, I found the "serious condition" involved the normal and healthy birth of my first child. Dr. Pearson had fudged the

telegram just to make sure I would be allowed to come home. When I got back to base, my punishment caused a delay in my completion of training. Then I got the measles, followed by pneumonia. All this kept me from leaving with my group. Instead, I had to go later with a bunch of Yankees!

A newly graduated Second Lieutenant, with pilot's wings

After graduation as a pilot, I went to Alexandria, Louisiana for crew training. On one of our flights from there, I learned that our flight path would be directly over Louisville. I called the folks to tell them I would be flying over the area. We got down real low, and I could see my Mother down below waving a towel at me. There were some other people down in the field, as well, including a farmer with his mules. I was really roaring the engines letting Mother know I was there. Then I saw those mules taking off with the wagon. I've always wondered if they ever caught the mules.

Scaring some Mississippi mules with a
brand-new B-17, Flying Fortress

When we left for England, I didn't know that Lucille was carrying our second child.

On D-Day, June 6, 1944, I was the co-pilot on two bombing missions over the English Channel; one in the morning and one at evening. When we flew over the Channel, there were so many ships down there it looked like you could walk across on them.

On a pass in London, I was staying at the Piccadilly Hotel when one of Hitler's buzz bombs (a V-1, robot plane) came over. I happened to hear it; and when the engine shut off I dived under the bed. The hotel was severely damaged. My crew looked everywhere for me. They thought I was in the morgue or hospital because they found my jacket, my cap and a little old handbag I had with me. When I realized I was alive, I went to the underground to try to get to the train station and get a train back to our base. There were so many people evacuating London, they wouldn't let me on the train. I got some GIs to pull me through the window and onto the train. My crew sure were surprised to find me back at our base.

When we first got to England and I began my service as co-pilot on a B-17, Flying Fortress, we were told that after 25 missions we could come home. You've never seen such an eager bunch of men to get missions. We would have flown 25 missions in 25 days, if they had let us, and would have been home before you knew it.

But, on our first mission, three planes and their complete crews were shot out of the sky; and we soon realized this wouldn't be as easy as we had anticipated. Soon the required number of missions was raised to 30 and then to 35 before we were allowed to go home.

Our plane that we used for most of our missions was "Raggedy Ann," a B-17F. We flew 14 missions in her. After that we moved to our own new plane, a B-17 G model, called "Badger Beauty." It was on this plane's 15th mission that our crash occurred.

We had successfully completed a bomb run over Munster, in Germany, and were on our way home. However, we had been hit over the target. We had three engines gone, and the crew was throwing out everything they could. Our waist-gunner was hit by shrapnel. He was only 16, because he had lied to get into the service. We should have bailed out, but he was unconscious; and we didn't want to leave him. Six of our crew were wounded, three were not (we had only a nine man crew, as our navigator had bailed out on an earlier mission when our plane was on fire). We decided to ride it down.

We got on the radio and started asking for a fighter escort, or "Little Friend," to escort us as we tried to make it back to friendly territory. Soon a P-51 fighter plane could be seen on our wing. The plane was called "Cherokee Kid."

He stayed with us for a long time, talking to us on the radio, until his fuel started running low. Then he said he was going to have to leave. I asked him to stay with us just a little while longer. He said, "No, I have got to go. I'm not going to have enough fuel to make it back now as it is. I've got to go." We told him good-bye; and as he started to pull up, he got a direct hit. All we saw was a puff of smoke, and he was gone. You can't imagine how all our crew felt!

The plane was losing several hundred feet of altitude a minute as we struggled to make it back into friendly territory. The Germans were shooting at us the whole time. And then it got quiet all at once. It was a little hazy outside, but we could see the ground about 1,000 feet below us. We could see American insignia on the jeeps below, and then we saw the Red Cross tent. We knew we had made it back, but we had passed the runway, and we knew we would just have to ride it down.

The flight engineer, who had been checking the plane over to see what damage had been done by enemy fire, reported the landing gear had been hit, was locked one-quarter of the way down and could neither be raised nor lowered. Also, the mechanism operating the flaps had been shot off.

The plane first hit the trees, then a water tower, then a brick building, and broke into three pieces. The tail section had a hole ripped through it big enough for three people to pass through easily.

Examining the remains of B-17 crash
of October 5, 1944

The gun turret crashed in on me and mashed me. When we finally stopped, the plane was popping and blowing. I knew I had to get out; I was bleeding like a stuck hog. I did manage to get out before I lost consciousness. I was taken to a front-line hospital where I was diagnosed with severe concussion and internal injuries.

Back home in Louisville, it was several days before Lucille learned anything about me, and even then she was only told that I was missing in action. She was pregnant, and she worried about what she would do if something happened to me. It was over a week before she got a letter saying I was safe and was in a hospital. It was another six weeks before I was able to make it back to the States, just in time for the birth of our second child.

Lucille deserves a lot of the credit for my coming home safely. She gets the credit, because she was on her knees every night praying to the good Lord to take care of me and bring me home. I am also grateful to the members of my church who prayed endlessly while I was away.

The Webb Pruitt Lee crew

THE JOURNEY

By Joan Wilson

This is the story of one English war bride's first solo journey. From war time England to Miami Beach was a vast leap, both in mileage and in culture. In retrospect, it is hard for me to believe that I actually undertook such a journey. There I was, a very young, only daughter of a middle class English family who had always been sheltered and protected and who had never been far away from home in her life. I had married my husband, Carl Wilson, in April of 1944. Carl was a Bombardier in the Eighth Air Force and upon completion of 35 missions had returned to the States in December, 1944.

On 12 February, 1945, I received my embarkation notice from Cooks Travel Agency in London, to my great excitement. After a few hectic days getting my passport and saying goodbye to my co-workers and others, my journey actually began on 16 February. My parents and my much loved Aunt Kay traveled with me by train to Swansea, in Wales, which was my port of embarkation. We traveled overnight in a crowded train, finally arriving in Swansea at the devitalizing hour of 4:30 A.M., and managed to find a hotel open so we could have some breakfast. We made our way to the shipping office and were told that we would have to make our farewells then and there as I would have to take a bus out to the ship and visitors were not allowed beyond a certain point. Saying goodbye to the three most important people in my life was horrendous and I have never been able to get that scene out of my mind. However, with the resilience of youth, once we were all seated on the bus, my spirit of adventure took over and I was able to choke back the tears and look ahead.

The name of our ship was the *Jamaica Producer*, and she was a British Merchant Navy vessel. Since the War was still going on we had to travel in convoy, at the speed of the slowest ship. I have always had the sneaking suspicion that ours was the slowest ship! There seemed to be an incredible amount of formalities and paperwork to be taken care of and an astonishing number of rules and regulations to be followed. Among other things, we were told that everywhere we went we must carry our gas masks, our purse and our brief case containing all our important papers. Fortunately, we had been pre-warned about the Important Paper ruling so most of us had some type of brief case with us. All of this, we were to discover, made taking a stroll on deck less of a joy than it should have been. Eventually we were assigned our cabins and got settled in. I remember there was music coming from some central location and the operatic aria, "Oh My Beloved Father," was one of the selections. This had long been one of my favorites and a huge wave of homesickness threatened to overwhelm me. I shared a cabin with two older ladies (probably in their fifties) and a girl about my own age or a little older who was a physician on her way to Montreal to join her husband. Her name was Marjorie Williams. Presumably, we were categorized along alphabetical lines!

We were at sea for exactly two weeks and had wonderful weather for that time of the year. It was warm and sunny, especially in sheltered parts of the deck and I was on deck as often as possible. I absolutely loved being at sea and thoroughly enjoyed the fresh air, the movement of the ship and just watching the horizon. We had one really bad night when we ran into a gale of hurricane force. We were all told to go to our cabins and on no account to venture out. My doctor friend prescribed a hefty sleeping pill for both of us and we slept soundly the whole night through. It was not until the next morning, when we once again ventured up on deck, that we realized what a severe storm we had weathered. One life boat had completely disappeared and another had been damaged and signs of the chaos were still apparent. All the members of the crew looked worn out and it became obvious, especially after talking to some of them, that we had come through a very bad storm, indeed.

We arrived in Halifax, Canada on Sunday 4th March, and were taken by bus to the railroad station and had our luggage bonded. We also booked sleepers on the evening train and were told we could send cables to our families. Unfortunately, my cable to Carl was so heavily censored that the only fact he was able to derive from it was that I had landed and the date. Marjorie and I and an American girl from New York, who had married an Englishman had formed a shipboard friendship. We stuck together through all the debarkation formalities and our first trip to the railway station. Three of the ship's officers asked us if we would like to make a tour of Halifax and then have dinner and we gladly accepted their suggestion. The walking tour of Halifax was fun. There was still a lot of snow around and the air was delightfully cold and crisp. Later they took us to the Nova Scotia Hotel for dinner. We all thought the food was wonderful. There seemed to be a bewildering array of little individual dishes given to each diner; but we watched our American friend and followed her lead! Our friends saw us safely to the train which was to leave at 7:30 PM and everyone got very sentimental and hugged everyone else. These men seemed to be our last link with England and the life we had known. They had done all they could for us and we all felt, after bidding them goodbye, that we were really on our own.

The train journey through Canada was exciting. We spent some time on the observation car looking at miles of snow and pine forests. We talked and exchanged addresses and I wrote, or rather finished, a letter to my family and at one station where there was a delay managed to get it into the mail. Marjorie left us there to continue on to Montreal.

We arrived in New York's Grand Central Station on the 6th March, where I discovered that my luggage was still somewhere en route from Canada. I had fully expected to be met by my husband and hopefully had him paged to no avail. There seemed to be a great many people meeting my fellow passengers. I just stood around for a while feeling lost: a bearded gentleman in a weird black hat said, "Are you one of our people?" and reached for my suitcase. I assured him that I didn't think I was one of his people and decided I had better do something! I remember my Mother saying, "Now if Carl isn't in New York, you had better go on down to Mississippi and to his Mother; she should know where her son is!" I ventured outside the station and hailed a Yellow Cab, feeling very much the world traveler, and asked to be taken to Cooks Travel Agency. The people there were very helpful and before too long I had acquired a ticket on a train to Monticello, Mississippi. Back I went to Grand Central Station and soon I was on another phase of my journey and heading for St. Louis. It was all quite exciting, and I had a little room all to myself, because it would be an overnight trip. I accidentally turned up the heat and almost roasted myself into a stupor. One of the porters came to my rescue and, upon hearing that I had arrived from England, was kindness itself and did all he could to help.

I arrived in St. Louis at 8:30 AM where I had to change to the GM&O Line. I was told to catch a bus to another station where I would board the Rebel which left at 12:30 PM. I innocently caused what could have been an INCIDENT. Remember, this was in the forties and segregation was in full force. I climbed aboard and sat myself down in the "Colored Section." I noticed there seemed to be a lot of black people about but thought that was the way things were in this strange land. I also noticed they seemed fascinated by me, but I still didn't know what was wrong. After a little while a conductor came by and suggested that I might be more comfortable if I followed him to a different area of the train. Once settled down again, the conductor, after hearing that I had just arrived from England, took me under his wing and asked questions about the War and my country whenever he had a spare moment. Somewhere along the way he got off the train, at his home town I presumed, and waved me a fond farewell as the train steamed off.

Finally, I reached Monticello early in the morning of 8th March, and once again there was no sign of anyone to meet me. My Mother had jokingly said, "When you get to Monticello, they will probably have a brass band there to welcome you." Not so. I have never felt so desolate as I did when the Rebel steamed away, leaving me and my luggage on the platform. After a few moments a gentleman in a uniform came up to me and asked if he could be of help. He told me he was Mr. Poole the Station Master. After he heard my accent he said, "I bet I know who you are; you must be Carl Wilson's wife from England. We knew you were coming but we all thought you were coming in to Jackson." Then he added that he thought that was where Mizz Bessie and Mary were. I felt that I would lose what little composure I had left if this kept up; but, fortunately, Mr. Poole said he would take me out to the house and see what was going on.

It was quite a moment. Very obviously, I was completely unexpected and my mother-in-law, Mizz Bessie, according to Mr. Poole, kept making little remarks like, "I declare, Honey, we thought Doris had met you in Jackson." My pretty sister-in-law had evidently just woken up and was sitting around looking puzzled in her bath robe. I had apparently gone through a different railroad station in Jackson from the one where Doris, my other sister-in-law had gone! I also met my father-in-law, who had just returned from a fishing trip and was cradling an enormous black fish in his arms. After a little while I was taken to a neighbor's house to use the telephone and, at long last, made contact with Carl. He seemed astonished to know where I was and said that he had a plane standing by to meet me in New York. I told him it was a bit late for that and asked why he couldn't just come up to Monticello and pick me up. I then had to fight my way mentally through a torrent of information about leave time, orders and distance. The upshot of which was that I agreed to go down to Miami via Biloxi and other points South. All of which sounded incomprehensible to me, but

Mary said she would go on the bus with me part of the way and make sure I got on the right bus for Florida. After a meal of freshly caught, fried fish, naturally, plus an interview with an excited little lady from the local newspaper, Mary and I boarded a bus that afternoon for Biloxi. I had arrived in Canada in a tweed suit plus a top coat and fur lined boots. Mississippi in March was to me like a Summer's day in England. I left my top coat and boots behind and, to the best of my knowledge, never saw them again. My husband's brother, Bob, met us in Biloxi and drove us to his home in Pascagoula, where we were to spend the night. I met his wife, Ruby, and his two year old son who was still up and full of life at 9:00 PM, which I thought was unusual. Children went to bed earlier at home. I seemed destined to make unpopular observations. I couldn't understand why the windows of the house seemed so dark and dirty. When I remarked on this to Mary when we were getting ready for bed, she looked at me oddly and said, "Oh, you must be talking about the screens." We didn't have window screens in England and, as I drifted off to sleep, I made a mental note to learn to keep my comments to myself or ask Carl at a later date!

I remember all during that long trip how warm the weather seemed to me. It had been a cold winter when we left England, and here I was magically transported into a warm Spring. I had even seen daffodils blooming in Monticello. It was like being on another planet. I seemed to lave nothing but winter clothes and wondered how things would be as I went further south.

The following morning, accompanied by my two new sisters-in-law, we set out in, what seemed to me like a fantastic car, for Mobile and the Greyhound bus station. In those days it was quite a lengthy ride and I was so impressed by Ruby having her own car and driving it with such ease. At that time of my life, I had no idea how to drive. On the way, we passed a wayside stall selling bananas. I was absolutely astonished, as we had not seen bananas in England for many years. So my new companions stopped the car and we purchased a large brown bag of the delicious fruit. We each ate a couple on the way and then when I boarded the bus they insisted that I take them with me to eat on the journey. This proved to be a mixed blessing. As the miles rolled by, the fruit became riper and more redolent. I remember we had made several stops and, finally, feeling very guilty, I disposed of them in a trash can, thinking as I did so how much my family would have enjoyed them and here I was throwing them away. At one point we had to change buses. There seemed to be an awful lot of servicemen trying to get home and apparently they took priority.

At one point it seemed doubtful as to whether I would be able to continue my journey. However, some young man in uniform suggested that I get on the bus with him and the conductor would think we were a couple and let us both on. I thankfully agreed to this and have always been grateful for the suggestion. Most of the people I was traveling with seemed very friendly and anxious to talk. One young girl told me she was going to meet her husband's family in Florida for the first time. She seemed very nervous about the whole thing, so I told her something of my recent experience, hoping to comfort her. I have a feeling that she couldn't understand my very British accent, because she gave me a long look and then gazed out of the window.

The miles rolled on and I was busy looking at the scenery and hoping that Carl would be there to meet me if I ever arrived at Miami. As night fell through the open bus windows I could smell the wonderful odor of orange blossoms. At long last we pulled into the bus station, and as I gazed anxiously out of my window, I saw Carl standing by the wall. The next thing I knew a very tall young man was pushing his way through the bus calling out, "Joanna, Joanna." I didn't really know if he was looking for me or not, but I said, "My name is Joan, are you looking for me?" He grabbed my bag and said, "Carl is outside looking on another bus and I am trying to help him. You wouldn't believe how many buses we have looked into this evening." It was then that I realized that my long journey was finally over.

James Dennis Hudson, Col. U. S. A. F. (Retd.), lives in Columbus with his wife, Margaret. James grew up in Birmingham, Alabama, and Columbus, graduating from Leigh High School in the latter. He grew up wanting to fly, following his role model uncle who was an Air Force Colonel. After completing pilot training as an aviation cadet, he went on to England where he flew as a lead pilot in the 492nd Bomb Group at North Pickenham and the 467th BG at Rackheath. James says his roughest mission was one to Magdeburg, when his B-24 came home with over 200 flak holes; none of the crew was lost and they got home with all four fans turning. He ended his service in England as a captain, flew 31 missions and was awarded the Distinguished Flying Cross with one Oak Leaf Cluster and the Air Medal with six Oak Leaf Clusters. He remained in the Air Force after the war serving in various operations and command assignments.

THE OSCHERSLEBEN MISSION

By William H. "Bill" Johnson

Thankful to be alive, and thankful to my fellow crew members and an Almighty God, I write this in recall of what I consider to be one of the "roughest missions" flown by the U.S. Air Force in World War II; perhaps second only to the August 14, 1943, mission to Schweinfurt on which my Group (381st Bomb Group, lst Division, 8th AF) sustained the highest losses of all Groups that participated, and since called an "aerial massacre."

Bill Johnson, second from left, standing

Early on the morning of January 11, 1944, we were awakened (about 3 A.M.) to go on a mission. Of course, we did not know the target, but knew it would be a long, rough one, because at breakfast (3:30 A.M.), we had real eggs instead of powdered ones as usual. Then, at briefing at 4:00 A.M., it was revealed that the target would be Oschersleben, Germany, on aircraft and industrial plants, deep in the heart of Germany approximately fifty miles southwest of Berlin. Our bomb load was ten 500 pound demolition bombs. Each of the other planes in our group had a similar bomb load. We assembled without incident. The weather forecast was for scattered clouds in the target area. We flew in formation as usual. The 1st Division of the 8th Air Force consisted of bombers from the 381st Bomb Group and the 91st Bomb Group. Our two

groups were to lead all other groups into the target area that day. As we flew across the English Channel and over France on the way to Germany, we began to notice increased cloud cover. As we crossed the border into Germany, there was almost solid cloud cover, making it difficult to see the ground, to find the target, and make a visual bomb run. In fact, although there is still some controversy about it, we were later informed that Bomber Command in England had called for the Second and Third Divisions to turn back to bases in England. At any rate, we proceeded to the target area and were able to spot the target through broken clouds. We had no fighter protection from our own aircraft, and began to have serious fighter attacks from the German Air Armada soon after entering Germany. Also German flak was extremely heavy. My Squadron (533rd Bomb Squadron - 381st Group) had nine aircraft flying that day in our regular group and in a composite group made up of our planes and planes from the 91st Bomb Group. In my Bombardier's compartment in the nose of my plane, I had twin 50 caliber machine guns and 1150 rounds of ammunition. German fighters were everywhere, coming right through the middle of our formation, some coming so close you could see the whites of the pilots eyes. B-17s were on fire and falling all around together with a large number of German fighters that our groups shot down. We could see numerous parachutes floating toward the earth, but also a number of our planes were on fire and some exploded before the crew could bail out. Of the nine planes of the 533rd Squadron, six were shot down from our main group and two from the composite group. Eighty airmen from one squadron were either killed or made prisoners of war after capture on the ground.

A number of my close friends were killed on that one mission. I shot every round of my ammunition

194

before we were able to get out of Germany. My squadron was the hardest hit of the two groups; out of 12 planes in the two groups, the 533rd lost 8. According to official reports our B-17 aircraft shot down 39 German fighters in the Luftwaffe going to, from, and over the target area. Incidentally, our bombs did destroy the target that day. Official reports show that other German targets hit that day were Halberstadt and Brunswick, and they accounted for a total loss of 60 B-17 bombers (600 combat crewmen). This came soon after the Schweinfurt raid of October 14, 1943, in which my group had the highest losses of all groups. Many died, and some were P.O.W.s. Those who died did so for the sake of freedom just as men have always done and will continue to do when liberty is threatened.

The Oschersleben mission was just one of many close calls for this writer, who went on to finish his 25 missions plus one (26 total), completed on May 30, 1944, one week before the Normandy invasion.

Following the Oschersleben mission, my squadron was shot up so badly, I was made the Squadron Bombardier and my navigator, John Bruning of Ohio, was made the Squadron Navigator. We were given a new crew and a new plane (Rotherhite's Revenge).

Lt. Bill Johnson, bombardier

District Attorney, William H. Johnson, Jr.

POLEBROOK, THE 351ST AND A MOVIE STAR

By Major General Robert W. Burns

Let me begin by presenting my credentials as a Mississippian. I was born in the Carolina community in Itawamba County. After a few intervening moves, my father, a doctor, settled at Ecru, in Pontotoc County. I was about five years old when this occurred. I graduated from Ecru High School and from what is now the University of Southern Mississippi. I enlisted as a Flying Cadet in the Army Air Corps in February, 1939, and became a 2nd Lt., in November of 1939.

After duty in the Panama Canal Zone and Central America, my first active duty, I was returned to the States in November, 1942, and was assigned to the then forming 351st Bomb Group which was to be equipped with B-17s. The Group was activated at Geiger Field, Spokane, Washington, and I was the Air Executive Officer. In effect, I was the deputy

Robert W. Burns of the 351st Bomb Group

Group Commander. I suspect that one of the principal reasons I got this job was because I had acquired a substantial amount of time in B-17s in the Canal Zone. In fact, I think I probably had more time than anybody else in the Group.

After passing through the several training phases, we were declared fit to move on to duty with the Eighth Air Force. We arrived at Station 110, Polebrook, England, in March, 1943.

Going to England with us, and as an integral part of the 351st, was a Hollywood photographic unit headed by Captain Clark Gable. They and all their equipment flew with us to the U.K. Gable's task was to produce a motion picture to be used in recruiting young American boys to enlist as gunners in the Air Corps. This unit finished its work at the end of 1943 and returned to the States to produce the film titled "Combat America." No doubt, you have seen it.

During his tour with the Eighth, Gable flew on five combat missions and he didn't pick them. He would simply announce that he would fly on a particular day, then he would fly wherever the target was. He flew his last mission with me to a target at Nantes, France. The oddball events that occurred on this mission is a story in itself, but that telling can occur at another time.

I was given command of the 351st in October, 1944, and retained command until March, 1945. I was relieved to make a command slot open for a senior colonel from the Pentagon who had spent the war there and needed a shot at combat before it was all over. This was my biggest disappointment of the war.

We knew the war was just about over, and I keenly looked forward to flying over Europe

196

without being shot at. Also, I had flown my own airplane to Europe, and I had dreamed the entire war of flying a plane back across the Atlantic.

As it turned out, I did fly home but as a passenger in the rear of a C-54. I was pretty indignant about this, at the time; and as a matter of fact, I still am.

I'm happy to get that off my chest.

Captain Clark Gable (left) after one of his missions with Colonel Burns.

"WE HAVE MET THE ENEMY AND THEY IS US...." *Pogo*

By Craig Harris

Sometimes combat crews in the Eighth Air Force could be caught up in crises of their own making, without any help from the enemy.

On April 14 and 15, 1945, bombers of the 8th AF were sent to a target in France, at the mouth of the Gironde Estuary which leads from the Bay of Biscay into the harbor of Bordeaux. Some German gun emplacements there had been by-passed during the occupation of France by the Allies but now were causing problems blocking the use of the Bordeaux harbor by the French Navy and interfering with needed commercial traffic. So, with targets in Germany hard to find, and with a poor weather forecast for Germany, the 8th AF decided to send over 1,100 B-17s and B-24s to Pointe de Grave across the Gironde Estuary from the town of Royan to take out the German positions.

Flak and other stuff!

At the 457th Bomb Group at Glatton the briefing for the mission to Royan brought forth smiles among the crews, for the news of a milk run was welcome indeed. The Group had lost two B-17s shot down by ME-262s at Oranienburg on April 10, and one of those lost was Lieutenant Colonel Rod Francis from Jackson, Deputy CO of the 457th. So the prospect of a mission without the threat of ME-262s was a pleasant one. B-17s of the 457th BG were among 388 that struck "....four enemy strong points and flak batteries..." in the Bordeaux area, dropping their bombs from 16,000 feet.

After the mission, however, the bombardiers, at least, were not too happy. Bombing results, despite the absence of resistance and with excellent visual conditions, were very poor. (One squadron achieved "fair" results.) The bombardiers and lead crews were strongly taken to task for their under-achievement. "You did more damage to the fish in the Bay of Biscay and the Gironde than you did to the target" was one sarcastic comment. "Tomorrow you WILL go back and you WILL destroy the target!"

So, the following day, April 15, the 8th AF was sent to targets in the same area, but with a different plan. The 457th Bomb Group was among those which, upon arrival at a point about 20 miles northeast of the target, would go into circular orbit, and be called in - in six-ship elements - to a target designated by a scout commander observing results from earlier drops. Five of the six 457th BG elements hit designated targets, with only the last element having to make a 360 degree turn to make a bomb drop.

However, for the author's crew, the same tight formation that insured that its bombs would hit near the element leader's bombs, caused a problem that required resourcefulness and a lot of luck to solve. We, in our own B-17, 42-97190, "Hitler's Milkman," were leading the lower three ships of the six-ship element, flying below and astern of the element lead. Having been admonished at briefing to "keep it tight," the co-pilot (the author), was flying the bomb run and, indeed, had it "in tight," with the nose of his aircraft almost below the tail of the lead ship. While commendable from the standpoint of "good formation," it really was not too smart, because I had forgotten that our element lead was a squadron lead before the breakout to the target, and as such was equipped with a smoke marker in its bomb load.

When bombs were dropped, 42-97190 flew through the smoke from the lead ship's smoke marker, apparently while the particles were still in combustion, for, instantly, our cockpit windscreen became solidly opaque. NO forward vision at all. I had been using the lead ship's ball turret for reference and now, suddenly denied this reference, I experienced a moment of severe insecurity. However, the cockpit's overhead panels were clear, and I was able to shift my reference to the lead-ship's tail guns, almost over my head. Despite the awkwardness of the situation, the element came off of the target intact, but with a key aircraft in the formation completely blind to the front.

After a brief cockpit conference between the co-pilot, pilot and engineer (who had been standing behind the pilots), it was decided to leave the formation. The co-pilot got the attention of the crews on each wing by a small wing-waggle, after which the pilot (on the left) and engineer (on the right) motioned the wing crews to move away and give some room. This accomplished, 42-97190 slowly let down, away from the formation, and made a wide turn to head for home.

To have an opaque cockpit windscreen is not really a desperate situation, because one lands a B-17 looking out the side windows more than the front. But the pilot and I reacted with real concern, because we had gotten used to seeing out the front, for such useful things as lining up on the runway for landing, keeping the aircraft on the runway during the rollout, etc. So, on the way home, we felt that we were compelled to find some way of clearing up that windscreen, frosted over on its outside or front, surface.

There were not a lot of solutions available. Finally, it was decided to try to scrub a hole in the frosting from the outside. The aircraft, with landing gear

down and full flaps deployed, was slowed as much as possible without stalling. This part really was easy, as 42-97190 was as beautifully rigged, easy-to-fly as any B-17 that ever flew. Mac, the engineer, had brought along some oranges to eat on the ride. I, the co-pilot, produced a pocket comb and a handkerchief. We folded the handkerchief over the comb, and saturated it with orange juice, in the naïve hope the acid juice would react with the smoke frosting. Sliding back the side window, I reached around to the front of the windscreen and scrubbed away with the comb, trying to make a hole in the frosting. (What a strange sight this would have been to any onlooker, this B-17 hanging nose-up in the air, landing gear and flaps down, with an arm reaching out around to the windscreen!) To the surprise and delight of the cockpit crew, it worked providing a viewport about the size of a coffee saucer. The pilot, now encouraged by success, reached out of his side and scrubbed free an even larger hole. We could see to the front!

Fighters at 8:00 o'clock high!

We didn't need front vision to see the RAF Typhoons that suddenly zoomed into formation with us. Apparently, during our preoccupation with the windscreen, we had wandered out of the briefed return route. Perhaps they were playing with us, but they acted downright mean and wanted identification. This led to a scrambling search for that little piece of rice paper with the flare codes on it, but the paper was found and the proper identification flares fired. After this the Typhoon pilots became quite friendly surely feeling condescending to those dumb Yanks who had gotten themselves into a bind and generously escorted us safely around London and on our way to Glatton.

It was a happy return; after our uneventful landing, we learned that the Group had redeemed itself with excellent bombing results. However, when our crew chief looked at his airplane and asked, "Lieutenant, WHAT did you do to my cockpit windscreens?" we had to tell him what had happened. He looked from one to the others, and saying nothing, sadly walked away shaking his head. We hoped he was not angry but feeling only sadness and sympathy for this dumb crew who could get themselves into a mess on a mission with no opposition by their own stupid stunts. We will never know, because he and his crew changed the windscreens overnight without comment, and they all had that same sad expression on their faces when we taxied away from the hardstand for the next day's mission.

Our navigator trying to figure out
where the heck we are!

Here we are; all ten of us!
That's me, standing, second from left

THE FATE OF "THE SPOOK" AND PHILIP CASCIO

Philip Cascio grew up in Leland, where he graduated from high school. He attended Ole Miss, and was there when Pearl Harbor was attacked. During his tour of duty, Phil was credited with two enemy planes shot down. He has been self-employed since the war, in Greenville, where he now lives with his wife, Cherry.

Phil's recollections of his fateful last mission as recounted below, were first published in the newsletter of the 303rd Bomb Group.

Philip Cascio, who lives in Greenville, saw a picture in the newsletter of the 303rd Bomb Group, in its April, 1991, issue: a crew photograph in front of an airplane named "Spook," with the cutline, "Unknown 358th Squadron combat crew." He wrote to the newsletter, "I was part of the crew. I am now home in Greenville, Mississippi. Thanks for missing us."

Philip was the ball turret gunner of that crew. He gave the following recollections of what happened to "Spook" and its crew after dropping its bombs on St. Nazaire in France, and "Spook" was attacked by 20 to 50 enemy fighters.

On returning after dropping the bombs on the target at St. Nazaire, we were nearing the English Channel. Dunnica, the pilot, called to our attention, over the intercom, that a B-17 about 15,000 feet below us was being attacked by ME-109 fighters. He asked if we wanted to go to their aid. We all agreed.

We left our formation at approximately 25,000 feet. Descending, we then circled the crippled bomber at approximately 10,000 feet. From a pack of 5 ME-109s, we accumulated 15 ME-109s in a matter of seconds!

The final long outcome - some members of the crippled bomber bailed out leaving us to face the worst that was to come. Being close to the French coast and the English Channel, we tried to make it to our home base at Molesworth, England.

We were eventually shot down and crashed twenty miles from the English coast in the English Channel. During that part of the air war, we had no fighter escort whatsoever.

On crashing in the water, our plane broke into parts. Tail gunner, Taylor, went down in the tail section. I feel he was shot and killed before we crashed. Waist gunner Dew and someone else were last seen floating in the high waves of the English Channel. I was able to get out of the ball-turret and crawl to the radio compartment. Holland was all shot up, and blood was coming from all over his flight suit. Tucker, upper-turret, and Co-pilot Pace and I escaped through the radio hatch. Of the two dinghies attached to the bomber, one did not inflate; the other did. We were lucky we grabbed the inflated one. The last I saw of the pilot, Dunnica, he was trying to get out the pilot window. He was pulled down with the front part of the plane.

The three survivors, while in the rubber dinghy, were strafed at least three times. We floated in the bitter, wet, cold, high waves of the English Channel for approximately fourteen hours. Yes, we flipped over many times; pulling each other back to the dinghy by a cord we had tied to our waists. We eventually drifted to the coast of Brest, France, in the early dark morning. We crawled to a small hut on the shore line. Being exhausted, tired and cold, we slept a short time under leaves and paper to keep warm.

Waking about six in the morning, we saw a French house in the distance. The French family gave us coffee, bread and an exchange of clothing. A splendid exchange for them. They made us leave because they were afraid of the German soldiers in the vicinity.

We were captured a few hours later and taken to the Bastille in Paris where we lost track of time in the tall, dark cells. A few days later, we were taken to Frankfurt, Germany, to an interrogation camp. A few days later we were transferred in a box car to STALAG 3B, 7A and eventually 17B. In the POW camp we met the members of the bomber that we tried to save. They were from the 306th Bomb Group.

Twenty-eight months later, the long awaited end of the war came.

Funny, isn't it; one typewritten page can cover two and one half years of prison life.

Alex A. Hogan grew up in Starkville, graduated at Mississippi State College in 1938 but was living at Jasper, Alabama, and serving as Assistant Scout Executive before he entered the Army Air Corps. He was in primary flight training when the war began with Pearl Harbor. His service in The Mighty Eighth was in the 94th Bomb Group at Bury St. Edmunds. Alex became a captain and a command pilot. He flew 14 missions before being shot down over Berlin on April 18, 1944. He then spent the rest of the war in P.O.W. camp at Sagan. During his tour of duty Alex was awarded the Distinguished Flying Cross, the Purple Heart and the Air Medal with two Oak Leaf Clusters. After a civilian career in the banking and securities business, he is now retired and is living in Jackson with his wife, Virginia. He is also retired from the Air Force with the rank of Lt. Colonel.

Bernard H. Coggins lives in Baldwyn where he grew up. He joined the Air Corps early and was a cadet at Maxwell Field when Pearl Harbor was attacked. He served as a navigator in the 60th and 315th Troop Carrier Groups. Bernard was shot down on March 24, 1945, bailed out of his crippled plane, was wounded and captured, while dropping paratroopers at the Rhine Crossing. He served as a P.O.W. at Munster for exactly six days, being liberated on April 1, 1945. After the war, he finished his college degree at Mississippi State University, taught school, coached little league baseball and served for 19 years as Mayor of Baldwyn.

A MISSION TO COLOGNE

By N. Kenneth Nail

The Great Cathedral of Cologne

The City of Cologne is crescent shaped and fits into a major bend in the Rhine. In the middle of the crescent sits the old Cathedral of Cologne.

Cologne is an ancient city. From the earliest times it has been a hub for pathways, lanes and roads to all of Northern Europe. The great Cathedral of Cologne was started in 1248 A.D. Work proceeded, with many interruptions, for over 600 years. It was finally completed as late as 1880.

There it sits, to this day, on its pedestal, majestically overlooking the great bend in the Rhine. Its twin towers rise to over 500 feet, among the tallest structures in all of Europe.

Across the street from the Cathedral is the railroad station and, behind that, stretching for quite some distance, are the marshaling yards. This has been, and still is, a major center of Germany's transportation system and of activity for Germany's industrial strength.

Because the marshaling yards in Cologne were of such importance to Germany's industrial production (war production during World War II) the Eighth Air Force made a number of missions to knock them out. Every time we hit the rail yards, crews moved in immediately to repair them and get them operable again. Thus, these missions had to be repeated over and over.

Like other targets which *The Mighty Eighth* hit several times, the flak kept getting worse and worse. Those crews operating the 88s were well trained and had a lot of practice before the war was over! As the Nazi armies pulled back out of occupied Europe into their homeland, they didn't leave their antiaircraft guns behind nor their highly skilled gunners. They brought them back to protect the vital targets in Germany. Cologne was no exception; it was considered a rough target right up until the end of the war.

On October 15, 1944, the 457th Bomb Group led a task force to hit the marshaling yards at Cologne. My Squadron, the 748th, was in the lead position in the Group that day; and I, as a newly promoted lead navigator, was flying in the lead ship as the DR or second navigator with our Squadron Navigator, Roland Byers. The other occupant of the nose that day was the Squadron Bombardier, Irwin Rosen.

From the time we left our base, Glatton, that morning, the skies were heavily overcast. We rode above that cloud deck all the way to Cologne, fully expecting that this would be a PFF, or radar-directed bombing mission. With the radar equipment which we had, we could really only hope to hit the center of the city of Cologne. This was not a hopeless choice, however, since the railroad marshaling yards spread themselves over the center of the city. There were, of course, a number of things which we didn't particularly want to hit. Chief among these was the fine old Cathedral of Cologne!

When we reached the initial point and turned onto our bomb run, flak began to burst around us. I've seen worse flak (Merseburg and Berlin, for two examples), but those gunners at Cologne were well-equipped and well-trained. They did a creditable job of shooting at us, though I don't remember any of us wanting to offer them our

kudos. We lost two B-17s to flak that day. I think, in heavy flak like that, any one of us would just as soon have turned around and gone home. But there were about 10,000 of us up there at 28,000 feet over the city, and we had a great tradition that *The Mighty Eighth* never once turned back in the face of enemy action; we proceeded to the target.

On a PFF bomb run, the bombardier and the PFF operator, who sits in the radio room back behind the bomb bay, are working closely together. The bombardier is in control; but as long as he can't see the target, he relies upon the "Mickey set's" picture to tell him the location of the target.

Our bombardier, Rosen, kept his eyes to the bomb sight; and, as we made it down the bomb run, the clouds began to break just a tiny bit. All of a sudden, Rosen hollered over the intercom; "I see the Cathedral!" I shall never forget those immortal words. From 28,000 feet, through only slightly broken clouds, Rosen saw the great old Cathedral of Cologne.

Rosen placed his cross hairs on the Cathedral, dropped our bombs with a shout of, "Bombs away." The B-17 gave its usual lurch as it was relieved of its 2,500 pound burden.

I don't know what Rosen thought as the bomb load sped earthward and Cathedral-ward. To be charitable, I've always believed that he was hoping that his aim was faulty enough that he would miss.

He did. We missed the Cathedral, but we knocked hell out of the railroad marshaling yards which started with the train station across the street. As the bombardiers in the other planes in our formation saw the bombs leave our bomb bay, they toggled their bombs. Since we were always flying in a tight formation over the target, wing tip overlapping wing tip, the bombs were strung out neatly over the target. In fact, the strike photos showed that we had done such a great job that we received a commendation from the Wing Commander for the day's work.

The lead crew for the day, standing, third from left, Rosen, standing, far right, Nail

When the allies took Cologne, they found a scene of utter desolation. From all the times that *The Mighty Eighth* had bombed Cologne, everything in the center of the city, including the train station and the marshaling yards were completely wiped out. Everything but the Cathedral!

I wish I had kept a copy of *Stars and Stripes* which came out the day after the allies took Cologne. I well remember the banner headline: "GALLANT AMERICAN FLYERS SPARE THE OLD CATHEDRAL OF COLOGNE." I have been thankful these last fifty years that we missed what we aimed at that day and, instead, hit our target. It couldn't help me rest at night to know that I had a part in destroying in one blow a historic monument, a shrine of pilgrims, a place of worship, built over a period of 600 years, to the Glory of God!

In 1982, thirty-eight years after that mission to Cologne, my wife, Ethelda, and I were spending a week in Amsterdam. One day we caught a train down to the City of Cologne, a pilgrimage to see the historic old Cathedral of Cologne. As we crossed the Rhine and came around the bend in toward the train station, all of a sudden, there it was! And how it hit me; it's like my first sight of the Grand Canyon; I was completely overwhelmed. My eyes automatically went up and up, to the top of those glorious twin towers.

We examined the Cathedral, inside and outside. It had not been damaged in 1944. The train station across the street was another matter. The train station was a post war building.

TWO OF THEM?

By Wallace Crumby

Since my brother passed away February 8, 1991, I am writing this for both of us.

In 1941, as seniors at Camp Ground High School in Water Valley, my brother, Hollis, and I were very aware of the bombing of Pearl Harbor. I remember that time very distinctly. After war was declared, our government started trade schools throughout the country to train people needed for our defense program. We attended a sheet metal school in Grenada, while we were still seniors in high school; and after graduation, we went to Baltimore, Maryland, to work in the Glenn L. Martin Aircraft factory. We participated in building U. S. Navy patrol bombers. We probably could have been exempt from the draft because of our defense jobs; but knowing that men with families were being drafted to fill the monthly quota, we felt that because we were single with no immediate family responsibilities, we should fill our own spots in the draft quota. After almost a year in Baltimore, we decided to come back home to Mississippi and volunteer through the draft board. This we did, not giving any thought to being separated from each other while in the service.

After completing the army physicals, we were faced with the decision of which branch of service we should choose. This selection depended on which one would let us serve together. Since we were physically qualified to enter any branch of service, our choice was to enter the Navy. However, to our disappointment, just prior to this time the five Sullivan brothers had been lost in the North Atlantic, which caused all the armed services to take a close look at keeping brothers together. We requested of each branch of service represented at our physicals whether we could serve in that particular service together. Without exception, they would not guarantee that this request could be honored. The representative from

the Air Force stated that he would give it a try. Since this was what we wanted to hear, we signed with the United States Army Air Force.

Wallace, left, and Hollis Crumby

After signing up, we went through basic training together at Miami Beach, Florida, then flew on to Denver, Colorado, for armory school. After completing armory school, we were sent to Panama City, Florida, for gunnery school. At this point, a severe problem could have developed. Hollis failed to get the percentage hits on the tow target and was not qualified to continue with our class. As soon as I found out, I went to the commander and told him that if my brother failed; then I could be counted as failing also. I wanted to be on the same shipping list regardless of our destination. Needless to say, we were really concerned until the actual shipping list came out, and we found that we were both given the same orders.

We were sent to Boise, Idaho, where combat crews were made up, and that was when we found that we were on the same air crew. From there we went to Casper, Wyoming, and took combat crew training. Then we went to Missouri and picked up a new B-24

206

Liberator bomber and flew it to England by way of South America and Africa. While in England we were assigned to the 445th Bomb Group, 8th Air Force. By the way, we enjoyed being in the same bomb group with Jimmy Stewart, the movie actor. After this assignment, we flew 35 combat missions together over Europe with experiences too numerous to mention. This assignment won for us the Distinguished Flying Cross and the Air Medal with three Oak Leaf Clusters, also the European Theater of Operations Ribbon with three Battle Stars, Marksman, and Good Conduct Ribbons.

It was always gratifying after each attack by German fighters and heavy anti-aircraft fire to hear Hollis on the intercom say, "Everything is OK." I flew the ball turret for twelve missions and the rest of the missions in the nose turret. Hollis flew all missions from the tail turret of our airplane.

When we finished our tour and returned to the States, we were discharged in 1945, and returned to our home in Water Valley.

Hollis, left, and Wallace Crumby

William L. Temple, who grew up in Lauderdale County, entered the Army Air Corps early: January, 1941. Thus, he was on active duty when the war began. He also went to England early on, serving in the 92nd Bomb Group at Bovington, and later at Alconbury and Podington. The 92nd was the oldest B-17 Group in England. He flew only three bombing missions, as a radio operator. However, his principal duty was the operation of a British Marconi Direction Finder and the sending and receiving of coded information. In civilian life after the war, Bill worked for the State of Mississippi as an electrical engineer.

John Earl Carter, now deceased, grew up in Calhoun County. His career of teaching at Ripley was interrupted by the war. He served in the 401st Bomb Group at Deenethorpe as a clerk typist. John was a graduate of the University of Mississippi with a B. A. degree and the University of Southern Mississippi, with an M. A. degree. He was a life long resident of Calhoun County and was very proud to be a 4th generation Calhoun Countian, whose grandfather fought in the Civil War in the 17th MS. Regiment.

SECRET SQUADRON MISSIONS

By Charles N. "Chuck" Williams

Born January 21, 1924
Sheffield, Alabama

Attended Sheffield City Schools and University of North Alabama

TRAINING

Entered military service January, 1943.
Basic training at Salt Lake City, Utah. Assigned to Army Medical Corps. Requested and received transfer to Army Air Corps.
Air Corps training:
Aircraft mechanic, aircraft instrument maintenance, flight engineer, aircraft phase check instructor (B-29) and aircraft gunnery school. Crew combat training at Pyote Air Base, Texas. Assigned as tail gunner.

Charles N. "Chuck" Williams

HIGHLIGHTS

March, 1944: Crew ferried a B-17 from Grand Island, Nebraska; to England via Bangor, Maine; Goose Bay Labrador; Iceland and Scotland.

Crew was assigned to 305th Bomb Group, 422nd Squadron.

Flew 5 combat missions with the 422nd. Squadron was reassigned and transferred to Cheddington Air Base near London and designated as the 406th Bomb Squadron (Unattached) for night flying, dropping leaflets and other special assigned top-secret missions.

Completed 47 night missions with the 406th and returned to the USA in November, 1944. Interesting but uneventful. The 422nd flew a mission (4 aircraft) over the D-Day invasion area of France, taking off about 2300 hours of June 5, 1944, and returning to England about day break on the morning of June 6, 1944 (D-Day). We did not know what was going on until we landed at our base, but we take pride in saying we were the first to fly on D-Day.

NIGHT COMBAT FLYING

Advantages: No formation, able to take evasive action against flak and fighter aircraft. Normal altitude 14,000 to 23,000 feet. Shorter time on missions, straight over and back.

Disadvantages: No fighter escort. Subject to search lights, flak looks worse at night (red), fighter aircraft has the advantage, attacking low from 5 to 7 o'clock. Have to be on constant alert since there is usually no warning of a night fighter attack, until you see the fire from his guns. Other friendly aircraft over the same targets (RAF) have to avoid collisions or bombs from above.

RETURNING TO THE USA

Due to combat fatigue, I was hospitalized after the 52nd mission and returned to the U.S. by hospital plane (ATC). Was hospitalized for three months at Miami, Florida. Upon returning home was married to Sara Stanley, my before-war sweetheart, on December 7, 1944. Following release from the hospital was assigned as a phase check instructor at McDill Field, Tampa, Florida, until three days following V-J Day when I received my discharge and returned to Sheffield, Alabama, to try to pick up where I had left off almost three years before.

POST WAR

Worked, played saxophone in honky-tonk band. Took advantage of GI Bill education and built a home. Looking for greener pastures took a job with an engineering company in Louisville, Kentucky. Traveled all over the US for 7 years. Then settled for the next 35 years in South Alabama with American Can Company and James River Corp. Engineering and management duties. Retiring (medical) in 1987. Moved to Tupelo, Mississippi, after traveling in a motor home for about a year in 1990 to be near our son's family.

EIGHTH AIR FORCE HISTORICAL SOCIETY AND REUNIONS

Our combat crew has successfully held reunions since 1976. Six of the ten are still living. We have managed to keep in touch since World War II. We enjoy the fellowship of the 8th Air Force Historical Society, State and local monthly meetings. Have made many new friends who have one thing in common: we served our country with THE MIGHTY EIGHTH AIR FORCE, something to be proud of.

Something that Chuck didn't tell about in the above, too modest, record of his experiences, is told in the following, taken from a combat report, dated August 19, 1944, compiled by Captain A. V. Pearson:

"Aircraft 791 (Fortress 42-30791, "Pistol Packin Mama"), piloted by Lt. J. R. Bailey, on a leaflet mission over France, August 16, 1944, was over the third of its five targets at 0049 hours when its No. 1 engine began throwing sparks and caught fire. The pilot put the aircraft into a dive and feathered the engine and leveled off at 23,000 feet, position 4909N - 0013W, time 0026 hours, extinguishing flames. Unable to hold altitude on three engines, aircraft began to let down and had reached 15,000 feet, position 4950N - 0050W, time 0049 hours, when it was engaged by lone unidentified aircraft which attacked from below at 5:30 o'clock. Presence of the attacking enemy aircraft was not known until he began firing immediately and his gun flashes were seen. The tail gunner commenced firing and called to the pilot to take evasive action to the right; whereupon the top turret brought his guns to bear upon the enemy aircraft, which exploded an instant before the top turret opened fire. There was a tremendous bright flash in the explosion and pieces of the enemy aircraft could be felt and heard hitting the fuselage of 791.

The tail gunner was S Sgt Charles Williams and he was given "One enemy aircraft destroyed."

The Crew of "Pistol Packin Mama." Chuck, first row, right

A FIRST FOR MISSISSIPPI -
A SPECIAL HONOR

William Edward Clancy grew up in Jackson, and learned to fly (private flying lessons) at Hawkins Field, the old municipal airport for Jackson. When Pearl Harbor was bombed, he was already trained and ready to leave for combat. In fact, while many of us were not only shocked by Pearl Harbor, but even wondered where it was, Bill Clancy was already in the Army Air Corps and was flying a B-17 E, at McDill Field in Florida.

Thus, Bill was one of the earliest members of the Eighth Air Force. When he went to England, he was assigned to one of the first units there, the 91st Bomb Group, 323rd Squadron, as a pilot. He attained the rank of Major while in the Eighth, flew 25 missions, many of them in a lead position, and was awarded the Distinguished Flying Cross and the Air Medal, both of these with Oak Leaf Clusters.

Captain William E. Clancy being given decoration by Colonel Wray.

One special honor which Bill Clancy received was the Order of the Rigid Digit; in fact, he was really the first recipient of that illustrious award. At this point, perhaps it would be well to recount some of the history of this exclusive order and give some explanation of its significance. To do this I am going to rely upon an article in the January, 1977, issue of *The Ragged Irregular*, the 91st Bomb Group Memorial Association newsletter.

Quoting directly from *The Ragged Irregular*:

"The Order started back in the winter months of 1942, a terrible time in the history of *The Mighty Eighth* and of the 91st Bomb Group. Colonel Stanley Wray, the Group Commander, designed an award to boost morale and lighten hearts during those dark days. There were fewer than six groups making up the entire bombing force of the Eighth, and those groups were just trying to get started with their B-17s in precision, daylight bombing. There was no fighter protection; the loss rate was high, often as high as ten percent on a mission and there were no replacement crews or replacement aircraft available. Someone calculated that if this kept up, the last crew would fly from Bassingbourn on April 19, 1943.

"However, replacement crews and aircraft did arrive, along with additional groups in the early Spring of 1943, providing much relief to those who feared the demise of the Eighth Air Force.

"The idea for the Order of the Rigid Digit, like many other ideas at the time, was inspired by the RAF. The RAF had a fictional character who epitomized ineptitude, what we would call a real screw-up: Pilot Officer Percival Algernon Prune. He is said to have completely destroyed 23 British aircraft in as many different ways during his flight training with the RAF. For that, he was awarded the "Iron Cross First Class," decorated with swords and diamonds from *Der Fuehrer*, since it represented more aircraft destroyed than had been done by the entire Lutwaffe in 1939.

"Col. Wray felt that a humorous award for assorted goofs, awarded with pomp and circumstance, would help bring some cheer into the dark days.

"The medal designed was of sterling silver, four inches in diameter, hung from a ribbon of the baby blue of innocence. At the top was engraved 'Wray's Ragged Irregulars,' and immediately beneath was the motto of the Order, 'My God, Am

I Right?' Since this was a play on the British Royal Motto, 'My God and My Right' this use had to be cleared with the Royal Family, which gave its approval. Below the motto was the clenched fist with upraised middle finger, and underneath was engraved 'Order of the Rigid Digit.' On the back was engraved the names of those to whom the award was given.

"Ten miniature copies, approximately one inch in diameter, were made to be permanently kept by the recipients. The medals were made by John Bull Silversmiths in Bedford and paid for personally by Col. Wray.

"The presentation was made before the assembled group officers and the unlucky recipient wore the large emblem around his neck for the night of the reception. Thereafter he wore the small emblem below his military decorations. A lengthy citation was read with each presentation, beginning with, 'In gross disregard for his own safety and that of his passengers and bringing great shame and discredit to the military service this medal is given to.......

"The initial award was planned for Capt. William Clancy for an episode during group training in the States. At Redmond, Oregon, Clancy's plane ran off the end of the short mountain runway and crashed in a ravine. Col. Wray was in the co-pilot's seat and suffered back injuries. (Actually, the brakes on the plane had carbonized and could not function, but Clancy took quite a ribbing from the group for trying to dispose of the C.O.) Some wags from headquarters, knowing of the upcoming award 'borrowed' the medal and had Col. Wray's name engraved at the top, and prepared a citation admonishing him for not stopping Clancy from not stopping the plane. So, the first recipient was Col. Wray himself, then Clancy, and others as circumstances merited. Lt. Col. Baskin Lawrence won the award for raising the landing gear instead of the flaps as he finished landing an A-20 tow-target plane. Brig. Gen. "Possum" Hansell got his for landing short of the runway by about 100 yards.

"After the war was over, possession of the Rigid Digit became a much desired decoration in higher echelons; so three of America's top generals have their names on the award.

"The headquarters group of the 8th Air Force - the Castle Coombe Group - met each year in Washington following the War. Members who had received every major military decoration felt that the Order of the Rigid Digit was needed to make them truly distinctive; so citations and medals were wrangled by Gen. Ira Eaker, Gen. Carl Spaatz and Gen. James Doolittle. So the award has gone full cycle, to finally become a sort of 8th AF Order of the Garter."

Bill Clancy was discharged in 1945, but was recalled to active duty during the Korean War, stationed at Bolling Field, Washington, DC. He came home from there to be Liaison to the Civil Air Patrol. He served as Wing Commander of the CAP for one year. He was honored by the Civil Air Patrol (called the "Silver Air Control" by the Clancy's maid) for finding a downed Navy pilot. While in this phase of his service, he attained the rank of Lieutenant Colonel.

Flight Commander Captain William E. Clancy with crew and E.J.H. Wright (RAF) with Paramount News assigned to film from Clancy's plane, 1942.

In civilian life, Bill was with John Hancock Insurance Company for 17 years. His job concerned the management of leases, all over the U.S. He and his wife, Janet McRae Clancy, lived in Boston for 15 years.

NO PARACHUTE ! ! !

By Wallace Crumby

I am writing this at the request of my family.

For some reason that I cannot recall, I was to be a replacement as a waist gunner on another crew. This was very common as, for lots of reasons, every crew member could not make every mission with his crew. I do remember that I was told I would be flying this mission. Since our crew was not flying, it seemed a little strange for me to take part. I remember going to briefing and finding out that the mission was to Bremen, Germany.

In the briefing, we were told that Bremen was the Pittsburgh of Germany. This was on the Rhine River and well protected with anti-aircraft guns.

When I reached the hard stand where the plane was parked, I immediately checked the chaff load. We did this to find out how rough the mission was going to be. I was dismayed when I found more than twenty cases on board. Normally, six or eight cases was enough. By the way, chaff was little bundles of foil icicles used to fool the enemy's radar. Needless to say, this was a major concern!

As we started engines for this flight, I started to look for my parachute. I don't know to this day why I didn't bring my parachute, but I evidently forgot it.

I didn't say anything because on our plane and in most other crews a spare was taken along. I made it fine until we started down the Rhine River and the ack-ack started. I reached for the spare chute and to my amazement, when I started to snap it on my harness, it wouldn't latch. After close examination, I found my harness and the chute had the same type connectors and could not be attached. Normally, the harness had rings and the chute had steel snaps; both had rings.

That really shook me up to be without a chute. I could see myself going down on a burning B-24 with no other choice. This is when finality may become a reality. My chest began to pound and throb. Even the ends of my fingers throbbed.

Anybody who says he didn't get scared on a mission needed medical attention. I looked around and found a flak jacket, but that didn't help much. Usually you threw out a bundle of chaff, counted to five, then another. Those instructions went out the window as I threw one every five seconds - a whole bundle every other second would do better. That didn't help the scare at all. Every way I looked there was a brick wall. The flak had turned the sky into a black cloud.

Needless to say, I thought about asking the Lord for protection. Then I remembered that when I was in grammar school, we had to learn the 23rd Psalm. I recited the part that says, "Yea, though I walk through the valley of the shadow of death, I will fear no evil for thou art with me." With this promise, what else could you ask for. All I know is that after I said this and really meant it, all the throbbing and pulses left and I felt as safe then as I do today after over fifty years.

But this is one mission I shall never forget.

8TH AFER FROM KILMICHAEL

By Linwood H. Elmore

I graduated from Kilmichael High School in 1942 and entered military service at Camp Shelby in October of that year. After induction, I was assigned to the Army Air Corps and sent down to Biloxi to Keesler Field for basic training.

When we left Biloxi, not knowing where we were going, we were not properly clothed for very cold winter weather in Chicago. Consequently when we arrived there by train to find it extremely cold and snowing I, along with a number of others, wound up in sick bay for about three weeks with pneumonia. When we were recovered enough to do so, we took our physical training at Soldier Field, dressed in overcoats and boots. We took physical exercise and marched, Monday through Friday, in rain, sleet, or snow.

I attended radio operator and mechanic technical schools in Chicago, and then began the long series of stops on my way overseas. These included Alexandria, Louisiana, a tent city; Salt Lake City; a stop in Nebraska and another at Pyote, Texas, where I joined a B-17 crew.

When our crew left to fly a new B-17 over to England, we went by Goose Bay, Labrador, where we were snowed in for three weeks. The next leg of our journey took us to England, the Eighth Air Force and the 305th Bomb Group.

We arrived in England in time to be in the Normandy Air Offensive. Our crew was assigned to Chelveston and to the 305th Bomb Group, 364th Squadron, to fill in until a permanent had been made. I served as the radio operator and right waist gunner.

This "fill-in" assignment went on for some time at Chelveston. We frequently changed crews. We flew a number of bombing missions in this way. Finally, the 422nd Group was formed at Cheddington and we were transferred there. At Cheddington our missions were at night and we flew eight missions, dropping leaflets over Germany.

I attained the rank of T Sgt and was awarded the Distinguished Flying Cross and the Air Medal with Oak Leaf Clusters.

I served in the Air Force slightly over three years and was discharged at Maxwell Field, Alabama, on October 29, 1945.

In civilian life, I worked for 35 years for the Bell Telephone System, and retired in 1984. I married Jimmie Lou Winstead in 1954. We have two children and three grandchildren.

My crew had a reunion in 1987 in Wichita, Kansas. I have heard from my navigator, Howard Bacon, of Boston, every year at Christmas time. He always brings me up-to-date on the events in the lives of my crew members.

Otho S. Johnson, Jr. was born March 7, 1924, in Jackson. He attended the University of Mississippi, better known as "Ole Miss." He was a junior engineering student and a member of the Advanced Corps ROTC when he was released from the ERC and joined the Army Air Force to become an aviation cadet. After graduation, he reported for B-24 pilot training at Smyrna AFB, Tennessee. He and his All-American crew (3 Southerners and 7 Yankees) trained at Charleston AFB, South Carolina. They flew the northern route to England and were assigned to the 445th Bomb Group at Tibenham. They flew six combat missions and flew back to the USA shortly after VE Day. After 30 days R&R they reported to Sioux Falls AFB, South Dakota. After VJ day the crew was separated; and he reported to the Harlingen AFB, Texas, where he flew gunnery school trainees. He was discharged in September and returned to Ole Miss and graduated with a BSE in Engineering. He continued to fly in the Reserve at the Jackson AFB until the base was closed. He then joined the Air National Guard at Key Field AFB Meridian, where he flew the P-47. He married his Ole Miss sweetheart Dot Day and worked as a Ceramic Engineer for 3 years. In 1952, he joined Lamar Life Insurance Company as an agent retiring after 45 years. He and his wife of 50 plus years have 3 children and 3 grandchildren and live in Jackson.

John L. Dugan grew up in Shuqualak where he still lives with his wife, Earline. He was working for the Navy Department in Washington when Pearl Harbor was attacked. He says he thought, "How could this happen?" After basic training at Keesler Field he completed radio mechanic training and gunnery school. When he arrived in England in January,1942, he took further gunnery training at the Wash. His first duty thereafter was at Headquarters, 12th Bomb Wing at Coggleshall, followed by service at Headquarters, 3rd Air Division at Elveden Hall. Finally, he flew combat missions with the 388th Bomb Group at Knettishall in 1943. John was shot down on his seventh mission, off the coast of Denmark and became a P.O.W. He was awarded the Silver Star, The Air Medal and The Purple Heart.

SMOKE BOMB !

By David M. Taylor

David M. Taylor was born and grew up in Grenada; following his World War II service he had a long and illustrious career in the Air Force. After completion of pilot training, he was assigned to the 95th Bomb Group where he flew 27 combat missions in the B-17 and earned the Distinguished Flying Cross and the Air Medal. He was again called upon to perform in a combat role in Korea where he flew 83 combat missions in C-46, B-26 and C-47 aircraft. During this period he was awarded the second Oak Leaf Cluster to the Distinguished Flying Cross, the Bronze Star, the Silver Star, and the eighth Oak Leaf Cluster to the Air Medal. His combat role continued in Vietnam where he flew 32 combat missions in TF-102A and C-130 aircraft. He continued his service in the Air Force where he held many staff and command positions, finally retiring with the rank of Colonel.

Colonel Taylor now resides part of the year in Charlottesville, Virginia, and part of the year in Santa Fe, New Mexico. After the death of his first wife a few years ago, he married the widow of his World War II ball turret gunner. Crews do tend to stick together!

After completing the Aviation Cadet program in the Gulf Coast area and receiving my pilot's wings, I was commissioned a Second Lieutenant at Ellington Field, Houston, Texas on May 24, 1943.

I was assigned to B-17s at Moses Lake, Washington and had completed training with a group that was scheduled to deploy overseas. However, this group was converted to a replacement training group. After being sent to two other replacement training groups, I finally got to go to the 8th Air Force as a replacement crew in 1944.

We were assigned to the 95th Bomb Group at Horham, England. There I flew 27 missions as pilot, 17 of which were as lead pilot. On at least three of these, we led the entire 8th Air Force. I flew a new B-17 with my original crew back to the States in May of 1945.

One of our missions that turned out rather surprisingly was a flight over a target in Germany (Nuremberg) where we started a sea of fire in the town below. The lead plane always dropped smoke bombs for the rest of the airplanes to see when to drop their bombs. It was procedure that we put our flak suits on before the initial point. My

engineer always put my suit on me, and he would fasten the flys on the left shoulder. This left my right arm free to adjust the autopilot since the bombardier would be guiding airplane to the target with the Norden bomb sight.

Things didn't go quite as I had planned. First, the engineer fastened the flys of my flak jacket on the right side instead of the left side. This allowed the jacket to slide off, hitting my right arm when I adjusted the autopilot. The second problem came when the flak jacket hit my arm causing the helmet to drop down over my eyes. This happened over and over: I adjusted the equipment, my flak jacket fell down, my helmet slid over my eyes, and I was peeking out at the war.

What I saw when I could see out was FLAK! That day the Germans were firing box flak saturating a particular altitude. They were hitting the flight ahead of us hard, right at the altitude of each squadron. The puffs of black smoke were so thick it looked like you could walk on them, and B-17s were blowing up and falling out of the sky. I couldn't look long because of my flak jacket problem, and the intermittent peeks from under my helmet, but what I did see each time I looked out was that the flak was getting worse and worse.

Our problems were not over for that day. Finally, the bombardier called, "Bombs away," and at that moment the cockpit was engulfed in smoke so thick that I couldn't see the Command Pilot. He thought the plane was on fire and hit the bail out button. He started snapping on his parachute. The tail gunner jettisoned the exit door, and the rest of the crew got ready to bail out. The scene below was no place to bail out! I called to the crew not to bail out and pushed the Commander back in his seat. Adjusting the autopilot to make a gradual turn, I pushed the button to open the bomb bay doors which sucked the smoke out of the airplane. Then, I went to the bomb bay and found that the smoke in the cockpit was caused by a smoke bomb hung up in the bomb bay door.

In my rush to get to the bomb bay, I hadn't taken time to snap on my parachute. As I kicked the smoke bomb out, I was balancing on a narrow ledge over the open bomb bay doors, and below was 25,000 feet of space and fire. Fortunately, I didn't fall. I got back to the cockpit and found, to my delight, that the airplane was still flying without any major problems, and I turned to the rally point.

The Germans had missed our altitude, and we had only scattered flak damage. Despite the problems of the day, it was a lucky one for us, and one certainly to be remembered; no one was hurt, the crew didn't bail out, the plane had only minor damage, and we returned to Horham a very happy crew.

The Crew at Horham. Taylor, standing , left

The crew at a recent reunion, Taylor, second from right

216

A HOME AWAY FROM HOME

By George G. Roberts

George Roberts was born in Wigan, England, and came to the United States at the age of three in 1924. His family settled in Johnstown, Pennsylvania, and he entered the Air Force from that city in August of 1942. Following training schools in radio and aerial gunnery, he was assigned to the 306th Bomb Group located near Bedford, England. He began his combat tour on October 8, 1943, and completed his 31st and final mission on July 9, 1944. After the war, George was employed by the Department of Air Force and worked as an electronics instructor at Scott AFB, Illinois. He relocated to Gulfport in 1958 when electronics training was transferred to Keesler AFB at Biloxi. He retired from Keesler as a Program Analyst in December of 1976.

George and his wife, Norma, have been married 52 years and still reside at their Gulfport home. They are the parents of two children: daughter Ellen, a professor at Columbus College, Georgia, and son Gary, a Pascagoula attorney. Having lived in the Magnolia State over 40 years, Mr. Roberts says he is a dyed-in-the-wool Mississippian!

My tour with the United States Eighth Army Air Force began in early September, 1943, when I was assigned to the 306th Bomb Group, 367th Bomb Squadron. Our location was seven miles north of Bedford, England, adjacent to a small village called Thurleigh. It was part of a farming area known as the bury fields. Local farmers grew Brussels sprouts, cabbage, sugar beets and cattle feed. Homes in the area varied from old primitive dirt floor huts with thatched roofs, to more modern brick, two-story apartments. Our base, identified as AAF Station 111, was constructed directly in the middle of two of the larger farms on a gentle knoll that provided a panoramic view of the countryside.

It was rather easy to get to Thurleigh Village, as we needed only to walk the quarter mile down narrow Keysoe Road. It was even shorter if we just ambled down one of the farm paths that circled the Squadron area. Unfortunately, there was little to see or do in the village for young men seeking "action." Two small churches, a combination petrol and grocery store, and The Jackal (village pub) were the prime attractions in Thurleigh. Accordingly, when evenings were free, most of the airmen ventured into the town of Bedford. Transportation was provided via large GI trucks. There was also a dependable cab company from Bedford that charged us ten shillings for the round trip. Early on, I rode the lorries, but switched to "Pop" Fuller's taxi when I discovered it meant staying in town an hour or two longer. I usually made the trip into Bedford about two nights a week. Sunday was always a "must" day for me as I liked to attend services at one of the Methodist churches. Saint Paul's on Harper Street proved to be the most enjoyable and satisfying. They had a group of young people that met following the formal service at 6:30 P.M. to sing, eat and chat about the war, the Yanks and any subject injected into the conversations.

After the service at about 7:30 P.M., I usually made my way back to the Red Cross Club to await the 9:30 P.M. trucks that took us back to the base. It was after a service one evening in October that I was approached by a lady of the congregation. She appeared to be in her early forties, plainly dressed and very polite. "I want to invite you to our home for supper," she said. I was a bit taken back, and not knowing what I would be getting into, I politely thanked her and told her that I needed to get back to the base early. She replied, "Well, perhaps next week then; if you can arrange it." The following Sunday evening, not wishing to avoid the issue, I accompanied her down the dark streets to 161 Waterloo Road. On the way, she informed me that her name was Olive Barkham, and her husband was a Captain in the British Army. She and her young children were residents of Hastings on the South coast but were forced to evacuate inland to Bedford when the Blitz began. At the door of the rather old two family brick dwelling, I was greeted by four charming young girls and a family dog. Mrs. Barkham introduced me to Joan, 15; Anne, 14; Doreen, 9 and Brenda, 6. After a few barks, I had to shake the paw of their small Spaniel, Sandy. I was overwhelmed and amazed by the warm welcome and friendliness I encountered. To say they made me feel at home would be putting it mildly. They served a light but delicious meal and then I was bombarded with questions about the States, where I lived, my family and how I managed to get to Bedford. They learned much about me, and I in turn got the history of their life before Bedford. Alas, it was 9:15 P.M. all too soon and time for the return to the Red Cross Club to catch a truck back to the base. They insisted on walking back with me as far as the town square; so a mother, four young daughters and a family dog accompanied me back to Bedford Town Centre. "You must come back, whenever you can get to Bedford," they all said. "We want you to feel that our home is yours." It was the finest evening I had experienced since entering the Service, and I really looked forward to returning.

I walked back to 161 Waterloo Road many times since that evening and really fell in love with the entire family. Brenda, the six year old, became my adopted daughter and the beneficiary of most of my "sweets" rations. All of us went for walks, visited the cinema, had a bite out and, of course, went to church every Sunday. Following church, we visited the homes of other friends to sing favorite hymns, eat cheese sandwiches and drink hot tea. However, the most satisfying times were those spent "at home" just laughing, talking, singing and playing charades. During those times, when missions interfered with trips into town, Mrs. Barkham would write a letter saying how they missed me but understood that it was not always possible to stop in. I was reminded that my favorite chair was always empty and waiting. In March of 1944, they had a surprise birthday party for me and made tarts, scones and a cake. Sandy,

the dog, was dressed up in a party costume, replete with a clown's hat and sitting up as I entered the home. Captain Barkham had arranged for a short pass from his military post on the coast, and I was delighted to chat with him. All of the personal information I had provided to the children had been passed on to him in their letters. Missions were soon forgotten when I was with my adopted family, the Barkhams.

My Adopted Children, 1943-1944

In early July, 1944, I told them I was nearing the end of my tour, would soon be returning to the States; and there would be little, if any, advance notice of my leaving. I purchased a small Bible for Mrs. Barkham and suitable gifts for each of the girls, then called via a neighbor's phone to say that I would be in the following day. Carrying my small gifts, I made my way down the narrow streets feeling sad that I would be leaving these wonderful friends, but anticipating that perhaps I would be returning to my parental home after a year away. Upon arriving I was met at the door by many church friends that came over to be sure that I had a proper going away send-off. After much laughter, a few songs and "remember whens" they were gone and then a mother, four daughters and a dog bade me a last good-bye. A few tears were shed, and Brenda, sitting on my knee, asked, "How long will it be before you come back?" Trying to swallow the lump in my throat, I said only "after the war." As fate would have it, two days later I boarded a train for Chorley Relocation Center in Lancashire. Then it was on the Holyhead, Wales, and a C-54 flight to the Zone of the Interior. Strange, I thought as we neared Presque Isle, Maine, one year ago I spent 17 days on the USS Argentina in crossing the North Atlantic as part of a convoy. I made the return trip by air in 17 hours and this included a refueling stop in Iceland.

It was 20 years later, July 4, 1964, before I would return to England and again make contact with those who overcame my loneliness and made my life so much happier during my 31 mission tour. The Barkhams had returned to their home in Hastings just after VE Day, and Mrs. Barkham and Anne had written me earlier to say how happy they were to get back to the South Coast. Now, all the girls were married, and two had children of their own. Little Brenda had moved to Scotland, and I did not get to see her, but I visited with the others for two short days. Twenty years later, in 1984, I again returned. Mr. And Mrs. Barkham had died, Joan and Anne were grandparents and Brenda was still in Scotland. Doreen, the 9 year old, was to die two years later following a sudden illness. My last visit was in 1992 when my wife, Norma, and I went to see Anne and her husband Dick who have a lovely home in St. Leonards-by-the Sea. They are retired, and their children and grandchildren live in other towns. We reminisced for hours, visited the historic villages on the South Coast and promised that we would again return. "Please come back next year and plan to stay with us for two weeks," they said. "We feel like we have been a part of your family for over fifty years." I am sorry to say we did not make that visit, but the ache to return is ever present. Perhaps "next year" is the thought that emerges each time I read their seasonal cards and letters that always ask, "When Are You Coming?"

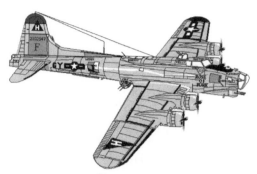

"Rose of York"

T Sgt George G. Roberts

MY EIGHTH AIR FORCE
BROTHER

By George A. Reynolds

George Reynolds has written this story about his brother especially for this publication. George has also authored a history of the 458th Bomb Group of which his brother Jerry was a member. He says he knows his brother would be pleased to be included in this collection of stories of Mississippians in the Mighty Eighth.

Jerry M. Reynolds, Jr. was born in Meadville, Franklin County, on March 2, 1920. After high school, he worked in some temporary jobs and attended Bowling Green Business College, Kentucky, part time. At the time of the attack on Pearl Harbor, he was manager of a cold storage plant in Natchez, and being leery of the draft sending him into the ground forces, he enlisted in the USAAF on January 8, 1942. He applied for cadets; and after basic training at Jefferson Barracks, Missouri, he went to Cuero, Texas, and Class 43-H. During final phases of cadets, he washed out, declined offers of bombardier and navigator schools and went to Tyndall Field, Florida, for gunnery school. After completing this training, he was sent to Lowrey Field, Colorado, for armorer's school.

Jerry M. Reynolds

Next, Jerry was sent to Boise, Idaho, and assigned to Lt. Harold B. Dane's crew for final phase training in the B-24. In late May, 1944, the crew left for the ETO by way of Goose Bay, Labrador, arriving in Northern Ireland on June 3, 1944. From here, they were assigned to the 458th Bombardment Group, 2nd Air Division of the Mighty Eighth, based at Horsham-St.Faith, just outside Norwich, England.

Now officially known as Crew 67, they began flying combat missions in early July and these continued until the gas hauls began in flying fuel over to Gen. Patton's tanks. After this, they became a lead crew and finished their 30-mission tour in late March, 1945. The crew came home by sea, and most were assigned to posts on the West Coast, for possible assignment to the Pacific Theater. But at Beale Field, California, Jerry's points came to 99, and he left the military service July 29, 1945.

Over the next year, Jerry was undecided on his career and took several unsatisfactory jobs. He began flight training and obtained his private pilot's license before deciding to enter military service again. He went to the recruiting station in Natchez to reenlist, but it was closed, so he stopped by the airport to get in some practice in instrument flying. During the flight, he came back to Meadville and started the return to Natchez. He was fatally injured in the crash of his light aircraft on September 12, 1947.

During their tour of duty with the Mighty Eighth, Jerry's crew experienced several interesting situations. They flew on some of the first attacks on the Nazi V-1 "buzz bomb" rocket sites.

On July 21, 1944, shortly after bombs away, a heavy, accurate flak barrage began and a later count showed 99 holes in the aircraft. Two engines were lost immediately, and the control system was shot out. The pilot ordered the crew to standby for the bailout bell in case he could not regain control. The co-pilot, in trying to assist the pilot, switched on the autopilot and the aircraft stabilized, but continued to lose altitude. All items possible were then thrown out, including the machine guns, to reduce weight. The aircraft continued descending but at a slower rate, then leveled off at about 10,000 feet. A control cable was found to be severed behind a section of heavy plywood in the waist. Available tools were used to dislodge the plywood to no avail. The waist gunner then ripped it off with his bare hands, the cable was spliced and normal control was returned. Over France, the crew joined with another damaged plane, running on three engines, but with machine guns still operating. Two enemy fighters turned toward the flight, and both ships entered a cloud bank for about 20 minutes. When Jerry's ship emerged from the clouds, there was no sign of the other B-24, and no radio calls were ever heard from them. Shortly, two P-38s intercepted the stricken plane and escorted it on to England at about 90 MPH.

On August 25, 1944, Jerry's crew flew a mission to Tertre, Belgium, to bomb an ammonia plant. G-2 had indicated two small towns in Belgium that were sites for heavy AA fire. The lead aircraft picked the wrong town to avoid, and the formation was subjected to a heavy flak barrage. The crew received several hits in the aircraft, and three of the fuel tanks were punctured. By reducing speed, the pilot was able to keep the ship airborne until it reached Allied lines in France, and they made an emergency landing at a British fighter strip, remaining there overnight. A small town close to the airfield was jumping with music and laughter after sunset, and the crew decided that was the place to be; however, one crewman would have to stay and guard the aircraft. The pilot, being fully democratic, decided to flip coins to see who stayed with the ship. When the flipping was over, it was

the pilot himself who remained as the guard; he was the only member of the crew who spoke any French!

About halfway through their tour, clear air turbulence caused a midair collision with the lead ship, which had to make an emergency landing. Crew 67 assumed the lead position and accomplished the mission.

On a mission to Hamburg, the 458th BG encountered an enormous flak barrage. Only the lead plane was lost on this sortie; and after the Group got back to base, the navigators calculated the flak area to be 20 miles long, 12 miles wide and about 10,000 feet in depth.

On their last mission to Berlin, flak punctured two fuel tanks, and gas was pouring out into the slipstream. The pilot polled the crew about bailing out when the fuel was exhausted. Again the genius of the engineer came into play. He transferred fuel to the remaining good engines and leaned out the mixture to the nth degree. Crew 67 landed at home.

All of the original crew members remained together for the entire tour except the co-pilot. He injured his back on the Munich mission trying to pull the ship out of its descent with the control system out. Otherwise, there were no injuries or wounds of any kind to the rest of the crew.

ALLISTON SLADE, 390TH BOMB GROUP, 570TH BOMB SQUADRON

By Bettye Duke Jackson

Alliston Slade was born near Purvis. His mother died when he was very young. His father worked for the railroad and was away from home often; so Alliston was reared by his maternal grandparents. In the early 1930s, the family moved to Vicksburg where jobs were available. Our country was in a depression, and jobs and money were scarce. Alliston dropped out of school in the 7th grade in order to help his grandparents.

In his early teen years, Alliston decided he needed to leave Mississippi and search for work that would give him a better income. He left Mississippi, walking; he was picked up in Alabama by a policeman who gave him the choice of being booked or going into the Army. He chose the Army.

Although Alliston had only a 7th grade formal education, he was an avid reader. He had wanted to be in the Air Force and asked for permission to transfer. His score on the entrance exam was so high that he was admitted and began pilot training. From then on it was a steady climb up the ladder.

In June, 1942, the now Captain Alliston Slade, was stationed at Blythe, California. He was flying a P-43 on a training observation mission when the engine failed and forced him to crash land in a remote area. A liaison plane looking for the lost plane spotted him, and the liaison plane dropped a message at a railroad station giving the plane's location. Captain Slade was found deep in the mountains south of Blythe.

Captain Slade was assigned to the Eighth Air Force and soon became part of the 390th Bomb Group based at Framlingham, in Suffolk, England. In the winter of 1943, he was the lead pilot of a B-17 squadron flying heavy bombardment missions against Germany. His plane with a crew of ten was hit over Germany on one of these missions.

Captain Slade headed back to England; but when all engines failed, he was forced to crash land in the ice cold North Sea. After going under water, the plane surfaced long enough for the crew members to get out. Only one of the life rafts was intact. Half of the crew rode in the raft, holding the rest of the crew in the water. One crew member died, and most of the others suffered frost bite, cuts and bruises. They were rescued after a couple of hours by a fishing boat watching for downed planes.

On another mission, Captain Slade's B-17 was again hit hard, and only one of the four engines was working. He brought the plane back to the field at Framlingham and safely landed with one engine. Captain Slade eventually was awarded the Distinguished Flying Cross with two Oak Leaf Clusters.

After the war, the now Major Slade flew air lift missions into Germany. Still reaching for promotions and topping the grade scale in all tests, Major Slade was sent to Ole Miss by the Air Force to study physics and mathematics. His duties were now in top secret training. (They still remain top secret from his family.) On entering Ole Miss, Slade signed for 38 hours of course work, but was told that he could not take that many hours. Having always found ways to achieve his goal, he fought the system and won, finishing in two years with a 4.0 G.P.A. The Air Force decided Major Slade should continue in physics and math, and he completed his Masters degree in one year, still maintaining a 4.0 average. His brilliant performance on all tests, in the Air Force and in academics, was more than outstanding. His family only knows that he was involved in nuclear physics and work with the Strategic Air Command.

After completing the college work, Lt. Colonel Slade attended staff school where he was a classmate of Chuck Yeager. While driving to his assignment in Colorado Springs, Slade's car went over a cliff, and he broke his back. Now a paraplegic, he was hospitalized for a year and a half. Unable to accept the fact that he would probably be permanently hospitalized, Lt. Colonel Slade chose to retire.

Many schools sought Slade for faculty positions, including M.I.T. and the Air Force Academy. Lt. Colonel Slade chose to come back home to Mississippi and teach physics and math at Ole Miss. He retired in 1976. In 1989, Lt. Colonel (Rtd.) Alliston Slade joined his comrades in the sky. What a legacy he left – a little Mississippi boy who dropped out of school in the 7th grade but never lost sight of his goals!

Lt. Col. Alliston Slade

Frank J. Mastronardi grew up in Vicksburg and went to school there. He had never flown before the war, but he entered the Air Corps wanting to be a fighter pilot. That was not to be, however, and his career turned out to be as a radio operator on a B-17, in the 401st BG at Deenethorpe. He completed 12 missions, but on unlucky number 13, he was shot down on a mission to Frankfurt on March 20, 1944, and served as a P. O. W. for the rest of the war. He attained the rank of T Sgt and was awarded the Distinguished Flying Cross. Three members of his crew are still living. Frank served as a credit manager for Sears for 34 years after the war. He also worked at Deposit Guaranty National Bank for 13 years. He is now retired from both.

"FEARLESS FORETICH"

By Gerald Foretich

I was a product of the Great Depression, which meant tough times for my respected lawman father and his family of 13, many of whom are still in Gulfport, where I grew up. After I had grown up and worked hard for some time at the minimum wage, I was drawn to the Army Air Corps, in 1940.

I was drinking a coke and listening to "Tangerine" on the jukebox at Bennett's Drug Store in Tallahassee, Florida, when an MP from Dale Mabry Field came in to tell us that Pearl Harbor was bombed. Someone asked, "Where is Pearl Harbor?"

Spurred on by this momentous event, I became an aviation cadet. Poor night vision washed me out, but by June of 1943, I was training as a radio operator-gunner. I was in Yuma, Arizona when I rode in my first B-17, the famous Flying Fortress. It wasn't long afterwards that my crew ended up training at the airfield at Gulfport.

I was fortunate to be taking my final training in my hometown. It was a unique experience for my family, especially Mom, to get to know each one of the crew with whom I was to go overseas. Mom was really proud of "her boys." However, this closeness to the fellows would make the events that were about to take place more difficult.

All of us, except the navigator, went by ship to Scotland, then by rail to the 384th Bomb Group at Grafton-Underwood in England. It was November, 1944. The 384th deserved its reputation for horrific raids on Germany, losing many men and planes in the process. I'll have to admit, terror was a companion aboard those bombers.

My first mission, which I flew with a different crew, came on November 27, a raid to the Offenberg rail yards. Three days later our Gulfport crew came together for our maiden assignment, one of 1,281 bombers. "Flak Alley,"

so named for its murderous return fire, lay ahead as our crew homed in on an oil refinery. After unloading the bombs, our B-17 was struck by flak. This was a very painful experience, as fire scarred my face, throat and wrists; and some of my buddies were killed. At one point, I was ready to quit. But as I lay there, I thought, "If I don't get out of this, Mama and Daddy will never know what really happened to me." It sounds silly, but I think that thought really saved my life.

The centrifugal force of the spinning plane hampered my escape efforts. An explosion finally threw me out. My parachute was hampered by my flak suit and only some fancy midair maneuvering allowed the chute to open about 100 meters from the ground. I fell into a freshly plowed field, dirt mixing with my bloody, burnt skin as two men ran toward me. One was a German soldier; the other, a farmer with a pitchfork. With German civilian sentiment being what it was, I prayed the soldier would reach me first. He did.

I later learned that two others of my crew survived: the tail gunner, Wesley C. Borgeson, who'd fallen down with the exploded plane's tail, and Jack Chidley, the bombardier, who parachuted without a scratch.

Eventually, I was hospitalized, lucky, I suppose, that with defeat looming, the Germans treated us P.O.W.s nicer. They wanted good treatment when the roles were reversed. I have only scraps of memory about those days: such as the time a P.O.W. corpsman pulled a bandage off my burned face, or the time I nonchalantly picked up a U. S. flight jacket that was likely the prize of a German. That jacket and a pair of wool socks I had brought overseas with me kept me from freezing that winter.

My memories also cover some of the realities of P.O.W. life: bad water, scant food, endless marches, men stuffed so thick on boxcars that sanitation was impossible, the demoralization of standing nude in freezing weather. I do remember some friendly German guards, meeting several boys from the Coast, and receiving Red Cross packages with goodies like spam and cigarettes - some of the slightly better memories.

I came to be known as "Fearless Foretich" after the Li'l Abner character, probably something to do with my sense of humor. One morning I deliberately confused the German guards doing a headcount by sneaking from one barracks to another. I reasoned that a good Kriegie (German for war prisoner) should harass the enemy every chance he gets.

On the day Hitler died, the P.O.W.s' clandestine radio was playing "Hit Parade" when BBC interrupted. Everyone cheered. A few moments later the announcement was made: "The moment has arrived that all the trapped parachutists at Barth have been waiting for - The Russians are here!" Whoopeeeeeee! I'll bet you could have heard that bunch back in the good old USA.

The following is an excerpt from the diary which I kept during the last days of my incarceration in the prison camp:

Today is March 28, 1945. Yesterday I had a hot shower, and today I shaved and have on a clean uniform throughout, complete with a shoeshine. I feel like a million bucks. Yesterday we received a Red Cross parcel for the first time since February 27th. Every one is happy and feels like he still has a stomach after all. For the past month we have been living on one meal a day. This meal consisted of approximately 12 tablespoons of dehydrated vegetables in the form of a watery soup, plus a few German rations. You can imagine how good that Red Cross parcel looks. I have lost more than 30 pounds since I was shot down last November 30. The reason for this diary starting with the title "April" is that April is going to be Victory Month. I predicted that April would be the month that the war would end when I

was in England last November, and it looks like I am going to be right. I started the diary today because Red Cross was an event second only to the end of the war in importance to the fellows here in Stalag Luft 1, at Barth, Germany. And, so with a good feeling all over, especially in my stomach, I decided to start today.

April 30: Today is Monday and the last day of the month. My prediction is up at midnight tonight.

1000 o'clock: We just got orders to dig fox holes. This looks like it. The Russians are coming – Ho. Ho.

1300: The Germans are setting off demolition charges at the radar school. It is used to train German antiaircraft gunners, radio and radar operators.

1400: Explosions at the air field now. I guess they are setting off demolition charges to all the equipment they don't want the Russians to have.

1740: I just saw a German looking through the fence. He was as drunk as a skunk and was yelling "Komarad" at us. Ha.

1800: We just heard that the German civilians are looting our Red Cross supplies at the radar school.

1900: It is rumored the German officers have no control over their men. All of our foxholes are completed now, and the area looks like a giant Swiss cheese. While I was digging my foxhole with a tin can (we didn't have anything else to dig with) one of those big explosions went off right outside the fence about 50 meters away. I had the hole about one foot deep when the explosion went off; but by the time the noise died down and the dirt quit flying, I was about three feet down.

2015: A drunken German starts shooting a pistol outside the barracks. Foxholes again. This looks like a lively night coming up.

2030: All the Germans are leaving now. This is an experience that comes once in a lifetime. I wouldn't miss it even if I could have.

2100: One of the German guards from our compound is in the barracks now. He is also drunk. He wants some of the fellows to hide him so he can stay with us and avoid being taken by the Russians. He has been one of the good guys and always treated us OK. His name is Ernst. I don't know what the outcome of his request was.

2320: We have full control of the camp now. White flags are flying, and a party has been sent out to contact the Russians to let them know the situation here. I guess I hit my prediction within 40 minutes. Pretty close, wasn't it???????

I guess, after that, we all whooped it up somewhat. My friend Pat and I decided to burn down a guard tower just for the hell of it. We picked a good one, the one that supported the main electric lines feeding the camp. We had just built a nice fire at the base of a tower leg, and it was beginning to burn when an MP (P.O.W.-turned military police) came running over and made us put out the fire. Then we were marched over to a building that had some jail cells in it. This turned out to be the place the Germans used when they put someone in solitary confinement.

For 24 hours we sat in the cell, unrepentant. It wasn't bad, though; and they fixed and served our food. It was better than outside. The next day we were turned loose and told that we couldn't burn down any guard towers.

No one except the guys who were there could understand the feeling of exhilaration of a bunch of men just released from a prisoner of war camp in the land of an enemy who was responsible for so much suffering and death. They started it. Now it was our turn.

At a nearby radar school, I confiscated a bed and mattress, the first I'd had. I liberated some German camp records and boxes of German armbands. The P.O.W.s all scoured Barth for souvenirs.

We were like little kids in a candy store who couldn't decide what we wanted to take or keep. Every one would keep picking up things until he couldn't carry any more, and then discard some items in favor of other things we wanted more.

I got more than I would be able to carry home. I think most of us just got a lot of pent up emotions and energy out of our systems.

I don't suppose anyone who has never been out of the U.S., or in a situation like we had been through, could imagine the feeling one has when he sees our flag for the first time after so long. I stood for a full 10 minutes just looking at the flag and thinking that we will be on our way **HOME!!**

John Allen Cockerham is a native of Hamilton, where he still lives with his wife Georgia. He flew 23 missions in the 100th Bomb Group at Thorpe Abbots, as a toggleer. He received the Air Medal with 4 Oak Leaf Clusters. The worst mission he had was on the submarine pens at Bremerhaven. After the war, he served in the Air Force until 1947. He later joined the National Guard and served on active duty in Germany during the Korean War.

LAK'A SACKY AND THE MEN WHO FLEW IT

By Herbert S. McRae

Herbert S. "Mac" McRae was born in rural Lauderdale County; when he was six years old his family moved to Meridian, where he grew up and finished high school in 1940. Since his draft number was low and no one wanted to hire him, Mac enlisted in the Army Air Corps as an aviation cadet. He says 80% of his class, Class 43G, was washed out in 3 days and all these cadets were sent to gunners school. He was discharged in 1945, and worked at several jobs before going to work in the Civil Service. Mac was married in 1948 to Louise Ellis, who was employed by the Social Security Administration. He took a job with the same agency and they moved to Birmingham, Alabama, where they worked until retirement in 1982. They have three sons and two granddaughters. Mac and Louise now live in Meridian.

Survival of a bomber crew during World War II was dependent on many things, not the least of these being a closely knit crew who had trained together and worked together until they had developed a relationship so close that each man knew that the other would react instantly and correctly in any emergency *without being told.*

As flight engineer of the crew, this was my theory; and I was delighted to find that Perry Smith, the airplane commander, shared my views wholeheartedly.

In early April, 1944, orders on the bulletin board advised me that I had been assigned to crew #20, and should report to the base theater of Rapid City Army Airfield, on a Monday morning. There I first met the 9 men who would be on the combat crew with me and with whom I would face death 35 times within the next few months. They were:

> Perry Smith, airplane commander
> Ed Betts, co-pilot
> Don Grivetti, bombardier
> Paul Oliver, navigator
> Joe Kibble, radio operator
> Frank Soley, ball turret gunner
> John Vincent, waist gunner
> Jess Williman, waist gunner
> Tom Glen, tail gunner

Early in our tour Jess Williman was removed from our crew by order of the Commanding General of the Eighth Air Force. We were told that we didn't need two waist gunners! (The generals didn't have to fly the combat missions.)

During the tour we lost Perry Smith as airplane commander when he was promoted to lead pilot. He went down over Kassel and was made a P.O.W., and he survived the war in prison camp. We lost Joe Kibble due to severe wounds; he was mustered out of the service. These latter two men were replaced by Jim Currran, co-pilot and Howard Langlois as radio operator.

We flew the missions required of us and won one Distinguished Flying Cross for heroism, two Purple Hearts and the Air Medal with many Oak Leaf Clusters.

The name? To every bomber crewman, his bed was his "sack" in which he "sacked out" and logged "sack time." We were awakened at 2:00 to 3:00 A.M. for missions, causing much loss of valuable "sack time." Hence the name of our plane: "LAK'A SACKY."

Our crew wasn't any more outstanding than any other crew composed of civilians, quickly trained and thrown into the jaws of death that was World War II. We were outstanding in that all 12 of the men involved survived.

Today, there are seven of us who are still living. We stay in close contact, get together for reunions often. These men are closer than brothers, and I cherish being part of the crew.

Standing, second from left,
Herbert McRae.

Noel Thomas Cumbaa grew up in Phoenix City, Arizona, but married a Mississippi girl, Eloise, and now lives in Greenville. Noel entered the Air Corps early; Pearl Harbor caught him flying a BT-13 from Keesler Field to Fort Benning. He graduated as a pilot in Class 41-D. His 8th Air Force service was in the 95th Bomb Group at Horham where he served as Squadron Commander and later Group Operations Officer, flew 19 Combat missions and attained the rank of Lt. Colonel. He was awarded the Distinguished Flying Cross with one Oak Leaf Cluster, and the Air Force Commendation medal with one Oak Leaf Cluster. After the war he continued to serve in the Air Force until retirement in 1961, with the rank of Colonel.

Carl Fred Wilson grew up at Monticello, in Lawrence County. He always wanted to be a flyer but had never been up in an airplane before entering the Army Air Corps in 1941. When the war started, Carl was stationed at MacDill Field, Florida. He was trained in air gunnery and as a bombardier, though the latter was not in a formal school. He was required to work as a bombsight maintenance engineer and, as such, had to fly and test the bombsight. From this activity he became a bombardier trainee by bombing targets erected for that purpose. He did dry run bombing on almost every building in the Tampa-St. Petersburg area. He went to England in 1942 and was there until 1945. He was assigned to the 92nd Bomb Group at Bovingdon and later to the 96th Bomb Group at Snetterton Heath. Carl worked in training bombardiers and also flew 35 combat missions. He attained the rank of M Sgt and was awarded the Distinguished Flying Cross, the Air Medal with 4 Oak Leaf Clusters, the Purple Heart and his group was awarded a Presidential Citation. He says his worst mission was to Schweinfurt where 60 heavy bombers were lost on the one mission. On a mission to Cologne, where he was operating the chin turret , Carl shot down two ME-109s.

Carl was married to the former Joan Kathleen Wilson before he left England. He and Joan now live in Ocean Springs and have two children and two grandchildren.

FROM THE DIARY
OF
CHARLES E. CLIBURN

Charles Cliburn grew up in Hazelhurst and joined the aviation cadet program before the war began with the Pearl Harbor attack. Therefore, he was one of the first Mississippians to serve in The Mighty Eighth. In fact, he was the first pilot member of the Eighth Air Force to complete 25 missions and come home. Charles now lives in Ada, Oklahoma, where he has lived with his wife, Mary Jane, since he retired from the Air Force in 1965. Since that date he served in education until he again retired in 1983,

During the war, Charles served as a pilot in the 91ˢᵗ Bomb Group based at Bassingbourn. He was awarded the Distinguished Flying Cross with one Oak Leaf Cluster, the Air Medal with three Oak Leaf Clusters, the Purple Heart, the Air Force Commendation Medal; and his unit was awarded two Presidential Unit Citations.

The following excerpt from his diary is dated, November 23, 1942.

We had another mission today, the target was the German U-boat base at St. Nazaire. We encountered heavy accurate flak at the French coast. All the planes turned back but five. About 30 miles inland, Major Zenowitz turned back. He is missing in action. After the run on the target, we were attacked by 15 FW-190s and ME-109s. A very bitter battle raged, one I will long remember.

We were flying in a diamond formation. The fighters attacked from all directions. All my control cables were shot away except one elevator and the aileron, rudder completely gone. The ship was riddled with holes. One 20mm shell exploded in the cockpit, severely injuring the co-pilot, Lt. Clyde DeBaun. I was also wounded in the left foot. The radio operator was severely injured (Sgt. Curtis Pyrah). The tail gunner's oxygen was shot out. The interphone was shot out. The automatic pilot was shot out. The electrical system was shot out. The radios were out. The tail wheel was damaged and would not come down. The elevator trim tab was damaged causing the plane to want to nose up. I placed my knees against the stick to hold it down. I was unable to fly formation; so I took the lead until we were out to sea, away from the fighters and let down to 1,000 feet. All of Major

Smelser's gunners back of the top turret were shot. Major Smelser went down at sea. Lt. Philip Palmer, the bombardier, took care of the injured men and served as co-pilot after removing Lt. DeBaun. Lt. Ray Kurtz, the navigator, did a great job to find the base after dark with no navigational aids. The visibility was less than one quarter mile and we had no radio or instrument landing system.

By a miracle, I was able to land. I landed with the tail wheel up with no damage to the plane from landing. We were the only plane to make it back to the base. Lt. Corman crashed 30 miles south of the base. Five of his crew are dead. Capt. Wallack made an emergency landing in southern England. I was confined to the hospital for a short time with a 20mm fragment in my left foot. Lt. DeBaun and Sgt. Pyrah were confined for an extended period. They received the Purple Heart. I received the Purple Heart and the Distinguished Flying Cross.

(Note: They gave me Lt. Jones' plane, "The Bad Penny." Lt. Jones and Major Smelser were flying another plane that day. Six months later, when I completed my combat tour, my plane, "Quitchurbitchin" was still in the hanger. They also gave me Lt. Garrett's co-pilot and radio operator.)

(*Editor's note: Charles Cliburn told me that when he landed the plane that day, he couldn't see the runway. He was able to pick out a beacon near the end of the runway and, also, could see very dimly the hooded lights of vehicles on a nearby highway. By his memory of the relationship of these two landmarks, he was able to line up with the runway, came in on his approach and hit it just right for a good landing. It is also said that the navigator, who had no navigational aids at all, sighted the highway signs and followed them to Bassingbourn! I think he was being facetious about that, though.*)

Charles E. Cliburn

After the mission, Lt.Cliburn (Standing Right)

230

JACK PHILLIPS' DIARY

Jack Phillips was a native of Tupelo. He graduated from Tupelo High School and attended Ole Miss. While he was in college, he was called into service and entered the Army Air Corps where he became a bombardier. Jack was stationed at Bury St. Edmunds; and during the time he was there, he met his future wife May. He flew his missions over Germany with the 94ʰ Bomb Group. Jack attained the rank of Captain, became the Group Bombardier and earned medals for his war service, including the Distinguished Flying Cross.

Following the war, Jack completed his education at Ole Miss obtaining a degree in Business/Accounting. While he was at Ole Miss, he also played the trumpet with the Ole Miss stage band, The Mississippians. Upon completion of college, Jack returned to Murton, England where he married May. They lived in Tupelo where he was employed with the telephone company. Later moving to Jackson, Jack continued to work for the telephone company and eventually entered into private tax accounting. Jack and May had two children; a daughter and a son.

Jack's favorite pastimes were listening to the opera and the symphony. He especially enjoyed spending time with his two granddaughters in Atlanta. He loved attending the periodic reunions with his WW II Group. Obviously, his war experiences and the accompanying comradeship with his crew remained an important part of his life.

Jack joined the Mississippi Chapter, 8ᵗʰ AFHS in 1992. He died in 1993 at the age of 72.

These diary entries are published here by permission of Jack's family.

December 11, 1943
Target: Emden, Germany

This raid was my first, and our first mission as one crew. At 3:30 A.M. we were awakened and told that breakfast was at 4:00 and briefing at 5:15. We all got up from bed and started to get dressed without much conversation from anyone.

For breakfast we had a bowl of hot cereal and two eggs fried the way you wanted them. Fresh eggs are a real luxury in the ETO.

At briefing, an intelligence officer had a very large map on the wall with our course plotted to and from the target. He began his talk by telling us that the target was Emden, Germany, the foremost port in Germany since Hamburg had been almost put out of action by earlier air raids. We were told to expect both heavy flak and German fighter opposition.

Lt. Jack Phillips, bombardier

Taking off at 8:30, we flew through a heavy overcast and had much difficulty finding and joining our group formation. At 11:00, we started out over the North Sea in formation. The sky was filled with heavy bombers. Shortly after we left the English coast, I went back to the bomb bay and began pulling the pins from the bombs. We were carrying 40 incendiary bombs, each weighing 100 lbs., and I got a little short-winded before finishing because we were flying above 15,000 feet.

About 12:15 we reached our bombing altitude of 24,000 feet. The temperature in the nose was 42 degrees below zero. We test fired our guns and all of them test fired OK which was a relief.

At 12:40 we could see the German coastline. The bomber Wing about 12 miles ahead of us was already turning in for the bomb run. At 12:50 we could see the flak bursting ahead of us. On my right, about 2 o'clock high, I saw several fighter planes racing toward another fighter formation. They were too far away to recognize, but one of the planes exploded and went down in flames.

Now we could identify German fighter planes as they maneuvered for a head-on attack. They were Focke-Wulf 190s. They began attacking from the rear. The tail gunner reported hits on a 190 that went down on fire. One of the bombers in our Group peeled off and started down. Several chutes opened. I could see ahead of us several planes going down in flames and all of them looked like B-17s. The flak was getting heavier and thicker.

I opened the bomb bay doors as we started down the run. The lead ship didn't drop. We had passed most of the harbor installations but Emden was still directly beneath us and I dropped, although ten of the bombs failed to release. Fighters were still making passes, but both the center and right nose guns had frozen and wouldn't fire. Frank's left nose gun jammed or froze - everything had gone wrong.

The tail and waist gunners' oxygen systems were shot out by flak, and they were unconscious from lack of oxygen. Gavit sent the engineer back to help them and told us to prepare for a fast descent.

At 2:10 P.M. we reached the Channel at 12,000 feet, and the two gunners had revived and were OK. We beat the rest of the formation to the field and landed at 3:05 P.M.

What a day!

****

The crew of *Miss Donna Mae*. Phillips, front row right.

December 13, 1943
Target: Kiel, Germany

We were awakened at 3:15 A.M., and ate breakfast at 3:45. It was powdered eggs this time. At 4:30 we assembled in the briefing room where the intelligence officer stood facing the large map on the wall. We immediately saw that this would be a long haul. We were told that the target was Kiel, the great shipbuilding center of Germany, and if every Group could hit the target, the effort would considerably shorten the war. We were told to expect heavy opposition. Our ship was to fly what is know as coffin corner, the lowest plane in the Group formation. This position makes the plane most vulnerable to flak and enemy fighters.

We took off at 7:45 and started climbing to join the formation. At 10:30, I went back and pulled the pins. We had 5,000 lbs. of TNT on board - 10 bombs each weighing 500 lbs.

We left the coast in good formation at 10:45 and started out over the North Sea. There were formations of B-17s that seemed to fill the sky. Everything rocked along smoothly until 12:30 when someone called out on the interphone, "enemy planes at 3 o'clock high." These turned out to be ME-110s and JU-88s, twin engine fighters that began firing rockets and 20 millimeter cannon shells at us. I began firing at those coming in at 10 o'clock. They passed under us about the time 6 white puffs with red flashes began bursting under our nose just a few feet away. The ball turret gunner reported he had hit and shot down an enemy plane, and the tail gunner called out that he had hit one pretty badly with smoke pouring from it.

Vapor trails began flowing behind the planes so heavily that it almost obscured visibility. This gave me the jitters because the enemy fighters could sneak in without being seen. We went up to 25,000 feet and the contrails diminished and so did the fighter attacks. They were running low on ammunition or fuel, probably. Heavy flak began bursting off to our right - coming up from New Munster.

At 1:05 we turned in for our bombing run on Kiel. At the same time everyone began hollering, "look at that flak out there." Ahead of us the flak was so thick it looked like a giant black cloud. I didn't think it would be possible to fly through it. It soon began to explode so close you could hear the loud bangs and feel the heat from the red flashes right through the Plexiglas in the nose. A big chunk of the stuff whizzed through the nose between the navigator and me. It was so close that I actually felt the heat sting my face as it passed.

I opened the bomb bay doors, and the flak seemed to be getting thicker and more accurate with only about thirty seconds to go before bombs away. After bombs were released and the doors closed I could see a little bit of clearing ahead of us. But the flak had been a real nightmare. We had flown through an almost solid wall of antiaircraft fire for more than twenty miles. There they go, "Bombs Away," and all of the planes dropped their bombs in unison - long strings of bombs falling in every direction you looked.

I closed the bomb bay doors. The flak was still pouring up at us, but I could see clear areas ahead of us. I was convinced that it was more than just luck that brought us through that barrage.

The return to base was fairly uneventful and we landed at 4:30 P.M. Our ship had holes all over it and it was a miracle none of us was hit. We all seemed to be dead tired and that drink of Scotch at the debriefing sure hit the spot.

****

A little the worse for wear and teaar, but we got back!

December 16, 1943
Target: Bremen, Germany

At briefing we were told that the target was Bremen, Germany, a city of about a half million people and a very important industrial area. We finally take off at 8:30 and assembled with the Group above the overcast. As we approach the coastline of England, you can see formations of B-17s all over the sky. As we leave the English coastline at 13,000 feet and head out over the North Sea, we begin to climb to 24,000 feet until we hit German territory. Down below, you can see a few small boats in the North Sea - probably fishing vessels. Our Group is leading the whole show this time and behind us dozens of other bomber groups bouncing along at 24,000 feet. There are heavy strato cirrus clouds that we are flying through that nobody likes because they make a good cover for the German fighters to sneak through for an attack.

We hit the turning point at 12:50. It looked as if several fighters, either enemy or allied, were approaching our formation. They veered away before I could identify them. Flak begins to come up on our right but still out of our range. Coming in our direction, I can see formations of about 200 planes of some kind - too far out to identify. They go right through the flak on our right, and the tail and waist gunners call out that they looked like American B-25 and B-26 bombers. What a relief!

At 1:02 we turn in on the bomb run. There's a solid cloud layer in this part of Germany; so we are depending entirely on the Pathfinder plane that is equipped to bomb through the clouds. I'm beginning to believe we've missed Bremen, but almost immediately the flak starts pouring up through the clouds. Bomb bay doors are opened. Using radar controlled guns, the Germans are trying to bracket the formation with 12 to 20 bursts in each bracket. They have our altitude now, and there doesn't seem to be a single square yard of area without a big black burst right in the middle. There are also hundreds of red streamers coming up through the clouds. This is a type of flak that leaves a red smoke trail as the shell comes up and explodes. Scary looking stuff! "Bombs Away" at 1:12.

The bomb bay doors are closed immediately. About five minutes later, a couple of the planes in our Group hit the deck - it must have been due to flak damage.

The tail gunner calls out that enemy fighters are attacking the Group directly behind us. I can now see great columns of smoke rising through the cloud layer in the general area where we dropped our bomb load. Ahead of us are several fighter planes that turn out to be friendly P-47s - a welcome sight; the Luftwaffe doesn't seem too eager to tangle with our fighters.

At 2:30, we pass over Holland and hit the English Channel. At 3:00, we begin circling the field and descending until we reach the cloud layer at 4,000 feet. Everywhere, you can see planes circling and going down and disappearing through the clouds. It reminds me of a swarm of yellow jackets going into their nest.

The field was almost closed in by a heavy fog and flares were being fired to mark the runway. We made a rough landing which wasn't bad at all

considering the poor visibility. We are back on the ground again after another mission that left me feeling a great relief but very, very tired. I suppose it's caused by the tension of the mission, no food and too little sleep.

****

December 25, 1943
Target: A stand down

About 11:00 A.M., Colonel Castle, our commanding officer, came in over the public announcement system while most of us were stretched out on our cots in the hut, and wished everyone a Merry Christmas with the hope that by next Christmas the war would be over, and we would all be home celebrating Christmas.

****

December 31, 1943
Target: Ludwigshaven, Germany

Awakened at 3:30, we got ready to be picked up by the trucks and taken to the mess hall where we had a good breakfast and then on to the briefing room. The map with our course marked out to the target indicated it would be a long haul into southern Germany. The intelligence officer wasted no time in telling us the target was Ludwigshaven, an important industrial city on the Rhine River in southeastern Germany. We were to be over enemy territory 4½ hours and on oxygen for 5 ½ hours.

After taking off and joining the formation, we headed south until we reached the English Channel, then turned due east toward France. There was a fairly heavy cloud cover below us, but we could see the French coastline ahead of us. We soon had a solid undercast blotting out all visibility of the ground. The reflection of the sun on the white clouds below gave off a terrific glare, and I tried to avoid looking down as much as possible.

We were scheduled to drop our bombs at 12:37, but I could tell that we were about 15 minutes behind schedule. Several times we changed our course to dodge the flak barrages thrown up as we approached large towns or cities. At 12:40, we turned in toward the target which we couldn't see for the cloud cover below and again depending on the pathfinder ship to determine when and where to drop. Then came the flak - very thick - two of our planes went down in a spin and no one reported parachutes being seen. "Bombs Away," all 40 of the 100 lb. incendiaries we were carrying. The formation closed up and got ready for enemy fighters. We had been lucky so far.

In a few minutes, the sky seemed to be filled by vapor trails from fighter planes. My heart did several flip-flops as they seemed to be turning directly toward us at a very high altitude. Within a few seconds that seemed like hours, everybody began to cheer at the same time as we recognized that they were P-47s and P-51s.

Another hour went by and still no enemy fighters, but we were still deep in enemy territory where anything could happen. Then, somehow, 6 German fighters sneaked in and attacked the formation behind us shooting down one B-17. They quickly broke off the attack as they tangled up with our fighters. Two fighters collided head-on in a big burst of flame and smoke. I watched the wreckage flutter toward the ground - not a pretty sight to see.

Time drags on and we finally reached the French coastline at 4:35. The clouds began breaking up as we crossed the Channel and could see the White Cliffs of Dover ahead. We landed at 5:35, dead tired, cold and hungry. They had hot chocolate and sandwiches waiting for us when we got out of the ship. But what I wanted most of all was sleep.

****

January 5, 1944
Target: Bordeaux, France, Airdrome

We were told that we could expect moderate to heavy antiaircraft fire over the target but little fighter opposition since there was nothing in the general area of the target except a Luftwaffe pilots training school. Fighter escort cover would be provided by both American and RAF squadrons.

We left the English coast and headed southeast for France. We reached the French coastline at 9:05 with a stiff tailwind giving us a ground speed of 320 miles an hour. P-47 fighters escorted us until we were about 100 miles from Bordeaux but left us when they began to run low on fuel. Only ten minutes after they had gone, German fighters came up and attacked the Group behind us. They also began to make passes at us from the rear as we approached the target. Our bombing altitude was only 18,000 feet and the AA guns were deadly accurate. I opened the bomb bay doors as we started the bomb run at 10:34. All at once, dozens of big black puffs burst all around us splattering the plexiglass nose with spent pieces of shrapnel. I reached down and put on my chest pack just in case. "Bombs Away at 10:38" and I lost no time closing the doors as the flak had become a solid black cloud. The ship off our right wing was hit and went down.

Just as we got clear of the flak area, dozens of enemy fighters swarmed around us, barreling in head-on and flying straight through the formation. They were coming in one after the other so fast that everyone was firing almost constantly. One Focke-Wulf 190 caught afire as he passed through the formation, and I believe I got a few slugs into him as he came in straight at our nose. There were planes going down all around us, mostly B-17s - a sickening sight.

These attacks lasted for over a half hour, and we were well out over the Atlantic before they turned back. But it wasn't all over then because as we crossed the Brest Peninsula, German fighters showed up again and began attacking. I watched the tail gunner of the coffin corner in the Group ahead of us shoot down a ME-109. But it was our Group that seemed to get the worst of it - we lost four crews.

****

January 21, 1944
Target: Pas de Calais, France

There has been quite a lull in operations since our last mission. I suppose it's partially due to the heavy damage received by our planes from the last raid.

But today we start out again on a very different kind of mission to Pas de Calais, France. This is the kind of mission we all dream of making but seldom do. Our target is a patch of woods 1,000 feet long and 500 feet wide. It is actually an orchard where the Germans are reported to have built rocket gun installations.

We are briefed at 9:45 and take off at 13:15. This mission was very uneventful except that we saw a group of German fighters coming our way but friendly fighters showed up at just the right time.

****

January 23, 1944
Target: Frankfurt, Germany

We were awakened extremely early at 2:30, breakfast at 3:00 and briefing set for 4:00. Our target is Frankfurt, Germany, a large industrial city. It has the reputation of being a tough target and everyone seems pretty tense at the briefing.

We take off at 6:45 and join our formation assisted by red flares fired from the lead ship. It looks like a 4th of July display of fireworks. By 10:00 AM, we are on our way into enemy territory with a heavy cloud layer below us. Coastal batteries are throwing up flak, and it's pretty accurate.

All the way to the target we have had good fighter protection from P-47s and P-51s. Again, we are bombing by Pathfinder with the ground completely blotted out by clouds. Flak is very heavy over the target area, but each ship is throwing out bundles of stuff that looks like long strips of tinfoil. It's called flak agitator. The gun batteries aren't able to use radar with any reasonable degree of accuracy because these strips of tinfoil interfere with radar readings and the device that calculates our altitude and speed.

Bombs away at 13:15, and we turn on our heading for home. We have a lot of trouble with vapor trails from the planes ahead of us, so we climb to 28,000 feet to get clear. We land at 16:03, tired and hungry of course but with another mission under our belts.

****

January 27, 1944
Target: Frankfurt, Germany

The mission today is just a repetition of the preceding one because it's Frankfurt, Germany, again.

****

January 28, 1944
Target: Brunswick, Germany

The target is Brunswick, Germany and everybody is sweating this one because the Group lost almost half of the planes that flew the last mission to Brunswick. Fortunately, we weren't scheduled for that one; and I was on a three-day pass at that time.

We take off and join our formation before the sun is up, and it is bitterly cold at the altitude we are flying. Crossing the enemy coast around 9:30, we get a warm reception from the coastal flak batteries. Our formation changes its course several times and outflanks most of the heavy stuff.

For the next two hours things are relatively quiet except for the appearance of friendly fighters making their rendezvous right on time. Bombs away at 12:18, and we immediately began to climb to get out of the heavy contrails pouring from the formations ahead of us. We almost collided with another Group that passed across and through part of our formation. Ice began to form on our wing tips but not enough to worry about at this time. Occasionally, a few enemy fighters would poke their noses through the clouds only to be driven back by the P-47s and P-38s in the area.

****

February 2, 1944
Target: Wilhelmshaven, Germany

Our target for today is Wilhelmshaven where the Germans keep several submarines based. The assembly was very nicely done and we started across the North Sea with hundreds of other B-17s and some friendly fighters in the distance. As we moved along, a few of the fighters came in and flew close to our formations.

We passed over the target at 11:09 and once again dropped our bombs through the clouds by Pathfinder. The trip home was uneventful except for the tense period when we had to disband the formation to descend through the heavy clouds that extended up to 27,000 feet. We all knew there would be hundreds of other planes milling around in those clouds and we couldn't see a foot in front of us. But we finally broke through the overcast and made it home OK.

****

February 3, 1944
Target: Frankfurt, Germany

Frankfurt, Germany is our target again. This makes our third visit to this city of 600,000 people. Frankfurt is known as the Pittsburgh of Germany and is located in the southwestern part of the country. This is a long haul, and everyone still looks a little tired from yesterday's mission.

We take off long before the sun comes up. There is a heavy overcast; and when we break through it, the lead ship can be seen firing red and green flares. The sky is still very dark. We climb in one direction at the rate of 250 feet per minute until we catch up to the Group. The formation begins to circle as other planes join us - 21 in all.

We have close fighter protection most of the way into the target. Over the target the flak got so heavy that it looked for a minute that our formation would break up. I saw two Fortresses blow up and the wreckage spin down in flames. We failed to drop our bombs and the formation began to make a

wide circle for another approach to the target. Just as we were about five minutes away from the target, the ship flying about 100 feet below and in front of us caught afire. It turned out to be Isner's crew.

It just so happened that we had a cameraman on board who sat right behind me on an ammunition box. I turned around and pointed out Isner's ship but he had his head down almost between his knees and wasn't watching anything. I shook him and again pointed to Isner's plane which had now pulled back and was flying only a short distance off our right wing. As the cameraman held up his camera to the window to take shots, I noticed his hands and the camera he was holding were shaking so badly, I doubt if he got any good pictures. Isner's crew began bailing out fast, and some of them opened their chutes too quickly. I saw a couple of the crewmen's flying boots fly off their feet when their parachutes popped open. After all of the crew had apparently bailed out, the plane continued to fly alongside us with flames spewing from one of the engines. I was afraid if it went out of control it might collide with us. We moved on ahead of the burning plane, and I never did see what finally happened to it. It was a sad sight. This crew had come over with us, and we knew the crewmen. They must have all got out because I counted nine men, and Allen Rakes counted ten. I suppose they were all taken prisoner as soon as they hit the ground.

The flak was extremely heavy, but we finally dropped our bombs and headed for home.

****

February 6, 1944
Target: Romlin Airdrome, France

Our target is an airdrome deep in France about 200 miles on the other side of Paris. It was called Romlin Airdrome, and it was our job to destroy it. I had a feeling this might be a pretty tough mission and I was right. The flak was heavy and extremely accurate. As we got closer to the target area, German Focke-Wulf 190s of the latest series streaked in and shot down one B-17 before we could even fire a shot. You could tell they were real veteran fighter pilots.

Visibility was perfect when we dropped our bombs, and they really clobbered the target. When we got home and examined the plane, it looked like we had more than our share of holes in the ship. Chalk up another mission for crew 20.

Apparently, Jack Phillips discontinued his diary after the last mission recounted above.

How could they get home in this one?

James Lawrence Caldwell, a native of Como, grew up there and was working on a dairy farm when Pearl Harbor was attacked. He completed gunnery school at Fort Myers, Florida, and radio school at Scott Field, Illinois. Since he joined the Air Corps early, August 1, 1942, he was in England flying during some of the toughest times seen by the Eighth Air Force. He flew as a radio operator-gunner in the 91st Bomb Group at Bassingbourn. His roughest mission was the second Schweinfurt raid on October 14, 1943; the flak was the worst he had ever seen. James was wounded twice; and, while he never had to bail out of his airplane, he did survive two belly landings. He was credited with shooting down two enemy planes. He was awarded the Distinguished Flying Cross, two Purple Hearts and the Air Medal with three Oak Leaf Clusters. James attained the rank of T Sgt and flew 27 missions, after which he was sent home to recuperate from his second battle wound.

BILLY DUKE

This is an experience of A/C Billy Duke who later received his wings and piloted "The Iron Duke" for THE MIGHTY EIGHTH. Lt. Duke's story is found elsewhere in this anthology.

A/C Billy Duke and Stearman

Dearest Folks,

Well, at least I have time to write to you and tell you all about what I have done since last time I wrote. Well, it all started last Thursday when my instructor and I were up for a dual instrument ride. We had just been up for ten minutes when the ceiling closed in on us faster than we could descend, and bingo we were covered with ice. We couldn't see out the front, so we radioed for instructions, and they told us to go to Terre Haute and they made a mistake, but didn't find out until too late. Instead of sending us away from the storm, they sent us right into the middle of it. We got to Terre Haute and found out we couldn't land. We started out for Indianapolis, hoping for the best. On the way over, my instructor told me that we were going to jump out when our gas was almost gone, so I began to resign myself to the idea

that I was going to make my first parachute jump, but things went different. We contacted Indianapolis airport (Stout Army Air Field) and asked for instructions. They talked to George Field and George said to attempt our landing, so we started to make our plans.

I broke my windshield with my mike and we tested the stalling speed. It usually stalls out at 60, but it stalled out at 120 with all the extra weight of the ice. We came in with both of us fighting the plane to keep it straight and keeping it from stalling out. We made our approach at 130 mph instead of the usual 90 and hit the ground at 120 instead of 70. When we got in they took some pictures of the plane because the Army officials up there couldn't believe it.

Anyway, to make a long story short, we were grounded there until Saturday and then we came back. Sunday I had another thrill - I again went up with my instructor for what I thought to be another instrument ride, but today he told me I had passed my 50-3 instrument check which qualifies me to fly an airplane in any type of weather and is the hardest check to pass in the whole course. I am pretty happy about the whole thing! I get an instrument card, if and when I graduate.

Oh, I forgot. As soon as I got back Saturday, I had to go on A.G. (Officer of the Guard) for 24 hours. Well, Monday it snowed like heck and we couldn't fly. Today I went to Lexington,

Kentucky and Evansville, Indiana and returned, so I have been kept pretty busy. By the way, your son, William A., was the first one in 44C in my class to pass his instrument check. I only lack 33 flying hours to graduate and I am hoping to cut that down to 20 by next Sunday.

I am afraid I won't go home with Goldie, so I want to know for sure whether you are coming or not so I can see about some rooms.

Be Sweet, and remember you have -

All my love,

Bill

Iver L. "Mike" Iverson lives in Tupelo with his wife, Marie. They have three children and five grandchildren. After attending Armorers School. Mike was sent to England where he served in the 95th BG at Horham and the 390th BG at Framlingham. He attained the rank of Sergeant and spent most of his years in England working as a butcher in the mess hall. Since the war he has worked in supermarkets, first in the capacity of butcher and later as store manager.

LETTERS HOME FROM T SGT HOMER C. DUKE

Sunday P. M.
3:30 and hot

Dear Folks,

Guess you think you'll never hear from me, but I am going to try to write at least once a week.

Today was my "day off." I sleep every chance I get so naturally I stayed in bed all morning. Got up at eleven, ate dinner, and went to the movie. I didn't go to town because we brief at 7 tonight and I don't guess we'll come down till about 2 A. M. It's to be a high altitude formation flight and for that we need plenty of rest. Can't afford to go to sleep on oxygen. Might have something go wrong, and at 20,000 it takes about 30 seconds to go out without oxygen.

I can't think of anything to tell you about what I'm doing except that they keep us on the go all the time. I guess Bill has pretty much the same thing to go through with. How is he? Tell him to drop me a line sometimes. He should be about two weeks behind me in R.T.U., but then I don't know how they work it on the West Coast.

Wish I could get out of these heavies into the new A-26s, but I guess almost all heavy men would rather fly something else. It is talk around here that we might all go to B-29s if things continue to click in Europe. Can't say I would like them either but the radio man has a snap on them I've heard. Everything works on pushbutton, they say. Although that's probably a latrine rumor, it makes nice thinking. We fly two days straight and go to ground school on the third day. Our flights are for eight hours; and I have to make position reports to the ground every thirty minutes, copy two weather reports every hour, etc. Most of our flights are 1000 mile cross country. I was in Ohio twice last week and Havana, Cuba once. Pretty as it is flying over the ocean, I'll take the land every time.

My pilot (Lt. Fillingame - Hattiesburg) says we'll get to see some of the Ole Miss games, but I doubt it. There was a piece in the Tampa paper this morning about the football team U of M was going to have. Looks like Meher is sticking his neck out, don't it?

I got the pictures and nice letter, Bettye. Thanks a lot. My tail gunner says "what, whenever." Don't get the big head - he's blind. Pretty nice looking kid 'tho. Twenty-one, Schenectady, NY, three years at Cornell. Too bad he's too old for you. Glad to hear you're having a good time with your sorority. Have fun and when school starts, go to school and study. I don't want to come back and find you still taking geometry!

How are Bennie Murle, Dean and ???? Hope they are O.K. and tell them "Hi" for me. Also Tanks and kids. You don't have much to cook now and I don't want you to work yourself sick. That goes for you too, Dad. Tell Betty Clifton Connor to keep her nose clean and she might drop me a line sometimes. Hello to Alpha and Julia in next letter. Someday, I'll get around to writing everyone. Must close and get down on the line. Try to get another off soon.

All my love,

Homer

Oh! Yeah! I haven't been to town in three weeks and four days. Some record for H. C., Jr.

****

October 13, 1944

Dear Folks,

Gee, but I guess you thought I would never write you. I know I went back on my word, but I don't guess I have any real excuse. It seems like it's been a long time since I've written a letter and I guess it has. I know I must write Billy and Bill this morning, if I have time.

I have been getting about six or eight letters a day from some kids at home; and for the life of me, I can't see what prompted them to start writing to me. They have been coming in for about a week at the rate of two to four from each of them and of course, I haven't had time to reply to any. They are from Olivia Lewis, Dorothy Butts, Lillian and Sue. I can't place this "Sue." They tell me all about how hard their school tests are; how they "trick" their teachers; and little Dorothy gives me the low down on the campus. They range in length from two paragraphs to three pages and the stationary goes from U of M paper, tricky colored stuff, monogrammed linen, down to just plain notebook paper. They must have some type of "write the G.I. club." That's the only way I can figure it out.

Sgt. Homer Duke

Well, I haven't been doing anything but flying and working. It seems like that takes up about 20hrs. of the day and I've been using the other four for eating and sleeping. I sent you our schedule so you can see for yourself that every available hour is utilized. This morning I was scheduled for a code and blinker class, but I passed that long ago and didn't have to go. We fly at eleven. When we have afternoon flights, we try to land about seven, but sometimes it is later. We are doing high altitude bombing and that means about six hours under oxygen. It doesn't get quite as cold here as it does at some other places, but at 20,000 for six hours on O2 with about 20-30 degrees below "0" and bomb bay doors open, this little ole rebel gets plenty cold. Of course, we have heavy winter flying clothes, but even then I nearly freeze.

One of the interesting things about it here, I think, is the fact that we use a lot of old combat ships for training. They are all ships that left from MacDill to go overseas and they bring them back here when they complete their missions. I have flown the original "Memphis Belle," "Old Scrooge," "Pistol Packing Mama," "Stardust," "Tillie," "Manly," and many others. They are still fine aeroplanes that have a wonderful tradition and background. In addition to these B-17Fs, we also fly new B-17Gs but most of us like the old ones best. I, for my part, prefer the old ones because the radio equipment works better.

I got my box day before yesterday and it was delicious. To prove my point, you'll be glad to know that it lasted just about 30 minutes. All the fellows enjoyed the cake and said it was delicious, also. Thanks a million.

Have to stop now. Don't either of you work too hard and tell Bug to be sweet. I'll try to write Murle Sunday. Hello to Bennie and Dean. Bug, Stinger says write him. How did you like Fillingame? He's a pretty good guy. Got to go now.

All my love,

Homer

****

March 29,1945

Dear Folks,

Just a line to let you know I'm OK. I feel like you have received my letter mailed on the 23rd of March, in which I tried to tell you all I know about Billy. I hope you gained some comfort from it. I could not write any letters for 30 days due to censorship regulations. I have done everything that is humanly possible to get any information. It is out of our hands (over here) now. If he is a P.W., the German Red Cross notifies the Red Cross in Switzerland, who in turn notifies the War Department in Washington. They will notify you and you can then let me know. It usually takes between two and six months.

It is impossible for you to realize how I felt. I was so shocked it made me sick. We had a 9 day rest furlough to a flak house in Southern England from the 12th to 22nd of March; and even when I was down there, I couldn't write you. I hope you can understand the reason for the long delay.

I am fine and the crew are all OK. We don't have so many more to go now, and I'm positive we will make it OK. Usually it is the first 20 missions that are the toughest. Billy was on his seventh. He would have made 1st Lt.'s pay as all first pilots are put in for 1st after 5 missions. They will probably give it to him officially in order that he can get his 1st Lt.s pay when we whip Jerry. After 20 missions, the Eng. And R.O. make Tech Sgts. They make Staff after five and fly from 5 to 20 as Staffs then finish as Techs. T/Sgt is the highest rank an enlisted man can hold and draw flying pay.

Yes, Mom, as you say, we are kept pretty busy now. But by the looks of things, it should be over soon over here. The boys in the ground forces are doing a swell job and it looks like they have Jerry on the run in most sectors, although the war is far from won. Hundreds of brave boys will die and be maimed yet. That's the part of it I can't understand. God alone must know the answer. You keep writing me "not to forget to pray." Mom, I've prayed more in the last three months than I ever did before in my life. I have put my life in God's hands, and I ask Him many times a day to let my crew return unharmed. I know there is a God who guides us all and that He will answer prayers. One day I was manning a waist gun and the flak was not too heavy. All at once, the gun was knocked out of my hands and the handles splintered. A piece of flak about as big as a hen egg had come through the bottom of the ship between Bill and I, torn between my feet, and ripped both my flying boots on the inside, gone up between my legs and hit the gun in my hands. Bill is Bill Morrow, my waist gunner. When we realized how close it had come to killing one of us, we both knelt and thanked God. Don't ever let anyone tell you that men in combat don't pray. We have had several very narrow escapes and I honestly believe that the prayers of the boys on my crew pulled us through. The reason I'm telling you this is that I want you to know that I'm earnestly praying for Billy's safety and I know you are doing so, too.

If you see Dr. Purser, you can tell him I have his last letter to Billy and I wish he would write me one about the same things. Just tell him that, and I'm sure he'll know what I mean.

I am forbidden to send any mail home, so I'll have to keep it all and try to bring it with me when I come or try to outsmart them some way.

I am glad to hear that you are a real farmer now, Dad. Good work and good for you; but don't try to overdo yourself. By the way, did you leave my money in the Bank of Oxford or transfer it to the First National? I wish you would let me know and send me a couple of blank checks on whichever bank it is in. I expect to be in N.Y. in two or three months and I know I'll be broke. I'll need some $$ to get home on and I guess I can get a check cashed there. I'm on the downhill grade now, Dad, and I don't mind telling you I feel a lot more confident that we'll finish. When I get home, you and I have a lot of hunting and fishing to catch up on, so prepare. We had a rest leave and I didn't get to do any fishing. They do quite a bit of fly (dry) fishing up in Scotland, but about all they hunt seems to be hares (big rabbits). They build snares for them because of the ammunition shortage. There are a great many pheasants over here and I see them every evening in a meadow just across the road from my hut.

Well, have to close now. Its getting late and we're up again tomorrow. They wake us at 2 A.M. and we usually get to bed about 8 P.M. and it's 10 P.M. now. Be sure to let me know if you hear anything and I'll do the same. Take good care of yourselves and try not to worry about me. If there is anything you don't understand about my letter, let me know and I'll try to explain. There were many things I had to hint at or go around. Bug, you better start writing me. Be sweet and take care of Mom and Dad. Send me a box if you can – meat, cakes, mayonnaise, olives, pickles, spam, film (620), toothpaste, (censored, censored) etc. Nite and a big hug for Dean. Hello to Bennie and Merle and Bill.

All my love,

Homer

****

April 11, 1945
England

Dearest Folks,

How's everything back home? I hope that you have been receiving my letters, and that they explained the reason for the big delay in my writing. Things are about the same over here now as they were. I have no news about Billy. You will be notified first as I told you, so I wish you would write me as soon as you hear anything.

We are O.K., although we had a pretty rough trip a few days ago. Fighters hit us and knocked out number one engine and we caught fire. We were ready to bail, but we got the fire out by diving the ship and leaving the formation. We had to come all the way across Germany by ourselves and without any fighter escort. We were all pretty scared that the Jerry fighters would jump us because we were by ourselves and pretty well shot up. I'm sure God answered our prayers because we made it back across the Channel by just about two miles. We had to crash land in a field because the ship was out of control. Fil and Don made a wonderful crash landing and certainly deserve some type of award. Not a one of us was hurt, other than bruises and minor scratches. Of course, it shook us up a bit, and we were all scared plenty; but the miraculous thing was that we made it back at all. We decided to stick with the ship and try to get back rather than to bail out in Germany and be certain P.O.W.s. Walt did a good job of bringing us out. That makes the second time he's navigated us back by ourselves from deep in Germany. He is on his own when we are deep, because Jerry jams all my radio equipment. We were all praying overtime and He certainly answered them. We had over two hundred holes in the ship and how it stayed in the air at all is beyond me. Our ship got two Jerrys. Chuck and Randy got one for Billy, and I got one for Ken and Billy. We are sure to get credit for one because he blew up right under us. When Chuck and Randy got him they said, "We got one of those ba---rds for Bill." They are all a swell bunch of fellows. Even when the chances looked pretty thin, they all kept their heads and I was sure proud of them. I'm on the best crew in combat in the E.T.O., and I am proud to be a member of a real bunch of men. When I get home, I'll tell you all about it. There is so much I can't write because of censorship. The main thing is that none of us were hurt and we have our rough ones behind us now. We only have a few left, you can count them on your hands, and we will come back O.K. Don't worry about me.

Well, Folks, it looks like Jerry is about whipped over here now. If they don't ship us all to the south Pacific, we should be home by June. That's all we eat, drink, and sleep – going home for that 20 day furlough. They say that if you have over 25 when the war ends, you get to go home anyway, so it really makes no difference to us if it should end tonight.
I want you to just keep that old chin up a bit longer and trust in God. I'm sure you will have good news before long. Well, guess I'll bring this to an end. Have to get up early in the morning. I'm sure

the other families will tell you more of the crash, but the main thing is we are not hurt and are all O.K.

I think of you all the time. Keep letters coming. I have never yet received an *Oxford Eagle*. Tell everyone "Hello" for me and give Dean a big hug. Don't work too hard, Dad. Be a good girl, Bug. And just stay as you are, Mom. Love to you three and remember –

I love you,

Homer

****

The following addendum to the above letter was written by Lt. Lyman C. Fillingame, the pilot of Homer's crew. It gives some more detail on the mission Homer C. Duke told about in the above letter.

April 10, 1945

25th Mission: Jet airfield at Burg-Bel-Magdeburg

We were flying in the lead plane of one of the elements in our Squadron when our formation was hit by seven ME-262, jet planes. They came in so fast and damaged our lead plane. He was hit badly enough he left the formation, so we pulled into his position to lead the other planes. The jets hit us almost immediately, just behind our #2 engine. We immediately attempted to feather the prop on #2 to stop it from windmilling and creating a drag on the airplane. The shell had severed the hydraulic lines and we were unable to stop the prop from turning, so in a very short time the oil starved engine caught fire and of course we were all worried that the fire would explode the gas tanks located in the wings. We immediately put the plane in a dive and were able to extinguish the fire and pointed back toward home base with the still windmilling prop and a new problem. We dropped our bombs except for the ones on the left side that had to be dropped

manually by one of the crew members standing on the very small walkway over the open doors. This tedious job was completed, then we tried to shake the windmilling prop loose by a procedure that caused us to lose more altitude, but not the prop. All this time we were very concerned that more enemy fighters would show up. We were in contact with a few of our own escort planes, but they were low on fuel and were headed back to base. Walter navigated us back home and skirted around known flak installations.

The account Homer described in his letter told you more about the feelings of the crew than I knew at the time, because believe me I was so busy with flying a crippled aircraft and encountered one decision after the other. Don was a very dependable co-pilot and part of his job was trying to inform the crew what was going on.

By the time we reached the English coast the windmilling prop was very loose and wobbling very badly, tearing loose chunks of the engine and tossing them through the sides of the airplane, endangering the ones who were nearest and causing a tremendous drag as the engine cowling was peeling back.

The decision to crash-land was difficult, but everything considered, we felt it was the best thing to do. With the help of God we made a successful wheels-up landing.

Land never felt so good!

****

April 21, 1945

Dear Folks,

Hello, and how are you three today? Hope you are all fine and feeling O.K. We are all well and very happy that we only have so very few raids left

before we get to come home. right now we are on pass, but I didn't go in because I'm broke and I didn't want to borrow any more money. I owe all my pay this month as it is and besides I needed the rest. With luck, we'll finish this month. We have 30 in now. Got another look at the capital of the Reich on my birthday. It was nice to think that we were paying just respects to another guy for his birthday also. Hope we clobbered him good. I'm sure that by now you have heard of our crash and I want to assure you again that we were not hurt. I wrote you of it right after it happened, but I was afraid you would think I was covering up and worry, so I want you to know we are all O.K. Hope I'll be able to tell you all about it in detail soon. We should be home by June or before.

Well, this is just a line to let you know I'm still kicking. Can't think of anything to write about so this will really be short. Write me all the news and send me an *Eagle*. I haven't read one in four

months so you see I'm really not up on the local news.

****

May 31, 1945

Well, I guess you have given me up for good, but I've been so busy for the past month that I've been running around like a chicken with his head cut off. I'm awfully sorry I didn't have time for even a short note, but you know me, and how bad I am about putting things off.

I guess you know by now that I won't get to come home – at any rate for a few months. We had our hearts set on it so much and it was really tough luck that our group was selected for occupation.

246

We lost Hrenko off the crew. He's leaving tomorrow for the States. Other than that, we are all together so far. Fil, Don, Walt, and I have been in Austria and France quite a bit the last month having liberated French P.W.s. Most of them have been prisoners for five years and it really does your heart good to fly them back to their homes in France. There are lots of rumors about when we get to go home. Tomorrow, we go to Casablanca for a couple of days, and as far as we know, that will be the type of work we will be doing. Patrol duty and transporting men and materials to Africa. If they go by the rotation plan, we will be one of the first crews to go home. We have 30 missions, as you know, and that will be up at the top of the list. The work isn't so hard except for the flying. I have about 600 hours in the air over here and let me tell you that's a lot of hours in the air. We have been over almost all the towns in Germany that we bombed and let me tell you we really pounded them to rubble. It doesn't seem possible that those people could have lasted as long as they did.

I haven't been able to go to Norwich lately so I have no news. Do you know anything? I'm sure that if the bombardier, navigator, chin turret got out that Billy bailed also. He and Bubba were probably the last to jump so they might have been at another camp. Please let me know as soon as you hear anything. Keep your faith in God and we'll have good news soon, I'm sure.

T Sgt Homer Duke standing second from left.

I REMEMBER, I REMEMBER

By Joan Wilson

I remember, I remember
The blackout, fog and rain,
The drafty railway platforms,
And waiting for a train.

And I remember ration books,
The spam, and powdered eggs,
And queuing up to get my sweets,
My chilly painted legs.

And, also, I remember ways
We used to do our hair
Piled high on top or hanging down.
We were young, we didn't care.

And I remember coupons
For all our clothes and shoes.
If I buy that dress, I can't get that.
Whatever shall I choose!

And I remember air raid sirens.
We called them "Moaning Minnie."
The whistle of a falling bomb
And wireless talks from Winnie.

I remember trips to London,
Barrage balloons above,
That varied sea of uniforms,
One of them my love!

And I remember dancing
To the tunes we loved so well,
The Lambeth Walk and *In The Mood*.
Glenn Miller tunes were swell.

And I remember vapor trails
And dog fights in the skies,
The night they bombed the London docks,
And Lord Haw Haw's lies.

I remember well our wedding,
A whole week's leave we had.
That "Bed and Breakfast" by the sea
We thought was not too bad!

I remember the Atlantic
And that February trip
When we traveled in a convoy
At the speed of the slowest ship.

And I remember way back when
How everything seemed new.
I hope that these few memories
Gave some joy to each of you!

MAY 28, 1944

By Willard Woodrow Rush

Willard Woodrow Rush was born in Tennessee but lived much of his first sixteen years in Grenada County, in Mississippi. He entered military service during August, 1942, as a private, unassigned. In March, 1943, he reported for duty as an aviation cadet; and on the following Christmas Eve, completed training as a navigator and was commissioned a second lieutenant. During January, 1944, he was assigned to the 486th Bomb Group (H) at Tucson, Arizona, for combat crew training in B-24 aircraft. His unit deployed overseas to a new base near Sudbury, Suffolk county, England, during March, 1944, as part of the Third Air Division of the Eighth Air Force.

He flew on the first combat mission of the 486th during early May. By mid-July, when the group converted to B-17 aircraft, he had completed thirteen missions in B-24s. His combat tour in B-17s was completed about mid-November, and he returned to the States and assignments in ATC and MATS.

He returned to civilian life in September, 1947, but was recalled to active duty in April, 1951. During 1952, he completed a tour of duty, including combat missions as a navigator in Japan and Korea. For the next several years, he served in aircrew and staff positions in Troop Carrier units of the Tactical Air Command.

After graduating from the Air Command and Staff School in 1959, he was assigned as a war plans officer in Headquarters Fifth Air Force in Japan with principal plans responsibility for Southeast Asia. Upon returning to the States in 1962, he served in various staff positions in Continental Air Command and Headquarters Air Force Reserve until retirement as a lieutenant colonel in 1971.

He and his wife, Eloise, reside in Perry, Georgia, not far from Warner-Robins Air Force Base, his base of last assignment in the United States Air Force.

This was to be my seventh combat mission as navigator aboard B-24 bombers of the 486th Bomb Group, an Eighth Air Force unit based near Sudbury, Suffolk, England. For the second time, I was to fly with my original crew, the nine men with whom I had arrived in England two months earlier aboard our plane, "Lady Lightnin'." On five of my earlier missions, including the first one flown by the 486th, I had served as one of the two navigators aboard a lead aircraft. Now I looked forward to being with my own crew again, men with whom I had trained and bonded, men whom I knew and trusted.

When aircrews assembled for an early briefing well before dawn that morning, there was little doubt in my mind that this was to be a good day for the crew of Lady Lightnin'. But when the curtain was pulled back from the board to reveal our target and the routes to and from, I knew we were in for a difficult and dangerous day. The target was to be an oil refinery near Lutzkensdorf in eastern Germany in the vicinity of Leipzig. It was a long way to go, and we would be over heavily defended enemy territory most of the time. On takeoff, our plane would be loaded to the maximum with the combination of fuel and bombs.

To some members of the crew, the takeoff may have been routine, but to me it was not. I was genuinely concerned about Lady Lightnin's clearing the trees that grew along our flight path. Only a week earlier two of the group's aircraft, similarly loaded, had crashed in the same area during takeoff on a foggy morning. Of the two

Flight Crew, Lady Light'nin I, taken at Davis-Monthan Air Force Base, Tuscon, Arizona, February, 1944
Woodrow W. Rush, 2nd from right, kneeling

crews there were only ten survivors; and, though the fog was gone, the loss of friends was still on our minds. The navigator's position during takeoff was on the flight deck, and I will never forget the face of Clarence "Pop" Vaughn, top turret gunner and assistant engineer, who was buckled in next to me. His countenance reflected the gravity of the fear we shared, yet the courage of one who sets fear aside to perform the duties he has been assigned.

Thanks to the skill and composure of our pilot, Ray Zuker, and copilot, Claudie Climie, we lifted from the runway and began our long climb to formation at a flight altitude of 20,000 feet. Since Lady Lightnin' was not a lead aircraft, my navigational duties were limited to keeping up with where we were perchance we had to take over the lead or to leave formation for some reason or other. Of course, I maintained a navigator's log, entering locations, times, and events which would be passed on to the debriefing officer upon completion of the mission. Sometimes that wasn't as easy as it may

sound, especially when there was turbulence, reduced visibility, and constant changes of heading.

Inbound to the target was never a picnic, and this was no exception. Personal comfort was not a real consideration. A heavy flying suit, fleece-lined boots, gloves, flight helmet, earphones, throat mike, oxygen mask, flak jacket, flak helmet, and parachute harness, together with related hose and wires, limited our movement but permitted us to survive and perform our duties at high altitude. Often the temperature would be thirty or more degrees below zero, and icicles would form on and around our oxygen masks from condensation of water in our breath. But I, for one, never complained about having to fly at high altitude; the higher, the better, for the threat of flak decreased rapidly as the altitude increased.

As our formation of 28 bombers moved further into Germany, I was concerned about the IP (Initial Point) which someone in headquarters had chosen for the bomb run. On my map, there was a red circle around it, indicating a heavy flak concentration. Flying as briefed, the formation leader led us on course to that point, and there his plane was brought down by flak. Another plane of our group was shot down a few moments later. We observed two or three parachutes as the lead plane went down, and silently prayed there would be survivors among the crew. I especially hoped that the lead navigator, a friend with whom I had talked at the aircrew briefing, would be among the living.

Deputy lead immediately took over, but the formation had strayed from the briefed course, and the new leader was unable to bring our formation back to the proper track for the bomb run. As a result, we were unable to pass over the target, and since it was impossible for the formation to turn around and try again, we were ordered to salvo our bombs in a wooded area. Then, before we could drop the bombs, still off the briefed course, we found ourselves in heavy flak; and at some point Lady Lightnin' was hit and the #3 engine had to be shut down. I assumed the problem was flak damage, but years later pilot Ray Zuker told me a 20mm cannon shell had cracked two cylinders, causing engine oil pressure to drop to zero. Apparently we had been hit by a German fighter which we never saw. Ray cut the engine and feathered the propeller before it had a chance to catch fire. Power had to be added to the other engines in order to keep up with formation, increasing our fuel usage significantly.

At "Bombs Away," we encountered a new problem. The pilots could not move the aileron or rudder controls. Something had jammed the control cables. Flying tight formation is difficult enough under normal conditions but suicidal without directional control. By using throttles alone, Ray and Claudie slowly maneuvered Lady Lightnin' away from the formation. Any other procedure likely would have resulted in an uncontrollable spin and the loss of all life aboard. We were then all by ourselves over enemy territory, out of the flak but slowly losing altitude and an easy prey for enemy fighters.

At 17,000 feet our bombardier, Gene Joslyn, whom we called "Josh," crawled back from his position in the nose to check the bomb bay. He soon reported that two of the bombs at the bottom of a rack had not released, and that six bombs higher on the rack had released and piled on top. Not only were the arming vanes free to spin on the released bombs, but the bombs had jammed the aircraft control cables which passed through the bomb bay. I remember how I felt when Josh reported this on the intercom. It was as if I sat atop a stack of dynamite with the fuse lit and burning rapidly beyond my reach!

How Josh did what he did, I do not know. Burdened with all the clothing and paraphernalia needed for survival at high altitude, but without an oxygen bottle, he quickly went to work from a narrow catwalk across the bomb bay. He was unable to attach a parachute to his harness or to use a portable oxygen bottle because of the constricted space in which he worked. Less than three weeks earlier, a fellow bombardier of our squadron, working without parachute, had fallen to his death while trying to safety bombs returned from a mission. Josh was fully aware of this, but didn't hesitate to take the risk because of the urgency of the situation. He knew well that as little as a five pound impact after the vanes had spun off would result in an immediate explosion - - and the vanes had spun while the bomb bay door was open.

After first safetying the bombs, Josh faced the difficult work of removing these 110 pound weights from where they lay in the bomb bay. At the time, he probably weighed no more than 130 pounds himself. With great care, he lifted and passed the bombs to crew members in the waist of the plane. These included ball turret operator Bob Buckner, who stepped down into the bomb bay to assist Josh, and two others, flight engineer Ralph Young and radio operator Tommy Truax, who also served as waist gunners. Nearing exhaustion, Josh and his helpers then dropped the bombs very carefully and one by one safely through the opened camera hatch. With the bombs removed, the control cables functioned properly and the pilots again had full control of Lady Lightnin'."

I will never forget how Josh looked when he returned to his position in the nose of the aircraft - - completely exhausted, ashen faced, greatly in need of oxygen and, like the rest of us, very relieved. How thankful we were for what he had done! When I asked him later how in the world he had done it, Josh gave full credit to the Lord who provided the almost superhuman strength and stamina needed to complete the job. I felt then, as I do now, that Josh and his helpers, with the help of God, had saved our lives. But we still had problems.

We were over enemy territory, alone, crippled, on three engines, fearing enemy fighters, and very concerned about our fuel supply. Maneuvering on three engines had used a lot of fuel, and we were still many miles from our base. I focused on doing the very best job I could as navigator, avoiding known flak areas and charting the best possible course of safety to England. But there was no way of knowing where enemy fighters might appear, and I was much concerned. I didn't see what Ray Zuker saw, that two of our own fighters, P-51s, had picked us up as escorts. Knowing that would have relieved my concerns greatly.

Just as Ray saw something I didn't see, apparently I saw something he missed seeing: another crippled B-24 and a B-17 joined us to the rear of our right wing in what I've called a "straggler's formation." They never moved in close to Lady Lightnin,' perhaps because they had control problems such as we had experienced. Nonetheless, I felt good about their being there, for we were close enough together to combine our defensive firepower if attacked by German fighters.

As we neared the English Channel, flight engineer Ralph Young called me on the intercom to report his estimate that our fuel supply would be exhausted in five or six minutes. If that turned out to be the case, we would not be able to reach England. Accepting his estimate as a real possibility, I computed a ditching position and relayed it to radio operator, Tommy Truax, for a "May Day" transmission. Ray called Air Sea Rescue for a heading to the nearest rescue ship on

station along our flight path. We were then descending at about 750 feet per minute.

We weren't the only aircrew in trouble. The B-17 which had joined us for a while pulled away and disappeared. I don't know whether the crew crash-landed, bailed out, or what. The other crippled B-24 lost altitude more rapidly than we; and, just after passing the enemy coast, I saw perhaps five or six parachutes as aircrew members bailed out over the Channel. Whether they drifted back to land, or whether they were rescued at sea, I do not know. Unless they were picked up quickly, survival would have been almost impossible in the frigid waters below. For any crew members who remained aboard the B-24 in a controlled ditching, survival was unlikely. The plane broke up when it contacted the water. Witnessing this, I decided to choose bailout rather than ditching, if I had a choice.

Minutes later we were still descending, and it looked doubtful we had enough fuel to reach land. In a desperate effort to lighten the plane, whatever was loose and not essential for flight was jettisoned into the sea. Ditching seemed inevitable, and pilot Zuker instructed the crew to take up ditching positions. For me this meant leaving the nose and going to the waist of the plane where there was a better chance of survival. Our tail gunner, Carl Williams, and nose turret operator, Bill Callahan, and possibly Pop Vaughn in the top turret, had remained in their combat positions up to this point, ready to defend against German fighters. Upon hearing the "prepare for ditching" order, Bill immediately tried to vacate the nose turret, but encountered a problem and by intercom called on me for assistance. I helped him line up the turret properly and open the access door, and he immediately pulled himself out and hurriedly scrambled to the waist.

Josh had already moved to the rear; so then I was alone in the nose. I was torn between going to the back or remaining on duty at the navigator's position where possibly I could still be a help to the pilots. I chose to wait just a little longer, constantly tracing our progress toward the friendly coastline ahead.

By this time we were down to about a thousand feet, and it appeared maybe we could remain airborne for a landing in England after all. So I remained at my position. When we passed over the beach, we were down to 500 feet, too low to bail out. Our fuel gauges all showed zero, but we were still flying and our base was not far away. Just in sight of the field, I moved to my landing position on the flight deck, and two emergency flares were fired to indicate our need for immediate landing. Then, on the landing approach, #2 engine ceased turning.

Now with two operational engines, our pilots lowered and locked the landing gear, and we touched down on the runway. But Lady Lightnin' didn't go much farther, for the remaining two engines quit just as we turned off the runway. What a happy time and place to run out of fuel! As I recall, it was Buckner and Callahan who immediately jumped from the plane and kissed the ground on which they stood! Later, while Lady Lightnin' was being towed to our hardstand, the crew reported for debriefing; and after that, my seventh mission was over. Only twenty-three more to go!

Two days later, crew chief, Chuck Wycoff, and his ground crew had replaced #3 engine, patched 200 holes, and the Lady was ready for another mission. Unfortunately, I never set foot aboard this great old bird again, nor was I to fly again with the great crew with whom I shared this adventure. My second and certainly most memorable mission with Lady Lightnin' and her crew had turned out to be my last. A few days later, on June 3, I was formally transferred to a lead crew and another B-24, the "Silver Dollar." But that's another story.

Now, over a half century later, I am still "navigator" of the Lady Lightnin' crew. The bonds we forged in training, and especially in combat, however brief the time may have been, have held us together these many years. Our pilot, copilot, bombardier, navigator, engineer, radio operator, tail gunner, and crew chief remain in contact with one another. For the past several years, until last year when infirmities became a greater factor, we met in reunions every eighteen months. We hope to meet again this year; but if we don't, I know that we remain drawn together by bonds which do not fail with the passage of time. These are the shared memories of a time when all worked together in trust and obedience to do their best for the great country they loved. How grateful I am that I was privileged to serve with them!

Willard Woodrow Rush
Perry, Georgia
February, 1999

Robert Frank "Bob" Masterson, Jr. grew up in several towns in Mississippi and finished school at Clarksdale's Bobo High School. He wanted to be a pilot as he grew up. When he joined the Army Air Corps, he was sent to radio school at Sioux Falls, SD, and then to aerial gunnery school at Yuma, Arizona. He did not arrive in England until March, 1945, assigned as a radio operator-gunner on a B-17 Flying Fortress in the 482nd Bomb Group at Alconbury. He never flew a mission, however, as the war was winding down at that time. When he was discharged a year later, he went to college and then worked for the State Highway Department. Bob, now retired, lives with his wife, Anne, in Yazoo City. They have two children and five grandchildren.

DID YOU SAY THE INFANTRY?

By Charles Lambuth Randle

Reverend Randle has now retired from the ministry and lives in the Golden Age Nursing Home in Greenwood. The story below, which he contributed, is an unusual one, but one which we knew of back in the cold wintry days at the tail end of 1944.

I was born in Vaiden, in Carroll County, November 3, 1921, the son of Ernest G. and Althe Puller Randle. I attended Vaiden High School and graduated there in April, 1940. I went into the Civilian Conservation Corps in January, 1941, and served until December, 1941. It was while serving in Brooklyn, near Hattiesburg, on December 7, 1941, that I heard the news that the Japs had bombed Pearl Harbor. I got discharged December 11, 1941, and heard President Roosevelt ask Congress to declare war on Germany, Italy and Japan. I went back to my home and was drafted into the Army on August 1, 1942. We were given a fifteen day furlough and had to return to Camp Shelby on August 15, 1942.

I was sent to Atlantic City, New Jersey, for basic training. I stayed in the Breakers Hotel while there. I was sent from there to Lincoln Air Force Base, Nebraska, to Airplane Mechanics School. We studied P-38 and P-40 planes. I can remember the cold Nebraska weather that we had in the winter time. I completed this school January 28, 1943, and was sent to Ephrata, Washington; I served there until July 15, 1943, and then was sent to Salt Lake City and reclassified for overseas. We were sent to Rapid City, South Dakota, where we received overseas training. We then were sent to Pendleton, Oregon, and from there to Walla Walla, Washington. We then came all the way across to Camp Shanks, New York. I remember eating Christmas dinner on the troop train in Nebraska.

We boarded the H.M.S. Queen Elizabeth on January 1, 1944, and left the next day. We arrived in Greenock, Scotland, January 9. We went by Glasgow and down to Deopham Green west of Attleborough, Norfolk, England. It took a while

to get to know my way around there, but I made it just fine. I was with the 452nd Bomb Group there in Norfolk. I can remember the first American raid on Berlin on March 6, 1944. Our boys said, "We really laid it on them." While in Berlin in the Occupation Forces, I asked a German lady if she remembered that day and she said, "Our house was like a ship out on a rough ocean."

I remember General Jimmy Doolittle coming to our base for the 100th mission party.

I served with the 452nd Bomb Group until the Battle of the Bulge, and then soldiers of the 8th Air Force and other units were transferred to the infantry and were sent to Tidworth Barracks for infantry training. A group of us was sent to Camp Ogbourne St. George near Swindon, England. I was at Camp Ogbourne St. George on April 12, 1945, when President Roosevelt died and Harry S. Truman became President. I can remember us having a mourning parade.

I shipped to Le Havre, France, with a Medical Corps Group. My first experience riding a "Forty & Eight" came here. We moved to Verviers, Belgium, where I was on May 8, 1945, when Germany surrendered. I remember the Belgian people saying, "Hitler Kaput!" meaning Hitler is finished. We had two nights street dancing to celebrate. When the displaced persons returned from Germany, a fight between them and the collaborators took place.

I remained at Verviers until June 10, when we boarded trucks for Marburg, Germany. We passed through Aachen and Duren and crossed the Rhine River at Cologne, Germany. There was destruction all the way. We moved from Marburg on to Halle,

254

Saxony, known to soldiers as "Midnight, Germany." That was July 1, 1945. The second night we were there the call came through that we would move into Berlin. Some of our soldiers were in town that night and the Russian MPs came in and started sending them back to camp. Fights broke out between them. The next day, July 3, we moved 110 miles through Russian territory into Berlin. About 10:00 o'clock that morning, we met this long Russian wagon train moving down into Saxony.

We got into Berlin that afternoon, and we were assigned to the First Airborne Army with headquarters at the Berlin District Telefunken. The Second Armored Division served Berlin and also the 82nd Airborne division.

Destruction was everywhere. It is reported that in 10 days of fighting 80,000 people were killed. You could see graves in the front yards of homes where people were buried and also a lot of them were under buildings that were bombed.

The Reichstag looked as though someone saw Hitler standing in the midst of it and planted a bomb so that it would get him. A bomb hit it and tore out a hole all the way through. The Reichbunker where Hitler and Eva Braun committed suicide was just to the left of it.

The Olympic Stadium was also torn to bits. While I was there I looked for the name of Glenn "Slats" Hardin, a Greenwood boy who won a gold Medal in the 1936 Olympics, and it was there.

I remained in Berlin until November 8, 1945, when I started the journey home.

I was discharged December 23, 1945.

James E. Garrison grew up in Pontotoc. In May, 1943, he and four close friends from Pontotoc went over to the air base in Columbus and joined the Army Air Corps. After basic training at Miami Beach and a stint in Norwich University in Vermont, Jim was classified for pilot training at the Nashville Classification Center. However, in primary flight school, he and many of his class were reclassified; and he ended up in gunnery school where he trained to be a toggleer. Jim flew in B-17s in the 379th Bomb Group at Kimbolton. He flew 14 combat missions before the end of the war in Europe cut his tour of duty there short. He remembers being attacked by German jet fighters on a mission to Berlin, something that was unheard of at that time. He feels very lucky, indeed, to have made it home from that one. Jim is very proud of his service in *The Mighty Eighth*. Aren't we all!!! Jim, now retired, lives in Murray, Kentucky; but he still has roots in Pontotoc and returns whenever he can do so.

2nd Lt. Curtis A. "Pee Wee" Reese was from Fulton. He was trained as a bombardier at Victorsville Army Air Field, California, graduating toward the end of 1942. In England, he was assigned to the 305th Bomb Group at Chelveston, where he became Squadron Gunnery Officer. He was credited with shooting down several enemy fighter aircraft from his position in the nose turret. Pee Wee was mentioned prominently in a story by MacKinlay Kantor in his December 18, 1943, *Saturday Evening Post* story "Letter to a Boy Back Home." Kantor tells in the story that he flew in the nose with Pee Wee and his navigator on a very rough mission with heavy flak and fighter attacks. Reese and his crew were shot down before this article appeared, on September 27, 1943. His pilot, Harvey Rogers of Clarksdale survived and became a P.O.W.; Pee Wee was killed in action.

A USO SHOW TO REMEMBER

By Jefferson W. Brown

(Winfred Brown came home from England in 1946 to start a career with Mississippi Valley Gas Co. He retired in 1990 and has spent his time since then working on cars, airplanes and houses as a hobby.)

In early April, 1944, I found myself in England, 19 years old and no training except basic training at Keesler Field. A few days later I was assigned to 985 MP Company, stationed just outside the gate at Bassingbourne. We did only town and road patrol and convoy escort. After about 6 months, I was transferred to Huntingdon - same job, just different location.

M.P. Brown with trusty steed

Late one afternoon another MP (I can't remember his name) and I were told to go to a given location to meet the Bing Crosby USO Show Group and escort them to a base a few miles North of town. I can't remember the name of the base. We were told to drop them at the front gate and return to headquarters for duty that night. As we approached the gate, the base

MPs motioned us in and said to follow them. We followed them into the base to a hanger that was already full of people waiting for the show. They took us inside, all the way around the crowd in front of the front row of seats, at the stage. Then we were given chairs and told to have a seat. We were then invited into Bing's dressing room to meet him, and he gave each of us an autograph. After the show was over, we returned to our headquarters, knowing we were in trouble. We got a rather severe chewing out, but nothing more.

J. W. Brown today with his favorite pastime

It was a once in a lifetime experience and a decision that I have never regretted.

PIECES OF NOSTALGIA

By William H. "Bill" Turcotte

Camp Shelby, Kelly and Randolph Fields, Ellington, Hondo, Salt Lake City, Blythe, Walla Walla, Grand Island, Bangor, Goose Bay, Iceland, Prestwick - these are familiar names and places - steppingstones to many aircrews of World War II. Reception, classification, pre-flight and advanced training, assignment, aircrew assembly and first phase, second and third phase, overseas staging, transfer and arrival to base for aerial combat overseas.

Our original aircrew of 10 men left Grand Island, Nebraska, with our Provisional Group on July 1, 1943. On to Bangor, Goose Bay and Iceland on July 4; Prestwick next day and Bovington for orientation; then to 91st Bomb Group, 322nd Squadron, Bassingbourn. There was more orientation and training flights over East Anglia, and our crew was split to fly first missions with experienced crews as replacements. The first combat mission is always memorable and ours was no exception when our bombardier Capen Simons and I were assigned to the Jack A. Hargis aircrew. The 91st was briefed on July 26 to bomb port facilities at Hamburg (350 plus ack-ack guns!).

Original crew at 91st BG. Turcotte, center, front row.

The Hargis crew was assigned as a spare ship to fill in any position aborted for mechanical or other reasons. After assembly at altitude and leaving the coastline, there were no aborts in our squadron or group. The pilot, having completed several missions, elected to fill a slot in another group heading to Hanover, our target, a synthetic rubber factory. Over enemy territory, the guns were test-fired. There were reports over the intercom of "bogeys" - two B-17s going down - the IP or turn on bomb run, flak barrage, "bombs away," and we were out of it. With a "mouth full of cotton" and the enemy coastline in view, fear turned to exhilaration and excitement over the North Sea, but not for long. We had left formation and were descending when we heard over intercom, "prepare for ditching." Looking down I could see the pattern of waves and that the sea was fairly calm. Taking up our positions, seated on the floor of the radio room and backs to the bulkhead wall, we soon felt a jolt as the ball turret hit the water, and plowed to a stop. We were out of the radio room hatch, and the pilots out the cabin windows. Two dinghies were launched, 5 in each. We dropped off the wingtips and watched as "Destiny's Tot" (42-3119) sank slowly, then broke at the radio hatch, making crunching sounds and went under, its "Triangle A" Group mark and tail gun the last to go. My first reaction? -- "there go my Luckies and Zippo under the compass cover."

Walrus amphibian Air-Sea rescue plane affectionately called Shagbat by the RAF and Royal Navy

"MayDay" by the radio operator before ditching and a handcranked radio signal soon brought two Spitfires circling low, then a converted Lockheed Hudson (Anson to the RAF) dropped a large dinghy, almost a bulls-eye between our two dinghies. Next, two single-engine, pusher-type Walruses (affectionately called "Shagbats" by the British) landed, taxied up and loaded 5 into each. They were plainly overloaded, like sardines packed in a can. We never saw the other Walrus after it taxied away.

The pilot and co-pilot wireless operator made a takeoff run, the waves had whitecaps, and swells were rough and jolting as we bounced along and came to a jarring stop. The wireless operator had a fainting spell and passed out. We pulled him into the hatch and stuffed a rag between his teeth, thinking he was having a seizure. Within a few minutes he came out of it, and the pilot tried another takeoff run, riding a swell until we plowed under a wall of water that momentarily submerged us. It broke off part of the horizontal tail plane. We taxied for hours over rough sea until a high-speed ASR motor launch picked us up along with the rest of the crew. The other Walrus took off back to base after unloading. Ours taxied behind until it took on water that caused an electrical short and had to be towed. After a 25-mile taxi ride at 6 knots and 15 more aboard the launch, and "Shagbat" following our stern light, we reached Yarmouth at 0400. The Walrus was beached and 18 inches of water drained. After repairs it flew back to Coltishall base. After the engine was taken down, the cylinders were found to be caked with salt. Some craft!

RAF Air-Sea Rescue high speed motor launch boat

About midmorning after a short nap there was a sort of celebration by rescued and rescuers; the

Hargis crew signed their names on a 50-franc note from our escape kit. A stripped-down B-17 picked us up at a nearby B-26 base. Back at the Group, we had our picture taken and a week of R & R at "Flak-city" near the Channel coast - customary for ditched crews at the time.

50- franc banknote from escape kit signed by all of the Jack A. Hargis aircrew after ditching a B-17 in the North Sea. The Walrus amphibian pilot still has the original note, signed at Yarmouth on July 27,1943.

Jack A. Hargis Aircrew after North Sea Ditching. Turcotte kneeling, far right.

Strategic bombing of industrial targets required deep penetrations into Germany with no fighter escort. The Luftwaffe fighter force was dreaded by bomber crews. Flak was usually just a few minutes of sweat over the target. The fighters hit you coming and going. They hit the lower elements in the low groups by choice. If you were in the high group, high squadron, your chances of getting back were better; and we knew it; and the high, lead and low squadrons and group positions were rotated.

So it was when the 322nd led the 91st Group on the first Schweinfurt mission, August 17, 1943, our 4th with all original aircrew. ME-109s and FW-190s attacked head-on, wings blazing, peeling off belly up below us. Repeated passes wing to wing and the Hargis aircrew on our left wing in "Dame Satan" (42-2990) was hit by a 109 that came barely over our left wing. I watched as it left the formation. Over the ball bearing factories at Schweinfurt, bombs raked the target area and great columns of brown smoke and dust were rising. I hardly noticed the flak in the absence of fighters. They met us again and again on the way out. All ammunition in the nose was expended. Hot cartridge cases were 3 inches deep and burned our ankles. We made it, but four of the 322nd crews went down, including "Dame Satan." Fifty years later I learned their fate although I had heard that some of the crew were P.O.W.s. We had 20mm shrapnel damage, a direct hit at the waist window, the gunner with shrapnel leg wounds, and a gaping hole in the left wing from flak. The mission cost 65 B-17s, 11 from the 91st Group. It was the first great air battle of the war. We were just scared and glad to be back as we watched a B-17 land safely with wounded aboard. We learned that Lt. James A. Judy had been shot down but pulled out of a slow spin, ordered the crew to bail out, then hedgehopped the crippled ship with only his badly wounded engineer aboard to crash land at Manston Airfield in "My Prayer" (42-5712).

All aircraft and aircrew losses were not due to enemy action. Not just a few were caused by pilot error, accidents, assembly at altitude, mechanical failure, bad weather conditions and just plain foul-ups.

After the Schweinfurt raid, aircrews flew "milk runs" to bomb airfields occupied by the Germans in France (a "milk run" was only when you were back on base).

On August 31, on missions to Amiens and Romilly airfields, the 91st went just over the Channel coast from England. As I watched the Squadron above and to our right, a B-17 started

to fill in a vacant slot. At the same time, another one attempted to fill the position from below, and they spanked together disintegrating and falling below. As I watched the falling debris and bomb loads, a damaged 'chute with part of a body floated to our right. I thought, "No survivors, 20 men gone to Glory." "The Eager Beaver" (42-29816) and "L'il Audrey" (41-24523) were no more; but by some miracle one of the tail assemblies spun downward, then leveled off and S Sgt Charles E. Allen, tail gunner, bailed out, surviving with slight injury. Eight bodies were recovered, the others M.I.A. in the Channel.

Upon getting back to base again, we learned that "Paddy Gremlin" (42-29972) was damaged by falling debris from the collision and crash landed at Polebrook. Three of the crew bailed out over the channel and drowned. Pilot, Lt. Jess D. Rogers, 322nd Squadron and four of the crew died in the crash.

After the Schweinfurt raid, we had about figured out the odds against completing a 25 mission tour - 3 to 1 - or after 7 missions your number was due up. On a long mission to Stuttgart, the 91st was briefed to fly above 29,000 feet where we had a 55 knot tail wind and a front over France reaching up to our altitude. Going in to the target with no fighter support, we saw no enemy fighters. The target was obscured by cloud cover, and our Group orbited for another unsuccessful bomb run. The leader turned southwest to an alternate, the marshaling yards at Kiel. After seeing bombs rake the railyard, we turned for home. In the high Group we saw enemy action below and two B-17s going down, another beelining for the distant Alps.

Over France we were getting low on fuel. The pilot was leaning the fuel mixture, and the engineer was switching fuel tanks before we left formation and headed for cloud cover. The pilot called for a heading. I had marked a temporary Spitfire landing field on Beachy Head before leaving base, the nearest point of land on the English coast. I started getting fixes on the G-box which, luckily, we had that day. In cloud cover the pilot ordered all loose baggage including our guns salvoed. Off went the nose hatch and unspent ammunition went out. I gave the pilot a heading and ETA to Beachy Head. When we broke through to scattered clouds, the Channel was ahead; and passing over it heading for the white cliffs, we saw two ditched B-17s and one about to ditch. Our pilot, LeRoy B. Everett, set us down on the mat runway, and we stopped just short of the cliff overlooking the Channel. We were one of the few B-17s to land there safely. It was abandoned soon afterward. While we were being refueled, the RAF gave us tea and cookies, and we were only a couple of hours late getting back to base. Fifteen Forts ditched in the Channel. The 91st lost two ditching and one to fighters over France. The crew of "Mizpah" (41-24497) ditched just offshore, and one dinghy paddled safely to shore. All the others were rescued by ASR. Another 91st Fort, "Bomb Boogie" (42-5763), the one hit by fighters, was abandoned by the crew and all survived, five as P.O.W.s. Five evaded, two to Switzerland, one to Spain, one to U. K., and one evaded but was captured in Paris in December, 1943.

After missions to Nantes and Romilly, France, in short order came Frankfurt, then Bremen, then Anklam, east Germany, on October 9. The 91st was briefed to lead a decoy diversion while the mainstream bombers with Tokyo and bombay tanks went on across the Baltic Sea to hit port facilities at Gydnia and a Marienburg, Poland fighter factory. Our target was across the enemy Baltic Coast on a heading to Berlin, then 60 kilometers to the IP, from there to a fighter assembly plant, target for today. Enemy fighters were waiting. Our ship was hit at the IP. No. 4 engine was out and afire when we left the formation. A single-engine fighter hit us in the cockpit at the co-pilot's foot. The cockpit was full of smoke from the shellburst and hydraulic fluid was leaking down from the cabin bulkhead into the nose and crawl space. I stood up behind the cockpit where the engineer was helping the co-pilot get his 'chute on and out the bombay with a crippled foot. The pilot hollered, "Get Out;" so I went back through the crawl-way soaked in hydraulic fluid. Our new bombardier

was on his first mission. We snapped on our chest packs and bailed out the nose hatch. Our original co-pilot Lt Alec Stewart, then first pilot, stayed at the controls of "Green Fury" (42-29778), and it went down with the rest of our crew except the engineer and co-pilot, Lt. Donald Strunk. Our original first pilot and bombardier were flying with other crews.

The bombardier, Lt. James Brown, and I landed in a rutabaga field near Stavenhagen where a woman was pulling and piling turnips. Home guards had us surrounded. After capture, the Luftwaffe took us to pick up our badly crippled engineer who landed and fell off the roof of a farmhouse. After leaving him at a prison hospital, the bombardier and I were put in separate cells at New Brandenburg air base. Late at night we were escorted down a hallway and saw our badly hurt co-pilot on a wooden bunk with a swollen foot and ankle. Next day we went by train with a noncom escort through Berlin to Frankfurt rail station, then by truck to Dulag Luft, the German interrogation center.

Needless to say, that 14th and last combat mission is always memorable to survivors. The 91st lost 6 aircrews on the Anklam mission, 36 total on the "diversion" and the main force was almost unscathed. Lt. Simons, our original bombardier, went down with Lt. Judy's "Old Standby" (42-5178), and all were P.O.W.s except the waist gunner who was killed in the air. The rest of 18 months, 20 days at Stalag Luft III and Stalag VII-A is too long a story to tell. Liberation came at Mooseburg on April 29, 1945, by the 14th Armored division, 7th Army, attached to Patton's 3rd Army. Evacuation on VE-Day was memorable to about 6,000 airmen, all evacuees from Luft III. We learned the war was over when the message came over C-47 (Goonie Bird) radio on the way out from the German airfield at Straubing to Liege, Belgium.

Fifty years later with wife, Dorothy, and a party of 250 ex P.O.W.s, I was on a return visit to Luft III and Stalag VII-A. Along with scenic tours we revisited the sites of our P.O.W. camps in Poland

and Austria. The Poles gave us memorial services and rifle platoon salutes. The Czechs and Austrians, gave us royal treatment. On April 29, at Mooseburg, to the day and hour, we commemorated our liberation with a memorial service at our P.O.W. camp site; also, with a large delegation of French ex-P.O.W.s at their memorial marker on a small green space by a weeping willow.

Dot and I left Munich on our own and stayed 10 days with friends in London. They treated us to return visits with friends gathered at a pub in Royston, near our old air base, to the Wall of the Missing at Madingley American Cemetery, and a return visit to the site of our forced landing on the former Spitfire base at Friston, now a large sheep pasture. Nostalgia flowed freely as we toured Beachy Head with our hosts and Bill Land, the Air Sea Rescue pilot that helped pick up our Hargis aircrew from the North Sea. He still has the 50-franc note signed by the crew. He and his wife, Joan, a well-known landscape artist, presented us with a treasured painting of the white cliffs of Friston and Beachy Head as we left their home in West Sussex.

Our good friends and hosts in London, John and Iris Bayles, were our guides to the sights and for all of the VE-Day commemorations in Hyde Park. We joined their neighbors and a group of seniors who experienced the Blitz and watched the flyovers of vintage warplanes on their "commons" or "green." We had weekend London Transport tickets, the only way to Hyde Park and reserved bleacher seats with other vets next to the VIP viewing stand. We saw the Queen's party arriving and all events to the closing ceremony when she lit a gas "beacon" and simultaneously 2,000 other flares or bonfires over the United Kingdom commemorating 50 years of peace in Europe and victory over aggression and oppression. Some tears and nostalgia flowed. WWII was history long remembered, and those who gave all never forgotten, and with thanks to our hosts who gave us red carpet hospitality reserved for Air Force vets.

They remember us, and the days when East Anglia skies and landscapes roared and were blanketed with U. S. warplanes. Lest we forget, they gave us their Celt and Anglo heritage; and we gave part of it back. Our comrades who lie in their hallowed ground and MIAs, they remember and join us, lest we forget.

Seniors commemorating VE-day, May 8, 1995 on the common, London. Those with arms linked are survivors of the London Blitz

Clayton Lee Betterton grew up in Calhoun County. During the war, he was assigned to a B-17 Flying Fortress crew who flew a new B-17 to England by way of Goose Bay, Labrador. His pilot, Tom Lee, says that Clayton was a quiet, unassuming fellow, always a gentleman and that he was very thorough in his work as a flight engineer, top turret gunner. As the crew left Goose Bay, in winter weather, he discovered that all four props were running away. Clayton quickly analyzed the problem, changed to the inverter, which corrected the problem so that they were able to switch back to instruments. Clayton was killed on his 22nd mission, by a 20mm shell, dying instantly. He was interred at Madingley, near Cambridge. After the war his body was brought home and now lies in the quiet and peaceful Oak Springs Cemetery near Derma.

FELTON SMITH'S STORY

By Roger F. Smith

Felton Lomax Smith was assigned to the 896th Military Police Company, stationed in the 8th USAAF Headquarters, High Wycombe, England.

Felton retired from Johnston Tombigbee Furniture Manufacturing Company in 1987, with 40 years service. He and his wife, Louise, celebrated their fifty year wedding anniversary on June 11, 1998, with their three children, Roger, Katrina and Sheila.

This article was written by his son, Roger.

I was born on February 8, 1922, in Fayette County, Alabama, and moved to rural Lowndes County, near Columbus at an early age. I led a normal farm life until December 7, 1941, when war changed the entire country. Several buddies and I tried to volunteer for the United States Marines in early 1942; however, my father refused to sign for me to join.

On December 23, 1942, I was inducted into the United States Army and entered active service one week later at Camp Shelby. I was sent from there to Miami, Florida, for basic training. My barracks was located in a beach house. I later found out that the tourist industry was shut down due to gasoline rationing, and the government had rented several large hotels and beach homes in Miami to house soldiers during their basic training. During my first few weeks I worked hard, but noticed that several recruits did not share the same attitude. Many went on sick call to get out of drilling. Some even went so far as to put soap under their armpits to elevate their temperature and fake an illness. Little did I realize that later on these actions would nearly cost me my life.

It was on January 20, 1943, when I became ill with a sharp pain in my right side. With sick call full of "gold brickers," I had a difficult time making anyone believe that I was really sick. For three days, I was sent back to the barracks with a CC pill in hand and told to rest. My appendix ruptured on January 23, and I was taken to the Nautilus Station Hospital at Miami Air Base.

Years later my son got my medical records which consisted of thirty-five pages covering two months in the hospital and one in a rehabilitation center. My appendix was never removed by Army surgeons, but they recommended that it be taken out at some future date. I guess that future date never arrived, as I still have what was left of my appendix.

I was discharged from the hospital and reassigned to duty on April 12, 1943. Since my basic training unit was long gone to the Pacific Theater by then, I was assigned to a Military Police Company of the Army Air Force at Orlando, Florida. I never did complete my basic training. After nine months of Military Police training, my unit boarded a troop train headed for Camp Kilmer, New Jersey. After that move, no one knew where we were going. On February 27, 1944, we boarded a ship which became part of one of the largest convoys ever to cross the Atlantic. This was due to the build up of troops and equipment for D-Day. Half way across the ocean we were told our destination was England, and we arrived there on March 9th.

I was assigned to the 896th Military Police Company. This was the headquarters company of the Eighth Air Force stationed at the now famous Wycombe Abbey, a woman's college at High Wycombe, England. Our officers informed us that General Doolittle, leader of the Tokyo raid, had taken command of the Eighth Air Force on January 5, 1944, and was now living on a large estate there. Our job was to guard this estate, Wycombe Abbey and the underground command post which consisted of a three story bunker having its own communications center and switchboard. The German Air Force tried to find this headquarters all during the war but never succeeded. We knew this because we heard their propaganda radio broadcasts from time to time. I remember seeing General Doolittle on his hands and knees looking at maps just before D-Day. The most danger we had was when the buzz bombs began to fall just after D-Day in June of 1944. We were told it was not necessary to take cover as long as you could hear the engine running. If the engine cut off, take cover because the buzz bomb could then fall anywhere. Another memory that I have is when King George VI and Queen Elizabeth inspected General Doolittle's home guard of which I was a member. This event was something a farm boy from Mississippi does not soon forget.

In December of 1944, during the Battle of the Bulge, all MPs were taken into the field and given an infantry training refresher course in case we were needed. Since I missed much of this basic training I learned quite a lot. Until the war in Europe was over, I saw hundreds of bombers coming back from missions each day, some with one or two engines out. I was greatly moved by the fine job these air crews did. After the war in Europe was over, thousands of ground personnel were given rides in the bombers to tour the European battlefield. This was quite a thrill for me. I expected to see a veteran air crew on my tour, but was surprised to see that they looked almost as young as I was. We were allowed to occupy the gun stations which were not loaded, and I manned the tail gun as we flew over London.

In August of 1945, we were getting ready to move to the new Eighth Air Force Headquarters on Okinawa when Japan surrendered. Our orders were then changed, and we stayed in England another six months. I departed for home on February 10, 1946, and was given a prisoner from Alabama to guard and turn over to the authorities at Camp Shelby. This prisoner had gotten drunk and had stolen an Army Jeep and run it into the side of a farmer's barn. He had already served half of his time and was to finish the rest of his sentence in the States. Once on board ship, he was placed in

the brig. I visited him and gave him candy bars to brighten his days. We landed in New York harbor, and seeing the Statue of Liberty was an unforgettable thrill for me. At Camp Kilmer, New Jersey, we caught a train to Camp Shelby; and I breathed a sigh of relief when I turned the prisoner over to the Officer of the Day. After I received my discharge and mustering out pay of one hundred fifty seven dollars and thirty-nine cents, I walked toward the bus station and heard someone calling my name. It was my former prisoner. He had been turned loose and wanted to know if he could come with me. We caught a bus to Columbus where my father and sisters were waiting for me. Of course, no one was waiting for my former prisoner, so we gave him a ride to the railroad station to catch a train to his home in Alabama.

Felton Smith in 1945

After General Eisenhower and his staff moved to France to direct the War, General Doolittle became the highest ranking American in England. All of us had great respect for him. While most of the MPs were privates, like myself, he would greet us if he was not too busy. In 1987, I wrote to him asking for some information regarding a genealogy project my son and his wife were writing. I doubted if I would get a reply, but was thrilled to receive an answer with General Doolittle's own signature. I later found out that until his death he insisted that all his correspondence be answered promptly.

I was proud to serve my country overseas for one year, eleven months and twenty-three days.

Felton, second in left line. A wedding in England.

The King and Queen inspect the troops. Felton Smith, second in line.

William P. Cassedy, a native of Brookhaven, flew in the 306th Bomb Group at Thurleigh. He was awarded the Distinguished Flying Cross after a mission which he never really should have flown. He was the regular co-pilot on his crew, but on this mission he was not scheduled to fly since his Squadron Commander, Lt. Col. J. W. Wilson was flying with the crew. As the crew was short one waist gunner, Cassedy volunteered to fly in the waist. On the bomb run, a 20 mm shell from an attacking German fighter, exploded in the cockpit, killing the pilot and severely injuring Lt. Col. Wilson. A fire was burning behind the top turret. The order to bail out was given and the crew members who were able to do so bailed out. Lt. Cassedy made his way to the cockpit and flew the plane home with several members of the crew too wounded to bail out. When they arrived at Thurleigh, it was found that the flare gun had been destroyed; and the radios had been shot out. With no communication with the tower, Cassedy landed the plane against the traffic of other arriving planes. Fortunately, the other pilots recognized an emergency and pulled up, allowing him to land safely. (*Editors note: We were unable to get a complete story of this mission as William P. Cassedy had died several years ago. Some additional details may be found in* First Over Germany: A History of the 306th Bombardment Group, *by Russell A. Strong.*)

ROYALTY CHRISTENS A FORTRESS
"The Rose of York"

By George G. Roberts

In early May 1944, Master Sergeant Ed Gregory, our crew chief, originally named our third new plane "The Princess" in honor of the eldest daughter of King George VI and Queen Elizabeth of England. After the first mission he decided to go all the way and changed the name to "Princess Elizabeth," thus removing any doubt as to his intentions. He then asked the Base Commander to invite Princess Elizabeth to Thurleigh Air Base to christen the B-17 Flying Fortress.

When the idea was submitted to the Lord Mayor of London, it was considered, but the suggestion was made that the name be changed somewhat because if the airplane were ever shot down it could be a bad omen. Thus the name of our plane was changed to "Rose of York." This would be a fitting name, as the Princess and her family were from the "House of York," and she was fondly thought of as a Rose. The symbol of the House of York was a white rose, and so Gregory had artist Sgt. Curry paint the new name and a white rose on our plane, B-17G #2102547. The Royal Family agreed to the christening, and the date was set for July 6, 1944. Being the only radio operator to fly on the plane at that time, I was notified to be available in Class "A" uniform to participate in the event.

The plane was washed and literally polished to perfection, and a person would think that it had just been delivered from Boeing Aircraft Factory. Actually by this time we had flown thirteen missions in the plane, it had been patched on numerous occasions, and it even suffered hanger queen status for two days. On her first mission, which was to Berlin on May 19th, she suffered flak damage and did not fly again until May 23rd. Maintenance had done a superb job.

An iron plate was fastened to the two nose turret gun housings, and a bottle of fine English cider wrapped in parachute silk was tied to a bright rope hanging just under the iron plate. We moved the "Rose" from her usual hardstand to one near to the flight line and opposite a big hanger. We went over every area of the plane one final time and were sure that every detail had been covered. All was in readiness, and since I was born in England, I was a bit more eager than the rest of the crew to meet and talk with the Royal family.

Air crew members Captains Perry Raster, pilot; Steve Tanella, bombardier; Lt.'s Talmadge McDonough, co-pilot; William Pleasant and Marian Northway, navigators; T Sgts Eugene Kelly, engineer; and George Roberts, radio; S Sgts Herman Shore and Donald Urban, waist; William Landrum, ball turret and Watson Vaughn, tail; lined up under the right wing of the big Fortress. The ground crew consisting of M Sgt Edward Gregory, Sgts Mark Madsen, E.C. Rowell and Pvt Thomas Boyd lined up under the left wing. We were ready for the big event by 11:00 A.M. even though the time set for the dignitaries to arrive was not until noon. At a few minutes past twelve, a large motorcade of black Daimler automobiles drove up to the perimeter track, made its way through the crowds of airmen and stopped directly in front of us. The British entourage included King George VI, Queen Elizabeth, Princess Elizabeth, and a host of other dignitaries, which included Lord Mayors and Members of Parliament. Lt. General Jimmy Doolittle, Maj. General Robert Twining, Brig. Generals Robert Travis, Howard Turner and Bartlett Beaman led the American contingent. Our base commander Col. George L. Robinson was the first to greet the visitors and served as host for the occasion. Just then a formation of 54 Flying Fortresses roared overhead in salute to the dignitaries. The drone of the 216 Wright cyclone engines fairly shook the ground and elicited many OH's and AH's from the assembled spectators.

The visitors led by the King then moved toward the flight crew. Each introduced himself to us, and Col. Robinson and pilot Raster provided our names and crew positions to them. Generally, it was a polite hand shake, one or two questions about our job and then to the next crewman. Queen Elizabeth spoke at length to me, asking me how many radios were on the plane, what some were used for and where they were located. Her final reply to my answers was, "Radios are such a mystery."

Princess Elizabeth, King George VI, Queen Elizabeth and General Jimmy Doolittle at christening of B-17G, Rose of York, Thurleigh Air Base, July 6, 1944.

Upon completion of the introductions to the air and ground crews, Princess Elizabeth stepped to the front of the plane and swung the silk wrapped bottle of cider against the iron plate. The first attempt resulted in a bounce back; but the second try broke the bottle, and the cider dripped through the wrapping to the ground. She then said quite firmly, "I christen thee Rose of York." King George and Gen. Doolittle then accompanied T Sgt Kelly and me into the waist section of the plane to have a look around. I remember that the King stooped over and very slowly and carefully made his way up to the radio room, but I don't recall Gen. Doolittle even bending his head down until he got to the radio room door. Members of the Press followed the king, but most of them were content to wait

outside the plane while he had his look around. I would estimate 15-20 members of newspapers, magazines, radio and newsreels recorded the event; and hundreds of pictures were taken. Ted Malone, a noted radio newsman, covered the event and a few days later beamed the program to the USA. It was a weekly show entitled: "Westinghouse Presents" and covered the actions of fighting men overseas. The March of Time included a segment in their newsreel, which at that time was shown at most theaters. Westinghouse was kind enough to mail my mother a recording of the event on a record, which I still have. Additionally, the Army Air Force sent a group of official photos to my home about a month later.

Princess Elizabeth meets crew, July 6, 1944

As I recall, the entire proceedings lasted about forty minutes. The dignitaries then went to the officers club for lunch and enjoyed some home made ice cream. The ice for the freezing was provided by a B-17 which took off with a few pots of water in the waist section. After flying around in the freezing temperatures it did not take long to change it to ice. Following the meal, the Royal family them motored to another 8th Air Force Base, I believe it was the 303rd Bomb Group at Molesworth. Pilot Raster, Co-pilot McDonough, Navigator Northway, Engineer Kelly and I as radio operator flew the plane to that base where it was viewed by many of their

266

personnel. We did not stay with the plane during this time and had free time until later in the day when we flew her back to Thurleigh. It was only a few days later that I again met Queen Elizabeth who made a surprise stop at the Red Cross Club located on Bronham Road in Bedford.

Two days following the christening on July 8th I flew my 30th mission and Engineer Kelly completed his combat tour. Kelly and I started together and remained on the same crew for 30 missions. He was the first man from our original crew to finish. I missed an earlier mission due to hospitalization and needed one more trip. That came on the following day, July 9th. On this day the "Rose" was piloted by Col. William Raper, group operations officer; and as was the case on many of her missions, she lead the First Bomb Division.

After my departure from the 306th Bomb Group on July 15th, the "Rose of York" continued to fly missions with new personnel at the controls and was usually picked as the lead aircraft for the Bomb Group. On February 3, 1945, she flew her 63rd and final mission. Ironically this raid was to Berlin, the same city where she got her initiation.

She received numerous flak hits while on the bomb run. One engine was smashed and another was leaking fuel as the big bomber turned for England and home. She kept lagging behind the main formation, finally another bomber crew reported hearing her last distress signals from an area over the Friesian Islands in the North Sea. Neither the plane nor any of its crew was ever heard from again. Eighteen other planes were shot down on this mission. On this occasion the "Rose" was carrying a passenger, Guy Byam, a BBC War Correspondent who had requested to make the flight. The 306th Bomb Group later named a plane for Guy Byam.

In 1997, Her Majesty, Queen Elizabeth II, dedicated the American Air Museum at Duxford England. A restored and greatly enlarged photo of the 1944 christening showing young Princess Elizabeth, King George VI, Queen Elizabeth and General Jimmy Doolittle was unveiled to mark the dedication. It is now on display at the entrance of the museum. A copy of this original photo accompanies this story of "Rose of York" a gallant plane, which I will always think of as "Princess."

"Little Jake" Epting grew up in Tupelo, and they say he was absolutely fearless on the football field even though the opposition he met might dwarf him physically. He was fast, he was shifty, he was fearless and he was smart. And so he was as he became the pilot of a B-24 Liberator, which his crew named "Tupelo Lass" in his honor. When Jake and his crew were starting their journey, flying their B-24 to England, Jake made it a point to fly over Tupelo; from what I hear about it, it was really more as if he "flew through Tupelo." They say he dropped down to treetop level and flew the entire length of Main Street at that altitude, catching everyone's attention just as he used to do on the football field.

Jake and his crew went on to fly in the 93rd Bomb Group at Hardwick. The Group was one of the ones shipped out to North Africa for special training and later the infamous raid on Ploesti. Fortunately, "Tupelo Lass" and her crew made it safely through that ordeal and returned to Hardwick to complete their tour. On the way they had engine problems and had to stop at Tripoli for repairs. While they were there, Jake met a fellow he knew from Tupelo and promised him a buzz job. You guessed it! Jake, true to form, gave them a buzz job of a lifetime.

"Little Jake" Epting is no longer with us, but he's still remembered in Tupelo; and, I would venture to say, among the veterans of the 93rd and the villagers in Hardwick, as well.

FIGHTER BASE DOC

By Dr. W. W. Walley

All my life I wanted to be a medical doctor. I got a job in a Junior College to pay my way through the two years of college there. At the end of the two years program, I was drafted into the Army. My spirits were somewhat down then because I thought that would be the end of my opportunity to go to medical school.

I was sent for basic training at Camp Wheeler, Georgia, where I was assigned to the 63rd Infantry Division and, also, the Medical Battalion. The latter made me very happy because at least I'd be working in the field of my greatest interest.

The Infantry Days

Two weeks before we were to ship out for the Pacific (we already had our orders to go to that theater) I was told to report to Headquarters, which I did. There I was told that I had been selected to go to Officers Candidate School. They explained that, if I was successful, at the end of my three-months training, I would be commissioned a 2nd Lieutenant in the Medical Administrative Corps. This sounded mighty good to me; I would be in the field I wanted to be in. However, I had no earthly idea what a Medical Administrative Officer's duties would be. I was just happy to be selected for an opportunity to go to school.

In O.C.S. I experienced some of the roughest and most intensive training of my career. It seems now, in retrospect, that they wanted to find out if they could break your spirit. If you couldn't take it, they felt you wouldn't be able to dish it out later. Two weeks before our class was to graduate, I was notified between classes one day, to report to Headquarters. What that usually meant was that you had "washed out." All of my friends started telling me good-bye and commiserating with me on such a terrible thing to happen after having gone this far. We knew, of course, that if we had to report to Headquarters, that we should change to a Class A uniform and report to the officer in charge. I reported with a rather snappy salute, expecting to be blasted, but this fellow hardly looked at me. He just said, "Candidate Walley, you lacked 32 cents paying for your laundry last week." I had been put through all that hassle to learn that I owed 32 cents. I really didn't know whether to blow-up or hug his neck! I just saluted, said "thank you," did an about face and returned to class. All my classmates were surprised to see me come back, since a call to report to Headquarters like that meant that you were never seen or heard of anymore; you just simply packed up all your stuff and shipped out!

At least I survived that and other ordeals and was commissioned a 2nd Lieutenant in the Medical Administrative Corps. When my assignment came I was totally surprised that I was being sent to the Air Force, and I would not have to go to the Pacific and into ground fighting as I was already resigned to do.

I was assigned to a Service Unit and stationed at Fowlmere, which is near Cambridge, in England; eventually I wound up with the 339th Fighter Group there at Fowlmere.

Lt. W.W. Walley, Fighter Base Doc.

I had a rather close call one day while I was on duty at the airfield at Fowlmere. I was riding from the flight line to the base hospital on my bicycle, when I heard one of those German V-1s, or "buzz-bombs" coming over. These unmanned bombs were a last gasp of the Germans and were sent over England in great numbers in those days. This thing sounded to me like a little one-cylinder engine attached to a bomb and directed toward England. When it ran out of gas, it just stopped. Then it just dropped where it was and, of course, exploded with a tremendous force. When I heard this "putt-putt" coming, I knew what to do - take cover! There was not much of a place to take cover in a big wide-open wheat field in which our base was located. I just resigned myself to what was going to happen, got off my trusty steed and lay down on the ground, covering my head with my arms. The bomb exploded about 100 yards from me. When I came to, I realized I had not been badly hurt, but I had a terrific headache and such a ringing in my ears that I couldn't hear anything. I don't really know how long this lasted, but I was able to get up, get on my bicycle and go on to my duty.

I did report to the Flight Surgeon on duty, told him what happened, and went through an examination to see if I was injured at all. He didn't find any bleeding or other evidence of serious damage and told me to go back to duty. My hearing was still affected; I couldn't hear the telephone ring; I couldn't hear anyone talking to me, but I could answer calls that came to me through my Sergeant who wrote them down for me. This lasted for some time. Gradually my hearing began to return, and eventually I could hear as well as ever. I was never on sick call and no record was ever made of my experience.

Fowlmere was a very small village, with maybe 400 residents. The main gate to our base was right in the middle of the village square. Also at the entrance was the village shop, run by a Mr. Jackson. He and I became close friends. I had some time on my hands because, when our planes were out, I had very little to do until they returned. Thus, I was able to spend some time with Mr. Jackson and became very friendly with him. I was invited to his home on several occasions and had Christmas dinner with him on the two Christmases I spent in England. He and his family needed cheering up since they had family members serving in the British armed forces far away; they also provided needed cheering up for me. Two of his daughters suggested playing tennis on one occasion. I thought this would be a snap as I brought a friend with me from the base to play. Even though I had never played tennis on grass before, I thought this would be easy; it wasn't. They made us look like rank beginners, beating us until it wasn't the least bit funny.

My duties as a Medical Administrative Officer were simple, mainly keeping medical records. One duty I had was to work with the Flight Surgeon who was on duty as he saw the men who reported to him for sick call. Sitting near him, I would handle one line of men while he saw another line of men. Of course, he was available to answer any real questions that came up; but most of the men I saw never knew that I was not another doctor. In fact, they all called me "Doc."

With some time on my hands, whenever I could it was my custom to go to mission briefings. On one of those days the Eighth put up over 1,000 bombers and many, many fighters. The air was so full of contrails it became completely overcast even though the day was fair to begin with. Before noon it was raining simply because of the condensation made by those contrails. It would take that huge bomber force quite some time to reach altitude and assemble in formation before crossing the Channel; sometimes they were circling and forming for an hour before starting across the Channel. On this particular occasion two B-24 bombers had a mid-air collision just overhead. I was a witness to the whole thing. There was a terrific explosion, because they were both loaded with bombs. Then out of the big ball of fire, two parachutes opened, then another. I quickly thought of the number of men flying in each plane, while only three had escaped. When the single parachute opened and was gradually descending, a burning bomber wing was spiraling down; and as it did so, it caught the parachute, dooming the descending airman. This was the most unnerving thing I ever saw during the War, even though I had seen numerous people killed, attended any number of airplane crashes and picked up pilots all over England to bring back to our base and eventually to the Cemetery near Cambridge. This young airman was one of only three who managed to get out of the two burning planes, with a total of at least twenty crew on board; the image of his burning parachute went over and over and over in my mind, and still does.

I remember another experience very vividly, because it made such an indelible impression on me at the time. We had a young replacement pilot going on his first mission. He was just as jolly as he could be, eager to go on his first mission. When he returned that day and landed, I don't think I've ever seen anybody as distraught as this man was. He was as near shock as anybody I've ever seen, not to be in total shock. I've wondered many times how he managed to land a plane like a P-51 on that fighter strip and survive!

It was my custom to help the returning pilots, get them out of the cockpits and get them back to base. We had whiskey available to give those who wanted it. On this particular occasion, this man was just too "shook-up" to undo his harness; I had to help him out of it. I then took him back to my office where he told his story. Since he was flying on his first mission, he said, "I really didn't want to shoot anybody, but everywhere I turned somebody got right in front of me." When it was all over, he had shot down five German fighter craft, and one almost certain "probable." He had become an ACE on his very first mission. He was a big part of the reason our Group was awarded a Presidential Unit Citation.

My participation in the events of D-Day were not memorable. A few days before the invasion began, I was sent on temporary duty to a British base down on the South Coast of England. I was to be there to help with the processing of expected casualties from the beaches of Normandy. As it turned out, no casualties were brought to this base. I had a pleasant time there with practically nothing to do, but I did have a sense of loss at not being back at Fowlmere where a lot of historic action was taking place.

At the end of the war in Europe my unit was moved back to the States. Shortly thereafter I received orders to report to a Very Heavy Bombardment Wing, stationed in Okinawa. I was promoted to Wing Medical Administrative Officer. However, while I was at home on a thirty-day leave, one of the planes from this Wing, by the name of "Enola Gay" dropped an atomic bomb on Japan. As it turned out, I never had to report to Okinawa. That was a very happy ending of my career in The Mighty Eighth.

I came home after the war was declared to be over, picked up my studies at the University of Mississippi, where I finished with a B.S. degree. I entered Medical School there and eventually entered the University of Pennsylvania where I earned a medical degree.

AN UNSUNG MISSISSIPPIAN IN THE MIGHTY EIGHTH AIR FORCE

By Craig Harris

This is the story of a Mississippian who carried out a vital role in the Eighth Air Force in 1943 through 1945, but whose story has not been told outside of historical accounts of the 457th Bomb Group. Roderick L. Francis, of Jackson, was assigned to the Group, newly formed in mid-1943; and by October, 1943, he was a Captain and the first commander of the 457th's 750th Bomb Squadron.

Before we start Rod's story, the author will share with the reader one reason for his interest in Rod Francis. Before the war, the author's father, Cecil E. Harris, was a school superintendent in Hinds County. Cecil Harris was a friend and colleague of Rod Francis's father, who also was a school administrator. When my father visited Mr. Francis, I would tag along and would visit with Rod, and we became friends. Later when my father organized a Boy Scout troop at the school in Byram, in Hinds County, Rod, already an Eagle Scout, pitched in to help. While he was the Assistant Scoutmaster, because of his age (less than 21), he had to be called, "Junior Assistant Scoutmaster." Intelligent, enthusiastic and good-looking, Rod was admired and respected by the little kids, of which I was one. We left Byram in 1938 for Port Gibson, and I lost track of Rod until February 6, 1945.

The 457th Bomb Group finished its Preparation for Overseas Movement (POM) and passed its POM inspection on January 12, 1944. Its aircraft and flying crews left Grand Island, Nebraska, on January 17, and arrived at USAAF Station 130, Glatton, between January 22 and February 1. Ground personnel arrived in early February, and ground and flight crew readiness was sufficient for the Group to go into action on February 21, putting aircraft over Lippstadt and Gutersloh.

By April 25, Major Rod Francis, 750th Squadron Commander, had been 457th BG Air Commander for four missions on which the 457th put up one squadron of a group. On that date he flew as AC with the crew of Captain Ed Bender on a mission to Essey airfield near Nancy, France. Sgt Laymon Mahan was the radio operator and Lt. Earl Woodard was Bender's lead navigator on that mission. Most of what we know of subsequent events come from Mahan's story in *Fait Accompli* (l) and from Woodard's unpublished story. (2)

The group encountered very heavy antiaircraft fire in the Nancy area; but, due to total cloud cover, no target could be identified sufficiently to make a bomb drop. So the group turned back toward the English channel, some 215 miles away, with bombs still aboard. South of Rouen, Major Francis's aircraft caught fire in the No. 3 engine. Sgt. Mahan looked in the bomb bay and fire was rolling between the bombs "... like logs in a fireplace." The bomb load was hurriedly dropped (near a small town, with the only injury being a skinned finger on a small girl). The crew parachuted from the burning aircraft (which burned without exploding long beyond the storied "37 seconds and she blows") and landed safely, scattered over a large area centered about 35 miles SSE of Le Havre, and about 5 miles SW of Bernay, in Normandy. The aircraft, a B-17G, 42-97070, crashed in the village of La Goulafriere and to this day is famous locally as "The B-17 of La Goulafriere." Major Francis came down near the village of St. Germain d'Aunay, which probably explains the official record of the crash as being in "St. Germain." As there are, by conservative estimate, at least seven towns named "St. Germain" within 30 miles of the actual crash site, first research erroneously placed the crash at St. Germain-la Campagne, about 3 miles north of St. Germain d'Aunay. A 1995 return visit to the area by Earl Woodard cleared up the confusion.(2)

Five of the crew - including Rod Francis, Laymon Mahan and Earl Woodard - evaded capture, and the rest - including Lt. Bender - were made prisoners of war. Mahan's narrative (1) tells in detail how the local French took the evaders in and turned them over to the Resistance, who helped the five take on false identities as Frenchmen and helped them make their way over several weeks, into Paris. In Paris , they caught a train to Toulouse, and thence were guided overland into the Pyrenees Mountains. After many tense moments while being shepherded by the guide, hopefully into Spain, they finally made their way into Spain on June 4, and into friendly hands. However, the evaders were very tense while in Spain, as Francis and Woodard were carrying information from the Resistance, such as the mining plan of Le Havre harbor, to take to the Allies. Unknown by them, they had been assigned to the Office of Strategic Services (OSS) a week after they were shot down, because of the secret information. Had they known, they would have been even more tense.

Upon arriving in London on June 17, Francis and Woodard were debriefed intensively for several days before they were allowed to return to Glatton. Back at Glatton, on July 5 Rod Francis was promoted to Deputy Group Commander, and to Lt. Colonel. By April 10, 1945, Col . Francis

had flown as Air Commander on eleven missions, while serving as Group Deputy CO.

On February 6, 1945, the author; his pilot, M.K. Burk; and navigator, J.T. Freese; were to report to the 457th Bomb Group CO, marking their "official" arrival at Glatton. Instead of reporting to the CO, the three were ushered into the office of the Deputy CO, who rose from behind a desk on which was a name plate that read, "Lt. Col. Roderick L. Francis, AC." I stared at this handsome man, who over the years that we were out of touch had put on more height, more weight and a mustache, and recognized Rod Francis. He stared at me in return and recognized me after which there were smiles and hearty handshakes (and a pilot and a navigator who wondered what in the world was going on).

Later, by asking around, I found that Rod Francis was well thought of by our colleagues, and had the reputation of being a good air commander who flew his share of the missions. We would meet only rarely at the officers club after that.

On April 10, 1945, Lt. Col. Francis was the air commander for the day's mission to Oranienburg, north of Berlin, with Captain Melvin Fox as pilot. Bombing was visual by squadrons in trail, and results were "generally good." No flak was encountered. However, just after the turn off the target, 3 or 4 ME-262s attacked the Group. Captain Fox's ship was hit between the No. 1 and No. 2 engines and left the formation with fire visible through a four or five foot slit in the wing, seemingly under control for several miles, when it circled, went into a spin and exploded. Fortunately, the crew had bailed out before the explosion; and only the radio operator failed to survive. Capt. Fox, Lt. Col. Francis (who landed on Hermann Goering's estate!), and the others were taken prisoner, but liberated some days later.

From *Fait Accompli* (3): "On May 28, 1945, Lt. Col. Roderick Francis, an evader and later a prisoner of war, was awarded the Silver Star. His citation is as follows:

"For gallantry in action while serving as air commander of heavy bombardment formations over Germany, 24 February 1944, 11 April 1944, 2 January 1945, 17 January 1945 and 10 April 1945. On these missions, Colonel Francis consistently overcame adverse weather, vicious fighter attacks, and intense flak to attack vital enemy installations. On several occasions, conditions and circumstances were so adverse that a less experienced and courageous leader would have faltered. On 11 April 1944, practically every aircraft was damaged, including Colonel Francis.' Unable to bomb the primary objective due to weather conditions, he maintained excellent air discipline and directed his units to another target of importance where a devastating blow was dealt to the enemy. The gallant leadership, forceful determination, and unyielding devotion to duty displayed by Colonel Francis reflects highest credit upon himself and the Army Air Force."**

I feel fortunate to have served under Rod Francis, and was happy to encounter him later in 1945, shortly after my separation from the service, on Capitol Street in Jackson. However, after that we lost contact, as he went on to a career, first in the Army Air Forces, then the US Air Force. We have been told that after retirement from the Air Force, he went into a second career as a high school administrator until his death in 1985.

Rod Francis was truly an outstanding "Mississippian in the Mighty Eighth."

REFERENCES:
(1) Mahan, Laymon. *In* Bass, JL & Briggs, HM: *Fait Accompli.* A Historical Account of the 457th Bomb Group (H) - The Fireball Outfit. JM Productions, Brentwood, TN 37024-1911, 1995. pp 273-277.
(2) Woodard, Earl. 918 Rochdale Dr., Kirkwood, MO. 63122-2414. Unpublished manuscript, loaned to author.
(3) *Fait Accompli.* Op cit. pp 317-318

Charles T. Williams grew up in Baldwyn but was living in Aberdeen and serving as a member of the Aberdeen Police Department when the war began. After completing his training in aircraft maintenance and gunnery, he was sent to England to work as a crew chief in the 487th Bomb Group. He attained the rank of M Sgt and received the Bronze Star for his outstanding service. He now lives in West Point with his wife Mamie. They have two children and two grandchildren.

JUST DROPPED IN AND STAYED A WHILE

By Bettye Duke Jackson

Ragland, second from right, kneeling.

James Leenard Ragland and his twin brother enlisted in the service April 20, 1942, and were sent to Camp Shelby. After three weeks, they were sent to Keesler Field, then to Pyote, Texas. Leenard was transferred to England and served with the 8th Air Force in the 379th Bomb Group. He was an upper turret gunner on a B-17 and attained the rank of T/Sgt. His plane was shot down over Gelsenkirchen, Germany in August of 1943. He was a P.O.W. in Stalag 17B, Barracks 39A for 21 months and was among the prisoners who marched over 250 miles through the Austrian Alps in the final days of World War II.

Leenard was shot down on his 7th mission – seven got out and three went down with the plane. He landed in a farmer's orchard and was knocked out momentarily. The next thing he knew, a German soldier had a gun between his eyes asking if he were American or British. The Germans were executing the British flyers. The

seven crewmen were interrogated and incarcerated in an old dungeon. They were kept there awhile and then, with a group of others, were loaded in box cars with fifty in a car and only standing room. The doors were barred and they had one bucket for a toilet. The boys had dysentery; so this was awful. They were in these cars for two days and nights before arriving at Stalag 7A where they stayed several months and then were sent to Stalag 17B for the remainder of the war.

Stalag 17B was an Air Force camp which housed 4,700 American enlisted men among a total of about 20,000 prisoners. Each barracks housed 300 men, 150 at each end divided into A and B sections by a common coldwater washroom. The barracks were very dark because there were only three bare light bulbs, and the electricity was turned off by 8:00 A.M.

274

Each end of the barracks was provided with a 20-gallon wooden pot which was used to carry food and water. There was usually a soup of cabbage, turnips, and horse meat (often spoiled), maybe a potato if they were lucky, and some kind of hard bread. If it had not been for the Red Cross, the P.O.W.s would have starved. They looked forward to the Red Cross truck coming on Friday with 10 pound packages of playing cards, books, powdered milk, Spam, corned beef, C-ration crackers, instant coffee, sugar, chocolate bars and 3 to 5 packages of cigarettes. The Germans would punch holes in every can so that food had to be eaten immediately and couldn't be stored for escaping.

The first winter was terrible – really rough. It was very cold, and the barracks offered no relief. One time it snowed for 62 days. About all they could do was stay in the barracks and play "stare."

A few tried to escape by digging tunnels under the barracks at night with empty food cans. Because the Germans would pull surprise roll calls, the men dug in the nude. When roll was called, they would have to hurry out of the tunnel and put on clothes that didn't have dirt on them.

Anxiety and depression were always there. Some went berserk and tried to go over the fence and were shot. Three who tried to escape were killed and their bodies were left lying in the snow for three days for all to see.

On April 9, 1945, with Germany falling to the Allies, 4,700 Americans in eight groups of over 500 began to walk west over 250 miles to liberation. They carried very little because they had nothing. The weather was cold and wet; sometimes 20 below zero. They slept on the ground, in barns when they found them, built shelters in the forest – many were sick and weary. The 13th Armored Division of General Patton's 3rd Army liberated them in May, 1945.

Leenard, when asked about his time in prison, always said, "I just dropped in and stayed awhile." Taps were sounded for this soft-spoken, gallant airman on July 30, 1997.

Congratulations on a job well done!

275

Otis G. Lancaster was born and grew up in Hamilton. He flew as pilot in the 490th Bomb Group out of Eye, in England. Otis only flew two missions, as the war in Europe ended shortly after his second mission. His first mission was a rough one, and he received the Distinguished Flying Cross for his part in it. His citation reads as follows:

OTIS G. LANCASTER,0830871, Second Lieutenant, Army Air Forces, United States Army. For extraordinary achievement while serving as pilot of a B-17 aircraft on a heavy bombardment mission to Kolin, Czechoslovakia, April 18, 1945. Prior to reaching the target Lieutenant Lancaster lost altitude when he drew only partial power from one of his engines. Noticing his position beneath the formation, an enemy fighter attacked, hitting another engine which became inoperative. Though prepared for an emergency landing, Lieutenant Lancaster brought his plane to the English coast where he lost the use of all but one engine. Undaunted, he skillfully landed his plane safely on the one remaining engine without incurring further damage to plane or crew. The outstanding airmanship, courage, and devotion to duty displayed by Lieutenant Lancaster on this occasion reflect the highest credit upon himself and the Army Air Forces of the United States.

Otis and his wife Irene live now in Columbus, where he is retired from where he worked in the State ASC office and, from 1950-1984 served as County Administrator.

THE METZ MISSION ON
NOVEMBER 9, 1944

By Willard F. Nester

(Note: This is the story of the Second Air division's B-24 heavy bombers that were assigned to destroy gun fortifications in the area near Metz, France, during World War II. The forts were hampering the advance of our U.S. Third Army by being strategically located deep inside the mountains, protected by a barricade of steel and concrete and defended by German troops. It would have been very costly in men and equipment to take these installations by ground forces; so the U.S. 8th Army Air Force was requested to use their heavy bombers to drop high explosive bombs on these forts to destroy them. My crew participated on this November 9, 1944 mission, with Fort L'Asine as our target. More that 400 B-24 aircraft were dispatched to bomb four (4) targets in the Metz area. Most of the detailed information in this story was obtained from official reports on file in the Air Force Archives, along with some of my personal recollections of this mission. Willard F. Nester)

There have been many individuals who have asked me: "What was it like to fly a combat mission?" Well, there were "good" missions and "bad" missions. No two were ever alike and no two individuals remember the same details. For me personally, the Metz mission was both "good" and "bad."

I was a B-24 bomber pilot, with a combat crew, assigned to the 329th Bomb. Sqdn, 93rd Bomb. Gp. (H), stationed at Hardwick, East Anglia, U.K., that was part of the 2nd Air division, 8th Army Air Force in Europe, during World War II. We had been trained in instrument bombing procedures (known as GH or Gee H) that permitted release of bombs on targets obscured by cloud cover or otherwise not visible. This placed GH crews in formation lead positions.

My story is about the mission my crew was on to bomb gun emplacements in the area near Metz, France, during WWII. Webster's dictionary identifies a gun emplacement as a "fortress, a large and permanent fortification." These fixed emplacements were built in strategic locations in the mountains, concealed and protected by a bombproof chamber of steel and concrete, with an embrasure in the wall which would allow a cannon

or artillery piece to be fired. (Note: I've been told, true or not, that these forts were never captured or destroyed during WWI. They were neutralized by encirclement.) This mission was flown on November 9, 1944, and the target was Fort L'Asine (Target # 27), located southwest of Metz.

The situation at the time was that the U.S. Third Army, commanded by Lt. Gen. George S. Patton, Jr., was approaching the German border where they began to encounter heavy resistance from German artillery, coming from gun emplacements located in the area near Metz. The U.S. Third Army requested heavy bomber attacks against the forts to silence their guns during passage of the U.S. Armored forces, seeking more favorable positions, for the eventual reduction of these fortifications. It was determined that approximately 1300 heavy bombers would be required to produce the desired results. The U. S. Eighth Army Air force could provide the required bombers from its three bombardment Divisions. The First and Third Divisions flew the B-17 aircraft, and they dispatched 904 B-17s. The Second Division flew the B-24 aircraft, and they dispatched 401 B-24s, for a grand total of 1305 heavy bombers to attack the Metz targets. An additional 10 B-17 aircraft were used to dispense their cargo of chaff over the entire target areas prior to arrival of the bombers and to disrupt sightings of the enemy antiaircraft guns. The B-17 aircraft groups attacked five targets, three in the Metz area and two in the Thionville area. The B-24 groups attacked four targets identified as Fort Nos. 17, 18, 23, and 27 (L'Asine). The remainder of my story will focus on the 2nd Air division's B-24 aircraft units.

The mission began on November 9, 1944 at 0300 hours when we were awakened and told to prepare for a mission that day. We dressed hurriedly but made sure that we wore the warmest clothing we had, leaving room only for heavy flying suits to be put on later. We stopped by the mess for breakfast knowing that our next meal would be at least 10-12 hours away. Our next stop was the equipment room in Operations to finish dressing in our flight gear and to pick up any equipment and supply items that would be needed on the flight.

Briefing was at 0400 hours, and that's when we found out where we were going and the target. The big map of Europe, mounted on the wall, was unveiled with colored strings marking the route in and out of the target area. The color of the strings indicated the different units involved. Briefings were very thorough. Weather conditions were explained in detail and covered from take off, forming, route in and over the target area to return home, including forecast landing conditions. The briefing officers briefed us on such things as the possibility of encountering enemy aircraft, areas of heavy flak, jamming of communications, and many other things to disrupt our mission. Also, they told us where we would pick up our fighters, and use chaff to disrupt their antiaircraft gun sights. To name it all is almost impossible, but it was just about everything that a crew needed to know.

On some of our missions, we were dropping our bombs only two or three miles in front of friendly forces, and doing that through cloud cover. This mission was the initial operational use of warning lines defined by SCS 51 localizer transmitters and the use of friendly antiaircraft bursts to mark the front lines. It was very important to know when we had passed friendly forces lines and not drop bombs prematurely. The transmitters were set up to give yellow indication on the approach to the warning lines and blue indication after crossing the line. The friendly antiaircraft bursts were spaced 500 yards apart for one mile on each side of the transmitters, firing 10 minutes before arrival of the bombers and continuing until 10 minutes after the attack was scheduled to end. The bursts were about 17,000 feet altitude and well below the bomber formations.

After the briefing, we were taken in the familiar GI trucks (canvas top, metal floor, fold down benches, etc.) to our assigned aircraft to prepare for the flight. The first inspection item was thorough "walk-around" of the aircraft and a status briefing by the plane's crew chief. Then followed a "look-around" inside the plane before settling into your crew position and making your first radio contact with the control tower. Next was a check of the aircraft's status forms, fuel load, radio and navigational equipment and intercom check with each crew member. Our crew consisted of the regular crew of ten men - plus on this mission an air commander and a pilotage navigator were assigned - for a crew of twelve. We carried 2500 gallons of fuel, two 2000 lbs. high explosive bombs and two smoke bombs. All other B-24 aircraft in the formation, except the GH lead crews, carried three 2000lbs. high explosive bombs and no smoke bombs.

Briefed times for the mission were: Station time - 0620; Start engines - 0640; Taxi - 0650; Take off - 0905; Zero hour - 0900. Take off weather at our base at Hardwick was: 2-4/10ths stratocumulus, bases 2-300ft., tops 5-7000 ft.; nil medium or high clouds; visibility 3-5 miles in light haze; surface winds W - WNW 15-20 mph.

We took off at 0700; and as soon as we were clear above the clouds, proceeded to the northern assembly area near Seething to join with the 448th Bomb. Gp (H) Weather prevented forming at the briefed altitude of 14,000 ft., and we had to move up to 18,000 ft. to form. That's where we took the GH lead of wing "A," consisting of 448th and 93rd Groups (H). Wing "B," consisting of 489th and 446th Bomb Gps (H), joined Wing "A" to complete the 20th Combat Wing formation. As leader of 448th Bomb Group (H), we left the English Coast at the assigned check point of Dungeness at 0909, at 18,400 feet. Enemy coast at 0917, at 20,000 feet.

Forecasted weather from the enemy coast to target area was briefly: Tops 12-14,000 ft., low clouds 5-8/10 coverage at target with occasional large breaks, tops 8-12,000 ft. Medium clouds formed rapidly 6-9/10 coverage, 16-18,000 ft., then becoming nil to 3/10 at target. Nil high clouds entire route. Visibility unrestricted aloft.

The Wing held a good formation and at approximately 0940, three Groups of P-51 fighters picked us up and provided fighter cover the rest of the way to IP, target, rally point and back to the point where they first picked us up. What a beautiful sight to a bomber formation to see those "Little Friends" in their familiar "figure 8" pattern about 2,000 ft. above our bombers. The P-51s never looked better.

The formation lead was briefed to be at the IP at 0946 - we were there at 0954 at 22,000 feet. Groups had gone into trail formation just prior to the IP and squadrons in trail formation just past the IP on the bomb run. Bombing altitude was 22,000 ft., IAS 160mph; - TAS - 225 mph; - winds 300 degrees at 90 mph; mag. Heading - 81 degrees - true Heading - 75 degrees; drift 6 degrees right; bomb sight - Norden; length of bomb run - 10 minutes; time of release - 1006; by GH procedures. Rally point at 1013 at 20,000 feet.

Prior to reaching the IP, we received a coded message that instructed all GH led units to drop their bombs using GH procedures, if at all possible. At the IP we made our run on course receiving a strong Gee signal and quickly established our course to the target area. About five (5) minutes on the bomb run, the navigator reported the Gee signals were fading badly and was concerned that he might not be able to use GH procedures for the bomb release. Shortly, he reported back that the signals had strengthened and were stable enough for use on the bomb run. He kept us on course

until the bombardier reported that he could see the target. Weather conditions had improved over the target area to 3-5/10 broken cloud cover, and downward visibility was unlimited. The bombardier, by use of the bomb sight, took us over what he had determined to be the target. Since we had been instructed to use GH procedures, and the navigator was confident he, too, was on course, the navigator released the bombs. After impact, the bombardier hurried from his position in the nose of the aircraft onto the flight deck and with great excitement told me, "I got a good look at the target and we knocked hell out of it." We made a smooth right turn making sure to keep our formation in close, and at the same time losing some altitude to be at the rally point at 20,000 feet. At this point the leader of the 93rd Bomb Group, after making a sharper turn to the rally point, was ahead of our formation off to the right and kept this lead back to our home bases. Weather conditions permitted the returning formations to slowly lose altitude, leaving the enemy coast at 1201 at 9000 ft. altitude and over the British coast at 1219 at 7,500 ft. altitude.

Weather conditions upon arrival at home bases were: 10/10 swelling cumulus and cumulonimbus, base 7-1200 ft., with rain and snow showers, tops unobserved. Visibility 3-5 miles except 1-3 miles in precipitation. Surface winds WNW-NNW, 20-25 mph with gusts to 35 mph. Since we were preparing for an instrument let-down and landing at Hardwick (our home base), I'm assuming that the 448th BGp was led by the deputy leader to their base at Seething for a similar type landing. There was no problem in landing, and we were home after a six hour thirty-five minutes mission. After debriefing the officers on my crew by staff personnel, the mission was at last complete.

If Paul Harvey, the noted news commentator and story teller, was telling this story, he would probably precede his remarks with "AND NOW FOR THE REST OF THE STORY." Except for the problems encountered while forming, caused by weather conditions, the mission had been a routine one until we were about half way on the 10 minute bomb run, when strange things began to happen.

First were the fading Gee signals; then moments later the signals strengthened to a degree of reliability and stability that could be used to maintain our course. Then the navigator began asking for course corrections, such as 2 degrees right, 2 degrees right, 3 degrees right, 2 degrees right, so close together that it was almost as if in a steady turn. We were on autopilot, and those corrections were made with precision. The heading on the bomb run started out as 81 degrees mag., 75 degrees true, 6 degrees right drift. At 22,000 feet wind direction was 300 degrees, velocity 90 knots, indicated air speed 160 mph, TAS 225 mph, ground speed 300 mph. About the time the course corrections had been made, the bombardier reported that he could see the target and engaged the C-1 Norden bomb sight on what he had determined to be the gun emplacement target. Both he and the navigator were confident that they were on course to the target. Bombs were released by the navigator on GH backed by the bombardier and his bomb sight - the ideal bomb run. Their skills by training, experience and dedication could not be questioned, for they, in my view, were at or near the top in their specialties. This was the crew's 13th GH lead mission - 5 squadron, 4 group, 3 wing and 1 division leads. We all thought at the time that we had hit our target with good results.

This mission had been on my mind for a long, long time as being the best of the thirty combat missions my crew flew during WW II. I felt that on this mission we did the most good to help our ground forces in reducing casualties and saving American lives, while bring closer the end of WW II. I was coaxed into writing my account of this mission, knowing that I was not capable of doing this story properly.

It was not until this year (January, 1996), while getting research data from the AF Archives at the Air University, Maxwell AFB, AL, and National Archives at College Park, MD, that I learned that the target we destroyed was a small town, or village (Goin, France), located approximately 2 miles southwest of the MPI (Main Point of Impact) for our assigned target (No. 27). Other GH lead navigators in the Wing also reported fading Gee signals, and one group completely lost their Gee signals and was forced to bomb targets in the Thionville area visually. We missed our target badly; and, as wing leader, caused other units dropping on our smoke bomb to miss, also. I deeply regret the very big error we made, but now you know "THE REST OF THE STORY."

On November 19, 1944, Lt. Gen. George S. Patton, Jr., wrote a personal letter to his friend, Lt. Gen. Carl A. Spaatz, Hq. U.S. Strategic AF Europe, to express his thanks for the heavy bomber support in the Metz area and advise him of the results when he inspected the forts.

A copy of this letter was endorsed through channels to the Commander, 329th Bomb Squadron, 93rd Bomb Group for all concerned personnel who were GH leaders on the Metz mission, of November 9, 1944.

Of the 401 B-24 aircraft dispatched for the 2nd Air Division to bomb four targets in the Metz area, 340 aircraft with GH leaders attacked the assigned targets, while sixteen aircraft were forced to visually bomb targets in the Thionville area. Of the four Metz targets, the B-24 units dropped a total of 2,139.000 lbs. (1069.5 tons) of high explosives, almost exclusively of the 2000 lb. HE type. We encountered no enemy fighters, flak was nil to meager and inaccurate, going in, over the target area and out, with only five aircraft reporting light damage. All aircraft returned safely and the 2nd Combat Wing reported the only fatality of approximately 3700 B-24 air crew members on this mission.

SERVICE OF THOMAS OWEN ROBERTS

By Thomas Owen Roberts

I lived in Cleveland and Shelby prior to service in World War II. I now reside in Brookhaven.

After enlisting for cadet training, I changed my residence to Boulder City, Nevada; and when called to duty in 1943, I reported to Fresno, California, for basic training, before proceeding through the various bases in California and Texas for further training; and I was commissioned as a navigator in December, 1943. I took combat crew training at Dalhart, Texas. When this was completed, we proceeded to England on the Mauretania, and were assigned to 369 Bomb Squadron, 306th Bomb Group, stationed at Thurleigh, near Bedford. I was on the crew of Lt. Richard F. Vogel, of Indiana.

Our first mission was to Saarbrucken on May 11, 1944; and our last mission on August 10, 1944, was to Chamant, France. I was fortunate to complete my assigned 32 missions without injury or problems, and my tour was rather uneventful, if you can call 32 B-17 missions uneventful.

Two of the missions were on D-Day and from June 17 through June 24, 1944, a period of 8 days, I flew 7 missions. My overall tour included two missions to Berlin, two to Hamburg, two to Munich, various other targets in Germany and France and one to Ghent, Belgium. The regular tour of duty was 30 missions when I started, and after 20 missions, the tour was increased to 35. I was given credit for three missions on paper to complete the tour.

A memorable part of my duty was the return to the U.S. on the Queen Mary; Winston Churchill was on board for the crossing. He disembarked in Halifax, Nova Scotia, to proceed to one of his meetings with President Roosevelt in Quebec.

I was promoted from 2nd Lt. To 1st Lt. during my tour of duty, and I was awarded the Distinguished Flying Cross and the Air Medal with three Oak Leaf Clusters. (The awards were standard for missions accomplished and not for any outstanding performance.)

While not a part of my Eighth Air Force duty, I did elect to stay in the reserve after the war was over; and I was recalled to duty during the Korean War as a captain with my job being that of a navigator-bombardier on B-26 aircraft. (This was the Douglas B-26, not the Martin B-26.) I completed 50 missions during the summer of 1952.

I have been an attorney since 1941, and later switched to the Air Force Judge Advocate Reserve. I retired from the reserve with the rank of Lieutenant Colonel.

Ray N. Bethune was born and grew up in Tennessee but lives with his wife, Jeanette, in retirement, in Biloxi. Ray was a pilot in the 493rd Bomb Group at Debach, in England, where he flew 35 missions as a pilot. He was awarded the Distinguished Flying Cross with two Oak Leaf Clusters and the Air Medal with 6 Oak Leaf Clusters.

OUT OF THE VALLEY OF THE SHADOW

By Catherine Gardner

Dan Gardner went through some deep valleys during his time in the 8th Air Force. He says, "I lost many friends and saw much suffering. We fought, bled and many died to protect our freedom."

In 1941, at the age of twenty-one, Dan joined the Air Corps. He was immediately sent to airplane mechanics school at Shepard Air Force Base in Texas. The United States was at war, and young men were being trained for combat missions. Leaving Texas, he traveled to Utah where he met his B-17 crew and began his assignment as a flight engineer.

In February, 1943, Dan began a circuitous journey to England. Stops along his route included Homestead Air Force Base, Florida; Trinidad; South America; Dakar in Africa; a French Foreign Legion camp in the Atlas mountains of North Africa; Morocco; and finally in England. There he was re-assigned to a B-24 group and flew three bombing raids into France.

One mission of the Allies was the destruction of the oil fields and refineries of Ploesti, Romania. These fields produced a big part of the oil supply for Hitler's war machine. In August of 1943, Dan's crew was scheduled to fly over these oil fields, but due to the loss of another plane, the mission was given to a more experienced crew.

After the Ploesti raids, Dan went back to England and Scotland and flew missions into Tunisia and Italy. They also flew missions directed toward German submarines of the coast of southern France.

On Dan's eighth mission over Germany, his plane took a direct hit between engines No. 1 and 2. Fire broke out and the plane began to lose a thousand feet of altitude per minute. The pilot ordered the crew to bail out. When Dan bailed out, he realized his parachute was not fastened correctly. He had to hold the chute with one hand and pull the rip cord with the other hand.

He landed in a field where a German farmer and a Polish prisoner of war were working. The two men took Dan to a big barn and alerted the German officials. The Germans placed Dan in solitary confinement, interrogated him for four days - December 20 - 24, 1943. Dan finally was joined by his crew; all had escaped from their burning aircraft and had been captured by the Germans. They were all interned in Stalag 17-B in Austria along the Danube River for eighteen months. Dan was in the P.O.W. camp with fellow Mississippians Lamar Rogers from Jackson, Harold Stalnaker from Tupelo; A. T. Bunch and Leenard Ragland from Oxford.

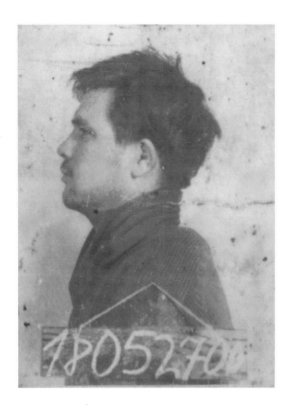

Around the 8th day of April, 1945, the Germans, fearing the approach of the Russian army, ordered the prisoners to take overcoats, blankets and any food they could carry and start marching. They marched 288 miles in 22 days - five days in rain and three days in snow. Having no shelter, they tore bark of trees and gathered moss to make shelters which always leaked. Sometimes they would find potatoes and turnips in fields along the way to eat. (Even now Dan shuns potatoes or turnips.)

The U. S. 13th Armored Division came into the P.O.W. camp on May 3, 1945, disarmed the Germans and freed the prisoners. They were flown to France and then home to the U.S.A.

After discharge, Dan served in the Mississippi State Highway Patrol. He served the Batesville district and was later transferred to the Starkville district. Dan retired as an Assistant Inspector after 30 years of service.

Luther Murray Dove was born and grew up in Louisiana, but he and his wife, Elma, now live in Jackson. Murray completed aircraft mechanics school, Boeing Flying Fortress School and gunnery school before joining his crew and proceeding to become part of the 92nd Bomb Group at Podington. He flew as the engineer-top turret gunner on his crew as they flew 34 missions and received one mission free! He was awarded the Air Medal with Oak Leaf Clusters. His missions included two trips to Berlin and the Kassel raid of December 1, 1944.

Crew picture, showing Charles Thomas Chambers standing, right.

A TRIBUTE TO CHARLES THOMAS CHAMBERS

By Olga Jones Chambers

I am the widow of Staff Sergeant Charles Thomas Chambers, ball turret gunner on 1st Lt. Robert G. Ritchie's crew, in the 385th Bomb Group. This is my story:

Tommy and I were childhood sweethearts. We were married when I was 17 and he was 20, We had a happy, fulfilling marriage that lasted 5 ½ years and are the parents of two sons, Charles and Thomas. Since Tommy was married with two children, his draft was deferred for many months. There was a great need for good men in the service and the time came for him to go.

Tommy was very patriotic and although he really wanted to stay with his family, it was his time to fulfill his military obligation. Once in the service, he volunteered for flying combat missions. He had heard horror stories about the danger in flying over enemy territory, but there

was a job to be done and my Tommy faced up to that challenge (he was that kind of guy).

Tommy told me about his trip overseas in a letter, as follows:

"When we left Gulfport, we went to Savannah, Georgia to Hunter Air Base. We were to get new B-17Gs and fly to England, but seven crews didn't get B-17Gs, ours being one that didn't get to fly over.

"Rather than sit around and wait for new B-17s, they said we were needed in England soon. We were at Hunter Air Base for about two days, then sent up the coast by train to Camp Kilmer, New Jersey. We were there for two or three days, then on a Saturday night before midnight all seven crews of us were taken by ferry boat to New

York docks and boarded the Queen Mary and sailed the next afternoon.

"It took only five days to get from New York to Greenock, Scotland (near Glasgow); from there by train to Eccleshall, England, for bomb group assignment. This took another two days; after that we were sent to Elmswell (Great Ashfield), our home base of the 385th Bomb Group. Each Bomb Group had four bomb ssquadrons; ours were the 548th, 549th, 559th and the 551st. We were assigned to the 548th Squadron.

"All this transpired from the time we left Gulfport until early in December of '44."

He was and still is my hero. I sensed that his job was very dangerous. Because of this, he told me very little about what was required of him. He didn't want me to worry. He had already gotten credit for two fighters he had shot down.

Charles Chambers, right, in squadron area.

On April 4, 1945, I received that dreaded notice that he was Missing in Action. It was a midair collision, off the coast of Holland; all the men in both planes were lost that day.

The shock of that message was devastating. My life has never been the same. In one moment I went from being a happily married woman to a struggling widow with the sole care of two young children.

Charles Chambers, right. Typical transportation.

When the news first came, other loved ones from the other crew members and I wrote letters to each other. At first, we were hopeful, but after a few weeks, when we realized all was lost, the tone of the letters changed to one of sorrow and sympathy for each other. (I still have those letters.) It indicated that all hope was gone. Tommy was never coming home.

I later learned that Tommy's death was the result of a midair collision. The following is an excerpt from a letter written by Mike Gallagher, an eye witness to the midair collision which took his life (Tommy was on Ritchie's crew.).

"Tim Crimmins was flying low section lead and Bob Ritchie was the element lead. This placed Ritchie directly below Crimmins and slightly to his rear. So Ritchie positioned himself slightly under and behind the tail of Crimmins' plane. He maintained his position by visual reference to the tail of the plane right above him.

"For some reason Ritchie's aircraft slid forward under Crimmins. To decelerate, he raised the nose of his plane. It then struck the aircraft right above. The impact was either right at the tail gunner's position or slightly forward. The tail separated from Crimmins' plane and became embedded in the nose of the Ritchie plane. The Crimmins aircraft nosed up for a second then went into a spin and went out of sight. Ritchie was able to maintain altitude momentarily, but he too went into a spin and spiraled down.

"No 'chutes were sighted from either plane."

With limited educational background, I had to find a profession that would support my family. I made a wise decision when I decided to go to Beauty School. At one point, there were a few men in my life, but none measured up to my Tommy, so I dedicated my life to rearing our children and running my own Beauty Shop.

Life slowly became easier: I had my own business and operators working for me. I managed to buy a comfortable home and stay reasonably debt free. Although life dealt me a cruel blow, causing me to be both mom and dad, the knowledge that Tommy would have expected me to face this challenge, was the driving force that helped me to accomplish my goal. I have always had a very deep and abiding faith in my God, and that along with a very strong determination got me through this horrifying experience. (One day at a time.)

I'm very proud of our sons. The older, Charles, was military, retired now after two tours in Vietnam. The younger is in Hospital Administration in a large hospital. My grandchildren are successful.

I spent many lonely, fearful hours, especially while Tommy was overseas. I never faced the reality of his not coming back until that day, April 4, 1945, when the official word came. I know now that he had to face the reality every day that this one might be the one from which he would not return. I heard of others not making it. But not my Tommy! This couldn't ever happen to us - but it did.

All was lost. Many wives, sweethearts, mothers and fathers were left behind. I've long since lost contact with the families, but there was a bond between us.

Tommy Chambers, my one and best love, was one of many unsung heroes, who gave up everything. I'm making sure that his memory will live in my children and grandchildren.

I'm quite proud of what I have accomplished since I lost him. I feel that I'm loved and admired. One compliment that stands out in my mind - when our youngest son said, "Mom, I never had a dad, but I never wanted for anything and I never felt in the least bit deprived, thanks to you."

BOMBS, BULLETS, BARBERING,
BOY SCOUTS AND
BEAUTIFUL DULCIMERS

This story is based on an interview with Hollis Long by Kenneth and Ethelda Nail.

Hollis E. Long was born in 1920, in Golden, where he also grew up, went to school and finished high school in nearby Belmont. His interests, as he grew to young manhood, began to center on music, particularly the guitar. All during his high school years, along with his brother and a small musical group, he played at parties, at schools and other engagements. Since there was no television in those days and most folks didn't even have radios, they often played in people's homes. After a Saturday night supper, the little band would furnish musical entertainment. That was the social life in the Golden- Belmont area in those days!

Hollis and his sweetheart, Nevil Senter, were married in September, 1941, less than two months before Pearl Harbor. He says that, because of the tense situation at the time, before he could be issued a marriage license, he had to sign a statement that he wasn't just getting married to avoid the draft. When Pearl Harbor was attacked, Hollis says he thought, "This is the last straw, but we are ready!"

At the time he was working as a painter, painting houses in the local area. This he continued for another year until he was drafted into the Army in December, 1942. Two of his brothers had asked for the branch of service they wanted and got what they wanted. Hollis decided not to ask for anything but just to accept whatever was assigned to him. When he took the prescribed tests, he made very good grades; because of his grades, he was assigned to the Army Air Corps. He was glad about this at the time; later he was *really* happy about it.

Basic training was at Jefferson Barracks, Missouri. He found living to be pretty rough for a newcomer to military service. The men lived in tents; it was

a cold winter, and they had few comforts. They didn't even have mattresses on their cots, only cardboard to sleep on. Walter Winchell described Jefferson Barracks as "Little Alcatraz." The men were advised that they had better not get sick and go to the hospital, or they would just have to stay in this place that much longer. Hollis says that they marched and marched every day, sometimes with terrible colds and near pneumonia. One of Hollis's friends did spend two weeks in the hospital, but when the rest of their group finished their six weeks, he was on the train with them anyway.

Dashing young Hollis Long

The next training was ordnance school in Savannah, Illinois, followed by armorer training in Pennsylvania. These two training experiences equipped him to handle bombs, fuse them, defuse them, load them. Bombs had to be maintained in good condition; fuses had to be changed out if there was any corrosion -- very dangerous work. They couldn't smoke; any small spark could set them off. Also, the men learned to link and load ammunition for machine guns.

It was December, 1943, before Hollis was ready to go overseas. They left from Camp Miles Standish at Taunton, Massachusetts, boarding their troop ship at Boston harbor. The ship was of the Liberty ship class, about 400 feet long. It was a former cruise ship, named *Crystal Ball.* They loaded about 5,000 troops on this small vessel. As was usual for ships of this size, especially in winter weather, the voyage was rough and many of the troops were seasick. Hollis never was. In fact, he says, the food was good. He was given a meal ticket for 25 meals; when the trip was over, he had had it punched 23 times.

Hollis was assigned guard duty on a 20 mm gun, all the way across the Atlantic, two shifts at night and two in the daytime. It was very cold out on deck and obviously, he didn't get too much sleep. The seas were so rough that, one moment he could dip up water over the rail with his cap; the next moment he was 75 feet in the air. It was so rough that the ship's crew tied ropes around the deck to hold to when you needed to get around.

The *Crystal Ball* was one of many ships in a convoy. Hollis says there were ships to the right and to the left of his ship, and there were ships as far as he could see in front of him and as far as he could see behind. A submarine followed the convoy for two days, and he saw destroyers dropping depth charges all around the convoy. This was very scary to all on board, but after two days the submarine gave up and left. One incident Hollis remembers was the sight of a man being buried at sea. He watched as a crew lifted a flag-covered body to the rail on a neighboring ship, tilted it up and the body slipped easily into the sea. Their ship landed at Glasgow on December 15. It was two months before Hollis learned that his and Nevil's first child, daughter Martha, was born on December 13 while he was still two days out at sea.

Leaving Glasgow, the Group went to Hull for 14 days for some overseas training, then to High Wycombe for 15 days for training on setting up a base (theirs was to be a new base). He found High Wycombe, the headquarters of the Eighth Air Force and General Doolittle's office, to be a very nice place: good living quarters, great food, a golf course – a veritable country club. While there his Group put together a small building for headquarters use. They also were trained to arm planes, before proceeding by train and GI trucks to their permanent home at Fowlmere, near Cambridge, the home base of the 339th Fighter Group.

The new base had Quonset huts for the personnel, but there was very little else there when the group arrived. The runways were simply metal mats laid out across a wheat field.

While the fighter pilots (P-51s) were on missions, the armorers spent their days linking ammunition. Before the planes left on each mission, they loaded the belts of 50 caliber ammo for each gun; they also loaded bombs under the wings in many cases. The base at Fowlmere was a frequent target for bombing attacks, and once a "buzz bomb" landed on the base, but aside from leaving a hole in the wheat field large enough to put a house in, it didn't do a great deal of damage. However, all this gave the ordnance men, like Hollis, some concern as they were loading bombs at the bomb dump.

Ready to load bombs for Adolph

Hollis recalls many instances of damaged P-51s returning from missions, belly landing in the wheat field. One day a plane was coming in for what looked like a perfect approach. However, it never leveled off, hitting the runway on its nose. The pilot managed to get out of the plane, staggered around dazed, ran into the edge of a wing, cutting

288

his nose so that he had difficulty breathing. Then the guns in the wings of the plane started going off. Hollis and the other armorers had to go in behind the plane and stop the guns from firing. The crash crew was then able to clear the wreckage while medics picked up the wounded pilot.

Sometimes planes came in with brakes inoperative. They weren't able to stop, running into barbed wire fences or into flight line huts which, fortunately, were unoccupied when planes were coming in. One day, on a take-off, a bomb under a plane's wing came loose, hit the runway and scooted about half a mile down it. It did no damage but gave a pretty good scare to everybody.

A slightly bunged-up Mustang

After seeing all the mishaps at Fowlmere, Hollis has been reluctant to fly ever since.

Hollis remembers very vividly the activity at Fowlmere on and around D-Day. During that period the P-51s flew almost around the clock, one mission after another. This really kept the ordnance people and armorers hopping, loading bombs, cleaning guns, loading belts of ammunition. (Hollis says that the pilots very seldom brought any ammunition home with them from missions, and they surely could use some ammo!) The time of the Battle of the Bulge was another memorable one. For the first few days after the German offensive began, the weather was so bad the P-51s couldn't fly. Then a day came when there was glimmer of hope for the weather. This meant the bombs and ammunition were loaded, only to get a signal that the mission was scrubbed. This meant everything

had to be unloaded. The same thing happened again the next day and the next and the next. When the weather finally did break, flights were two-a-day or three-a-day, just like on D-Day.

During the time Hollis was at Fowlmere, the 339th flew escort on a bombing mission to the Ploesti oil fields in Romania. This was their longest mission, an almost unbelievable trip for fighter planes. For this mission, the 339th Fighter Group received a Presidential Unit Citation.

Hollis and his fellow ground personnel knew who most of the P-51 fighter pilots at Fowlmere were, but didn't get to know them personally. When they came out to the flight line, they usually got aboard their planes and took off right away. He does remember Major George Preddy and Colonel Gravette, two of the leading aces. When the pilots had a delay of a mission they would go into a building nearby to wait. During this time they would write letters, many of them writing as if this might be their last letter home. Many times it was. The pilots would also censor the ground personnel letters for them while they were waiting to fly.

Not too long after arrival at Fowlmere, Hollis had the opportunity to try out for the dance band being organized on the base. He says, "Since I was the only guitar player applying, I was selected for the band." The members of the band named themselves "The Rocketeers." They were not part of Special Forces but, rather, were strictly volunteers. When they had a dance to play for, they often were out most of the night. Nevertheless, they still had their work to do on the flight-line the next day. The "Rocketeers" became rather famous and were much in demand. They played for parties at all the nearby bomber bases and fighter bases: Ridgewell, Bassingbourn, Duxford and, of course, at Fowlmere. They also played in London at the "Stage Door Canteen." They played all the popular songs of the day, especially Glenn Miller arrangements, though they had their own arranger. If they played for a party for enlisted men, each band member was paid $4.00; if for an officers' party the rate went up to $8.00. Most of the parties were lively, but Hollis remembers one party that turned into a drunken, rowdy melee. Once they joined with an RAF band to play for a dance.

The Rocketeers

Hollis and his guitar

On band trips to London, Hollis met a number of celebrities, including British singer Vera Lynn. He also met Bing Crosby and Frances Langford.

The members of the Rocketeers have tried to keep up with each other since the War; some have been to Golden to visit Hollis and Nevil. During his two year stay at Fowlmere, Hollis became friends with several of the British people who lived in the village and in the vicinity. He was invited to the home of

one man who was a government employee living near the base. He enjoyed tea, "biscuits," and creamed honey. He also enjoyed his host showing him his (flower) garden. He says this gentleman, who was widely traveled in Europe and elsewhere, had never been to America, and was full of questions about what it was like in the States.

Hollis and the other ground personnel at Fowlmere were especially interested in the children who lived in the village. There was a school very near the base. On special occasions, especially Thanksgiving and Christmas, these GIs would load up big boxes of food and gifts to take to the school. A few years ago, Hollis' brother, who is a school man, visited England and visited schools. When he visited the school at Fowlmere, he found that the children had put up a plaque at the school in memory of the GIs of the 339th Fighter Group.

When the Group left Fowlmere to return to the States, even though they left around 3:00 A.M., all the villagers lined the roads to bid them goodbye. All the houses in the village had their lights on; everybody was out to say farewell, old and young, especially the children. Many cried. Hollis remembers one friend, a villager who worked as a maintenance man on the base, crying and saying, "Everything is over. All the Yanks are leaving. Things are now going to be like it used to be."

When Hollis was growing up back in Golden, his father used to cut his hair along with that of his four brothers. Sometimes the boys cut each others hair. So it was at Fowlmere; Hollis cut hair for some of his friends during breaks in the work in the linking shed. One day the Captain, his Squadron C.O., called Hollis in and told him he wanted him to cut his hair. Hollis didn't want to do that, didn't want to mess up a haircut for the Captain! The Captain got his haircut. Evidently he liked the haircut he got, because Hollis had to cut his hair several more times. When the War was over and the Group was about ready to head back to the States, Hollis was ordered to Europe to cut hair for recently freed P.O.W.s at Camp Lucky Strike at Le Havre. He didn't want to go and miss going home with the Group. The Captain swore he didn't recommend Hollis for this job; in fact, he said he almost got in trouble trying to keep him from having to go. Who knows how great a barber Hollis was before; at Camp Lucky Strike he was faced with 80,000 P.O.W.s badly needing haircuts and de-lousing! Hollis did get through with his giant haircutting job and got back to the base in time to come home with the Group.

In civilian life, Hollis has continued his life with Nevil in Golden. He continued as a house painter and also served for a year as the postmaster in Golden. He also attended night school and got two years of college from extension classes taught by Ole Miss.

Many years ago Hollis became interested in Scouting although he had not been a Boy Scout in his youth. He has served as Scoutmaster of his troop in Golden for 49 years and still continues to serve today. As such he has amassed an enviable record, making trips with his troop to Philmont Ranch in New Mexico, and attending the National Boy Scout Jamboree at Valley Forge. He also has completed the requirements and has been awarded the Wood Badge. He also holds the Silver Beaver award in scouting.

Another interest Hollis has developed since the War is a musical one. He not only has become very active in making music the "old-timey" way; after attending dulcimer festivals in the Appalachian Mountains and observing, he went home and made one for himself. Now he is a regular at those festivals, enjoying the music of dulcimers, mountain banjos, hammered dulcimers, guitars, all of which is glorious. After making a dulcimer for himself, he began making them for others. He, at last count, had finished his 494th. He and his friends in this kind of music perform at many venues, not the least of which is at the meetings of the Eighth Air Force Historical Society!

Looking back to the days of World War II, Hollis says, "It was a bad time, a terrible time – but in some ways it was a pretty good time too."

This is Hollis R. Long: bomb loader, bullet stringer, barber, Boy Scout leader and beautiful dulcimer maker; and, he's a gentleman of the old school, always kind, always straight as an arrow, always cheerful, always Hollis!

Johnnie Sartor, Jr., is from Hamilton. He was a junior in high school there and was in church with his family when the news broke about the Pearl Harbor attack. After basic training in Gulfport and Armorers School at Denver, he trained with his crew at Tampa before they flew their brand new B-17 to England. Johnnie describes the mission to Bohlen, Germany on November 30,1944, as his worst. He says they were supposed to have a visual mission, but could not see the target due to smoke and clouds. Even though flak was very heavy and there were many holes in the plane, they did a 360 degree turn and went back over the target with the same results. Johnnie's ammo belt to his gun and his oxygen hose were shot out. They bombed a target of opportunity on the way home.

Johnnie's crew, plane named "Bad Time, Inc, II," may have been the last crew to have all ten original crew members living. Two are now deceased.

MIDAIR COLLISION: B-47 AND F-86H, FEBRUARY 5, 1958

By Howard Richardson

Editor's note: This is an account of a bizarre happening during the Cold War; it is still a story of The Mighty Eighth.

During February, 1958, the 19th Bombardment Wing, Homestead AFB, Florida, scheduled a USCM (simulated combat mission) which used B-47 aircraft loaded with nuclear weapons, the M-15. However, the weapon did not include the detonating capsule so that the weapon would not explode in an accident or if it was released in flight. We were fueled to the maximum which included full wing tanks. Takeoff took almost all of the 12,000 foot runway and was assisted by water injected during the takeoff roll. Aircraft proceeded in pairs, a loose formation. Climb was made up the middle of Florida. In the B-47, a normal level-off altitude is around 28,000 feet. As the mission progresses and the aircraft becomes lighter the B-47 will end up at around 40,000 feet at the latter part of the mission. Of course, when you complete air refueling you have descended and then gradually climb as you burn off your fuel.

Our crew consisted of me as aircraft commander, co-pilot, 1st Lt. Robert Lagerstrom, and radar-navigator, Captain Leland Woolard, who was flying as a substitute for our regular radar navigator. As we approached the Cape Canaveral area, we always watched and sometimes saw the launch of a missile. We turned on a westerly heading, proceeding to our KC-135 tankers, where we completed our scheduled air refueling. We continued westward, then turned north on a route which took us close to the Canadian border. We then turned on a southeasterly heading for our target at Radford, Virginia. We were exposed to enemy fighters and used our ECM gear.

After our target release we headed on a southerly heading, toward friendly territory. We were past the enemy around the Carolinas, and we were relaxed as we proceeded toward our home base, Homestead AFB. Our cruising level was around 39,000 feet; the weather was clear, visibility was excellent, but we were pulling contrails. The temperature was extremely cold at this altitude. All during the flight I had been busy making radio calls to FAA, selecting fuel tanks and watching the CG and moving fuel around. The co-pilot was busy recording the fuel log, operating the ECM and taking celestial shots for the bombardier-navigator. We started noticing fighter aircraft flying below and underneath us, going west then east. We were in friendly territory and were not too concerned about enemy aircraft.

About 30 minutes after midnight EST, February 5, 1958, as we approached the South Carolina-Georgia border, we felt a terrific jolt and a bright flash of light occurred off our right wing. The co-pilot and I saw the #6 engine slanted down 45 degrees, hanging by the front part of the engine to the wing. It appeared that it might fall off at any time. The right wing tank was missing.

Our cockpit was forward of the wing so that we could not see the surface of our wing, but we could see metal sticking up on its trailing edge. I don't know why, but the co-pilot and I said it had to have been a midair collision. He started calling "Mayday - Mayday" and trying to reach someone on the radio guard channel. We knew our nearest SAC base was Hunter AFB, GA. I told both crew members to forget about using our ejection seats until we determined how flyable the B-47 was. Lagerstrom contacted the Hunter tower, gave them our condition and asked them to relay this to SAC HQ and Homestead.

Major Howard Richardson, left

I then told the crew that I was going to descend to 20,000 feet altitude, put flaps and gear down and determine at what airspeed we could control the aircraft. I asked the radar/navigator to let me know when we could drop the left wing tank to hit in a wooded area rather than some home or highway. We dropped the tank and lowered the flaps and gear. I slowed the B-47 to around 220 knots and figured I could control the aircraft at that speed for approach and landing. I had been an instructor pilot, had in excess of 1500 hours in the B-47 and had a pretty good knowledge of its flying characteristics. We brought the gear and flaps back up and descended toward Hunter AFB. We talked about whether to keep the Mark 15 bomb. Tactical Doctrine listed the safety of the crew as the number one priority, if a decision was to drop the weapon. The Hunter tower told us that the runway had been under repair, and the beginning of the runway was about a foot above the ground and had not been smoothed out. We thought that if we landed a little short, the aircraft would catch the front of the runway and the Mark 15 might proceed toward the cockpit like a bullet through the barrel of a gun. We would also quickly lose 7600 pounds of weight, which might help the airspeed. Thus, we decided to jettison the Mark 15. We called the Hunter tower and told them what we were planning to do and asked them to call SAC HQ and get their blessing. We descended out over the Atlantic Ocean, then made a wide turn back toward the airbase. We had not heard from SAC, but decided to drop the weapon. Right after this the tower called us and said that SAC approved the drop but ordered us to go 20 miles offshore. We advised the tower that we had already released the weapon. I asked Woolard to make sure that he had the coordinates of the release. We made a wide base leg and turned on final, lining up with the runway. The wind was no problem; but my airspeed was high, on purpose. Since the #6 engine was slanted down, we didn't know whether it would drag on the runway. With gear and flaps down, I reduced the airspeed to 220 knots. I estimated my landing speed would be around 180 knots or less.

Trying to keep the right wing up and continuing to keep lined up with the runway became quite a problem. As we reached the runway, I reduced the airspeed more. When we did ease down to the runway, we were still fast and did a small skip. When we reached the runway again I pulled the brake chute, eased on the brakes and brought the B-47 to a slow speed, slow enough to turn off the runway. Fire trucks and ambulances were all around, plus the operations automobile with the ops officer and safety officer.

We all got out of the aircraft, and I think we all kissed the tarmac. Reviewing the B-47, we found the right aileron pushed in 20 inches deep and 4 feet long. We found out later that the main spar was broken. There was a big hole in the vertical stabilizer, in the empty fuel tank and another hole in the horizontal stabilizer right by the ECM plates on the right side of the fuselage and the tail turret. We learned later that the aircraft never flew again.

We were taken into base operations and given a room in the VOQ. When we arrived at our rooms I asked both of the crew members to write down everything that they could remember about the collision and landing. I had been exposed to other accident reports and knew how the crew members were grilled about every detail. By this time we had conditioned ourselves to the fact that we would be around Hunter for some time until the Court-Martial was completed.

We had landed about 0126 EST, went to bed, slept a couple of hours before we were awakened and told to get ready to brief General Power, Commander of SAC who was on his way from Homestead in his KC-135. We proceeded back to Base Operations, back down on the flight line. We reviewed our notes and prepared for the worst. I briefed the General and his staff with the help of a map, showing them about where the mid-air had occurred and our flight path to a landing. After the briefing and after answering all of the questions, General Power told us to get our gear and board his aircraft and that he was taking us with him on the flight back to Homestead.

General Power always did the takeoff ; after he leveled off, he came back and talked to the three of us. He said that he had talked to General LeMay, who was CINC, USAF and asked for permission to pin a Distinguished Flying Cross on me and Commendation Medals on the other two crew members. General LeMay said that HQ, USAF did not operate that fast but that we would get the medals later.

General McConnell, the 2nd Air Force Commander, was on board. He returned to Homestead later and, at a formal formation, he presented the Distinguished Flying Cross to me and Commendation Medals to Lagerstrom and Woolard. Later on, I was working at Division headquarters when the accident report was forwarded to 2nd AF and SAC. I added a recommendation to the report that anticollision lights should be considered for all military and commercial aircraft to help prevent midair collisions. The 19th Bomb Wing commander, Col. Cloyd, offered me a spot promotion to Lt. Colonel. I asked him to consider me for the next squadron commander vacancy that needed to be filled. He did this soon thereafter.

We were told later that the pilot of the F-86H had ejected immediately after the collision and descended in a thin summer flying suit, landing in a small clearing in the biggest swamp in Georgia. He was found by some locals who took him to the house of a forester. This individual brought out the family whiskey and gave him some shots that probably saved his life. He spent over a month recovering from wounds and frost bite. We learned that he, Clarence Stewart, also stayed on active duty, retiring in 1977.

I later checked out in the B-52H and served in operations and other staff positions. I completed 31 years service and retired in 1973 as a colonel. Leland Woolard died in 1986 and Bob Lagerstrom went on to become a captain for American Airlines where he retired not long ago.

APPENDIX A
Mississippians Killed In Action

Name	Home	Date of Death	Crew Position	Rank	Group
Abel, John H.	Meridian	23 Mar 44	CP	2 Lt	92 BG
Algee, Robert D	Hylulla	26 Aug 44	NT	Sgt	446 BG
Anderson, Douglas P.	Tupelo	7 Apr 45	CP	Capt	452 BG
Ball, John A.		23 Nov 42		2 Lt	
Beasley. Herman E.	Utica	20 Jun 44	BT	S Sgt	492 BG
Benson, Isaac D.		26 Feb 43		1 Lt	
Betterton, Clayton L.	Calhoun County		TT	T Sgt	457 BG
Blackmon, Clarence H.	Yokena	17 Aug 43	N	2 Lt	91 BG
Blount, Edward H.		6 Dec 42	RW	S Sgt	305 BG
Boggan, Wade H.		31 Aug 43		T Sgt	
Boyles, Charles D.		1 Jan 45		Cpl	446 BG
Branum, Buford	Hattiesburg	22 Feb 44	B	Lt	306 BG
Brock, Daniel J.	Jackson	7 May 44	B	T Sgt	389 BG
Brooks, Lloyd R.		28 Jul 43	BT	S Sgt	95 BG
Brooks, Robert L.	Duncan	30 May 44	RO	T Sgt	401 BG
Broome, Garland R.	Prentiss	29 Jul 44	TT	Sgt	44 BG
Brown, Charles W.	Aberdeen	14 Oct 44	BT	Sgt	305 BG
Bryan, George M.	Starkville	17 Aug 43	CP	2 Lt	91 BG
Buckley, William E., Jr.	Cleveland	10 Oct 43	P	2 Lt	95 BG
Burnette, James T.	Columbus	8 Apr 44	P	2 Lt	94 BG
Byrnes, Hartwell P.	Biloxi	26 Nov 44	TG	S Sgt	491 BG
Caldwell, Frank A.	Baldwyn	29 Jul 44	WG	S Sgt	100 BG
Camp, Charles E.	Guntown	2 Oct 44	RW	S Sgt	34 BG
Campbell, Robert L.		26 Jul 44	P	Lt	92 BG
Carr, Floyd D.	Louisville	27 Jun 44	RW	S Sgt	448 BG
Casey, James E.	Jackson	8 Mar 44	B	2 Lt	446 BG
Castle, Orville L.	Louisville	26 Nov 43	P	2 Lt	351 BG
Cavett, Clinton M.		8 Sep 44		2 Lt	351 BG
Chambers, Charles T.	Macon	4 Apr 45		Sgt	
Clark, Clyde R.	Vaiden	27 May 44	RW	S Sgt	389 BG
Clark, Joe T.		24 Mar 44	B	FO	379 BG
Clarkson, Billy T.	Enid	24 Feb 44	TT	T Sgt	445 BG
Collins, Wilbur H.	Ellisville	9 Sep 44	CP	2 Lt	390 BG
Corbin, Eugene W.		20 Oct 43		2 Lt	390 BG
Counce, James T.	Corinth	4 Jan 44	N	S Sgt	381 BG
Courtwright, Roy M.	Palmyra	25 Feb 44	BT	S Sgt	305 BG
Crump, Arch M.		16 Apr 43		T Sgt	
Dale, Sam B., Jr.		4 Jul 44		2 Lt	
Davis, John Y.		17 Jun 45		FO	
Denning, David H.	Saucier	25 Mar 45	NT	Sgt	448 BG
Downie, Donald S., Jr.	Jackson	29 Jun 44	BT	Sgt	390 BG
Downing, Virgil S.	Jackson	21 Mar 45	TT	S Sgt	100 BG
Duke, William A.	Oxford	22 Feb 45	P	2 Lt	458 BG
Durbin, John L.	Falkner	21 Jul 44	LW	S Sgt	93 BG
Edelstein, Herbert C.	Caledonia	22 Feb 44	NV	Lt	306 BG
Ellis, William F. Jr.	Rome	10 Jan 45	TT	T Sgt	379 BG

Emmons, Rufus	Meridian	26 Feb 44	TT	S Sgt	453 BG
Esters, Cecil C.	Magnolia	10 Apr 44	TG	S Sgt	401 BG
Etheridge, James C.		13 Jul 44		FO	489 BG
Everitt, Lloyd E.	McComb	25 Aug 44	BT	S Sgt	487 BG
Farmer, James M.		19 Jul 44	P	Capt	78 FG
Faulkner, James L.	Louisville	2 Dec 44	LW	Sgt	44 BG
Fitch, William D. Jr.	Marks	11 Sep 44	N	2 Lt	448 BG
Fitzgerald, David L.	New Albany	10 Feb 44	RW	Sgt	452 BG
Fleming, Dover C., Jr.		14 Aug 45		2 Lt	
Foster, Lane	Jackson	6 Apr 45	RO	T Sgt	303 BG
Foster, Thomas J.		7 Jun 44		1 Lt	
Franks, Jesse D., Jr.		1 Aug 43		1 Lt	
Garrard , Curtis F.		24 Mar 45		S Sgt	
Garrard, James M.		2 July 43		S Sgt	
Gartman, Woodrow W.	Gulfport	19 Apr 44	TT	S Sgt	448 BG
Gill, James M.		2 Aug 44		Lt	93 BG
Gilmore, James H., Jr.	Hattiesburg	25 Mar 45	RW	Sgt	448 BG
Gnesin, Harold M.	Gulfport	25 Jun 44	N	2 Lt	398 BG
Goodman, Lawrence		29 Jan 44	RO	T Sgt	392 BG
Gookin, WaLter A.		5 Jan 44		2 Lt	96 BG
Green, James W.		5 Jul 45	CPL		
Grisham, Hughlon K.	West Point	1 Aug 44	B	2 Lt	401 BG
Hand, Victor		23 Jan 43		Sgt	
Hanks, Weldon M.		25 Dec. 44		2 Lt	467 BG
Hardin, James C.		11 Mar 44		S Sgt	
Harris, Eugene P.	Winona	1 Dec 43	P	Capt	351 BG
Harris, Egar P.		11 Nov 44	WG	Sgt	303 BG
Harrison, James M.	Laurel	11 Sep 44	PN	2 Lt	93 BG
Hathorne, Clyde		24 Jun 44		T Sgt	
Hay, William R.	Biloxi	4 Jan 44	NT	T Sgt	392 BG
Hewes, Charles D.	Biloxi	18 Dec 44	P	Capt	4 FG
Hirsch, Charles B.		1 May 43		T Sgt	
Hollis, Terrell L.	Derma	19 Oct 44	N	2 Lt	389 BG
Homer, Harold H.	Biloxi	12 May 44	P	2 Lt	452 BG
Howell, Harold H.		3 Mar 44		2 Lt	
Hurdle, John P.		25 May 44	TT	T Sgt	388 BG
Johnson, James H.		16 Mar 44		Sgt	
Johnston, Gerald W.	Summit	14 Jan 45	P	Lt	390 BG
Jones, Edward L.		21 Jan 45		S Sgt	
Jones, V. Y.		10 Feb 44		2 Lt	
Jordan, John W.	Hollandale	20 Mar 45	N	2 Lt	445 BG
Kennedy, John H.	Meridian	2 Mar 45	CP	FO	96 BG
Knotts, Emery L.		1 May 43		T Sgt	
Knox, James L.	New Albany	29 Apr 44	B	2 Lt	306 BG
Lee, Edward P., Jr.		8 Jun 44		1 Lt	
Leggett, Edgar A.	Brookhaven	16 Aug 44	N	Lt	389 BG
Leist, Leroy E.	Lucedale	4 Feb 44	TG	S Sgt	100 BG
Lewis, Lonnie		10 Feb 44		S Sgt	
Linton, Peter	Hattiesburg	12 Jul 44	TG	S Sgt	385 BG
Littleton, Freddie H.		28 Jul 44	P	2 Lt	466 BG
Loflin, Harry C.	Jackson	11 May 44	N	Lt	379 BG
Lott, Edgar G.		19 Aug 43		S Sgt	
Lovell, Clyde D.		24 Sep 43		S Sgt	
Lyle, Charles L.		12 Feb 45		Capt	

Name	Hometown	Date	Position	Rank	Group
Mannon, James B.	Potts Camp	24 Dec 44	RW	Sgt	447 BG
McCall, Frederick C.		10 Jan 45		1 Lt	
Mc Kewen, John W., Jr.	Jackson	4 Jan 44	B	2 Lt	91 BG
McWhorter, Vivian B.	Waynesboro	28 Sep 44	B	2 Lt	457 BG
Melhado, Charles G.	Gulfport	21 Nov 44	N	2 Lt	385 BG
Mitchell, Howard L.	Bogue Chitto	5 Dec 44	P	Lt	91 BG
Mixon, George E.	Jackson	30 Dec 44	N	FO	447 BG
Moran, Chester L.		26 Feb 43	B	S Sgt	91 BG
Morris, Ollie L.	Sumrall	28 Sep 44	TT	S Sgt	389 BG
Morrow, James G.		20 Jun 44	BT	Sgt	492 BG
Morton, Neil H.	Hattiesburg	24 Apr 44	CP	2 Lt	392 BG
Mullens, Bluford B., Jr.	Greenville	25 Jun 43	CP	2 Lt	100 BG
Munroem, Archibald B., Jr.	Batesville	22 Feb 45	CP	2 Lt	458 BG
Naron, Talmadge C.		17 Aug 43		S Sgt	
Nelson, Augustus, Jr.	Meridian	7 Oct 44	P	Lt	401 BG
Newton, Lloyd E.	Starkville	3 Mar 45	TT	S Sgt	448 BG
Nored, George L.		8 Mar 43		T Sgt	
Parker, William J.		28 Jul 43	CP	Lt	95 BG
Pate, Dexter B.	Booneville	8 Oct 43	LW	Sgt	100 BG
Payne, Joseph A.		10 Dec 44		Cpl	388 BG
Pearce, Iren R.	Tremont	20 Jun 44	LW	S Sgt	492 BG
Pearson, Byron T.	Gulfport	19 May 44	LW	S Sgt	392 BG
Pennal, James R.	Nettleton	11 Apr 44	CP	2 Lt	388 BG
Pest, David	Hattiesburg	4 Oct 43	RW	Sgt	44 BG
Pettus, Albert F.	Bentonia	25 Feb 44	LW	Sgt	305 BG
Phillips, Edward L.	Holcomb	11 Apr 44	TG	S Sgt	95 BG
Potter, Robert O.	Hattiesburg	21 Nov 44	CP	2 Lt	96 BG
Proudfit, Richard D.	Grenada	8 Apr 45	B	S Sgt	91 BG
Ray, John H., Jr.		24 Feb 44	LW	S Sgt	389 BG
Redd, Harold L.	Jackson	20 Jun 44	BT	S Sgt	392 BG
Rice, Thomas L.	Meridian	15 Mar 44	BT	S Sgt	392 BG
Richard, Harold G.	Crystal Springs	20 Feb 44	P	Lt	306 BG
Riley, Darrell	Sardis	21 Nov 44	TT	T Sgt	91 BG
Roebuck, Harry C.		13 Jun 43		T Sgt	351 BG
Rogers, Martin C.	Ripley	16 Sep 43	BT	S Sgt	384 BG
Rosenblum, Charles M.		12 Sep 44		Sgt	
Ryan, Troy L.	Baldwyn	26 Nov 44	NT	S Sgt	491 BG
Schaen, James W.	Pontotoc	27 Sep 44	P	Lt	445 BG
Schlesinger, Gilbert J.	Mattapan	30 Nov 44	P	Lt	379 BG
Scott, James C.		17 Jul 45		1 Lt	
Shaffer, Robert S.	Vicksburg	12 Jul 44	RO	S Sgt	379 BG
Sharp, Robert H.		10 Jun 45		Capt	
Shaw, Charles M.	Liberty	11 Dec 43	B	2 Lt	44 BG
Smith, Teddy A.	Tchula	28 Sep 44	B	Lt	303 BG
Stanter, Herman L.		24 Feb 44	LW	S Sgt	303 BG
Steele, William H.	Itta Bena	10 Dec 42	RO	T Sgt	91 BG
Stewart, Paul C.	Meridian	24 Apr 44	P	2 Lt	303 BG
Stochl, William B.	Bay St. Louis	24 Feb 44	CP	2 Lt	445 BG
Stovall, William H., Jr.		7 Apr 45	TG	S Sgt	389 BG
Straus, Marks R.	Meridian	7 Apr 45	TG	S Sgt	389 BG
Suarez, Edward B., Jr.		2 Oct 44		Sgt	447 BG
Tapley, Thomas W.		11 Nov 44	NT	Sgt	303 BG
Taylor, Charles A., Jr.		5 Jul 45		Sgt	
Taylor, Fred		17 Feb 44		Sgt	

Terry, John B., Jr.	Kosuisko	17 Mar 45	BT	Sgt	490 BG
Thornton, Stanley B.	Union	7 May 44	RO	T Sgt	389 BG
Tickell, George D.A.		9 Jul 43		S Sgt	
Tidwell, Billy M.		31 Dec 43	TG	Sgt	446 BG
Tillman, Harvey K., Jr.	Tillatoba	11 Apr 44	TT	S Sgt	94 BG
Walley, Henry P.	Houston	21 Feb 44	CP	2 Lt	392 BG
Webb, James T.	Tupelo	30 Mar 45	RO	Sgt	486 BG
White, John B.	Grenada	8 May 44	P	Lt	96 BG
White, Rufus C.	Morton	14 Mar 45	TT	S Sgt	398 BG
Wilkinson, Oscar H.		27 Jan 43		Capt	
Williams, Buren C.		1 May 43		T Sgt	
Williams, Clifton M.	Escatawba	31 Dec 44	P	Lt	100 BG
Wiltshire, Ellington W.	McComb	10 Jan 45	CP	Lt	490 BG
Wing, Robert D.		9 Oct 43	B	2 Lt	95 BG
Winstead, James W.		8 Jul 44		S Sgt	
Worthy, Lawrence C.		13 Jun 43	RW	S Sgt	94 BG

APPENDIX B
MISSISSIPPI PRISONERS OF WAR

NAME	HOME	DATE	JOB	RANK	GROUP
Adcock, Ernest J.	Ridgeland	6 Mar 44	BT	S Sgt	445 BG
Allen, Henry H.	Vicksburg	29 Apr 44	BT	S Sgt	467 BG
Allen, Charles E., Jr.	Nitta Yuma	4 Jul 43	B	2 Lt	305 BG
Barry, Warren H..	New Albany	8 Apr 44	P	2 Lt	44 BG
Barton, Samuel W.	Calhoun City	14 Jan 45	TG	S Sgt	390 BG
Beasley, William C.	Georgetown	5 Sep 44	N	Lt	389 BG
Belcher, Amos	Walnut	25 Feb 44	TT	T Sgt	446 BG
Berry, Clyde A.	Houston	25 Feb 44	BT	S Sgt	389 BG
Bond, Thomas L.	Weir	9 May 44	P	2 Lt	94 BG
Boyd, Richard	Gautier	28 Jan 45	PN	Lt	93 BG
Breckenridge, Wilmer L.	Preston	28 Sep 44	TT	T Sgt	388 BG
Brinson, Ralph C.	Prentice	6 Mar 44	RW	Sgt	95 BG
Brown, John D.	Holly Springs	6 Mar 44	TT	T Sgt	445 BG
Bunch, Amos T.	Oxford	9 Apr 44	LW	S Sgt	457 BG
Burnett, Forrest N.	Charleston	18 Apr 44	B	Lt	447 BG
Burstein, Martin	Moorehead	5 Dec 44	CP	2 Lt	305 BG
Campbell, Zancel Y.	Leakesville	25 Feb 44	RW	T Sgt	379 BG
Carlisle, James T.	Houston	14 Oct 44	BT	Sgt	458 BG
Christy, James I.	Holly Springs	22 Jan 44	CP	Lt	457 BG
Clark, James E.	Meridian	8 May 44	RW	S Sgt	452 BG
Clary, Leonard E.	Mataban	7 Oct 44	BT	S Sgt	384 BG
Coody, Matthew E.	Louisville	16 Aug 43	BT	S Sgt	384 BG
Darden, Edwin J.	Hernando	9 Feb 45	RO	S Sgt	303 BG
Davidge, William F., Jr.	Hattiesburg	6 Feb 44	TT	T Sgt	447 BG
Day, Norman L.	Hickory	18 Mar 44	LW	S Sgt	44 BG
Dearman, Roger D.	McComb	25 Feb 44	BT	S Sgt	96 BG
Dickerson, George A.	Jackson	9 Oct 43	B	2 Lt	379 BG
Foretich, Gerald F.	Gulfport	30 Nov 44	RO	Sgt	384 BG
Francis, Roderick L.	Jackson	10 Apr 45	CP	Lt. Col.	457 BG
Franklin, Reedas G.	Jackson	12 Jul 44	RO	S Sgt	94 BG
Freeburgh, Charles H.	Philadelphia	24 Feb 44	TT	S Sgt	44 BG
Galloway, John A	Pontotoc	6 Mar 44	B	Lt	452 BG
Gimmel, William R.	Hattiesburg	6 Mar 44	RW	S Sgt	92 BG
Gates, Lloyd H., Jr.	Jackson	14 Feb 45	WT	S Sgt	379 BG
Gatlin, Waukeen G.	Meridian	19 May 44	RW	S Sgt	492 BG
Gibbs, Tyrus C.	Fulton	28 Jan 45	LW	S Sgt	93 BG
Gisham, Colbert W.	Seminary	24 May 44	LW	S Sgt	100 BG
Hamilton, William C.	Byhalia	22 May 44	B	2 Lt	388 BG
Hampton, Lee A.	Springfield	23 Jan 44	RO	S Sgt	492 BG
Harris, Secar J.	State Line	16 Mar 44	P	2 Lt	93 BG
Harris, William V.	Greenville	22 Feb 44	RW	S Sgt	306 BG
Havard, Lewis M.	Lucedale	21 Mar 45	N	Lt	490 BG

Hogan, Alex A.	Starkville	18 Apr 44	MP	Capt	94 BG
Hudson, Harry, Jr.	Louisville	28 Jul 43	TT	T Sgt	96 BG
James, Lee R.	Gulfport	11 Sep 44	CP	2 Lt	305 BG
Jones, Amzie A.	Ruleville	16 Mar 44	TG	S Sgt	95 BG
Jones, Hardy	Vicksburg	14 Oct 43	RO	T Sgt	351 BG
Jones, John M.	Macon	28 Apr 44	N	2 Lt	100 BG
Jones, John J., Jr.	Corinth	11 Jul 44	P	Lt	458 BG
Jordan, Wilbur M.	Carthage	18 Apr 44	TG	S Sgt	94 BG
Juchheim, Alwin M.	Grenada	28 May 44	P	Capt.	78 FG
Kayes, John L.	Brookhaven	6 Oct 44	RC	T Sgt	94 BG
Lamar, Horace B.	Pontotoc	7 Aug 44	TT	T Sgt	34 BG
Lamkin, William M.	Gloster	12 Sep 44	BT	Sgt	493 BG
Lee, O'Ferrel E.	Eskono	8 Apr 44	TG	S Sgt	453 BG
Liedtke, Ralph H.	Dossville	7 May 44	RO	Sgt	91 BG
Littleton, George J.	Tyro	22 Feb. 44	B	2 Lt	384 BG
Lott, Homer L.	Holcomb	8 Jan 45	B	S Sgt	384 BG
Martin, Claude C.	McComb	12 May 44	P	2 Lt	452 BG
Massie, Gerald S.	Ellington	5 Jan 44	TG	S Sgt	96 BG
Mastronardi, Francis J.	Vicksburg	20 Mar 45	RO	T Sgt	401 BG
McGee, Ray	Hickory	8 Apr 44	LW	S Sgt	446 BG
McInerney, Simon T.	Jackson	8 Jun 44	TG	Sgt	493 BG
Metcalfe, Thomas Q., Jr.	Canton	28 Sep 44	B	2 Lt	457 BG
Miller, George F.	Hattiesburg	3 Feb 45	P	Lt	91 BG
Moore, Thomas L.	Hattiesburg	20 Mar 45	P	2 Lt	303 BG
Murdock, William J., Jr.	Laurel	2 Nov 44	P	Lt	457 BG
Murray, Malcolm, G.	Grenada	20 Feb 44	TG	Sgt	305 BG
Nickles, Mercer C., Jr.	Aberdeen	30 Jan 44	LW	S Sgt	384 BG
Oakman, Jack H.	Panther Burn	5 Nov 44	B	FO	487 BG
Oldham, Jesse Z.	Carrollton	19 Mar 44	LW	S Sgt	384 BG
Owens, Norris R.	Laurel	29 Jul 44	RO	T Sgt	384 BG
Parker, Kenneth I.	Union	2 Mar 44	RO	T Sgt	379 BG
Parkinson, George F.	West	8 May 44	RW	S Sgt	96 BG
Pennington, Charles O.	Nettleton	27 May 44	NT	S Sgt	389 BG
Pettey, George C.	Shannon	12 May 44	LW	S Sgt	93 BG
Piazza, Emile G.	Bay St. Louis	15 Aug 44	TT	T Sgt	466 BG
Pool, John V.	Ellisville	21 Jun 44	TT	S Sgt	453 BG
Price, Ellis R.	Laurel	1 Jan 45	B	Sgt	305 BG
Price, Prentiss H.	Brookhaven	24 Jun 44	NT	Sgt	448 BG
Quick, Harold	Oxford	8 Mar 44	RW	T Sgt	388 BG
Ragland, James L.	Oxford	12 Aug 43	TT	T Sgt	379 BG
Richardson, Clyde E.	Purvis	2 Jan 45	RW	S Sgt	452 BG
Scott, Charles A.	Jackson	30 Jan 44	P	2 Lt	305 BG
Shaw, Lawrence C.	Natchez	10 Jan 45	N	FO	306 BG
Shults, Clennie C.	Corinth	22 Feb 44	TT	S Sgt	401 BG
Shumski, Edward J.	Bay St. Louis	22 Mar 44	CP	2 Lt	466 BG
Simonton, William M.	Natchez	31 Dec 44	CP	2 Lt	94 BG
Simpson, Ira L.	Jackson	14 Feb 45	N	2 Lt	389 BG
Smith, James E.	Booneville	16 Apr 45	TT	Sgt	448 BG
Spencer, Joe B.	Slate Springs	24 Dec 44	P	2 Lt	92 BG

Stalnaker, Harold L.	Springville	8 Apr 44	TG	S Sgt	458 BG
Steele, Edward L.	Tishomingo	13 Apr 45	RW	S Sgt	398 BG
Stephenson, Arris D.	Smithville	7 Apr 45	TT	T Sgt	452 BG
Sutherlin, Fordie E.	Pass Christian	7 Oct 44	TG	S Sgt	94 BG
Swain, Charles E.	Canton	22 Mar 45	RW	Sgt	390 BG
Teat, Harry J.	Jackson	6 Mar 44	CP	2 Lt	388 BG
Thornton, M.C., Jr.	McComb	27 Sep 44	RW	S Sgt	445 BG
Till, Rufus W.	Pelahatchee	22 Feb 45	RW	S Sgt	379 BG
Walsh, Earl C.	Jackson	6 Nov 44	P	Lt	4 FG
Ward, Rufus A.	Columbus	12 May 44	TG	S Sgt	96 BG
Wells, James E.	Kreole	24 Jun 44	TT	S Sgt	448 BG
Williamson, Jack D.	Ruth	15 Mar 44	RW	S Sgt	44 BG
Wilson, Donald L.	Pascagoula	1 Dec 43	TG	Sgt	92 BG
Wilson, Robert E.	Magnolia	26 Nov 44	RO	S Sgt	305 BG
Winter, Lonis V.	Lula	28 Jan 45	TG	S Sgt	389 BG
Wolak, Pete		24 Mar 44	BT	S Sgt	305 BG
Wolfe, Lillian E.	Smithdale	19 Jun 44	LW	S Sgt	93 BG
Wood, James M.	Tunica	6 Mar 44	TT	T Sgt	95 BG
York, David L.	Corinth	29 Apr 44	BT	S Sgt	389 BG
Young, Thomas E. Jr.	Pickens	26 Mar 44	CP	2 Lt	379 BG

APPENDIX C
MISSISSIPPI EVADERS

Name	Home	Date Shot Down	Crew Position	Rank	Group
Barlow, Archie R.	Hattiesburg	21 Jan 44	TT	T Sgt	44 BG
Blaylock, William T.	Grenada	26 Aug 44	BT	Cpl	446 BG
Brand, Wayne E..	Dublin	27 Jun 44	TT	T Sgt	445 BG
Byrd, Victor L.	Pineville	1 Apr 44	LW	S Sgt	389 BG
Cox, Harvey G.	Vaiden	23 Jun 44	CP	2 Lt	95 BG
Heafner, H. L.	Greenwood	29 Apr 44	RW	S Sgt	466 BG
Mason, Webber I.	Lucedale	8 Feb 44	TG	Pvt	482 BG
McCrarry, Joe E.	Columbus	29 Jan 44	RW	S Sgt	392 BG
Shook, Marcus L.	Belmont	18 Sep 44	RO	T Sgt	390 BG
Smith, Autley B.	Perkinston	28 May 44	LW	Sgt	486 BG
Whitlow, William B.	Jackson	10 Oct 43	P	2 Lt	385 BG

APPENDIX D
MISSISSIPPI INTERNEES

Name	Home	Date Shot Down	Crew Position	Rank	Group
Brown, George F.	Tupelo	25 Feb 45	N	2 Lt	351 BG
Fermo, Augelo	Clarksdale	20 Jun 44	NT	S Sgt	453 BG
Grafton, Harry E.	Laurel	20 Jun 44	P	2 Lt	446 BG
Laird, John C.	Decatur	18 Mar 44	NT	Sgt	44 BG
Leggett, Thomas A.	Laurel	11 Jul 44	CP	2 Lt	492 BG
Martin, John A.	Meridian	20 Feb 44	LW	S Sgt	100 BG
Sconyers, James H.	Yazoo City	20 Jun 44	N	2 Lt	492 BG
Winter, Clarence E.	Lula	24 Jun 44	TG	S Sgt	448 BG
Young, Thomas J.	Oma	21 Jul 44	CP	2 Lt	44 BG

INDEX

INDEX (CONTINUED)

INDEX (CONTINUED)

INDEX (CONTINUED)

INDEX (CONTINUED)